CHRONICLE OF THE MAYA KINGS AND QUEENS

SIMON MARTIN AND NIKOLAI GRUBE

CHRONICLE OF THE
MAYA
KINGS AND QUEENS

DECIPHERING THE DYNASTIES
OF THE ANCIENT MAYA

WITH 368 ILLUSTRATIONS
86 IN COLOR

Thames & Hudson

In memory of Linda Schele
(1942–1998)

© 2000 Thames & Hudson Ltd, London

First published in hardcover in the United States of America in 2000 by Thames & Hudson Inc., 500 Fifth Avenue, New York, New York 10110

Library of Congress Catalog Card Number 99-69615
ISBN 0-500-05103-8

Printed and bound in Slovenia by Mladinska Knjiga

CONTENTS

The great crucible of Maya civilization, Tikal's immense ruins reflect an 800-year dynastic history that ran the gamut from regional ascendancy to abject defeat

Founded by the Tikal exile B'alaj Chan K'awiil, the Dos Pilas kingdom took the name of its mother city Tikal and fought a relentless series of wars against it

A kingdom rarely free from foreign attack, Naranjo enjoyed its greatest success under the 'warrior queen' Lady Six Sky and her five-year-old son K'ak' Tiliw Chan Chaak

Playing a significant part in the military and diplomatic exchanges of the 6th century AD, the Caracol dynasty controlled a densely settled region

Enjoying a 'golden age' of over 130 years, the kingdom of the 'snake' eclipsed its arch-rival Tikal to create the most important political hegemony covering a great swathe of the Maya realm

PREFACE: DISCOVERING THE MAYA PAST

Of the moral effect of the monuments themselves, standing as they do in the depths of a tropical forest, silent and solemn, strange in design, excellent in sculpture, rich in ornament, different from the works of any other people, their uses and purposes and whole history so entirely unknown, with hieroglyphics explaining all but perfectly unintelligible, I shall not pretend to convey any idea.

Those are the words of John Lloyd Stephens, the American diplomat, journalist and explorer who, in 1839, together with English artist Frederick Catherwood, was one of the first outsiders to penetrate the rainforests of Central America. What the pair had encountered were the remains of ancient Maya civilization, which had lain smothered by vegetation, derelict and abandoned for almost a thousand years. Built by the ancestors of the modern Maya – who live today where they did in ancient times, in the area now covered by Guatemala, Belize, the eastern portion of Mexico and the western extremities of Honduras and El Salvador – no other culture in the New World has aroused such intense interest or posed so many puzzles.

Initially, scholars preferred to attribute Maya wonders to Phoenicians, Israelites or Atlanteans, but even after their indigenous origins had been established, ideas almost as fanciful took their place.

In this atmospheric, but also highly accurate lithograph by Frederick Catherwood, we see Copan Stela D and its accompanying 'zoomorphic' altar. Both were commissioned by the king Waxaklajuun Ub'aah K'awiil in AD 736.

The ancient Maya were now a people without precedent, unworldly pacifists who worshipped time itself. Their great ruins were not cities but empty 'ceremonial centres', simply stages where priest-astrologers performed awe-inspiring rituals for a peasantry scattered in the forest. The monuments carried portraits of priests and their gods; the hieroglyphs – less a form of writing than a clumsy aide mémoire – encoded only numerology, star-lore and incantations. All these misconceptions were shattered in the early 1960s. Proper mapping revealed that, far from being empty, the ruins were the cores of dispersed cities with populations that could run into tens of thousands. More decisively still, in a few key articles Tatiana Proskouriakoff demonstrated that the carved figures were actually kings and queens and that the inscriptions included biographies of their lives and names of the captives they had seized. At a stroke, the Maya had become an historical people.

Recent decades have seen an ongoing revolution in our understanding of the Maya, as archaeological research has burgeoned throughout the region and tremendous progress has been made in deciphering the writing system. The 'breaking' of the Maya code, though still incomplete, has offered unique insights into Maya thought and society, ranging from grand visions of the cosmos to the pragmatic structure of government. Although the challenges are considerable – monuments and their inscriptions have often been shattered by tree-fall or eroded by centuries of tropical downpour – the reward is the chance to peer into an otherwise lost annal of Precolumbian America.

This example of Early Classic portraiture depicts the Tikal king Chak Tok Ich'aak I (*c.* AD 360–378), identified by the hieroglyph painted in his headdress.

The Maya were never politically unified and during the height of the Classic period (AD 250–909) were divided into a patchwork of more than 60 kingdoms. Each ruled by a 'divine lord', they were locked in a constant struggle to preserve their autonomy or achieve dominance over their neighbours. Especially successful rulers might establish themselves as 'overkings' operating far-flung networks of political patronage – but in this turbulent landscape no kingdom achieved a permanent hold on power.

In *Chronicle of the Maya Kings and Queens* we examine 11 of the most influential and best-known kingdoms, and the dynasties that did most to shape the highpoint of Maya civilization. Behind the vast ruins of Tikal and Calakmul lie the stories of two of the most important, implacable rivals whose competition had an influence on the whole region. But much smaller sites such as Dos Pilas have fascinating tales of their own. Created by the Tikal exile B'alaj Chan K'awiil, it represented a 'splinter state' traitorously in league with Calakmul. His daughter Lady Six Sky, one of very few ruling queens, went on to establish a new dynasty at distant Naranjo, securing her realm with a determined series of conquests. One of the more dramatic changes of fortune took place in the far east. Copan's Waxaklajuun Ub'aah K'awiil presided over his city's greatest flowering of art and culture, but met his end in decapitation at the hands of a former vassal, the king of little Quirigua. Great rivals for supremacy in the west, Tonina and Palenque produced rulers of contrasting style. The former's B'aaknal Chaak is now best known for his relentless warring, the latter's Janaab' Pakal for the unparalleled grandeur of his burial.

Yet, for all its vigour, splendour and high culture, the world of the divine kings ended in a spectacular fall. By the early 10th century AD the royal dynasties were gone, populations had slumped dramatically and the greatest cities were abandoned to the forest. Our survey concludes with a look at the latest evidence about this enigmatic episode and the shadowy Postclassic era that followed it.

Carved jade stones, such as this fine example found at Nebaj, were highly prized by the Maya nobility. Here we see an enthroned ruler gesturing towards a court dwarf.

INTRODUCTION: MAYA HISTORY – THE MAJOR PERIODS

The first portraits of Maya rulers emerged during the Late Preclassic. Kaminaljuyu Stela 25 shows one wearing the mask of the sky god Itzamnaaj, itself topped by the leaf-crowned deity Huunal, a royal patron with Olmec origins.

The chronology of Mesoamerican civilization – following on from an Archaic period of hunter-gatherers – is traditionally divided into three eras: the Preclassic, Classic and Postclassic.

THE PRECLASSIC: 2000 BC–AD 250

The Preclassic (or Formative) period covers the emergence of complex societies and is itself divided into three major sub-periods, the Early (2000–1000 BC), Middle (1000–400 BC) and Late (400 BC–AD 250). The first great civilization, the Olmec, reached its apogee during the Middle Preclassic along the swampy estuaries of the Mexican Gulf Coast. Widely regarded as the 'mother culture' of Mesoamerica, Olmec concepts and art styles spread far beyond their homeland and were a major influence on emerging Maya societies. It was among the Zapotec, whose civilization arose in the mountainous Oaxaca region, that historical portraits were first joined by hieroglyphic writing around 600 BC. During the Late Preclassic scripts were developed in several parts of Mesoamerica, most notably among the successors of the Olmec, the Epi-Olmec, and the Maya.

By now the Southern Maya Area of highlands and coastal piedmont were developing into the distinctive Miraflores and Izapan societies respectively. The pictorial stelae found at Izapa itself are notable for including the first recognizable scenes from Maya mythology. As early as 500 BC, the Maya of the lowland forests were establishing their first major cities, raising at their cores great red-painted temple platforms decorated with ornate stucco god masks. Nakbe was among the first but was ultimately superseded by El Mirador, the largest concentration of monumental architecture ever built by the Maya. For reasons as yet unclear, this vibrant culture failed around the 1st century AD and most of its greatest cities were abandoned.

The main characteristics of the Classic civilization that followed – the use of the Long Count calendar, together with the carving of hiero-glyphic inscriptions and historical portraits – reflect the rise of a new political ideology and ideal of dynastic kingship (pp. 11–13; 17). In the Maya region these features first made their appearance in the Southern Area between AD 37 and 162, at sites such as Kaminaljuyu, El Baúl and Abaj Takalik, while Classic-style dynasties established themselves at Tikal in the Central Area by around AD 100 (p. 26). For reasons still unknown, the south experienced a premature decline, and by 250 the momentum of Maya culture shifted decisively to the lowlands.

THE CLASSIC: AD 250–909

It was over the next six centuries or so – predominantly in the Central Area – that Maya civilization reached its greatest florescence, forging the landscape of kingdoms examined in this volume. Yet the Maya were never isolated from developments in central Mexico, which by now was

The huge city of Teotihuacan, high in the Valley of Mexico, exerted a powerful influence over the Classic Maya. Among its many cultural exports perhaps the best known is the architectural style called *talud-tablero*. Amply illustrated in this view of central Teotihuacan, platform façades were made up of alternating levels of sloping batter and projecting panels, once brilliantly painted.

dominated by the vast metropolis of Teotihuacan, housing at its peak more than 125,000 people. Few if any parts of Mesoamerica were to be unaffected by its cultural, political and economic might; and its distinctive, rather angular style of art and architecture can be found in all Maya regions. Contacts were at their most direct during the 4th century AD, when Kaminaljuyu was revitalized under heavy Teotihuacan influence, and a swathe of the lowlands came, if only briefly, within its political ambit.

The year 600 marks the transition between the Early and Late Classic periods (today mostly defined in terms of art style), roughly coinciding with the fall of Teotihuacan. The Late Classic saw Maya civilization reach its peak population, greatest social complexity and artistic and intellectual highpoint. Yet this success did not endure and as early as 800 there are signs of significant distress: dynasties begin to collapse and population levels suffer a precipitous decline (for fuller treatment of these and later events see the Epilogue pp. 226–7). This traumatic era, a sub-period known as the Terminal Classic, ends with the last recorded date in the Long Count calendar in AD 909. The crisis was not immediately reflected in the north, however, where cities such as Chichen Itza and Uxmal show growth at this time.

THE POSTCLASSIC: AD 909–1697

By the dawn of the Early Postclassic (909–1200) Maya populations were largely concentrated in the Northern and Southern Areas, with the old Central heartland only sparsely inhabited. Chichen Itza continued as a regional power in the north, now showing close ties with the new masters of central Mexico, the Toltecs. The hybrid Maya-Mexican architecture of Chichen reflects its cosmopolitan make-up, while historical sources tell of its wide political influence. The succeeding Late Postclassic (1200–1697) witnessed Chichen Itza's decline and its ultimate replacement by Mayapan. This lesser imitator held sway over at least some of Chichen's former domain until internal discord caused its abandonment around 1441. In the Southern Area, the latter stages of the Classic had seen large-scale movements in population, with western arrivals creating a new series of statelets. The most powerful of these were the Quiche, though by 1475 they were being overtaken by their former vassals, the Cakchiquel.

The Postclassic came to an end in Mexico with the fall of the famed Aztec Empire to Spanish invaders and their native allies in 1521. But Maya resistance proved stubborn and it was only with difficulty that the Spanish brought the southern communities to heel in 1527 and their northern brethren largely by 1546. Maya kingdoms in the isolated forests of the Central Area proved more dogged still, and held out until their final conquest in 1697.

The Maya region covers three major geographic zones: a Southern Area of highlands and adjoining Pacific coastline; a humid Central Area of lowland tropical forest; and a drier Northern Area, a flat lowland of forest and scrub forming the greater part of the Yucatan Peninsula. The Maya were one of the peoples that made up Mesoamerica, a cultural sphere extending from northern Mexico to Honduras and El Salvador.

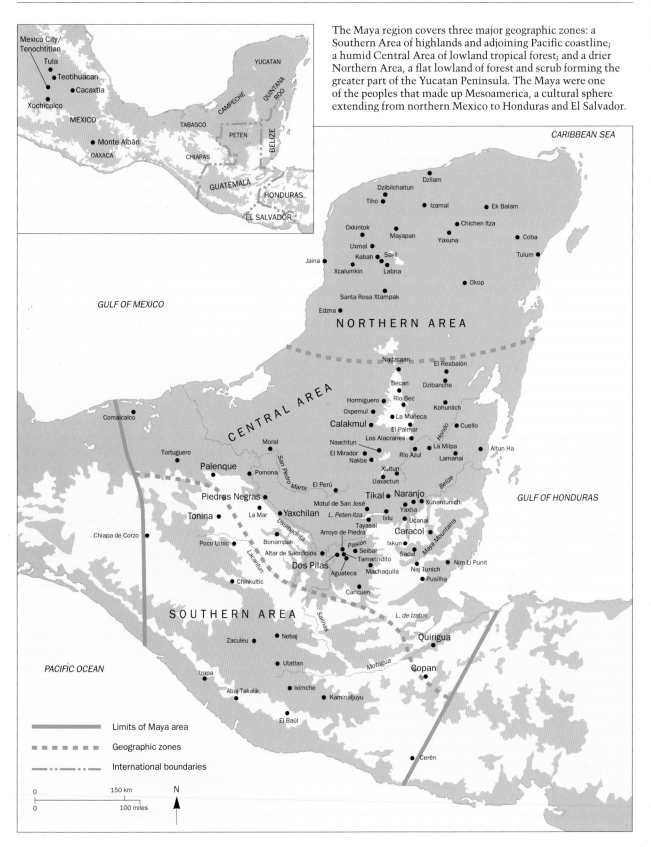

Mexico City/Tenochtitlan
Tula
Teotihuacan
Cacaxtla
Xochicalco
MEXICO
Monte Albán
OAXACA
TABASCO
CAMPECHE
YUCATAN
QUINTANA ROO
PETEN
BELIZE
CHIAPAS
GUATEMALA
HONDURAS
EL SALVADOR

CARIBBEAN SEA

GULF OF MEXICO

Dzilam
Dzibilchaltun
Tiho
Izamal
Ek Balam
Oxkintok
Mayapan
Chichen Itza
Yaxuna
Coba
Uxmal
Kabah
Sayil
Jaina
Xcalumkin
Labna
Tulum
Okop
Santa Rosa Xtampak
Edzna

NORTHERN AREA

Nadzcaan
El Resbalón
Becan
Dzibanche
Río Bec
Hormiguero
Kohunlich
Oxpemul
La Muñeca
Calakmul
Cuello
El Palmar
Los Alacranes
Naachtun
La Milpa
Moral
El Mirador
Río Azul
Altun Ha
Nakbe
Lamanai
Xultun
Comalcalco
Uaxactun
Tortuguero
El Perú
Palenque
Pomona
Tikal
Naranjo
Piedras Negras
Motul de San José
Xunantunich
Yaxha
Tonina
La Mar
Yaxchilan
L. Peten-Itza
Ixlu
Ucanal
Tayasal
Caracol
Chiapa de Corzo
Arroyo de Piedra
Ixkun
Poco Uinic
Bonampak
Pasión
Sacul
Altar de Sacrificios
Seibal
Naj Tunich
Nim Li Punit
Dos Pilas
Tamarindito
Machaquila
Aguateca
Pusilha
Chinkultic
Cancuen

CENTRAL AREA

San Pedro Martir
Usumacinta
Lacantun
Salinas
Hondo
Belize
Maya Mountains
L. de Izabal
Motagua

GULF OF HONDURAS

SOUTHERN AREA

Zaculeu
Nebaj
Quirigua
Utatlan
Copan
Izapa
Iximche
Abaj Takalik
Kaminaljuyu
El Baúl
Cerén

PACIFIC OCEAN

Limits of Maya area
Geographic zones
International boundaries

0   150 km
0   100 miles

N

MAYA WRITING AND CALENDARS

Whenever the intellectual achievements of Precolumbian America are discussed, the famed writing system and timekeeping of the Maya are always well to the fore. While the origins of both hieroglyphics and the calendar are obscure, there can be no dispute that the Maya took them to their highest level. The source of their particular passion can be traced to the social and political developments that transformed the Preclassic into the Classic. The new emphasis placed on dynastic descent, and ultimately divine kingship, created a need for permanent records to proclaim genealogy, ritual and great deeds – legitimizing the rule of individuals by fixing their lives within a sacred time order.

HIEROGLYPHIC WRITING

Maya hieroglyphs present the reader with a richness and visual elaboration unrivalled by any of the world's ancient scripts. The system as we know it today was evidently developed by the speakers of Ch'olan, one of the principal Mayan language groups, sometime in the Late Preclassic. Although it was later adapted by groups such as the Yucatecan-speaking Maya of the north, royal inscriptions in all areas remained predominantly Ch'olan, suggesting that this served as a kind of pan-Maya prestige speech, much as French did in the courts of medieval England, or for that matter 18th-century Germany and Russia.

The discovery of the phonetic basis of hieroglyphic writing, largely the work of the Russian Yuri Knorosov, has proved the key to its decipherment. Like most other hieroglyphic scripts, Maya writing is a 'mixed system' that uses signs called logographs for whole words, with others representing syllables and vowels. Part of its complexity lies in the variety of its spelling conventions, which allowed a single term to be written in a number of different ways. For example, the title *ajaw* 'lord, ruler', could be composed of: a) one of several alternative logographs; b) a logograph complemented by a syllable giving a phonetic clue to its reading; or c) constructed entirely from syllables (themselves often selected from a choice of signs). Individual signs could also be manipulated graphically, as when one is 'infixed' into another, with no effect on the reading of either.[1] At any one time the system used no more than 500 signs, of which 300 or so of the most common are now deciphered. Though this process is well advanced, many questions remain unanswered and some important areas, such as its verbal structure and the marking of features like vowel length, are only now succumbing to investigation.[2]

Spellings of *ajaw* 'lord, ruler':

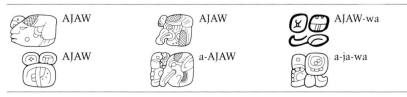

GUIDE TO ORTHOGRAPHY AND PRONUNCIATION

A feature common to all Mayan languages is the 'glottal stop'. This sudden constriction of the throat distinguishes, for example, *kab'* 'earth' from its glottalized counterpart *k'ab'* 'hand'. In the writing system this is reflected in a separate set of syllables (*k'a, k'e, k'o* etc.). The type of vowel, whether short, long or modified in other ways, is another important distinction and recent work suggests that this too was indicated in the script. In this volume long vowels are marked with a doubled letter, separating *chak* 'great/red' from *chaak*, the name of the Rain God. The Maya also made a contrast between hard and soft 'h' sounds: the former closest to the final 'h' in the Gaelic 'loch', the latter to the 'h' in 'house'. In line with the standard orthography, 'j' represents this hardened or 'velar' version (e.g. 'ja' as opposed to soft 'ha'). It is also important to know that in Mayan 'x' is used for the sound 'sh' (thus yax is 'yash' and Xunantunich is 'shu-nan-toon-ich'). In an older orthography that persists in many place-names, 'c' is better understood as 'k' and 'u' is pronounced as a 'w' (the site of Uaxactun is thus wa-shak-toon). Many archaeological sites have Spanish names and it is worth keeping in mind here that 'j' is also a hard 'h' (Naranjo is thus 'naran-ho'). Two non-Maya names with different conventions are Oaxaca ('wa-haka') and Teotihuacan ('tayo-ti-wa-kaan').

SPELLING CONVENTIONS

The flexibility of Maya script is well illustrated in the spelling of the name of the 7th-century king of Palenque, K'inich Janaab' Pakal (pp. 162–8). We variously see substitution (the use of alternative signs which have the same reading), complementation (syllables attached to logographs not as part of the reading but as phonetic clues to their value or marking a quality of the vowel) and infixation (the combination of two signs). Hieroglyphic transcriptions of each ruler's name appear in the 'glyphic spelling' section of their personal datafile and follow an established system. Logographs are set in capitals, while syllables and vowels appear in lower case. Hyphens join signs that are grouped in the same 'glyph block'. Square brackets indicate infixed signs, while this volume uses round brackets to mark elements that are present but omitted from the spelling. Colons indicate long or other 'complex' vowels in logographs (these features are still imperfectly understood and spellings are currently in some degree of flux). In the following examples, it is worth remembering that apostrophes mark glottalized sounds, while the letter 'j' is always pronounced as a hard 'h'.

Spellings of K'inich Janaab' Pakal 'Great-Sun ? Shield':

 chi[K'IN]-ni JANA:B' pa-ka-la

K'INICH-[JANA:B']PAKAL-la

K'INICH-ni ja-na-b'i pa-ka-la

Dynastic records were most often inscribed on the tall monoliths called 'stelae' (sing. stela), but are also found on stone wall panels, altars, thrones and door lintels and in similar contexts modelled in stucco plaster or carved in wood. Texts were also engraved on objects of jade, shell and bone, usually as marks of ownership on items of jewelry. But it is as well to remember that most writing was on perishable media, especially the bark-paper books known as codices (of which only four Postclassic examples, all non-historical almanacs, survive). Maya hieroglyphs developed from the tradition of brush painting, and scribes – who held a prestigious place in society – were called *aj tz'ib*, literally 'he of the painting'.[3] Their fine calligraphy is preserved on a few wall murals and, much more commonly, on ceramic vessels.

Surviving texts are dedicated entirely to the doings and concerns of the elite class. Public inscriptions tend to be terse affairs, with much use of formulaic expressions and redundant duplication of known facts. This gives us a rather skewed idea of Maya literature. Only rarely do we see first-person quotations, more animated or poetic language, or glimpse the wider range of topics discussed in long-lost books.

THE MAYA CALENDAR

The basis of any sophisticated time reckoning is a numerical system. Maya numbers were made from combinations of just three symbols: a dot for 'one', a bar for 'five' and a variable sign that represented 'zero'. The largest single digit was 19, composed of three bars and four dots. For larger numbers a system of place notation was employed, working in base 20 rather than our own base 10.

At the heart of the Mesoamerican conception of time lay a 260-day calendar of 20 named days and 13 numbers, now known in the Maya area as the Tzolk'in. This ritual count was usually intermeshed with another based on the solar year, a 365-day 'vague year' called the Haab. This was composed of 18 months of 20 numbered days, with a short month of five spare days at the end of the year. Since it fell short of the true solar year by about a quarter of a day, it slowly 'slid' against the seasons (although the Maya were well aware of this they made no attempt to correct it). The combined Tzolk'in and Haab is known as the Calendar Round, in which no combination repeats for 18,980 days or 52 vague years.

Recording greater expanses of time required a further system, one especially associated with the Classic era, called the Long Count. Normally the highest unit was the Bak'tun (of roughly 400 years), followed by the K'atun (of about 20 years), the Tun (360 days), Winal (20 days) and finally K'in (single days). Confusingly, the Winal position works to base 18, probably so that it could approximate the solar year at 360 days. Mayanists notate the Long Count as a scale of descending value, separated by periods beginning with the Bak'tun. The penultimate day of the 10th Bak'tun is thus written today 9.19.19.17.19, the next day completing the cycle as 10.0.0.0.0. Although these historical dates contain five

THE INITIAL SERIES

Monument inscriptions usually begin with an Initial Series date. The large introductory sign reads *tziik haab(?)* 'count of the years', always combined with the name of the relevant patron of the Haab month. Thereafter it reads in double columns, as below.

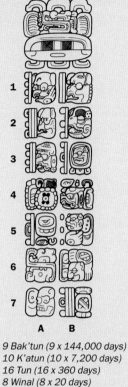

	A	B
A1	9 Bak'tun (9 x 144,000 days)	
B1	10 K'atun (10 x 7,200 days)	
A2	16 Tun (16 x 360 days)	
B2	8 Winal (8 x 20 days)	
A3	14 K'in (14 days)	
B1	7 Ix (Position in the 260-day Tzolk'in cycle)	
A4	G3 (Third Lord of the Night – 9-day cycle of patron gods)	
B4	F (Linked to G, meaning still unclear)	
A5	27E/D (27 days since the 'arrival' of the last New Moon)	
B5	3JC (Part of an 18-month cycle of lunations)	
A6/B6	X/B (The 'young' name of the appropriate lunar patron)	
A7	10A (30 days in the current lunation)	
B7	17 Sip (Day and month in the 365-day Haab or 'vague year')	

This Initial Series represents the date 9.10.16.8.14 7 Ix 17 Sip, equivalent to 24 April AD 649 (GMT+2 correlation and Julian calendar).

places, there were in fact 19 higher ones, the full system reflecting a quite unimaginable scope of time.

This five-place section of the Long Count had a starting point in 3114 BC, perceived as the creation of the current universe. The system was actually devised sometime in the 8th Bak'tun (7.0.0.0.1–8.0.0.0.0, 354 BC–AD 41) – popularly known as Cycle 7 – the earliest surviving date falling in 32 BC at Chiapa de Corzo, between the Olmec and Maya zones. The first known date that is probably Maya appears at El Baúl, on the Pacific Coast, in AD 37. The earliest from the lowlands falls in the following Cycle 8, at Tikal in AD 292. The great majority of Long Counts record dates in Cycle 9, with the last coming in Cycle 10 in AD 909. Maya stelae were erected primarily to commemorate key stages in the Long Count, most often whole K'atun-endings (such as 8.18.0.0.0 or 9.13.0.0.0), but half- and quarter-K'atuns were not uncommon, occurring every 10 and 5 years respectively (e.g. 8.18.10.0.0 and 9.13.5.0.0).

The opening date on major monuments is called the Initial Series. This includes the Long Count and its appropriate Calendar Round, but was further elaborated with various kinds of lunar data and other ritual cycles (see panel). This served as a base from which the chronology of the rest of the text was calculated, expressed in Calendar Rounds linked by precise day counts.[4]

The correlation question

Converting the Long Count into the Christian calendar was a key concern of early scholars and to some extent the question remains with us today. Rather cryptic statements from 16th-century Spanish chroniclers, native histories from the Colonial period and remnants of the ancient calendar still in use in parts of the Guatemalan highlands have all been compared with astronomical data in the inscriptions and archaeological techniques such as radiocarbon dating. The correlation that best fits these diverse criteria, and is now almost universally accepted, is that of Goodman-Martinez-Thompson (GMT).[5] It is likely that any deviation from this is only a matter of a few days and, in fact, most specialists currently use a two-day shift from GMT as standard.[6] The key to a final placement undoubtedly lies in celestial records of the Classic era. Unfortunately, these rarely offer single-day precision (most phenomena taking place over a number of days and their observation affected by the vagaries of cloud cover). Notable exceptions are eclipses. A monument at Poco Uinic, in the Chiapas highlands of Mexico, ties the Long Count 9.17.19.13.16 to a term known from Postclassic codices to represent a solar eclipse. Just such an event took place on 16 July 790, falling three days after the original GMT, one day after the standard amendment. It is still unclear if this correlation was one used by all Maya kingdoms or whether, as elsewhere in Mesoamerica, there were deviations across the region. All Christian conversions in this volume keep to the common GMT+2 and are given in the Julian calendar, the system in use throughout Europe during the relevant period and the standard for astronomical calculation.

THE ROYAL CULTURE OF THE MAYA

The Classic Maya developed a complex and highly refined royal culture which was reflected in all areas of their art, architecture and writing. Rulers combined supreme political authority with a quasi-divine status that made them indispensable mediators between the mortal and supernatural realms. From ancient times they were especially identified with the youthful Maize God, whose bounty of corn underpinned all civilization in Mesoamerica. Each stage of life – from birth to death to resurrection – found its parallel in the cycle of the maize plant and the myth that served as its metaphor (p. 222). In this way, the interests of the humble farmer and high king were entwined and basic sustenance set at the heart of Maya religion.[1]

The path to divine power

Royal succession was strongly patrilineal and the rule of queens arose only when the dynasty might otherwise be extinguished. As far as we can tell, primogeniture was the norm: eldest sons had preference. Princelings were termed *ch'ok*, originally meaning 'unripe, youth', but later extended to the wider sense of 'noble'. The heir himself was distinguished as the *b'aah ch'ok* 'head youth'. Childhood was marked by a series of initiation rites, one of the more important being a bloodletting usually performed at the age of five or six (see pp. 60–1). Although blood was their main claim to legitimacy, candidates still had to prove themselves in war. A bout of captive-taking often preceded elevation to office and the names of such prisoners were sometimes incorporated into the kings' name phrase, in the formula 'Master/Guardian of so-and-so'.[2]

Kingly investitures were elaborate affairs made up of a series of separate acts.[3] There was an enthronement, the heir's seating on a cushion of jaguar skin, sometimes atop an elevated scaffold bedecked with celestial symbolism and accompanied by human sacrifice. A scarf bearing a jade image of *huunal*, the 'Jester God' (so called because of the leafy three-lobed top to his head), an ancient patron of royal authority, would be tied to the forehead.[4] An elaborate headdress of jade and shell mosaic, trailing green iridescent plumes of the quetzal bird, would follow. A sceptre carved into an image of the snake-footed deity *k'awiil* was taken. The name carried in childhood was now joined by a *k'uhul k'aba'* 'divine name', usually taken from a predecessor, sometimes a grandparent (in modern Maya communities children are seen as reborn grandparents, a single word *mam* meaning both grandparent and grandchild) (see panel).

The rites of kingship

From here on, the calendar dictated a lifelong regimen of ritual and performance. The most enduring relics of these rites are the multi-ton stelae the Maya called *lakamtuun* or 'big/banner stones'. Their engraved texts describe their own erection, the binding of the altar set before it and the scattering of blood or incense it received. These ceremonies replicated primeval acts that first set the universe in motion. Carved with the king's image, often shown standing on a bound captive or iconic location, their

(*Opposite*) In this 'roll-out' photograph of a cylinder vase we see a ruler of Motul de San José relaxing in his palace surrounded by courtiers. A dwarf holds an obsidian mirror to his gaze, while musical entertainment is provided by a group of horn and conch-shell trumpeters outside.

(*Below*) This incised bone shows an accession ceremony. A young lord seated on a throne holds a simple headband, while an aged figure lifts a royal headdress aloft. It is unclear if the scene is real or mythical. Dallas Museum of Art.

ROYAL NAMES

The names we associate with particular Maya kings and queens are only parts of much longer sequences of names and titles. Very often they are based on those of gods and other supernatural characters, the most common of which were K'awiil, the reptilian, snake-footed patron of royal lineages; Chaak and Yoaat (or Yopaat), axe-wielding rain and lightning gods; Itzamnaaj, the aged supreme deity of the sky; and K'inich, the cross-eyed sun god (also used as the honorific title 'Great Sun'). Variants or aspects of these deities often appear in verbal forms – as in the 'god who does such-and-such' – usually in conjunction with features such as Chan/Ka'an 'sky' and K'ak' 'fire'. Powerful or prestigious animals are other common components: B'alam/Hix 'jaguar', K'uk' 'quetzal bird', Mo' 'macaw', Kaan/Chan 'snake', Ayiin 'caiman, crocodile', Ahk 'turtle' and Chitam/Ahk 'peccary' (the native American boar). The names used in this volume reflect the varied histories of their discovery and the current state of their decipherment, ranging from full translations, to nicknames, to those identified only by letter or number.

inscriptions go on to chronicle the major historical events that have occurred since the last stone was set up.[5]

Most ceremonies were conducted in the guise of appropriate deities, identified by a full costume and usually a mask (almost always depicted in cutaway form to show the wearer's face).[6] Some required specialized dance rituals, each identified by its own name and paraphernalia (one involved live snakes).[7] The accompaniment would consist of singing, the blowing of trumpets and conch shells and the beating of drums and turtle carapaces. More privately, rulers and their families sought to enter the spirit world through vision and trance induced by hallucinogenic drinks and enemas. They also performed auto-sacrifice, drawing blood from their tongues and genitalia with the aid of thorns, stingray spines and blades of the volcanic glass obsidian.[8]

Every major Maya city included at least one ballcourt. In the game itself two teams would attempt to keep a large (and very hard) rubber ball from touching the ground, scoring points by means of floor markers and wall-mounted rings. Equipment included padding for the knees and elbows and a wide waist belt or 'yoke'. Kings might style themselves *aj pitzal* 'ballplayer', though their real interest lay in the game's mythic significance. The ballcourt of the Underworld was the place of sacrifice described in the Popol Vuh (the 16th-century creation epic of the Quiche Maya) where the Maize God met his death, but from which he was ultimately reborn (see p. 130).[9]

The royal court, governance and war

Kings held court in palaces set in the heart of their capitals. Painted vessels show evocative scenes of courtly life, with enthroned lords surrounded by wives and retainers, often receiving the homage of vassals

Fulfilling their role as 'warrior kings', Maya rulers evidently took part in hand-to-hand fighting. In this scene painted on a cylinder vase from the Nebaj region we see the capture of an opposing lord seized by the hair.

VENUS: THE WAR STAR

For Mesoamericans the celestial patron and harbinger of war was not Mars but Venus. Known by the Maya as Chak Ek' or 'Great Star', its motion across the sky was carefully charted and the subject of much prognostication. Tables to this effect can be seen in a Postclassic book called the Dresden Codex, where Venus' malevolent effect is represented as darts spearing unfortunates below. During the Classic period key points in its progress were seen as favourable for warfare and some battles were timed to exploit this supernatural advantage. The appropriate hieroglyph, a still undeciphered verb known as 'star war', shows a star showering the earth with liquid – water or perhaps even blood (pp. 79, 95, 106, 109). It usually marks only the most decisive of actions, the conquest of cities and the fall of dynasties.

delivering mounds of tribute.[10] Maya kings seem to have been polygamous, but marriage is not a topic much discussed in the inscriptions (p. 131). Also in attendance were musicians and dwarves. The latter were more than simple jesters, they enjoyed a high status derived from their special association with caves and entries into the Underworld.[11] Scenes showing the feasting and entertaining of both visiting lords and local nobility reflect not so much leisure activities as the operation of government and diplomacy.

A key responsibility of kingship was to lead one's forces into battle against rival kings. Although the timing of attacks was essentially a tactical decision, there can be no doubt that auguries were strenuously examined in search of the most auspicious moment (see panel). To be taken captive was the greatest disaster to befall a Maya king. Public humiliation was obligatory and many seem to have been tortured before their execution by beheading, burning, or being tied into balls and cast down flights of steps. Occasionally, however, they appear to have survived their ordeals and even returned to their thrones as vassals of the victor.

Journeys to the gods: death and burial

Advanced age was seen as especially prestigious, and long-lived kings would invariably carry titles stating how many K'atuns they had seen. Death, when it came, was viewed as the beginning of a journey, a retracing of the Maize God's descent into the Underworld, where victory over the gods of decay and disease would lead to rebirth and apotheosis (pp. 167, 222). In preparation for this odyssey, dead rulers were laid in well-built tomb chambers. Stretched out on a wooden bier, the corpse was dressed in the weighty jade jewelry worn in life, wrapped in textiles and jaguar pelts and given a heavy dusting of the blood-red minerals hematite and cinnabar. Accompanying offerings included: ceramic vessels holding foodstuffs and drinks made from *kakaw* (cocoa beans), shells and other marine 'exotics', the effigies of gods in clay or wood, mirrors of polished hematite or pyrites, bark-paper books, musical instruments, items of furniture and, occasionally, human sacrifices. In many cases a steep pyramid would be raised above the tomb, its upper temple a shrine for the king's veneration as a deified ancestor. These temples were maintained over successive generations, forming a collective repository of dynastic power. In later years tombs might be ritually re-opened, their contents scattered about and the defleshed bones scorched with fire or removed as relics.[12]

CLASSIC MAYA POLITICS

A fundamental question we ask of any ancient civilization is 'how was it organized politically?' In the case of the Classic Maya we are fortunate in having both a strong archaeological record and, even more importantly, a unique collection of contemporary inscriptions. Their decipherment provides key insights into Maya conceptions of kingship and statehood, of political rhetoric and authority.

Though the significance of the Preclassic–Classic divide can be overstated, the distinction does seem to reflect a transformation from one social and political order to another. The emerging Classic tradition certainly drew from existing practice, incorporating ideals of rulership – even specific forms of regalia – that can be traced back to Olmec times. But it also had a keen sense of itself as an innovation, as a break from the past. Authority in the Preclassic Maya lowlands was generally manifested in broad, impersonal terms, with huge architectural programmes emblazoned with god masks and cosmic symbols.[1] The Classic, by contrast, emphasized the individual. The relationship between kingship and the cosmos was re-articulated, even reconceived. The monolithic stela, an ancient form, was now used to fix royal identity and life-history within a sacred order defined by the calendar. Ceremonial architecture underwent a similar development, as temple pyramids became mortuary shrines for the veneration of dead kings. These changes find explicit mention in the written histories, where Classic dynasties were established by named founders, sometimes on specific dates of 'arrival'.[2]

Elements of this system took root in various parts of Mesoamerica between 100 BC and AD 100. In the Maya area they first appear in the south, at El Baúl, Abaj Takalik and Kaminaljuyu, where stelae carved with royal portraits, dates and historical texts were in place by at least AD 37. The emergence of the first dynastic kingdoms in the lowland Central Area can now be traced to around AD 100 (p. 26).

For the Maya, governance was invested in the rank of *ajaw* 'lord, ruler'. By the end of the 4th century, paramount rulers were distinguishing themselves from a larger lordly class by calling themselves *k'uhul ajaw*, 'divine lord'. Though this was initially confined to the most ancient and powerful centres in the form we know now as the 'emblem glyph' (see panel), it ultimately spread far and wide.[3] Another title, *kaloomte'* (long known as 'Batab') was of special importance and restricted to only the strongest dynasties during the Classic proper.[4] When prefixed by *ochk'in*, 'west', as is often the case, it asserts a legitimacy derived from the great Mexican city of Teotihuacan, whose special role in the Maya area has still to be fully uncovered.

EMBLEM GLYPHS

The first real window on Classic Maya politics came in 1958, when Heinrich Berlin (who also identified personal names in the inscriptions) discovered what he called 'emblem glyphs'. These hieroglyphs share a common structure, but have versions that are unique to each of the major sites. Today we understand them as royal titles composed of three elements: two constants, *k'uhul* 'divine' and *ajaw* 'lord', and a variable, the name of a particular kingdom or polity. Over 50 are known from the Central Area alone (p. 19), while a much smaller inventory from the Northern Area is now growing rapidly.

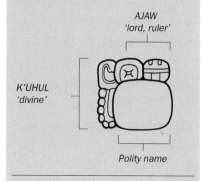

AJAW
'lord, ruler'

K'UHUL
'divine'

Polity name

Ajaw   K'uhul Ajaw   Kaloomte'   Ochk'in Kaloomte'

CHANGING PERSPECTIVES ON MAYA POLITICS

Although early scholars speculated vaguely on a system of 'city states', it was only with the discovery of emblem glyphs and dynastic history that a proper study of Classic Maya politics could begin. Thomas Barthel, working in the 1960s, noted that an unusual grouping of four emblems recorded at Copan in AD 731 (Copan itself, Tikal, Palenque and what we now know to be Calakmul) were each associated with a cardinal direction (p. 203). He took this to represent a four-way division of political authority in the Central Area based on cosmological principles. A second set of four, recorded at Seibal 118 years later, appeared to show the replacement of peripheral Copan and Palenque by centrally placed Seibal and Motul de San José, suggesting a contraction of the Maya realm in the Terminal Classic (p. 227).[5]

This perspective was expanded by Joyce Marcus in the 1970s. By noting which city mentioned the emblem of another, and which did not, she reconstructed ranked hierarchies of sites that made up large 'regional states'. She went on to propose an historical development in which a landscape of small Preclassic

chiefdoms coalesced into four or five true states (and one lesser confederacy) during the Classic period, before splintering again under the pressures of the approaching collapse.[6] Meanwhile, Richard Adams examined the relative size and distribution of Maya sites across a swathe of the lowlands, coming to the view that regional-scale entities could indeed be detected and their domains broadly charted (see below).[7]

As a better understanding of the emblem glyph emerged in the 1980s, conceptions underwent a sea change. Now recognized as a personal title defining the 'divine lord' of a particular city or area, it could be seen as an equivalent rank shared by a great many Maya rulers.[8] When Peter Mathews charted emblem glyph distribution across the region he defined a landscape divided into 40 or more small, self-contained statelets (see below).[9] Further advances in the decipherment only served to emphasize the diverse histories of each and the recurring warfare between them.

To a number of scholars, most notably David Freidel and Jeremy Sabloff, this seemed like a system of 'peer polities'. In this kind of environment statelets are equally matched, relations between them oscillating rapidly between peace and war with no enduring patterns or

meaningful hierarchies developing.[10] To better explain why, scholars including Arthur Demarest, Stephen Houston and Norman Hammond looked to political models developed for other cultures, principally in Africa and Southeast Asia. Here there were states which placed ritual performance at the heart of their existence, echoing the great emphasis the Maya placed on such themes. Dubbed 'weak states' by some, these units were inherently unstable. Paramount rulers wielded ceremonial and religious authority, but real political strength lay with a class of competing magnates. Charismatic kings could expand the boundaries of the state for a time, but feeble rulers risked its very existence, as the nobility switched their allegiance to neighbouring kingdoms or established powerbases of their own.[11]

In the 1990s, however, new evidence from the texts began to indicate that some of these petty kingdoms were consistently 'more equal than others'. While falling far short of organized states, it now seems clear that a number of the strongest were capable of establishing dispersed and rather dynamic hegemonies – a system which predominated throughout the Classic era (pp. 17–21).

Differing conceptions of Classic Maya political organization:

(*Left*) A reconstruction of regional states (after Richard Adams)

(*Right*) The divided landscape of small polities (after Peter Mathews).

The dynastic system of the lowlands was initially slow to spread from the heart of the Central Area known as the Peten. But after a phase of Teotihuacan intervention, towards the end of the 4th century, the pace quickened noticeably. New kingdoms, many of them established at existing Preclassic centres, ultimately filled most of the productive lands in the Maya area. Each was fiercely individual, adopting its own patron deities and mythic history, many doubtless drawn from existing Preclassic traditions. These polities were the largest stable units to emerge over the six centuries of the Classic and, despite continual conflict, the Maya landscape was never unified under a single authority.

New perspectives

Over the years scholars have differed both about the size of Maya polities, whether there were just a few regional-scale states or many small statelets; and their corresponding administrations, whether they had strong, centralized governments or weak, decentralized ones. As as result

Sajal   Usajal

Ajaw   Yajaw

The standard formula 'Divine Lord of x' predominates in this sample of 44 emblems from the Central Area. Rare exceptions may hint at organizational distinctions or represent archaic, perhaps Preclassic, forms.

there has been a choice between two contrasting views of Maya society (see panel). But the emergence of new information from the inscriptions, in which the Maya directly describe their political world, allows a re-assessment of the topic. Our own research – much of it summarized in this volume – points to a pervasive and enduring system of 'overkingship' that shaped almost every facet of the Classic landscape (pp. 20–1).[12] Such a scheme accords closely with wider Mesoamerican practice, while seeming to reconcile the most compelling features of the two existing views, namely the overwhelming evidence for multiple small kingdoms and the great disparities in the size of their capitals.

It has been known for some time that hierarchical relations appear in the texts, where they are expressed by the use of possession. Thus *sajal*, an office held by some of the leading nobility, becomes *usajal* or 'the noble of' when linking such a lord to his king.[13] The same structure can be seen with the kingly rank of *ajaw*, which becomes *yajaw* 'the lord of'.[14] While this demonstrated that one king could be subordinated to another, the small number of examples made them seem, at first, ephemeral and of limited significance. But another kind of expression proves to be equally important, greatly expanding the number of such ties. Here, a normal statement of royal accession is appended by a second phrase headed *ukab'jiiy* 'he supervised it', followed by the name of a

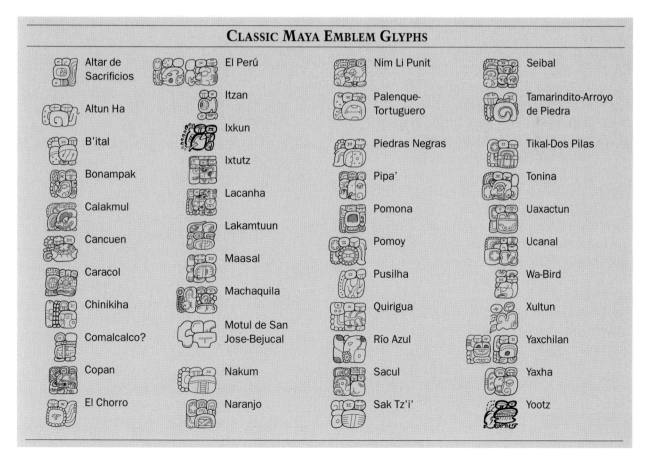

CLASSIC MAYA EMBLEM GLYPHS

Altar de Sacrificios	El Perú	Nim Li Punit	Seibal
Altun Ha	Itzan	Palenque-Tortuguero	Tamarindito-Arroyo de Piedra
B'ital	Ixkun	Piedras Negras	Tikal-Dos Pilas
Bonampak	Ixtutz	Pipa'	Tonina
Calakmul	Lacanha	Pomona	Uaxactun
Cancuen	Lakamtuun	Pomoy	Ucanal
Caracol	Maasal	Pusilha	Wa-Bird
Chinikiha	Machaquila	Quirigua	Xultun
Comalcalco?	Motul de San Jose-Bejucal	Río Azul	Yaxchilan
Copan	Nakum	Sacul	Yaxha
El Chorro	Naranjo	Sak Tz'i'	Yootz

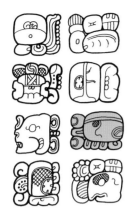

The status of client kings is revealed when they take office under the auspices of their political masters or 'overkings'. Here a king of Cancuen is *chumwan ti ajawlel* or 'seated into lordship' in AD 677. But a supplementary phrase, introduced by *ukab'jiiy* 'he supervised it' (highlighted), provides the name of his sponsor and patron, the mighty Yuknoom the Great of Calakmul (p. 109).

foreign king.[15] This identifies the dominant 'overking' to which the local king was beholden. Similar practices are documented across Mesoamerica and explicitly described for some Maya of the Postclassic (p. 228). When combined with new examples of the *yajaw* relationship, and the ever growing bank of data on diplomacy and warfare, it is possible to construct an outline anatomy of interaction and political power for the Classic Maya Central Area (see opposite).

As one would expect, relationships fluctuated over time, but long-lived patterns are also apparent. It should be emphasized that the Late Classic is much better represented in this kind of display than the Early Classic, for which fewer inscriptions are known and, in any case, political interaction is less discussed. The early influence of Tikal is under-represented as a result, while we get a much better picture of Calakmul's pre-eminence in the 7th century. While these were twin superpowers, as the chart shows, they were by no means the only polities to produce 'overkings', and lesser hegemonies developed in every region.

Rule of the 'overkings'

How did this system work and what were the principles that lay behind it? Talk of states and kingdoms tends to bring borders and territories to mind, but these were not the primary ways in which Maya polities defined themselves. More important was the dynastic seat at their core, their ceremonial and commercial focus and the hub from which ties radiated to lesser lordships in their periphery.[16]

Political expansion, where it occurred, was not an acquisition of territory per se, but rather an extension of these elite networks. The most powerful dynasties brought rival 'divine lords' under their domination, with ties often reaching far outside their immediate region. The bonds between lords and their masters were highly personal and remained in effect even after the death of one party. But whether cemented by oaths of loyalty or marital unions they were, in practice, rather tenuous and more reliant on military threat and the benefits available to subject lords. Apart from direct gains, war victories would encourage new recruits to enter the sphere of a successful protector, while inspiring fear and respect among existing clients. With an intimidating reputation in place, diplomatic persuasion could exert influence without the need for fighting.[17]

Where possible, dominant powers would operate through established local dynasties, but where these proved resistant, 'overkings' were not above manipulating the local succession to their advantage. The degree of influence they exerted undoubtedly varied from case to case, but their involvement in internal affairs otherwise seems slight. Surprisingly perhaps, the great 'overkings' rarely boasted of their possessions in their own inscriptions and we largely rely on vassal rulers to describe their subordinate status. Often such information only emerges when some subsequent event requires explanation or background, such as when patronage was overthrown by force (e.g. pp. 88–90, 218–19). The fact that subordination could be suppressed on clients' monuments hints at how

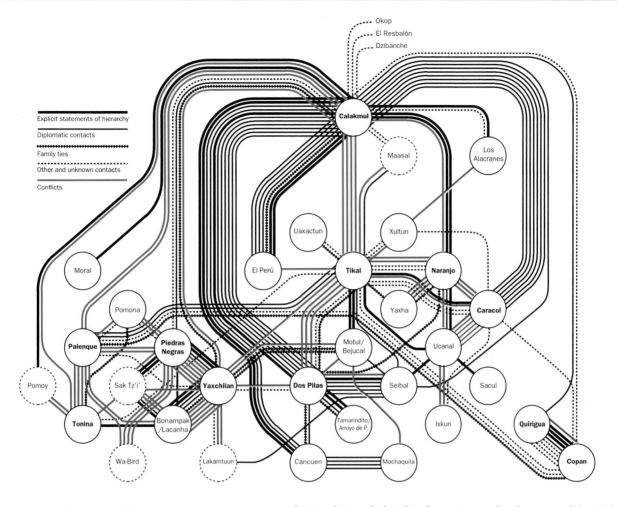

Explicit statements of hierarchy
Diplomatic contacts
Family ties
Other and unknown contacts
Conflicts

In many ways the political landscape of the Classic Maya, with its complex hierarchical and family linkages, and its shifting patterns of alliance and warfare, is better expressed by a schematic view of state interactions than by any territorial map (dashed circles represent polities of uncertain location – for the sake of clarity, some kingdoms have been omitted).

many more relationships of this kind remain to be discovered (p. 89).

In common with all documented societies of Mesoamerica we can take it that an economic dimension was integral to the system – a flow of goods and services from lord to overlord that would account, at least in part, for the great differences in size and wealth between cities. Unfortunately, though scenes of tribute payment are very common on painted vases (where numbered sacks of cocoa beans, heaped textiles and feathers serve as iconic currency) carved inscriptions make very little mention of inter-kingdom arrangements. Indeed, our understanding of Maya economics in general, including the highly significant topic of long-distance trade, is frustratingly poor.

The political landscape of the Classic Maya resembles many in the Old World – Classical Greece or Renaissance Italy are worthy comparisons – where a sophisticated and widely shared culture flourished amid perpetual division and conflict. Like their closest cousins, the small city-states that dominate major parts of Mexican history, we see a complex world criss-crossed by numerous patron–client relationships and family ties, in which major centres vied with one another in enmities that could endure for centuries.

COMPARATIVE TIMELINES

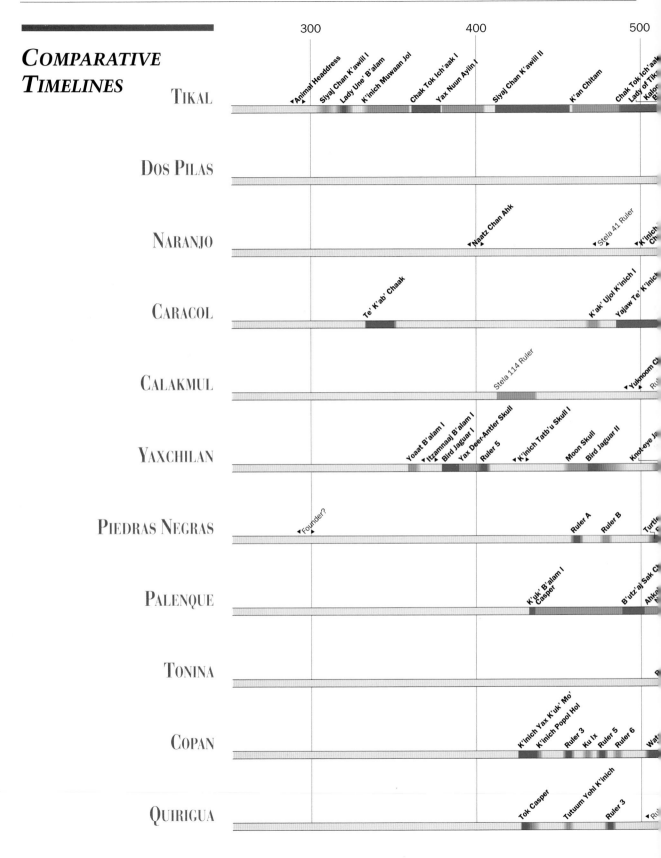

300　　　　400　　　　500

TIKAL
▼Animal Headdress · Siyaj Chan K'awiil I · Lady Une' B'alam · K'inich Muwaan Jol · Chak Tok Ich'aak I · Yax Nuun Ayiin I · Siyaj Chan K'awiil II · K'an Chitam · Chak Tok Ich'aak · Lady of Tikal · Kalo B

DOS PILAS

NARANJO
▼Naatz Chan Ahk · ▼Stela 41 Ruler · ▼K'inich Ch

CARACOL
Te' K'ab' Chaak · K'ak' Ujol K'inich I · Yajaw Te' K'inich

CALAKMUL
Stela 114 Ruler · ▼Yuknoom Ch Ru

YAXCHILAN
Yoaat B'alam I · ▼Itzamnaaj B'alam I · Bird Jaguar I · Yax Deer-Antler Skull · Ruler 5 · ▼K'inich Tatb'u Skull I · Moon Skull · Bird Jaguar II · Knot-eye Ja

PIEDRAS NEGRAS
▼Founder? · Ruler A · Ruler B · Turtle

PALENQUE
K'uk' B'alam I · Casper · B'utz'aj Sak Ch · Ahka

TONINA
R

COPAN
K'inich Yax K'uk' Mo' · K'inich Popol Hol · Ruler 3 · Ku Ix · Ruler 5 · Ruler 6 · Wat

QUIRIGUA
Tok Casper · Tutuum Yohl K'inich · Ruler 3 · Ru

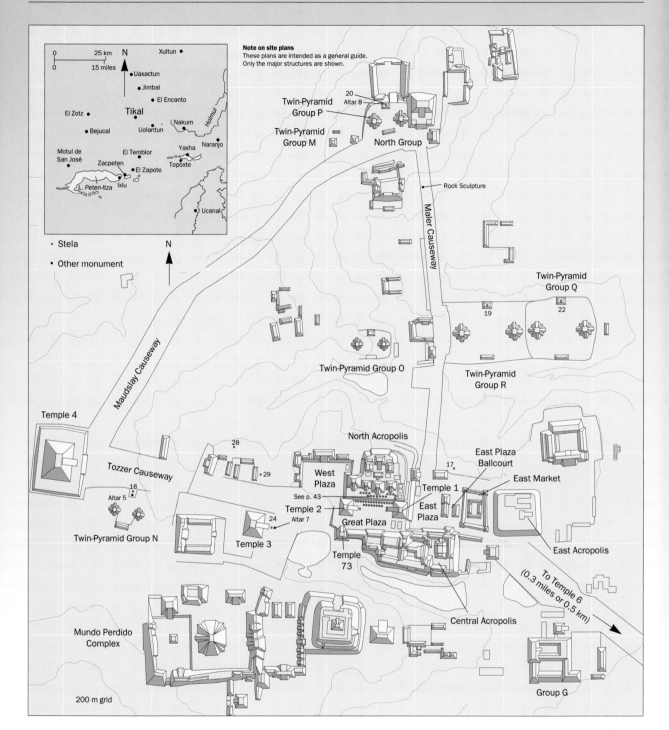

Note on site plans
These plans are intended as a general guide.
Only the major structures are shown.

0 — 25 km
0 — 15 miles
N

Xultun
• Uaxactun
• Jimbal
• El Encanto
El Zotz • Nakum
Tikal Holmul
• Bejucal Uolantun •
Naranjo
Motul de El Temblor • Yaxha
San José Zacpeten • Topoxte
L. Peten-Itza Ixlu • El Zapote
Ucanal •

• Stela

• Other monument

N

Temple 4

Maudslay Causeway

Maler Causeway

Twin-Pyramid Group P
20 Altar 8
Twin-Pyramid Group M
North Group
Rock Sculpture

Twin-Pyramid Group Q
19 22
Twin-Pyramid Group O
Twin-Pyramid Group R

North Acropolis
28
Tozzer Causeway
29
West Plaza
East Plaza Ballcourt
17
East Market
See p. 43
Temple 1
16 Altar 5
Twin-Pyramid Group N
24 Altar 7
Temple 2
East Plaza
East Acropolis
Temple 3
Great Plaza
Temple 73
Central Acropolis
To Temple 6 (0.3 miles or 0.5 km)

Mundo Perdido Complex

Group G

200 m grid

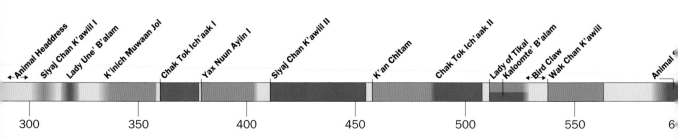

Animal Headdress
Siyaj Chan K'awiil I
Lady Une' B'alam
K'inich Muwaan Jol
Chak Tok Ich'aak I
Yax Nuun Ayiin I
Siyaj Chan K'awiil II
K'an Chitam
Chak Tok Ich'aak II
Lady of Tikal
Kaloomte' B'alam
Bird Claw
Wak Chan K'awiil
Animal

300   350   400   450   500   550   6

TIKAL

N̲O SIGHT GIVES A BETTER IMPRESSION of the past glories of Maya civilization than the towering ruins of Tikal. At its 8th-century peak a score of red-painted pyramids dominated the heart of a dispersed metropolis housing as many as 60,000 people. It claimed a dynastic succession of at least 33 rulers, spanning as long as 800 years. Its political fortunes, which, like all Classic kingdoms, oscillated between triumph and disaster, are central to any understanding of Maya history.

A survivor of the Preclassic collapse, Tikal became a crucible of the new lowland Classic tradition, with a dynasty in place as early as the 1st century AD. Towards the end of the 4th century it fell, like many other parts of Mesoamerica at the time, under the sway of the Mexican superpower Teotihuacan. If anything, the fused Mexican-Maya dynasty that resulted only consolidated Tikal's leading position in the region. But an erosion of its strength in the 6th century led to its defeat and conquest and a resulting 'dark age' of troubles lasting 130 years. Its fortunes were restored late in the 7th century and it resumed a key position in the Maya world until the general unravelling of Classic civilization 150 years later. Comprehensive excavations, first by the University of Pennsylvania and later by the Guatemalan Institute of Archaeology (IDAEH) have amassed incomparable details of Tikal's story.

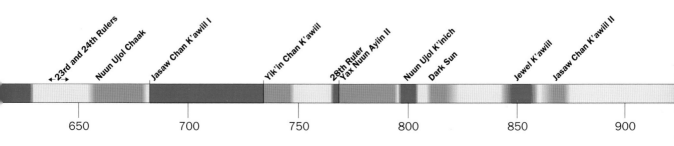

650 · 700 · 750 · 800 · 850 · 900

Yax Ehb'
Xook
c. 90

 Foliated
Jaguar
?

 Animal
Headdress
?

 Siyaj Chan
K'awiil I
c. 307

 Lady Une'
B'alam
>317>

 K'inich
Muwaan Jol
?–359

 Chak Tok
Ich'aak I
Jaguar Paw
360–378

YAX EHB' XOOK	
Glyphic spelling YAX-E:B' -XO:K? ('First Step Shark?')	*Also known as* Yax Moch Xok, Yax Chakte'l Xok *Dynastic title* Founder

FOLIATED JAGUAR	
Glyphic spelling ?-B'ALAM ('?-Jaguar')	*Also known as* Scroll Ahau Jaguar

ANIMAL HEADDRESS	
Glyphic spelling ? K'INICH-E:B'-? *Wife* Lady Skull	*Son* Siyaj Chan K'awiil I

SIYAJ CHAN K'AWIIL I	
Glyphic spelling SIYAJCHAN[K'AWI:L] CHAK-ICH'A:K? ('Sky-born K'awiil Great Claw') *Dynastic title* 11th in the line	*Father* Animal Headdress *Mother* Lady Skull *Monuments* El Encanto Stela 1

THE DAWN OF DYNASTY

Preclassic Tikal, if not a giant on the scale of El Mirador, was a city of some significance, and several of its later architectural landmarks have their origins in this era. The superimposed layers of the most important of these, the North Acropolis (a cluster of temples that began life as early as 350 BC, see p. 43) provide an invaluable record of the city's evolution. A major expansion of the complex in the 1st century AD was associated with Burial 85, an especially rich interment that signals some important social or political development.[1] Tikal inscriptions trace the origin of its Classic dynasty to a lord called **Yax Ehb' Xook** ('First Step Shark').[2] Unfortunately, no source pinpoints his rule in time, but estimates drawn from average reign-lengths now suggest a beginning for the sequence in the late 1st century AD, making Burial 85 a viable contender for his tomb (see panel).[3]

Nothing is known of Yax Ehb' Xook's immediate successors and the first contemporary date, on Stela 29, does not appear until 292. This monument provides our first sight of a Tikal *ajaw* – a richly garbed figure bearing regalia which would remain essentially unchanged for the next 600 years. In a form that has its origins in Olmec art, his father is shown

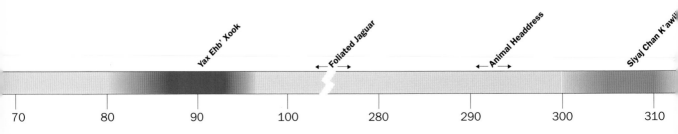

LADY UNE' B'ALAM	
Glyphic spelling	[IX]UNE'B'ALAM ('Lady Baby Jaguar')

K'INICH MUWAAN JOL	
Glyphic spelling K'INICH- [MUWA:N]JOL ('Great-Sun Hawk Skull/Head') *Also known as* Mahk'ina Bird Skull, Feather Skull	*Dynastic title* 13th in the line *Death* 23 May 359? (8.16.2.6.0 11 Ajaw 13 Pop) *Son* Chak Tok Ich'aak I

(*Left*) This small greenstone masquette was found in Burial 85.

Tikal Stela 29 carries the earliest Long Count date in the Maya lowlands: 8.12.14.13.15 (AD 292).

TIKAL'S COUNT OF KINGS

With no surviving foundation date for Tikal's Classic dynasty, estimates of its antiquity can only be drawn from the city's numbered count of kings – its 'successor titles' – and by calculating their average length of reign. While a long-standing interpretation has seen Chak Tok Ich'aak I as 9th in the line, there is good reason now to place him as 14th. Such a revision adds a century or so to the sequence, placing the rule of the founder to around AD 90. This has the advantage that it makes for a closer fit to the archaeological record, where both architecture and burial practices begin to show 'Classic'-style developments at just this time.

This listing of the 11th, 13th and 14th rulers of Tikal appears on a painted vase (p. 41).

looking down on him from the sky. Headdress designs commonly spell personal names and here may well identify him as a Chak Tok Ich'aak, one of several recurring royal names at Tikal. The name of the king himself falls on a missing section of the rear-face text, though he has been linked by some to the early but undated rule of **Foliated Jaguar**.[4] The same name, in a suitably early style, appears on one of many jade plaques recovered in distant Costa Rica, several of which seem to have originated at Tikal. A diminutive monument found well outside the city, at the peripheral site of El Encanto, provides our next clue. Most likely dated between 305 and 308, it carries the name **Siyaj Chan K'awiil I** ('Sky-born K'awiil'), presumably the same king named as 11th in the Tikal line on a later painted vase (see panel).[5] Both his parents are listed and the fact that his father, **Animal Headdress**, carries the Ehb' 'ladder/step' component of the founder's name suggests that he preceded him as ruler.

A breakdown in the male line seems to have taken place by 317, since the 8.14.0.0.0 K'atun-ending was conducted by an apparent queen, **Lady Une' B'alam** ('Baby Jaguar'). Her name is that of a local goddess, in this case an infantile feline with Olmec antecedents.[6] A fine jade celt known as the Leiden Plaque, recording the accession of a king in 320, is often linked to Tikal although a firm connection is lacking. The next attested figure was **K'inich Muwaan Jol** ('Great-Sun Hawk Skull'), Tikal's 13th ruler. He is named on Stela 39 as the father of his successor Chak Tok Ich'aak I and appears alongside him in an iconic array of ancestral rulers on the later Stela 28.[7] Another outlying centre, this time Corozal, contains an important stela describing Muwaan Jol's death, which probably took place in 359.[8]

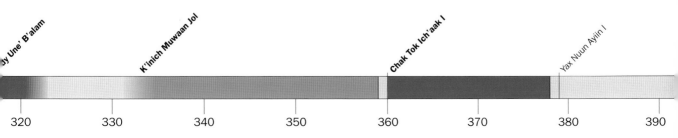

CHAK TOK ICH'AAK I	
Glyphic spelling	11 Ik' 10 Sek)
CHAK-TOK-ICH'A:K?	*Death*
('Great Burning?	15 January 378
Claw')	(8.17.1.4.12
Also known as	11 Eb 15 Mak)
Great Paw, Great	*Father*
Jaguar Paw, Jaguar	K'inich Muwaan Jol
Paw III, Toh Chak	*Mother*
Ich'ak	Lady B'alam Way
Dynastic title	*Monuments*
14th in the line	Stelae 26? & 39;
Accession	Hombre de Tikal?;
7 August 360?	Corozal Stela 1
(8.16.3.10.2	

This ceramic figure of Chak Tok Ich'aak I, a two-part censer, features his name glyph painted in his headdress (for another fine depiction see p. 1).

CHAK TOK ICH'AAK I

With a rich collection of inscribed ceramics and monuments, Chak Tok Ich'ak I is easily the best known of Tikal's early kings. His name seems to read 'Great Burning Claw', though it shows some variety in its spelling, with the *ich'aak* 'claw' element sometimes represented by the normal paw sign, and at others by a paw-nosed skull. His accession date has yet to be fixed with certainty, although a later statement of his reign-length suggests a placement in 360. A damaged stela found at distant El Temblor might be his inaugural monument, though its style may point to his earlier namesake instead.[9]

One or possibly two Chak Tok Ich'aak monuments have been recovered at Tikal, deposited as cache offerings in later construction. The lower section of the fine Stela 39, discovered in the Mundo Perdido complex, was carved in 376 to commemorate the 8.17.0.0.0 K'atun-ending, and shows the king trampling a bound captive.[10] His name appears on a second fragment, Stela 26, found in the North Acropolis' Temple 34. It has no surviving date, but includes an important listing of patron deities and ancestral kings. The high quality of these carvings is also reflected in the ceramic production of the time. Chak Tok Ich'aak is named on a lidded vessel incised with elaborate mythic scenes excavated from the Central Acropolis – Tikal's royal palace – while a series of finely incised offering plates and a superb portrait figurine also carry his name.[11]

Chak Tok Ich'aak presided over the largest and most progressive of the new Classic Maya cities. Part of this success was undoubtedly due to long-distance trade, not only that with the Maya highlands to the south but with distant Mexico and the powerful city of Teotihuacan. There are signs that imported Mexican architectural styles had already taken root at Tikal by this time and even hints of intermarriage between the two ruling elites. But Tikal's relationship with its western partners was about to change dramatically, and the lowland Maya would soon be drawn into a much wider Mesoamerican scheme.

THE LOST WORLD

Lying at the western edge of the city centre, the Mundo Perdido ('Lost World'), was the largest ceremonial precinct of Preclassic Tikal. A large four-sided pyramid was aligned with an eastern platform topped by a row of three temples, a configuration known as an 'E-Group'. Some were aligned as

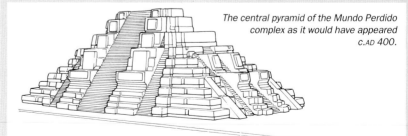

The central pyramid of the Mundo Perdido complex as it would have appeared c.AD 400.

TIKAL AND TEOTIHUACAN

Tikal enjoyed enduring contacts with Mexico and the great metropolis of Teotihuacan, 630 miles (1013 km) to the west. Trade items such as green-hued obsidian were being imported from there as early as the 3rd century AD, and local versions of the stepped masonry façade known as *talud-tablero*, a distinctly Mexican design, emerged at Tikal at about the same time. But towards the end of the 4th century there was an unprecedented surge in these foreign styles and artifacts, with distinctive ceramics – lidded tripods coated in stucco and painted with a range of Teotihuacan motifs – together with overt Mexican costume and symbolism on a group of monuments dated to this period. Tatiana Proskouriakoff dubbed the episode an 'arrival of strangers' and even countenanced the invasion of a 'foreign army'. These developments were certainly part of a much wider phenomenon across Mesoamerica at this time – equally evident at the Zapotec capital of Monte Albán and the highland Maya city of Kaminaljuyu – part of what Clemency Coggins has called the 'Age of Teotihuacan' and a 'New Order'. Recent breakthroughs in understanding the glyphic passages at Tikal that describe these interactions, in which David Stuart has taken the lead, offer a unique window into what took place here.[13]

This scene from a blackware vessel found at Tikal appears to show a group of armed Teotihuacanos arriving in the Maya area.

THE *ENTRADA* OF AD 378

Few, if any, events had such a transforming effect on the Maya lowlands as the arrival at Tikal of a lord called Siyaj K'ak' ('Fire Born') on 31 January 378. This episode would bring not only Tikal, but a whole swathe of the Central Area much more directly into the political, cultural and economic sphere of Teotihuacan, then at the height of its powers.

The journey, or *entrada*, of Siyaj K'ak' can be traced via the city of El Perú, 49 miles (78 km) due west of Tikal, where he is mentioned eight days earlier. This suggests a route that brought him from the west along the San Pedro Martir River, the natural approach from Mexico and Teotihuacan. A carved vessel uncovered at Tikal has long been interpreted as a stylized account of just such a journey, showing a line of armed Mexican warriors and vase-carrying 'ambassadors' travelling from a *talud-tablero*-style city towards another identified with an ethnic Maya figure. While the term 'arrival' might seem to have a reassuring neutrality, in this case it constitutes some kind of political takeover, even military conquest. For the Maya, like other Mesoamerican cultures, 'arrival' was used in both a literal and metaphorical sense to describe the establishment of new dynasties, and this was certainly its consequence here. In what would appear to be an instance of direct cause and effect, Chak Tok Ich'aak met his death – expressed as 'entering the water' – on the very same day. His demise was also that of his entire lineage, to be replaced by a completely new male line which seems to have been drawn from the ruling house of Teotihuacan itself.[14]

The New Order in the Peten

The radical new broom that now swept Tikal is apparent in a number of

solar observatories and used to chart solstices and equinoxes, though many were not oriented in this way and point to a different origin. The complex was rebuilt many times and its massive central pyramid shows the influence of Mexican styles as early as AD 250. The Mundo Perdido vied with the North Acropolis as the focus of Early Classic Tikal and, between 250 and 378, might even have supplanted it as the royal burial ground. In the 1980s a number of wealthy, though unidentified, graves were found within its three eastern temples.[12]

An unusual scene from a mural at Uaxactun shows a black-painted lord in gesture of greeting or submission to a warrior in full Mexican attire.

ways. Most of its monuments were destroyed (almost every broken fragment retrieved from construction fill pre-dates 378 in style). Others were dispersed from the city to peripheral locations, not just to El Encanto, Corozal and El Temblor, as we have seen, but to Uolantun (where an early monument had a new text added to it) and to the distant group where Tikal Stela 36 was found.[16]

Elsewhere, signs of the Teotihuacan intrusion are clearest at the nearby city of Uaxactun (see panel below). Here an important mural, uncovered in the 1930s but now destroyed, showed a lord in a gesture of greeting or submission to a Mexican-garbed warrior. Siyaj K'ak' is named on two Uaxactun stelae, one of which, Stela 5, celebrates the same arrival event seen at Tikal. Its portrait of an armed Teotihuacano is not Siyaj K'ak' himself but apparently another 'incomer' he had set in power. Such installations would take place at Tikal itself in 379 and at nearby Bejucal around 381. Siyaj K'ak' also appears at Río Azul in 393, probably in much the same context (see also p. 156).[17] The ethnicity of most of these subordinate rulers is hard to determine, but the central Peten was firmly in the grip of Siyaj K'ak' at this time. The extent of the New Order remains unclear, though isolated Mexican artifacts and motifs have been found as far north as Becan and to the east at Yaxha. A text from a looted jade ear ornament demonstrates that the city of Maasal (perhaps the large ruin of Naachtun) was part of this scheme, since its ruler is said to be the *yajaw* or 'vassal' of another important foreigner called Spearthrower Owl.[18] His significance is underlined again on a fine stucco-coated vessel – a typically Teotihuacan design – where he is said to be the overlord of an unknown Maya noble.

Unlike Siyaj K'ak', the intriguing Spearthrower Owl bears an overtly Mexican name possessing direct ties with Teotihuacan. There we see numerous anthropomorphic owls armed with shields, darts and the wooden sling the Aztecs later called the *atlatl*, whether painted on murals or sculpted in stone or clay. This imagery gives every impression of embodying some military concept, caste or deity, but its context at

Tikal suggests it had some titular function as well. The Tikal monument of greatest relevance to these issues, and a pivotal discovery of recent years, is the splendid Marcador. It was excavated by Juan Pedro Laporte in a residential group modelled in pure *talud-tablero* style, perhaps a special compound housing the incomers. It represents in stone a feather-trimmed standard, virtually identical to one uncovered at Teotihuacan save for a single item, its lengthy Maya text.[20] This tells of its own dedication in 416 by another vassal of Siyaj K'ak' and supplies a detailed, if still largely cryptic, account of the *entrada* of 378. In every other respect it is a totem dedicated to Spearthrower Owl. The owl, armed with an *atlatl*, appears at the heart of its feathered medallion, while the lord of this name features prominently in the text – including, significantly, a description of his accession to 'rulership' in 374.[21] Where, we must ask, did Spearthrower Owl reign? Crucially, later sources reveal that he fathered the next Tikal king, a character, as we shall see, depicted in Mexican dress. One damaged text could even indicate Spearthrower Owl's marriage to a Tikal lady.[22]

The idea that the 'rulership' concerned was that of Teotihuacan itself is tempting indeed and, if correct, would constitute one of the first real insights into the government of this mighty but mysterious city. Siyaj K'ak', the practical agent of the *entrada* mission, seems more like a general sent to further Teotihuacan's ambitions among its Maya neighbours.

(*Above*) This important tripod vessel was made for a noble who identified himself as the *yajaw* or vassal of the enigmatic Spearthrower Owl, here ascribed the title *kaloomte'*.

(*Above right*) Excavations into a Mexican-style residential compound south of the Mundo Perdido uncovered this 3-ft(1-m)-high stone banner known today as the Marcador.

Name glyphs for Siyaj K'ak (left) and Spearthrower Owl (right).

SIYAJ K'AK'	
Glyphic spelling	*Also known as*
SIY(AJ)-K'AK'	Smoking Frog, K'ak'
('Fire-born')	Sih

SPEARTHROWER OWL	
Glyphic spelling	*Accession (not Tikal*
?-KU?	*throne)*
(other spellings give	4 May 374
ja-?-ma ku)	(8.16.17.9.0
('Spearthrower	11 Ajaw 3 Wayeb)
Owl')	*Death*
Also known as	10 June 439
Atlatl-Cauac,	(9.0.3.9.18
Spearthrower	12 Etz'nab 11 Sip)
Shield	*Son*
	Yax Nuun Ayiin I

One of the more famous examples of Mexican style at Tikal is this fragment of Stela 32. It would seem to show a lord of Teotihuacan wearing the tasselled headdress and goggle-eyes of the Storm God Tlaloc.

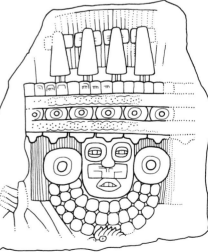

Yax Nuun Ayiin I
Curl Snout
379–404?

Siyaj Chan K'awiil II
Stormy Sky
411–456

K'an Chitam
Kan Boar
458–486?

Chak Tok Ich'aak II
Jaguar Paw Skull
c. 486–508

YAX NUUN AYIIN I	
Glyphic spelling	*Wife*
YAX-NU:N–AYI:N	Lady K'inich
('First? Caiman')	*Father*
Also known as	Spearthrower Owl
Curl Snout, Curl	*Son*
Nose	Siyaj Chan K'awiil II
Accession	*Monuments*
12 September 379	Stelae 4 & 18
(8.17.2.16.17	*Burial*
5 Kaban 10 Yaxk'in)	Temple 34 (Burial
Death	10)
17 June 404?	
(8.18.8.1.2	
2 Ik' 10 Sip)	

YAX NUUN AYIIN I

Although Siyaj K'ak' was now master of Tikal, he did not take the throne for himself but rather installed a son of Spearthrower Owl. Traditionally known as Curl Snout, his name can now be read as Yax Nuun Ayiin ('First ? Caiman').[23] The figure of Siyaj K'ak' continued to loom large over the new king's reign and he is twice named as his overlord, most likely because Yax Nuun Ayiin was little more than a boy at his elevation in September 379.

Yax Nuun Ayiin's two monuments, Stelae 4 and 18 – both erected for the 8.18.0.0.0 K'atun-ending of 396 – make few concessions to their Maya environment, depicting him in Mexican attire and in an unusual seated pose. Portraits on his son's Stela 31 make his affiliations equally overt, showing him as a fully equipped Teotihuacano, complete with plated helmet, spearthrower and square shield emblazoned with the goggle-eyed face of Mexican deities (see p. 35). By contrast, the titles of his wife suggest that she was a local woman, making theirs a strategic match designed to forge a new, culturally fused bloodline.

Few other records from Yax Nuun Ayiin's time survive, but the most interesting appears on a sculpture called the Hombre de Tikal ('Man of

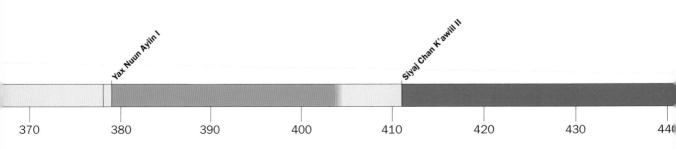

(*Above*) This lidded vessel from Yax Nuun Ayiin's Burial 10 represents an interesting fusion of Maya form and Mexican decoration.

(*Opposite*) With his face framed by a jaguar helmet and string of shells, Yax Nuun Ayiin I appears on Stela 4 in pure Mexican costume.

Tikal'), a rather portly, and now headless, seated figure. Its text, etched across its back like an elaborate tattoo, details events in 403 and 406, where Yax Nuun Ayiin shares prominence with a lesser lord called K'uk' Mo' ('Quetzal Macaw'). Glyphs carved on each shoulder provide the name and *tajal chaak* 'Torch Rain God' epithet of Chak Tok Ich'aak I, and this shows every sign of being a piece re-used from his reign, presumably a personal portrait.[24]

The chronology surrounding Yax Nuun Ayiin's death is none too clear. An accounting of his reign-length on the later Stela 31 might place his burial in 404, though the aforementioned Hombre de Tikal could indicate that he was still alive in November 406. A sign that he did not live to see the 8.19.10.0.0 ceremony of May 406 might come from its association with the otherwise unknown Siyaj Chan K'inich ('Sky-born Sun God'). This character may have presided over an interregnum before the enthronement of Yax Nuun Ayiin's son Siyaj Chan K'awiil II in 411.

Burial 10

Both of Yax Nuun Ayiin's stelae were found reset at the foot of Temple 34, the first pyramid to break the confines of the North Acropolis proper and intrude onto its fronting terrace. Deep within, in a large chamber hollowed from bedrock, lay Burial 10, a grave of extraordinary richness and diversity. The king's corpse was laid on a wooden bier, surrounded by the bodies of no fewer than nine sacrificed youths. Offerings included a spectacular assemblage of pottery vessels, many decorated with Mexican deities and motifs. One of these bears the legend 'the drinking vessel of the son of Spearthrower Owl'. There was also a ceramic effigy of an old trident-eyed god, who sits on a stool of bound human longbones. In one corner lay five turtle carapaces of increasing size, three still arranged on a rack in the form of an ancient *marimba* (a percussion instrument much like a xylophone). A small jade ornament carved into the head of a curl-snouted caiman provides a further link with Yax Nuun Ayiin, as does the offering of a headless caiman laid next to the body.[25]

(*Left*) This ceramic censer of an aged deity is one of the more characteristically Maya objects found in Burial 10.

K'an Chitam

Chak Tok Ich'aak II

Lady of Tikal
Kaloomte' B'alam

450   460   470   480   490   500   510

SIYAJ CHAN K'AWIIL II	
Glyphic spelling	10 Ajaw 13 Muwan)
SIY-AJ-CHAN	*Wife*
K'AWI:L	Lady Ayiin
('Sky-born K'awiil')	*Father*
Also known as	Yax Nuun Ayiin I
Stormy Sky, Manikin	*Mother*
Cleft Sky	Lady K'inich
Dynastic title	*Son*
16th in the line	K'an Chitam
Accession	*Monuments*
26 November 411	Stelae 1, 28? & 31
(8.18.15.11.0	*Burial*
3 Ajaw 13 Sak)	Temple 33 (Burial
Death	48)
3 February 456	
(9.1.0.8.0	

SIYAJ CHAN K'AWIIL II

For more than thirty years, Tikal's New Order had presented itself in the distinctive trappings of Teotihuacan imperialism. But with the accession of Siyaj Chan K'awiil II or 'Sky-born K'awiil' in 411 this was set to change, as the regime sought to absorb these traits and re-invent itself as a flagbearer of continuity and tradition.[26] The transition is evident on the distinctly Maya-style Stela 1, where his symbolic regalia may serve to chart his matrilineal ancestry. Stela 28, a likely commission, provides a similar listing, this time kings from the line of Chak Tok Ich'aak. This strategy of assimilation finds no better expression than Stela 31, a truly dexterous piece of political footwork.

Stela 31's front face shows Siyaj Chan K'awiil II swathed in the riotous ornament of Maya kingship. It is consciously archaic in style and largely a copy of Stela 29 from 150 years earlier. His complex headgear carries the crest of Yax Ehb' Xook, making his claims of dynastic revival explicit (on two vase texts he lists himself as 16th in his line).[27] In his right hand he holds aloft a headdress which, though Maya in form, bears a tiny medallion with the Teotihuacan emblem of owl, shield and spears, making it some kind of composite crown linked with his grandfather. His father Yax Nuun Ayiin is shown three times on the monument. Above the king he floats as an ancestral sun god, a purely Maya form; while on each stela side he wears the contrasting uniform of a Teotihuacano warrior. In sum, Stela 31 proclaims the rebirth of orthodox kingship, neither sullied nor diluted by its foreign blood, but reinvigorated.

The stela's rear-face text, which is of extraordinary length for this period, sets out Tikal's history leading up to the *entrada*, passing through the establishment of the new dynasty and on to Siyaj Chan K'awiil's own reign. Special mention is made of the 4th-century queen Lady Une' B'alam, who seems to provide an important precedent for the transfer of the founder's bloodline through a woman.[28] His own part is surprisingly small, with reference only to his accession, the completion of the 9th Bak'tun (9.0.0.0.0) in 435, and the stela's dedication in 445. One of the last legible events is the

(*Above*) This engaging 'full-figure' hieroglyph appears in the headdress of Siyaj Chan K'awiil II on Stela 31. It shows K'awiil, a patron god of royal lineages, emerging from a split in the sky – spelling the king's name 'Sky-Born K'awiil'.

(*Right*) This tripod vessel, incised with a vivid mythological scene, refers to Siyaj Chan K'awiil by his title '16th in the line of Yax Ehb' Xook'. Significantly, he is here named as some kind of overlord to its owner, the ruler of Ucanal.

We see here the front and sides of Stela 31, showing Siyaj Chan K'awiil flanked by two portraits of his father Yax Nuun Ayiin.

SPREAD OF THE DYNASTIC SYSTEM

While Maya kingdoms traced their conceptual origins back into the vast expanse of mythical time, the foundations of ruling dynasties were given dates in the here and now. By charting these we can see that the dynastic tradition was initially slow to spread from the central Peten, but gained considerable impetus after the Mexican *entrada* of 378. A spurt of new foundations include those of Palenque, Copan and Quirigua (and the earliest date at Seibal) during Siyaj Chan K'awiil II's reign alone. These sites share either inscriptional or stylistic links with Teotihuacan or Tikal and seem to reflect a specific movement to exploit underdeveloped regions under their patronage.

death of his grandfather Spearthrower Owl in 439, by then a grand old man. This was of enough importance to be noted at El Zapote, one of Tikal's important early clients (on Stela 5).[29]

The full extent of Tikal's domain at this time is difficult to gauge. Its great size and cultural energy have been seen to denote some kind of 'leadership' of the lowland Early Classic, and we cannot doubt its pre-eminent place in the New Order scheme. The limited number of early inscriptions outside the Tikal-Uaxactun area hampers the search for direct evidence, but Siyaj Chan K'awiil did exercise power at least as far as Ucanal, 32 miles (51 km) to the southeast, since a carved vessel from there places him as overlord to its king.[30]

The painted tomb

Siyaj Chan K'awiil's death seems to have occurred in February 456. His grave has long been identified as Burial 48, found on the key central axis of the North Acropolis beneath Temple 33.[31] It shows certain continuities with Burial 10, being the only other royal tomb at Tikal to possess human sacrifices (just two this time), though the Mexican influence in its offerings is much reduced. Rarely for Tikal, the chamber was painted, predominantly with a series of glyph-like symbols that define it as lying

TEMPLE 33: THE KING'S MEMORIAL

Siyaj Chan K'awiil's rock-cut tomb, Burial 48, was capped by a mortuary shrine, Temple 33. Its first incarnation in a 200-year history featured a broad basal platform with large stucco masks flanking either side of its stairway. Still within the Early Classic, a new superstructure and a fresh set of masks and panels were added (A). This second version was overbuilt by a third during the Hiatus period (pp. 40–43) (B), which involved tearing out the old staircase and setting the royal but unidentified Burial 23. At the same time, Siyaj Chan K'awiil's Stela 31 was brought up to the former sanctuary and ceremonially entombed within it. Construction of the new pyramid was still underway when the death of another high-ranking person necessitated a new entry into its rubble core and the dedication of Burial 24. Temple 33 now rose uninterrupted to its final height of 108 ft (33 m) (see p. 43).[32]

Executed in a cursive, even hurried hand, Burial 48 was decorated with extensive painting. Here excavator Aubrey Trik examines the Long Count date 9.1.1.10.10 (AD 457) recorded on its back wall.

in the flowery ether of divine space. Its north wall includes a Long Count date from March 457, the tomb's completion over a year, it seems, after his death. There may be some connection between this extended interval and the condition of the body, which was tightly bundled but missing its head and, it seems, its hands too. Whether this points to a violent death, or to some poorly understood ritual purpose, is hard to determine.

The king's original mortuary shrine, the first Temple 33, was soon remodelled and its stucco decoration replaced by a new programme of masks and panels. This second structure stood for perhaps two centuries before its burial beneath a third and final version in the Late Classic (see panel). As part of this project Stela 31 was dragged up to the former sanctuary, set almost directly above the deeply buried tomb and, accompanied by much burning and smashing of pots, sealed within the new pyramid.

(Right) Cutaway drawing of Temple 33 showing its earliest phases encased in a massive 7th-century pyramid.

(Far right) One of two large basal masks from the first Temple 33 discovered behind a later remodelling.

A

Stela 31

B

K'AN CHITAM	
Glyphic spelling [K'AN] CHITAM? ('Precious/Yellow Peccary') *Also known as* Kan Boar, K'an Ak *Birth* 26 November 415? (8.18.19.12.1 8 Imix 14 Sak) *Accession* 8 August 458 (9.1.2.17.17 4 Kaban 15 Xul)	*Wife* Lady Tzutz Nik *Father* Siyaj Chan K'awiil II *Mother* Lady Ayiin *Son* Chak Tok Ich'aak II *Monuments* Stelae 2, 9, 13 & 40

The recently discovered Stela 40 shows a lavishly attired K'an Chitam (note the name glyph in his headdress). AD 468.

CHAK TOK ICH'AAK II	
Glyphic spelling CHAK-TOK-ICH'A:K? ('Great Burning? Claw') *Also known as* Jaguar Paw II, Jaguar Paw Skull *Death* 24 July 508 (9.3.13.12.5 13 Chikchan 13 Xul)	*Father* K'an Chitam *Mother* Lady Tzutz Nik *Son* Wak Chan K'awiil *Daughter* Lady of Tikal? *Monuments* Stelae 3, 7, 15 & 27

K'AN CHITAM

The Tikal title next passed to Siyaj Chan K'awiil's son K'an Chitam ('Precious/Yellow Peccary') in 458. Until recently very little was known of him, but in 1996 a Spanish conservation project working at the base of Temple 29 – a west-facing pyramid on the terrace of the North Acropolis – unearthed an exceptional monument from his reign.[33] Dating to 468, Stela 40 closely follows the canon of Stelae 29 and 31, showing K'an Chitam holding aloft a headdress, though this time it is a plated, Teotihuacan-style helmet. The sides of the stone carry fine portraits of his father and mother, while its rear-face is covered by another long text. Though damaged, a reference to his birth might be reconstructed as 415, followed by an accession (apparently to some junior rank) in 434. It includes a very brief, but useful, accounting of his father's reign, before describing his own accession in August 458.

Stela 2 mirrors his father's Stela 1 where, once again, its symbolism is devoted to matrilineal descent. But he was also prepared to innovate. The 'staff stelae', small in stature and brief in text, portray the king impersonating fire deities, each equipped with a ceremonial 'fire-drill' and jaguar-mask studded cape.[34] They begin with his Stela 9 from the 9.2.0.0.0 K'atun-ending of 475 and the undated Stela 13. These monuments were the earliest found in their original positions in Tikal's Great Plaza. K'an Chitam's texts make no mention of external affairs, but if he was still in power in August 486 he would have presided over Tikal's attack on the northerly city of Maasal. Known from a later source, this is one of the first wars to be described in a Maya inscription.

CHAK TOK ICH'AAK II

K'an Chitam was succeeded by his son, Chak Tok Ich'aak II. His earliest mention is in October 486, the occasion of his 'first sacrifice' (usually a childhood rite of passage), and he was certainly in power by the time he erected Stela 3 in 488. Seven years later he marked the 9.3.0.0.0 ending of 495 with a flurry of three monuments, though their brief texts add nothing in the way of biographical detail. All are firmly in the 'staff stelae' style, though distinguished from his father's by the greater elaboration of their fire-drills. The last two references to Chak Tok Ich'aak come from outside Tikal. The city of Tonina records his death in July 508, while just 13 days later one of his vassals was captured by Yaxchilan (p. 120).[35] This surprising turn of events – Yaxchilan was a real minnow at the time – paints a picture of Tikal's vulnerability at this key juncture, perhaps part of a much wider military and political setback ignited by emerging rivals. Certainly the next half-century, sometimes called Tikal's Middle Classic, is an era of dynastic disturbance, and it was some 30 years before Chak Tok Ich'aak's son took his inheritance.

Lady of Tikal
511–527>

Kaloomte' B'alam
c. 511–527>

Bird Claw
?

Wak Chan K'awiil
Double Bird
537–562

Stela 10 carries a portrait of the 19th Tikal king, Kaloomte' B'alam, probably dedicated in the year AD 527.

LADY OF TIKAL	
Glyphic spelling IX-KALO:M[TE'] IX-yo-K'IN?	8 Ak'bal 11 Mol) *Accession* 19 April 511
Also known as Woman of Tikal	(9.3.16.8.4 11 K'an 17 Pop)
Birth 1 September 504 (9.3.9.13.3	*Monuments* Stelae 6, 12 & 23

KALOOMTE' B'ALAM	
Glyphic spelling KALO:M[TE'] ?[?]	*Dynastic title* 19th in the line
Also known as Curl Head	*Monuments* Stelae 10, 12 & 25

BIRD CLAW	
Glyphic spelling ?-TE'?	*Monument* Stela 8
Also known as Animal Skull I, Ete I	

THE TROUBLED 'MIDDLE CLASSIC': AD 508–562

Although its record is beset both by poor preservation and deliberate damage, a better understanding of Tikal's murky 'Middle Classic' period is now emerging. The era is epitomized by Stela 23, which had been re-erected, broken and incomplete, in a residential compound some distance from the Great Plaza. It bears the defaced portrait of a woman dubbed the **Lady of Tikal**, its rear text recording her birth in 504 and elevation to the rank of *ajaw* in 511, a queen at just six years of age. Almost certainly a daughter of Chak Tok Ich'aak II, her once shadowy reign proves to have been both substantial and politically complex. Although using a different regnal name, she is presumably the same female mentioned on the fragmentary Stela 6, where she celebrated the end of the 4th K'atun (9.4.0.0.0) in 514, and again on Stela 12 from 527. She seems never to have ruled in her own right and was instead partnered by one or more male co-rulers.[36]

On Stela 12 the Lady of Tikal is linked with the '19th in the line', a lord named, in part, **Kaloomte' B'alam** (the queen does not seem to have a place in the sequence). While the text describes her performance of the key year-ending rituals, the stela itself was dedicated in his honour and

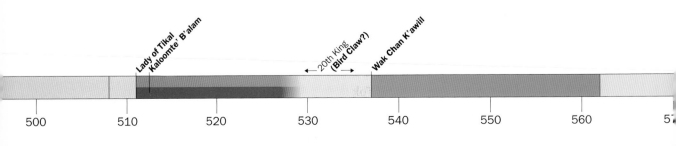

carries his portrait. Stela 12's twin is Stela 10. Badly damaged, it carries a particularly difficult text. It includes a royal accession, presumably Kaloomte' B'alam's own, but otherwise deals with early events in his career. In 486 he was involved in the 'axing' of Maasal and the capture of the prisoner shown on Stela 10's front face. We might infer from this that he had long experience as a Tikal general before his elevation to consort or guardian of the young queen.[37]

The name of the Lady of Tikal appears again on the equally perplexing Stela 8, the only monument of the lord, presumed ruler, that has been dubbed **Bird Claw**. A 'staff stela' in the style of Chak Tok Ich'aak II, neither its date nor this lord's relationship to the Lady of Tikal can be deciphered at present. The 20th Tikal ruler, for which Bird Claw is a candidate, ruled at some point between 527 and 537, but is otherwise unknown. Architecturally, we know that there were major developments during the Middle Classic era, with the building of the large East Acropolis platform and new plaza floorings throughout the central zone. The first twin-pyramid complex, a special arena for K'atun-ending ceremonies, was also added in the East Plaza at this time (see p. 51).[38]

The undoing of Tikal

Long known as Double Bird, Tikal's 21st ruler was **Wak Chan K'awiil**. We know that he was a son of Chak Tok Ich'aak II, probably born in January 508. His only surviving monument, Stela 17, was commissioned in 557 to celebrate the K'atun- (20-year-) anniversary of an event in 537. Though badly damaged, the context suggests that this marked the king's 'arrival' at *yax mutal*, Tikal itself. No ordinary accession, this is surely the return of a one-time exile, only enhancing the general picture of intrigue and irregularity in the 6th-century succession.[39] His use of the founder's name, on one occasion substituted for his own, is probably significant in this regard.

Despite its internal machinations, Tikal remained a major force. Wak Chan K'awiil sponsored the accession of Yajaw Te' K'inich II, ruler of distant Caracol in 553 (pp. 88–9). But by this time a notably closer kingdom, Naranjo, had come under the sway of Calakmul and a serious challenge to Tikal's power was taking shape. Caracol Altar 21 chronicles the rapid decline in Tikal fortunes, beginning with the collapse of its patronage over Caracol just three years later – apparent when Wak Chan K'awiil 'axed' a Caracol lord in 556. His own undoing was only six years away. Tikal was overrun in a 'star war' attack in 562, a date coinciding with a stationary node in the motion of Venus (p. 16).[40] The name of its perpetrator is badly damaged, but surviving details make Calakmul the prime suspect (pp. 89–90, 104). Tikal's mastery of the Peten was at an end and the city plunged into a long 'dark age'. Subsequent sections of Altar 21 probably deal with the ritual killing of Wak Chan K'awiil, who is not heard of again. Stela 17 itself met an unfortunate end: broken at its base and erased in part, it was found dumped by the side of one of the city's main causeways.

This painted plate, a Teotihuacan owl emblazoned at its heart, makes a dynastic point for Wak Chan K'awiil. He uses it to connect his celebration of the K'atun-ending 9.6.0.0.0 in 554 to his father Chak Tok Ich'aak II's commemoration of 9.3.0.0.0 in 495.

WAK CHAN K'AWIIL	
Glyphic spelling	(9.5.3.9.15
WAK-CHAN K'AWI:L	12 Men 18 K'ank'in)
Also known as	*Father*
Double Bird	Chak Tok Ich'aak II
Dynastic title	*Mother*
21st in the line	Lady Hand
Accession	*Monument*
29 December 537?	Stela 17

Animal Skull
>593–628>

23rd and 24th Rulers
c. 640

Nuun Ujol Chaak
Shield Skull
>657–679>

This fine painted plate, similar to two found in his tomb, shows Animal Skull holding a K'awiil-topped staff.

For the next 130 years not a single dated monument – or even a potential fragment of one – has been identified at Tikal and this long silence has come to be known as its Hiatus period AD 562–692. The phenomenon has been linked to the fall of Teotihuacan (which took place at this time) and even to the idea of a 'little collapse' across the Maya area.[41] But today we can point more specifically to Tikal's military humbling and the corresponding rise of a rival power in the Peten: Calakmul. At the same time, a better understanding of the Hiatus itself shows that far from being a moribund or uniform era, it was one full of incident and change.

ANIMAL SKULL

Wak Chan K'awiil was succeeded by Animal Skull, the 22nd ruler of Tikal, at some unknown point after 562. Despite outward signs of continuity, there is good reason to doubt that the new ruler was from the existing royal patriline. With no surviving monuments, our knowledge of him mostly relies on the bountiful collection of painted ceramics from his reign. Here his pedigrees give special emphasis to his high-ranking mother, an *ix ajaw* (literally 'lady lord') of B'alam ('Jaguar'), but minimal attention to his father, who is named only once and without title.

ANIMAL SKULL	
Glyphic spelling K'INICH-?[TE'?] ('Great-Sun ?') *Also known as* Lizard Head, Animal Skull II, Ete II *Dynastic title* 22nd in the line	*Father* Fire Cross *Mother* Lady Hand Sky of B'alam *Burial* Temple 32 (Burial 195)

Animal Skull

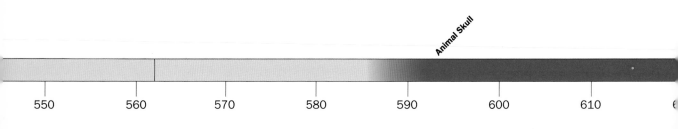

(*Above*) A painter from the court of Animal Skull created this vase with a list of early Tikal kings, decorated, appropriately enough, with the royal mat pattern rendered in regal red.

(*Below*) One of four effigies of the god K'awiil retrieved from Burial 195. Their stucco surfaces are original, surviving the complete decay of the wood they once coated.

Clearly, Animal Skull's matrilineal background was his major claim to legitimacy.[42] It may be significant that it was one of Animal Skull's painters that produced the vase listing early Tikal kings – the line directly preceding the Mexican arrivals – perhaps a sign that he sought to ally himself with the city's *ancien régime* (p. 27).[43]

There is a recurring link between conquests of the 'star war' variety and lengthy silences. While internal disarray may account for short periods of inactivity, longer spans are better attributed to foreign subjugation, to the rule of usurper dynasties or to later struggles between such interlopers and resurgent local lines. Animal Skull's exact role in these difficult times is uncertain. He might represent the first faltering steps towards renewed Tikal independence, or, conversely, he may have ruled as a puppet of the city's conquerors.

Burial in the North Acropolis

Although not one of the richest graves at Tikal in terms of jade or other precious goods, Animal Skull's Burial 195, embedded within Temple 32 of the North Acropolis, is certainly one of the most fascinating. Fortunately for us, the tomb was flooded soon after its dedication and a thick layer of mud deposited throughout the chamber. Painstaking excavation revealed hollow cavities, all that remained of decayed wooden grave goods. Filled with Plaster of Paris, many could be recovered in whole or in part, providing a unique glimpse of the perishable riches that once accompanied the dead. Among the more important were four large panels (perhaps a dismantled box) onto which the body had been laid. Each was carved with a central scene showing the king holding a double-headed serpent bar, flanked on either side by glyphic cartouches. Retrieved in the same way were four stucco-painted models of K'awiil, a small throne once decorated with glyphs, and the remains of a 'yoke', the protective belt used in the ballgame (found close to what could be a perished rubber ball). The body itself had been generously wrapped in layers of cloth saturated with a red pigment.[44]

The wooden boards feature a damaged but legible date of 9.8.0.0.0 or 593, and go on to provide Animal Skull's name, titles and Tikal emblem, as well as his status as a 3 K'atun Ajaw (i.e. aged between 39 and 59 years). Though obscured beneath a later repainting, the same date was written on one of two large plates in the tomb. The date of his interment is unknown, but an appearance of his distinctive name sequence at the city of Altar de Sacrificios, in the Pasión region, could suggest that he lived as late as 628.[45]

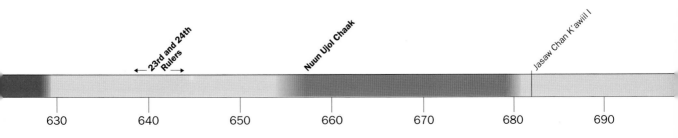

23rd and 24th Rulers

Nuun Ujol Chaak

Jasaw Chan K'awiil I

630   640   650   660   670   680   690

THE TIKAL EARTHWORKS

In 1966 archaeologists mapping Tikal's northern outskirts came upon a substantial ditch and embankment 2.8 miles (4.6 km) from the centre of the site. Cut 10 ft (3 m) into bedrock and 11 ft (3.5 m) wide, the resulting spoil had been heaped onto its southern side to form a rampart. Running from east to west and traversing undulating terrain, the feature proved to be at least 6 miles (9.5 km) in length and crossed at four or five points by causeways. At either end it disappeared into the major *bajos* or seasonal swamps that flank Tikal. As a single construction effort it surpasses anything found in the grander setting of the ceremonial core (its excavated volume of at least 118,047 cu. yards (90,250 cu. m) can be compared with the 23,884 cu. yards (18,260 cu. m) used in the building of Temple 1). Limited explorations to the south of the city have since found corresponding sections of earthwork. If complete, this would more than double the size of the project.

Forming a combined obstacle 19 ft (6 m) high and almost certainly topped by a further wooden parapet, this elaborate and expensive barrier shows every sign of being an active fortification. The vast area demarcated by the two lines, some 46.3 sq. miles (120 sq. km), makes it clear that rural farmland, rather than the urban core, was the primary object of its defence. Such remains are notoriously difficult to date, but ceramics retrieved from the northern line suggest that it was built in the Early Classic, when the crossing points were few or absent altogether. The one excavated causeway was added in later years, but initially was very narrow. This was widened significantly during the Late Classic and the line seems to have fallen into disuse at this stage.[46]

NUUN UJOL CHAAK	
Glyphic spelling NU:N-(u)-JOL CHA:K ('?-headed Chaak') *Also known as* Shield Skull, Nun Bak Chak	*Wife* Lady Jaguar Seat *Son* Jasaw Chan K'awiil

THE REIGNS OF THE 23RD AND 24TH RULERS

Animal Skull's reverential entombment and grand memorial pyramid point to an orderly succession, presumably by a member of his own lineage. While Animal Skull's demise had not immediately sparked a dynastic crisis, a profound schism soon opened in the Tikal elite and a contest for rightful use of the Mutal title ensued. Perhaps as early as 648 a disaffected or ousted faction decamped 70 miles (112 km) southwest to a region called the Petexbatun. Here a figure called B'alaj Chan K'awiil established the site of Dos Pilas as the capital of a rival Tikal state. It is of no small importance that this was under the tutelage and protection of Calakmul (pp. 56–7, 108–9). Neither Tikal's 23rd ruler, nor the subsequent 24th, can be identified with certainty, though characters named at Dos Pilas may represent this missing section of the dynasty.

NUUN UJOL CHAAK

Once an obscure figure, known only from a few short mentions at Tikal, we now recognize Nuun Ujol Chaak as a major ruler during some of his kingdom's most star-crossed years. If he erected any of his own monuments they did not survive the traumas of the Hiatus, but a surprisingly detailed picture of his life comes from references inscribed elsewhere.

It is tempting to read Tikal's internal discord as a struggle between a Calakmul-sanctioned line and one striving to restore its independence, though the truth of the matter may never be known. Whether legitimate claimant or usurper, Nuun Ujol Chaak now faced not only a rival for his title in the shape of B'alaj Chan K'awiil, ruler of breakaway Dos Pilas, but fresh opposition from Calakmul, protector and overlord of the fledgling exiles. The scene was now set for a personal conflict that would endure 22 years and dominate Nuun Ujol Chaak's troubled reign.

Nuun Ujol Chaak's first major setback occurred in 657, the earliest date we have for him, when Calakmul's Yuknoom the Great launched an attack on Tikal in the form of another 'star war'. Nuun Ujol Chaak fled the city, at least for a time, while Tikal itself may have been compelled to render tribute.[47] Whether garnering support among distant allies or, more probably, in exile, he next makes an appearance at the western city of Palenque. Two years after the war, in 659, he is mentioned there in some kind of military episode and seven days later goes to Palenque itself, in the company of its famous king K'inich Janaab' Pakal (p. 165).[48]

In time, Nuun Ujol Chaak managed to restore himself to Tikal, probably by means of some campaign now lost to us. It was 13 years, however, before he could mount an effective riposte, capturing Dos Pilas in 672 and ejecting his rival. His hold over the Petexbatun lasted five years, but another defeat at the hands of Calakmul forced him to relinquish the rebel seat in 677. Two years later the decisive engagement of the series took place when Nuun Ujol Chaak was defeated by B'alaj Chan K'awiil, most likely in concert with his Calakmul allies.

NECROPOLIS OF KINGS

At the very heart of the city lies the North Acropolis, one of the most complex and enduring edifices of Maya civilization. Beginning life in the Preclassic, *c.* 350 BC, it developed into a necropolis for Tikal's Classic dynasty. Each successive kingly interment sparked further modification and enlargement, with new temples enveloping older ones like Russian dolls. After AD 400 it expanded from the confines of its original Northern Platform to add a row of tall pyramids to its terrace, progressively obscuring the early complex from view. Jasaw Chan K'awiil's entombment in Temple 1 (*c.* AD 734), on the east side of the fronting Great Plaza, marked a final break with the old pattern and thereafter royal burials were dispersed across the city. By the 9th century, the complex held a complement of 43 stelae and 30 altars, of which 18 were carved with royal portraits and historical texts. Receiving burials even in Postclassic times, the North Acropolis was a scene of mortuary activity for at least 1,300 years.

Interestingly, the conflict took place exactly one K'atun – 20 Maya years to the day – after the arrival event recorded at Palenque. Carved some years later, the Palenque scribes may have contrived the earlier date to draw a particular parallel.[49]

The ultimate fate of Nuun Ujol Chaak remains uncertain. Following the battle there was an interment of bones at Dos Pilas, though the victim seems to have been another Tikal lord called Nuun B'alam (p. 57). Burial 23, the tomb which gave rise to the third version of the North Acropolis' Temple 33, has long been thought a candidate for Nuun Ujol Chaak's final resting-place, though the unexplored Temple 35 might be another contender.[50]

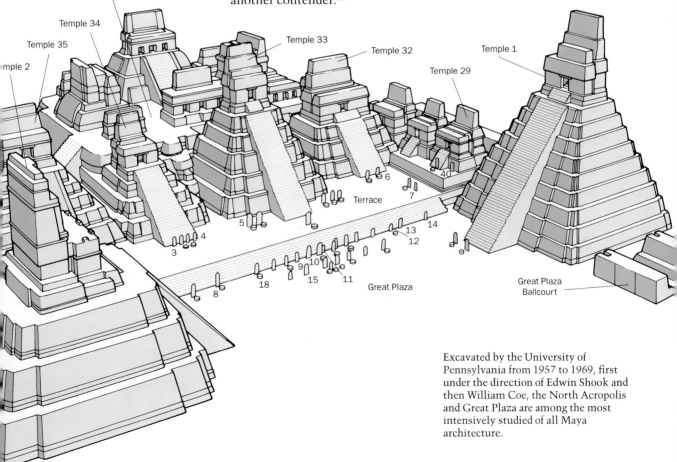

Excavated by the University of Pennsylvania from 1957 to 1969, first under the direction of Edwin Shook and then William Coe, the North Acropolis and Great Plaza are among the most intensively studied of all Maya architecture.

Jasaw Chan K'awiil I
Ruler A
682–734

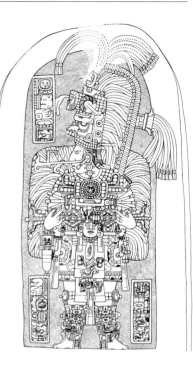

Erected in the northern enclosure of his second twin-pyramid complex, Group N, in AD 711, Stela 16 shows a richly attired Jasaw Chan K'awiil at the height of his powers (the 'j', it will be recalled, always represents a hard 'h' sound).

JASAW CHAN K'AWIIL I	
Glyphic spelling ja-sa-wa CHAN-na-K'AWI:L-ia ('K'awiil that Clears? the Sky') *Also known as* Ruler A, Ah Cacao, Sky Rain *Accession* 3 May 682 (9.12.9.17.16 5 Kib 14 Sotz') *Father* Nuun Ujol Chaak *Mother* Lady Jaguar Seat	*Wife* Lady Kalajuun Une' Mo' *Son* Yik'in Chan K'awiil *Monuments* Stelae 16 & 30; Altars 5 & 14; Temple 1 Lintels 2 & 3; stucco façade from Structure 5D-57 *Burial* Temple 1 (Burial 116)

JASAW CHAN K'AWIIL I

However serious the defeat of 679 might have been, it did not lead to the overthrow of Nuun Ujol Chaak's lineage and three years later he was succeeded by a son, Jasaw Chan K'awiil I. Under his direction Tikal was to experience a spectacular reversal in its fortunes and a resurgence that would restore much of its Early Classic glory. This is not simply the view of modern scholarship, but an image Jasaw Chan K'awiil clearly envisaged for himself, linking his reign to the heyday of Tikal's past and era of its closest contacts with central Mexico.

The defeat of Calakmul

Crucially, he succeeded in an exploit that eluded his father, a decisive victory over Calakmul. On 5 August 695 he 'brought down the flint and shield' of its illustrious king Yich'aak K'ak' ('Fiery Claw'). While its phrasing is formulaic and unremarkable, this clash was to prove a real turning point, sparking off the decline of Calakmul's wider hegemony and Tikal's rebirth as a militant power.

The battle is recorded high in the ceiling of Temple 1 – that great icon of Maya architecture – on one of two intricately carved wooden lintels.[51]

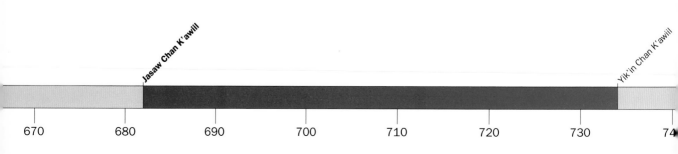

Jasaw Chan K'awiil

Yik'in Chan K'awiil

670   680   690   700   710   720   730   74

Prominent mention is made of the capture of *yajaw maan*, one of Calakmul's leading patron deities. Maya armies, like their cousins across Mesoamerica, carried effigies of their gods into battle, pitting rival deities against one another in much the same way as they did mortal men. The lintel scene shows a victorious Jasaw Chan K'awiil enthroned on a processional litter, dwarfed by the towering jaguar effigy at his back. The event was a commemorative 'triumph' (in its original Roman sense) that took place a month after the conflict. The king let blood and 'conjured a god' as part of a pageant, a colourful affair in which the story of the battle, both its historical and mythic aspects, was evidently performed. Masked pageants in highland Guatemala today retell the story of the Spanish Conquest in much the same way.[52]

A stucco tableau from the façade of Structure 5D-57, in the heart of Tikal's Central Acropolis, describes more of the aftermath. The Tikal king is shown holding the tether of a bound captive, the subject of an 'adorning' event 13 days after the battle (apparently preparations for the victim's sacrifice). Yich'aak K'ak' is named in an adjacent caption, but it is unclear from this broken text whether the prisoner is the Calakmul king, one of his nobles, or a foreign ally (p. 76).[53]

Symbols of renewal

Jasaw Chan K'awiil articulated Tikal's revitalization in a very particular way by reviving the symbolism of the once mighty, but now fallen, Teotihuacan.[54] In so doing he evoked direct comparison with the New Order that seized and galvanized the Peten three centuries earlier. His lineage might even represent a literal restoration of this Mexican-derived dynasty. While the stucco façade shows him bedecked in Teotihuacan motifs, the most vivid example of this programme appears on the second wooden lintel from Temple 1. Here in a direct counterpart to the triumphal procession, the scene is repeated in entirely Mexican form. Dominated this time by a giant effigy of the bejewelled war serpent the Maya called *waxaklajuun ub'aah chan* ('18 images of the snake'), the king wears a mosaic helmet and is armed with spearthrower and darts – every inch a Teotihuacano warrior.

Though the battle lintel itself is devoid of such 'mexicana', an allusion is buried in the text. The day selected for the commemoration, 14 September 695, was the 13th K'atun-anniversary (256 years) of the death of Spearthrower Owl, the Mexican overlord and father of Yax Nuun Ayiin I.[55] Jasaw Chan K'awiil's calendrical ties with this great lord began with his accession, just one day short of 308 years after Spearthrower Owl's own crowning.

Jasaw's realm

While Tikal was a force to be reckoned with once more, the scope of its direct influence was still rather modest. What seems to have been its traditional control of Motul de San José – the neighbouring kingdom to the south that encompassed Lake Peten-Itza – is reflected in a text

Jasaw Chan K'awiil is here shown enthroned on a great palanquin or ceremonial litter, dwarfed by a monumental effigy of a supernatural jaguar called *nuun b'alam chaaknal*. The occasion is a celebration of the recent victory over Calakmul, timed to coincide with the 260th anniversary of Spearthrower Owl's death. The key portion of the text (detail) describes the 'downing' of the arms and insignia of Yich'aak K'ak', king of Calakmul in AD 695.

from 711 naming Jasaw Chan K'awiil as its overlord.[56] But clashes with Naranjo in early 695 and Dos Pilas in 705 define the limits of his authority to the east and south, while El Perú, Tikal's nearest western neighbour, was still firmly in the clasp of Calakmul at this time. Increased influence to the north, however, beyond Uaxactun, may be reflected in an unusual exhumation ritual detailed on Altar 5. Here the Tikal king is joined by the ruler of Maasal – one of Tikal's Early Classic victims and perhaps the city of Naachtun – to disinter the bones of an unknown lady.[57] Maasal otherwise shows consistent ties with Calakmul, and control of this site may well have been an important gain of the main 695 war.

The later stages of Jasaw's rule seem stable and prosperous and his energies were now directed towards construction projects. His three K'atun-endings in power, falling in 692, 711 and 731, were marked with the twin-pyramid complexes M, N and O. He may also have been responsible for replacing the earliest arena of this kind in the East Plaza with a ballcourt and its associated Teotihuacan-style temple.[58] Other projects included major additions to the Central Acropolis and the building of Temple 2, a squat but massive pyramid on the west side of the Great Plaza. Its single carved lintel and now shattered stela (once placed high on its superstructure) depict a royal woman and it has been suggested that the temple memorialized Jasaw Chan K'awiil's principal queen and mother of his heir, Lady Kalajuun Une' Mo' ('12 Macaw Tails').[59] Excavation in its interior failed to find a tomb.

(Above) Tikal Altar 5 partnered Stela 16 in the walled precinct of twin-pyramid complex N. It shows two figures, Jasaw Chan K'awiil himself and a lord of Maasal, conducting an exhumation ritual with the bones of a high-ranking lady seen between them. AD 711.

(Right) Recovered from the king's tomb beneath Temple 1, this jade mosaic vessel was originally formed around a wooden cylinder, each segment held in place by its own tiny jade pin.

(Below) Of the 37 exquisitely incised bones found in the king's tomb, some of the more engaging are those illustrating mythological events. In a still obscure episode, the Maize God (centre) is borne by canoe, guided by the so-called 'Paddler Gods' (contrasting patrons of light and darkness). Other bone scenes show the canoe later sinking into the watery depths of the Underworld.

Rising 154 ft (47m) above the Great Plaza, Tikal Temple 1 has been an icon of Classic Maya architecture since Alfred Maudslay first cleared it from the forest's grip in 1882. Though barely visible today, its high roofcomb is decorated with a seated sculpture of Jasaw Chan K'awiil. AD 734.

The king's body was laid to rest in Burial 116, discovered directly beneath Temple 1 in 1962. It was heavily laden with jade jewelry and accompanied by an especially rich collection of rare shells, pearls, mirrors, jaguar skins and painted vessels.

Within Temple 1

On the east side of the Great Plaza, directly opposite Temple 2, an earlier version of Temple 1 was demolished to make way for Jasaw Chan K'awiil's 154 ft (47 m) mortuary pyramid. In 1962, after much exploratory tunnelling, excavators penetrated the roof of his vaulted crypt, now designated Burial 116. Its greater part was devoted to a masonry bench on which the king's body lay, adorned by a vast haul of jade, shell and pearl jewelry. The main necklace, made up of 114 spherical jade beads and weighing 8.5 pounds (3.9 kg), closely resembles the broad collar he is shown wearing on several of his images. Among a lengthy inventory of grave offerings was a spectacular jade mosaic vessel, whose lid offers a delicate portrait of the king.[60]

The most interesting find was a collection of 37 bone objects engraved with minute glyphs and pictorial scenes, highlighted in red cinnabar. Subjects range from the historical to the mythological, the latter involving lively renderings of rain gods fishing and the voyage, and then sinking, of a canoe carrying the dying Maize God and an array of anthropomorphic creatures. One bears a long list of death-dates for foreign nobility, while others supply intriguing, but still largely opaque, references to the kingdoms of Copan and Palenque. The last clearly historical date on a bone is from 727, though another might provide one in 733, suggesting that the king's death and burial can be placed shortly before the inauguration of his son the following year.[61]

Yik'in Chan K'awiil
Ruler B
734–746>

28th Ruler
>766–768

Yax Nuun Ayiin II
Ruler C
768–794>

YIK'IN CHAN K'AWIIL	
Glyphic spelling ?-(ya)-CHAN- K'AWI:L-la ('K'awiil that Darkens the Sky') *Also known as* Ruler B, Yaxkin Caan Chac, Sun Sky Rain *Dynastic title* 27th in the line *Accession* 8 December 734 (9.15.3.6.8 3 Lamat 6 Pax) *Father* Jasaw Chan K'awiil I	*Mother* Lady Kalajuun Une' Mo' *Sons* 28th Ruler, Nuun Yax Ayiin II *Monuments* Stelae 5, 20? & 21; Altars 2, 8? & 9; Column Altars 1?, 2? & 3; Temple 4 Lintels 2 & 3; Lintel from Structure 5D- 52; Tikal Rock Sculpture?

YIK'IN CHAN K'AWIIL

While Jasaw Chan K'awiil deserves the major credit for Tikal's upturn, it was his son the 27th ruler, Yik'in Chan K'awiil (perhaps 'K'awiil that Darkens the Sky'), who brought its imperial ambitions to real fruition and turned the city into one outshining all its rivals. Since his father's tomb could not have been added intrusively into Temple 1, this must have been among the new king's earliest works. In the years that followed he constructed or remodelled most of the major causeways linking key parts of the city, built Temple 6 (the Temple of Inscriptions) and the East Market complex, and made significant additions to the Central Acropolis. As if this was not enough, most of the great palaces ringing central Tikal were built or renewed at this time.[62]

Restoring Tikal's power
Equal to his reputation as its greatest builder, Yik'in Chan K'awiil stands among Tikal's greatest military heroes. His inaugural monument, Stela 21 of 736, is partnered by Altar 9 and its image of a prostrate captive from Calakmul. While the accompanying caption is damaged and it is hard to know if the royal title mentioned refers to the victim or his

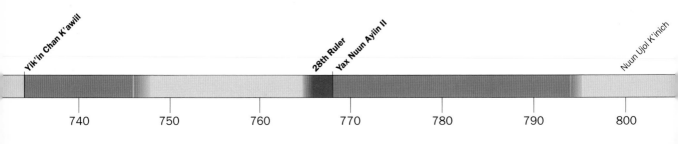

Yik'in Chan K'awiil

28th Ruler
Yax Nuun Ayiin II

Nuun Ujol K'inich

740   750   760   770   780   790   800

(*Above*) A magnificent example of Classic Maya wood carving, Lintel 3 from Temple 4, was hewn from extremely hard Sapodilla wood. It shows Yik'in Chan K'awiil seated on a great litter with a celestial serpent effigy arching over his head. The carving was commissioned to celebrate his victory over El Perú in 743.

(*Opposite*) This fine jade mosaic vessel was found in Burial 196 from Temple 73 and may be a portrait of Yik'in Chan K'awiil or one of his sons in the guise of the Maize God (see panel p. 50). We are fortunate that the Postclassic plunderers of Tikal abandoned their tunnel into Temple 73 just 28 in. (70 cm) short of this rich tomb.

overlord, there was a change of rulership at Calakmul at just this point (p. 113).

Further triumphs lay ahead, with his most trumpeted campaigns straddling the years 743 and 744. These are detailed on two wooden lintels from the upper sanctuary of Temple 4. At 212 ft (65 m) this is not only the tallest pyramid at Tikal, it is the single largest construction of the Late Classic period. In July 743 he attacked a city called Yaxa' ('Blue Water'). Originally thought to be the lakeside city of Yaxha to the southeast of Tikal, it is now clear that this was a namesake to the west, a satellite of the El Perú kingdom. The El Perú ruler Jaguar Throne was defeated and the effigy of his patron god captured and delivered to Tikal the following day. Just 191 days later, Yik'in Chan K'awiil turned to the east and attacked the kingdom of Naranjo, seizing a city called Wak Kab'nal ('Six Earth Place'), probably its capital. The Naranjo king Yax Mayuy Chan Chaak was taken prisoner and appears bound and prostrate on Stela 5. Its partnering Altar 2 is much destroyed but its rope border may once have secured a captive Jaguar Throne.[63]

These victories succeeded in breaking a hostile encirclement of the kingdom that had endured for at least a century. Since both victims were

THE PROBLEM OF BURIAL 196

Within Temple 73, a rather unimposing pyramid at the southwest corner of the Great Plaza, excavators found a rich interment, Burial 196, with many similarities to that of Jasaw Chan K'awiil. In particular, a stunning jade mosaic vessel closely resembles the one found in Burial 116 (p. 48). An inscribed stingray spine provides a firm date from 754 and Yik'in Chan K'awiil's name appears on a finely painted drinking cup. However, the modest scale of Temple 73 is troubling and there have always been those who argue that the crypt of Yik'in Chan K'awiil lies undisturbed within the unexplored bulk of Temple 4 – mirroring the burial arrangements of his father inside Temple 1. Certainly, Tikal's mightiest pyramid would be a memorial more befitting the great king's achievements. A better candidate for Burial 196 might be his son, the obscure 28th ruler.

A small drinking cup from Burial 196 names Yik'in Chan K'awiill.

leading Calakmul affiliates, their rapid defeat seems easiest to explain in the light of their patron's waning powers. The long-lasting disruption at both (El Perú was silent for as long as 47 years; Naranjo, bar one stela, for 36) might well suggest that they languished under lengthy periods of Tikal supervision. It was surely this renewed ascendancy over the Peten that fuelled Tikal's construction boom, whether through the flow of booty, tribute or even conscript labour. A heightened sense of security at this time may correspond to the disuse of the defensive earthworks.

The North Group

The length of Yik'in Chan K'awiil's reign has yet to be determined. The question is an important one, since its answer would allow us to assign another war and construction phase either to the final years of his rule, or to the first of his son, the shadowy 28th ruler. Twin-pyramid complex P, built in the North Group to commemorate the 9.16.0.0.0 ending of 751, pairs Stela 20 and Altar 8. The commissioning king's name is no longer legible, but the name elements Chan K'awiil are spelt out in his portrait headdress. The altar shows a prisoner, Wilan Tok Wayib', known from two other monuments: Column Altar 1 and the great Tikal Rock Sculpture (a limestone outcrop measuring 20 by 13 ft (6 x 4 m)). These describe his capture on 8 December 748 and sacrifice two days later. The *wuk tzuk* title he carries represents a firm link with the Naranjo-Yaxha region and points to continued conflict in this direction.[64]

28TH RULER

Very little is known of the monarch whose reign fell between that of Yik'in Chan K'awiil (the 27th in the line) and his son Yax Nuun Ayiin II (the 29th) – even his name is barely preserved. What we do know is that he was another of Yik'in Chan K'awiil's sons and presumably his successor's elder brother. The only two dates that can be certainly linked to his tenure come from the great glyphic façades of Temple 6, which he seems to have added to a pyramid begun by his father at the extreme southeast of the site core (incredibly, this major structure was only discovered in 1951). Falling within three days of each other in 766, the first marks the dedication of Temple 6 as a *wayib'il*, literally 'sleeping house' (a symbolic dormitory for a god or, more probably, the place in which its effigy was kept in seclusion), the second the three-quarter K'atun of 9.16.15.0.0.[65] Exposed to over 1,200 years of inclement weather, this truly monumental inscription – rendered in glyphs almost 3 ft (85 cm) wide – is now badly eroded but deals with a legendary past in which the character Sak Hix Muut 'White Jaguar Bird' appears as the local ruler. In a chronology worked out by Christopher Jones, the first scholar to chart out the Tikal dynasty, this figure presides over ceremonies performed in 1143, 456 and 157 BC.[66]

K'ATUN MOUNTAINS

The passing of the K'atun – 20 Maya years – was the abiding rhythm of Maya civilization. A specific architectural form was developed at Tikal to host their commemoration. Known as twin-pyramid complexes, the first was built in the East Plaza in the early 6th century. This was used for several successive K'atun events, but during the Late Classic, complexes were constructed for each new ceremony, with six built in the years, 692 to 790. In addition to their eastern and western pyramids, they typically had a nine-doored building to the south and a northern enclosure with a carved stela and altar pair. The stela recorded the name of each, all varieties of *witz* 'hill/mountain'. Such assemblages are rare outside Tikal and where found may reflect the extent of its later political orbit. There is an example at Yaxha and recent mapping at the southern satellite of Ixlu has revealed another.[67]

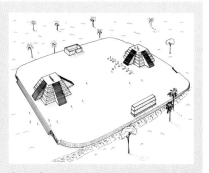

Group Q was one of the largest twin pyramid complexes, raised by Yax Nuun Ayiin II to mark the end of the 17th K'atun in AD 771.

This small bone was found in Burial 190 from Structure 7F-30, an outlying compound to the northwest of the site core. It names an otherwise unknown Tikal ruler called *?-k'awiil sak te' ajaw*. MT167.

YAX NUUN AYIIN II

The next ruler revived the name of one of the city's most important kings, Yax Nuun Ayiin, the Mexican usurper of four centuries earlier. Yax Nuun Ayiin II's most noticeable contributions to the city were his two twin-pyramid complexes, today labelled Q and R. Conventional in design but of enormous size, they were stages for the celebration of the K'atun-endings 9.17.0.0.0 and 9.18.0.0.0, falling in 771 and 790 respectively. Most of what little we know about him comes from the single carved stelae found in each of their walled northern compounds. The second son of Yik'in Chan K'awiil, Yax Nuun Ayiin II came to power in 768. In Tikal's last clear successor title, he is given as 29th in the line of the dynastic founder. These short, formulaic texts give no clue to the wider health of the kingdom, but the grandeur of their settings seems to reflect its confidence and wealth. However, long periods of dormancy at El Perú, Naranjo and Caracol all come to an end during his reign and Tikal's grip on the central region seems diminished. Yax Nuun Ayiin II survived until at least 794, the date on a painted vessel excavated from the Central Acropolis, which shows him in a palace scene, accompanied by his wife and courtiers.

(Right) This scene of Yax Nuun Ayiin II among his courtiers (note the curl-snouted caiman in his headdress) comes from a painted vase excavated in Tikal's Central Acropolis.

YAX NUUN AYIIN II	
Glyphic spelling	(9.16.17.16.4
YAX-NU:N-AYI:N	11 K'an 12 K'ayab)
('First ? Caiman')	*Father*
Also known as	Yik'in Chan K'awiil
Ruler C, Chitam	*Brother*
Dynastic title	28th Ruler
29th in the line	*Monuments*
Accession	Stelae 19 & 22;
25 December 768	Altars 6 & 10

Nuun Ujol K'inich
c. 800?

Dark Sun
>810>

Jewel K'awiil
>849>

Jasaw Chan K'awiil II
>869>

In this detail from Temple 3 Lintel 2 we see a late Tikal ruler, probably Dark Sun, engaged in a dance pageant, *c.* AD 810.

NUUN UJOL K'INICH	
Glyphic spelling NU:N-u-JOL K'INICH ('?-headed Sun God')	*Son* Dark Sun?

DARK SUN	
Glyphic spelling tz'a?-no?-CH'E:N?-na *Father* Nuun Ujol K'inich?	*Monuments* Stela 24; Altar 7; Temple 3 Lintel 2?

JEWEL K'AWIIL	
Glyphic spelling ?-K'AWI:L-li	

JASAW CHAN K'AWIIL II	
Glyphic spelling ja-sa-wa-CHAN K'AWI:L ('K'awiil that Clears? the Sky')	*Also known as* Stela 11 Ruler *Monuments* Stela 11; Altar 11

TERMINAL CLASSIC TIKAL

As we enter the 9th century, signs of a profound crisis come suddenly to the fore as dynasties across the region disappear and population levels start to plummet. As the pressures begin to mount the clarity of Tikal's dynastic picture diminishes considerably. Temple 3, at 180 ft (55 m) the last of its great pyramids, contains another elaborately carved roof lintel. It shows three figures in a rather florid style, with a ruler dressed in a corpulent jaguar costume flanked by two dancing attendants, originally named in accompanying captions. Only one of two longer glyphic panels survives, and this is rather decayed. A parentage statement can be identified, providing us with the name of the protagonist's father, a king called **Nuun Ujol K'inich**. He could have ruled for only a relatively brief period sometime between 794 and 810 (unless he is the missing 28th ruler).

The next monument, Stela 24 – commemorating the 19th K'atun of 810 – was not erected in the traditional twin-pyramid group but instead stood at the foot of Temple 3. It once bore a text of perhaps 136 glyphs, with a further 48 on the accompanying Altar 7. Both were badly smashed in antiquity, but the ruler's name, **Dark Sun**, survives on three stela fragments. A carved bone unearthed in Group G, an elite compound close to

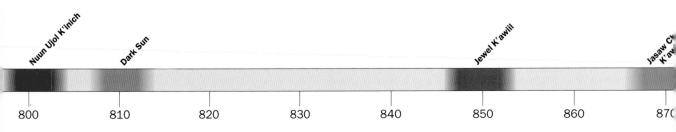

This evocative painting shows Tikal some 50 years after the collapse of royal power. By now, a much reduced population squatted in the deserted palaces, eking out a simple living amid a fast-returning forest.

THE END OF TIKAL

By the end of the 9th century Tikal had experienced a fate shared with its peers across the Maya realm. With all vestiges of royal power gone and deserted by the great bulk of its population, its elite quarters were taken over by squatters and simple thatched homes sprang up on its ceremonial plazas. These late inhabitants pursued their own, often elaborate ritual activities, moving and re-using earlier monuments for purposes quite estranged from those of the fallen nobility. By Tikal's last days any regard for the sanctity of the old order had long since dissolved and the North Acropolis was mined in search of its tombs and their jade riches. The more accessible were discovered and ransacked. Finally abandoned in the 10th or 11th century, the forest completed its takeover of the city, choking it with root and vine for the next millennium.

the city centre, provides the only other record from his reign.[68] In all likelihood, it is Dark Sun who wears the fabulous jaguar suit on the lintel high above in Temple 3, which could well be his mortuary shrine.

The next calendrical juncture, the turning of the key 10th Bak'tun (10.0.0.0.0) in 830, went unrecorded, part of a 60-year hiatus that seems to mark the end of any cohesive central authority at the city. One monument that does celebrate this date is a large altar (once part of a stela-altar pair) recently uncovered by Don and Prudence Rice at Zacpeten, to the south of Tikal, on Lake Salpeten. It includes the name of Yik'in Chan K'awiil, apparently tracing ancestral ties between the Zacpeten dynasty and its one-time political masters.[69]

The southern city of Seibal, on the Pasión River, provides our only reference to **Jewel K'awiil**, an otherwise unknown 'divine lord' of Tikal, in 849 (see p. 227). His journey to 'witness' the Seibal king's commemoration of the 10.1.0.0.0 K'atun might seem to reflect a dramatically transformed political reality for the Terminal Classic. But by now high titles are little guarantee of high kingship and with Tikal itself cast into silence we see its authority splinter among a range of provincial magnates. This is best seen at the satellites of Ixlu and Jimbal, which begin monumental programmes after 859 featuring their own rulers, both using the once exclusive Mutal title.[70]

There was at least one attempt to re-establish royal power at the old and increasingly depopulated capital. The ruler who commissioned Stela 11, erected for the 10.2.0.0.0 mark of 869, revived a name from better times, **Jasaw Chan K'awiil II**. Set in the Great Plaza, in front of the hallowed North Acropolis and alongside stelae from Tikal's long and glorious past, this was an appropriate setting for the city's final sculpture. The peripheral lordships survived for only a few more years, with the last of their stelae erected at Jimbal in 889. This same year saw Uaxactun erect its final effort, Stela 12. Though it includes the Jasaw Chan K'awiil name seen at Tikal, he may be a local namesake.[71]

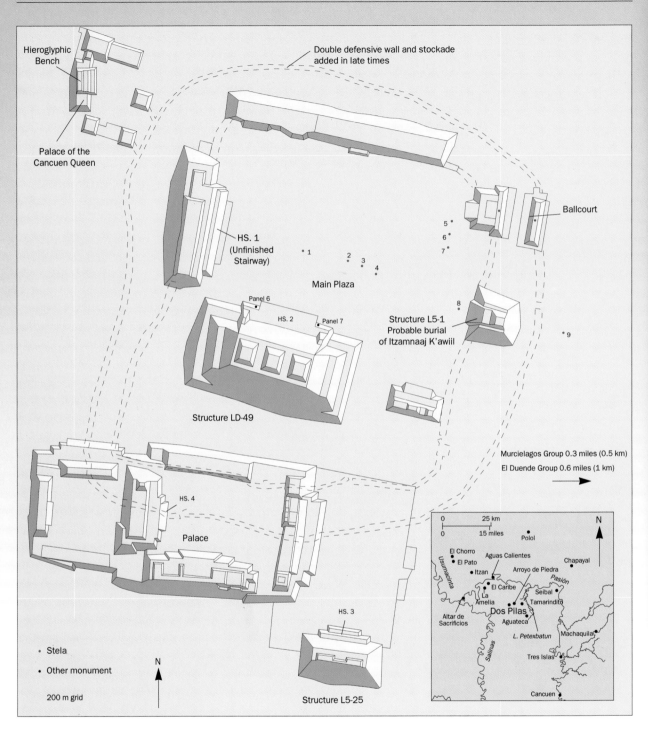

Hieroglyphic Bench

Double defensive wall and stockade added in late times

Palace of the Cancuen Queen

HS. 1 (Unfinished Stairway)

Ballcourt

5
6
7

1

2
3
4

Main Plaza

Panel 6

HS. 2

Panel 7

8

Structure L5-1 Probable burial of Itzamnaaj K'awiil

9

Structure LD-49

Murcielagos Group 0.3 miles (0.5 km)

El Duende Group 0.6 miles (1 km)

HS. 4

Palace

HS. 3

• Stela

• Other monument

N

200 m grid

Structure L5-25

0   25 km
0   15 miles

N

Polol

El Chorro
El Pato
Itzan

Aguas Calientes

Chapayal

Arroyo de Piedra

Pasión

Usumacinta

El Caribe

Seibal

La Amelia

Tamarindito

Altar de Sacrificios

Dos Pilas

Aguateca

L. Petexbatun

Machaquila

Salinas

Tres Islas

Cancuen

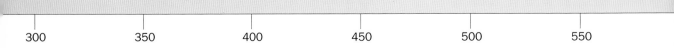

300   350   400   450   500   550

DOS PILAS

UNLIKE MOST LEADING CAPITALS, Dos Pilas was of no great size and its occupation brief, confined almost entirely to the Late Classic period. Yet its modest appearance belies a history of considerable importance and no small measure of intrigue. Its spectacular rise has much to tell us about both the grander strategies of the most powerful kingdoms and the bitter divisions that developed within them – while its equally spectacular fall provides an unrivalled glimpse into the strife that tore Classic society apart in its region.

Dos Pilas lies between the Pasión and Salinas rivers, in an area called the Petexbatun. From Early Classic times this was home to a kingdom centred on two sites, Tamarindito and Arroyo de Piedra. By about 650, however, its territory had effectively been co-opted by an intrusive dynasty which established the site of Dos Pilas in its very midst and quickly came to dominate the entire region. The key to this phenomenon, initially most puzzling to scholars, was its use of an emblem glyph identical to that of mighty Tikal. After a region-wide research project headed by Arthur Demarest and first Stephen Houston and then Juan Antonio Valdés, we can reconstruct much of what happened here, often in detail unparalleled in the Maya realm.

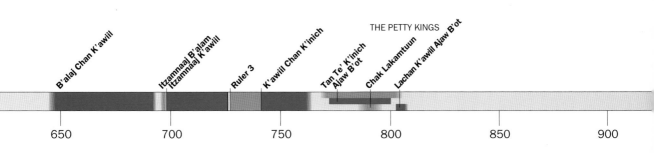

THE PETTY KINGS

B'alaj Chan K'awiil | Itzamnaal B'alam / Itzamnaaj K'awiil | Ruler 3 | K'awiil Chan K'inich | Tan Te' K'inich Ajaw B'ot | Chak Lakamtuun | Lachan K'awiil Ajaw B'ot

650   700   750   800   850   900

B'alaj Chan K'awiil
Ruler 1
c. 648–692>

Itzamnaaj B'alam
c. 697

Itzamnaaj K'awiil
Ruler 2
698–726

Dos Pilas Stela 9 carries the only known
portrait of B'alaj Chan K'awiil. AD 682.

B'ALAJ CHAN K'AWIIL	
Glyphic spelling b'a-la-ja CHAN-K'AWI:L	*Wives* Lady of Itzan, Lady B'ulu'
Also known as Ruler 1, Flint Sky God K, Malah Chan K'awil, Lightning Sky	*Sons* Itzamnaaj K'awiil, Itzamnaaj B'alam
	Daughter Lady Six Sky of Naranjo
Birth 15 October 625 (9.9.12.11.2 8 Ik' 5 Keh)	*Monuments* Dos Pilas Stela 9; Panels 6 & 7; Hieroglyphic Stairway 4
Father K'inich Muwaan Jol II of Tikal?	

ITZAMNAAJ B'ALAM	
Glyphic spelling ITZAMNA:J-ji-B'ALAM-ma	*Mother* Lady of Itzan
Also known as Shield Jaguar	*Brother* Itzamnaaj K'awiil
Father B'alaj Chan K'awiil	*Monument* Dos Pilas Hieroglyphic Stairway 2?

B'ALAJ CHAN K'AWIIL

The emergence of the Dos Pilas polity is one of the rare cases in which an internal struggle – the kind of factional dispute within a kingdom that would normally leave no trace in the inscriptions – erupts into something more visible and enduring. Its origins lie in the intrigues of Tikal's 'dark age', its 130-year Hiatus period, and an exodus from the great city that brought a lord called B'alaj Chan K'awiil to the Petexbatun to found a rival Tikal state. While his relationship to the incumbent Tikal ruler Nuun Ujol Chaak is unclear, he makes his genealogical claim to the Mutal title plain on Dos Pilas Panel 6, where a Tikal king (probably the missing 23rd or 24th ruler) is named as his father.[1]

Of crucial importance to this rupture is the involvement of Tikal's great adversary, Calakmul. In a passage dated to 648 the Dos Pilas king describes himself as the *yajaw* or vassal of his counterpart at Calakmul.[2] This would seem an extraordinary act of treachery for someone claiming membership of the Tikal royal line. Was it the isolated betrayal of a frustrated pretender, or should we look for a deeper relevance to the politics of the Hiatus era? In the wake of Tikal's conquest in 562 a new lineage of uncertain legitimacy established itself at the city (pp. 40–41).

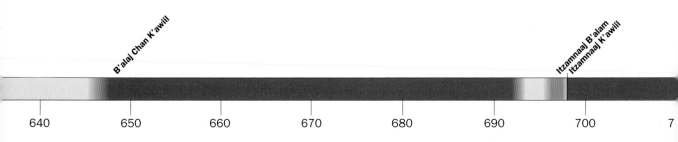

B'alaj Chan K'awiil

Itzamnaaj B'alam
Itzamnaaj K'awiil

| 640 | 650 | 660 | 670 | 680 | 690 | 700 | 7 |

In this key passage (abbreviated for the sake of clarity) B'alaj Chan K'awiil is said to be the *yajaw*, the subordinate or 'vassal lord' of the Calakmul ruler Yuknoom the Great. Dos Pilas Hieroglyphic Stairway 4, *c.* AD 684.

A large jade bead bearing the name of B'alaj Chan K'awiil (here in an alternative spelling) was found in a tomb at distant Tonina in 1852.

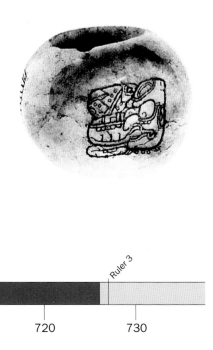

Plausibly, B'alaj Chan K'awiil was of this same line, perhaps as a full Tikal king, ousted in a coup that brought a rival lineage to power. Whatever the background, without Calakmul's support it is hard to imagine how this small group in the Petexbatun could have long resisted a foe more than ten times its size. For Calakmul, Dos Pilas represented, at the very least, a thorn in Tikal's side, at best, the prospect of neutralizing its greatest enemy by restoring a compliant regime to the city (pp. 108–9).

Civil war

What followed is, in Stephen Houston's words, Tikal's 'civil war', the most detailed campaign narrative we have from the Classic period. Its first act, in 657, saw a Calakmul attack on Tikal and the ejecting of Nuun Ujol Chaak (pp. 42–3).[3] No lasting control of the city resulted, however, and the exiles conspicuously failed to make good their return. The war came to the Petexbatun in 672, when a revived Nuun Ujol Chaak succeeded in taking Dos Pilas, this time forcing B'alaj Chan K'awiil into ignominious retreat. His five-year exile ended in 677, though since his return took place on the same day as a further Calakmul success over Tikal, his dependence on his patron is only too obvious.

Tikal and Dos Pilas engaged forces once again in 679, this time with quite different results. Nuun Ujol Chaak was defeated and one of his lieutenants, Nuun B'alam, taken prisoner. Though Dos Pilas presents this victory as the climactic final act of the war, neither side had achieved real satisfaction. Any hopes the Dos Pilas group may have had to topple the lineage of Nuun Ujol Chaak were not fulfilled, while mighty Tikal proved unable to smother its unwelcome sibling at birth.

A new Tikal

The location chosen for Dos Pilas, just 2.5 miles (4 km) from the existing centre of Arroyo de Piedra, was a 'green field' site with little prior occupation. Its modest scale reflects both its short history and the limited manpower at its disposal (at its peak, its population would not have exceeded 5,000). B'alaj Chan K'awiil's construction projects defined the site core, arranged about a main plaza and a large pyramid (LD-49) topped by a line of three sanctuaries. Beginning in 682, he laid out a programme of associated monuments that set his own actions in a glorious light and, as befitting a subject lord, paid due homage to his Calakmul patrons. He records two visits made to Calakmul itself. In 682 he joined his overlord Yuknoom the Great in a ritual dance to celebrate the 9.12.10.0.0 event; four years later he returned to witness the accession of Calakmul's next king, Yich'aak K'ak'.[4]

B'alaj Chan K'awiil took at least two wives. One provided him with a daughter, Lady Six Sky, who was to gain great fame in later years when sent to forge a new dynasty at distant Naranjo (p. 74). What may have been a further daughter, or sister, married into the local lineage of Arroyo de Piedra. B'alaj Chan K'awiil's other marriage, to a royal woman from the nearby Itzan kingdom, seems to have produced two sons. The name

Ruler 3

720   730

Itzamnaaj K'awiil as he appears on the face of Stela 15 from AD 721. His elaborate mask and headdress closely resemble the shell-mosaic fragments found in his (probable) tomb.

of one, **Itzamnaaj B'alam**, survives in a single battered passage, but seems to have been his direct successor.[5] If so, his reign was a short one, falling between his father's last mention in 692 and the installation of his brother Itzamnaaj K'awiil in 698.

ITZAMNAAJ K'AWIIL

Having survived its turbulent birth, Dos Pilas would now see a move towards consolidation under the 28-year rule of Itzamnaaj K'awiil. This is not to say that its militaristic ambitions were curtailed, or that there was to be any early rapprochement with Tikal – on the contrary, fighting continued – but there was a distinct shift in emphasis from long-range, macro-political tensions to local affairs, and we receive our first glimpses of the wider hegemony it now enjoyed over the Petexbatun and Pasión regions.

Itzamnaaj K'awiil's birth in 673 took place at the very height of the Tikal war, in fact, during his family's enforced exile from the Petexbatun (very probably at Calakmul). This seems to have caused some embarrassment and is the likely explanation for discrepancies in his recorded birth-date. The inscribed Long Count conflicts with the Calendar Round chronology and 'erroneously' places it in 679 – when safely ensconced back at Dos Pilas.[6]

The first part of Itzamnaaj K'awiil's reign saw further wars with Tikal – his first monument, Stela 1, recording an engagement in 705.[7] Here a Tikal lord was *jub'uy* 'brought down', and is shown as the prone captive under the king's feet. Interestingly, the text credits the success not to Itzamnaaj K'awiil himself, but to Ucha'an K'in B'alam or 'Master of Sun Jaguar', the future Ruler 3. A second monument, Stela 14, describes this lord's close involvement in rituals performed by the king, and it is clear that he was a powerful lieutenant and military captain a full 20 years before his rise to the throne.

El Duende and a Petexbatun hegemony

While his father had concentrated his building efforts in establishing the central core, Itzamnaaj K'awiil gave greater attention to an outlying portion of the site known today as El Duende. Here a natural hilltop was enlarged with the addition of a surmounting pyramid, while its lower slopes were modified to form a sequence of supporting terraces, giving the impression of a single massive structure (all lying above a natural cave). These terrace platforms held five stelae and altar pairings. Their surviving texts record victories over unknown and presumably quite minor victims in 717 and 721, as well as an account of a ritual circuit involving other centres in the region. In this tour, a stela is said to have been erected at Aguateca – a secondary site that was to be of increasing importance in the years ahead – and a god image dressed at Seibal, a large city and capital of its own kingdom 17 miles (27.5 km) to the east of Dos Pilas.[8] Itzamnaaj K'awiil is also mentioned on monuments at the original

ITZAMNAAJ K'AWIIL	
Glyphic spelling	11 Kawak 17 Mak)
ITZAMNA:J-K'AWI:L	*Father*
Also known as	B'alaj Chan K'awiil
Ruler 2, Shield	*Mother*
God K	Lady of Itzan
Birth	*Brother*
25 January 673	Itzamnaaj B'alam
(9.12.0.10.11	*Son*
13 Chuwen 19	K'awiil Chan
K'ayab)	K'inich?
Accession	*Monuments*
24 March 698	Dos Pilas Stelae 1,
(9.13.6.2.0	11, 12, 13, 14, 15
11 Ajaw 18 Wo)	& 16
Death	*Burial*
22 October 726	Dos Pilas Structure
(9.14.15.1.19	L5-1?

Stela 8, the elegantly carved memorial to Itzamnaaj K'awiil, provides an interesting 'error' in his birthday, given here as 9.12.6.15.11. Usually ascribed to miscalculation, in this case it would seem to have a rhetorical purpose, obscuring (to the casual observer at least) his foreign birth-place.

Petexbatun centres of Tamarindito and Arroyo de Piedra. A text at the latter describes the local king as his vassal.[9]

Death and burial

Itzamnaaj K'awiil died in October 726 at the age of 53. Curiously, this event is recorded not only at Dos Pilas, on the magnificent Stela 8, but also on one of the minutely incised bones found in the tomb of his contemporary and rival Jasaw Chan K'awiil, ruler of Tikal. Perhaps it was some blood-tie that made this event of interest to Tikal – though it is of little surprise that he is referred to only as 'He of Dos Pilas' and denied the Mutal title under such bitter dispute.[10]

The long and finely styled inscription of Stela 8 was commissioned by the incoming Ruler 3 as a tribute to his predecessor. It recounts Itzamnaaj K'awiil's birth, accession and contacts with the dynasty of Calakmul (the details of which are sadly destroyed), before recording his death and subsequent burial four days later 'at night' and 'within Dos Pilas'.[11] The positioning of this text in front of the now ruined Structure L5-1, on the east side of the main plaza, suggested that his tomb lay inside and guided archaeologists to a vaulted crypt 30 ft (9 m) beneath its summit. It held a body garbed in a heavy jade collar and wristlets, surrounded by fine painted ceramics and almost 400 pieces of shell mosaic, once adorning an elaborate headdress. While no accompanying text was found to prove his identity beyond doubt, all other evidence points to this as the king's final resting place.[12]

Dos Pilas pyramid L5-1 contained a royal tomb that seems certain to be that of Itzamnaaj K'awiil. Seen here under excavation by Arthur Demarest, the body was accompanied by numerous offerings (painted plates visible at the body's head and feet).

Ruler 3
727–741

K'awiil Chan K'inich
Ruler 4
741–761>

This painted vase shows K'awiil Chan K'inich – identified simply as 'Master of the Ahkul Lord' – enthroned in his palace. His use of a full royal title, six years prior to his actual accession, may be a sign that Ruler 3's rule amounted to a form of regency.

RULER 3	
Glyphic spelling	*Death*
?-ni-TI'?-K'AWI:L u-CHAN-? K'IN-ni-B'ALAM	28 May 741 (9.15.9.16.11 13 Chuwen 14 Xul)
Also known as	*Wife*
Scroll-head God K, Spangle-head, Jewelled-head	Lady GI-K'awiil of Cancuen
Accession	*Monuments*
6 January 727 (9.14.15.5.15 9 Men 13 K'ayab)	Dos Pilas Stelae 2, 5 & 8; Panel 19; Aguateca Stelae 2 & 3

RULER 3

'Master of Sun Jaguar' assumed the throne in January 727, 67 days after the burial of Itzamnaaj K'awiil. From here on he used an acquired regnal name (one that currently resists full decipherment), though his long-standing warrior's title continued to see occasional use throughout his tenure. If the next ruler of Dos Pilas, K'awiil Chan K'inich, was indeed a son of Itzamnaaj K'awiil (and our source on this is rather eroded) then the new king was not in direct line to the throne. Nevertheless, his elevation seems less a coup d'état by a military strongman than a form of regency, fulfilling a need for mature leadership at a time while the heir was still a child.

A remarkable, though now heavily broken panel depicts the bloodletting of a young boy, referred to as *ch'ok mutal ajaw* 'Prince of Dos Pilas' in the text above, and most likely K'awiil Chan K'inich himself. It may reflect Ruler 3's special concern for his eventual succession. Designation rites such as this are sometimes referred to in texts, but not otherwise given the emphasis of representation. At the centre of the scene we see a richly attired youth whose penis has been perforated by a kneeling lord, probably a ritual specialist, while four

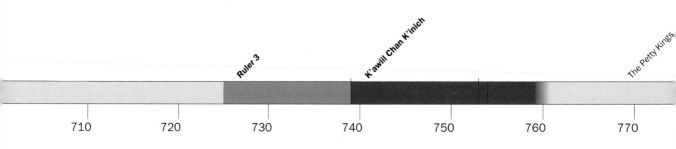

Ruler 3

K'awiil Chan K'inich

The Petty Kings

710   720   730   740   750   760   770

A CHANGE OF EMBLEM

From AD 735 onwards Ruler 3 shows a marked preference for a second, alternative version of the Mutal emblem glyph, one rarely used at Tikal itself (below).[13] The motivation behind this development is unclear (the new sign was of identical pronunciation) but may signal moves towards a more distinctive identity for Dos Pilas and reflect reduced competition with Tikal after the decline of Calakmul's power.

(*Below*) To mark his victory over Seibal, Ruler 3 is pictured in full battle attire, a Teotihuacan-style mask projecting from his face. Dos Pilas Stela 2, AD 736.

(*Below right*) Ruler 3, second from left, presides over the ritual bloodletting of a young boy, probably K'awiil Chan K'inich. Dos Pilas Panel 19 (restored), AD 729–740.

figures look on. To the left stands Ruler 3 and his wife. In her name she carries the female variant of the Cancuen emblem glyph, signalling a strategic alliance with a kingdom that controlled the upper reaches of the Pasión, a gateway to the resource-rich highlands to the south. To the right, in a slightly more animated pose, stands a lord with a complex title string including the term *aj kaanal* 'He of Calakmul'. His phrase ends with a further title, 'Guardian', or perhaps 'Master of the Prince'.[14] Such epithets usually refer to important captives, but here has been interpreted as his custodianship of the high-ranking child and a further sign of Calakmul's enduring influence at this centre. The final figure bears an important name or title, *unaab'al k'inich* ('Watery Place of the Sun God'), in a spelling normally only seen at Tikal.

The conquest of Seibal

Ruler 3 claims only one war success during his reign, but it was to be an important one. In August 735 his forces attacked the city of Seibal, the largest and most ancient capital in the region. It may already have come under Dos Pilas influence during the time of Itzamnaaj K'awiil – at the very least relations seem to have been amicable – but its full conquest would represent a major prize. The following day there was a still poorly understood 'axing' event, performed by some other important lord. Two stelae were commissioned to commemorate the victory, one at Dos Pilas and another at Aguateca. Their closely matched scenes show a triumphant Ruler 3 in full warrior attire standing atop the captured Seibal king Yich'aak B'alam ('Jaguar Claw').

The simultaneous erection of monuments at both sites heralds the development of Aguateca as something of a 'twin capital' under

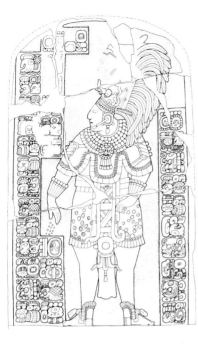

K'awiil Chan K'inich is here shown in the act of ritual 'scattering'. Aguateca Stela 1, AD 741.

K'AWIIL CHAN K'INICH	
Glyphic spelling K'AWI:L-CHAN-K'INICH	13 Kaban 20 Yaxk'in)
	Father
Also known as Ruler 4, God K Sky Mahk'ina	Itzamnaaj K'awiil?
	Monuments
Accession 23 June 741 (9.15.9.17.17	Dos Pilas Stela 4; Hieroglyphic Stairway 3; Hieroglyphic Bench 1; Aguateca Stelae 1 & 5

Ruler 3. Dramatically sited on the edge of a 40 ft (12 m) escarpment overlooking the swampy margins of Lake Petexbatun, and split in two lengthwise by a deep chasm, its attraction doubtless lay in its defensive qualities. Ruler 3's death in May 741 is recorded on Aguateca Stela 1. The whereabouts of his tomb is unknown, but the association of this monument with a large pyramid mound, Structure 6, might suggest that his burial lies within.[15]

K'AWIIL CHAN K'INICH

The new ruler, K'awiil Chan K'inich, was installed in June 741, 26 days after the death of Ruler 3. Early monuments include an inaugural stela at Aguateca and a hieroglyphic bench at Dos Pilas, the latter the centrepiece of an elite compound just outside the main plaza. Its text is a memorial recording the recent deaths of three leading figures: Ruler 3, his Cancuen wife and the Dos Pilas-born queen of Naranjo, Lady Six Sky. The Cancuen queen is clearly the focus of the inscription and her well-stocked burial was discovered directly beneath it.[16]

Conflict was a prominent feature of K'awiil Chan K'inich's reign. An early, pre-inaugural success was against the nearby area of Ahkul 'Turtle', and 'Master of the Ahkul Lord' became his personal epithet.[17] More impressive triumphs are detailed on Hieroglyphic Stairway 3, part of a temple pyramid (LD-25) that was his largest contribution to the site core. It describes the capture of lords from El Chorro (in 743), Yaxchilan and Motul de San José (both in 745), depicting their bound and writhing bodies on the stairway risers.[18] While it might appear that K'awiil Chan K'inich began his reign with a bout of particular aggression, these battles could as easily represent the repulsion of neighbours keen to test the young king.

Following the marital ties established by Ruler 3, K'awiil Chan K'inich was closely involved with the city of Cancuen, and is cited there

A 'rolled-out' view of the vase pictured on p. 60; the young K'awiil Chan K'inich is here shown conversing with two of his vassals. A similar scene, also featuring the Dos Pilas king, was excavated at Tikal, though how it got there is unknown.

In 745 K'awiil Chan
K'inich fought the western
kingdom of Yaxchilan,
capturing the lord pictured
here on Dos Pilas
Hieroglyphic Stairway 3.

THE UNFINISHED STAIRWAY

*Hieroglyphic Stairway 1 has areas of text
that were outlined but never completed.*

One of the hieroglyphic stairways at
Dos Pilas (HS.1), sited on the west
side of the Main Plaza, was left
unfinished by its sculptors. While this
is not the only monument the Maya
abandoned in this way, it is certainly
the largest and most prominent.
Completed sections are now damaged
and difficult to interpret, but include
parentage statements that link B'alaj
Chan K'awiil, Itzamnaaj K'awiil and,
seemingly, K'awiil Chan K'inich. The
final portion deals exclusively with
Itzamnaaj K'awiil, suggesting that
it was he who commissioned the
monument. Conceivably, work was in
progress at his death and halted as a
mark of reverence. More intriguingly,
however, other clues might point
towards K'awiil Chan K'inich as its
main protagonist, suggesting that its
abandonment may have been rather
later and correspond to the moment
of downfall at Dos Pilas.

The end of Dos Pilas hegemony finds
some mention on this hieroglyphic stair
at Tamarindito. Events dated to 761 refer
to K'awiil Chan K'inich (highlighted),
perhaps concerning his ousting or exile.

presiding over some event that took place at Dos Pilas. More overt
political control can be seen at Seibal, first conquered by Ruler 3 and still
under close Dos Pilas supervision. A series of glyphic tablets make no
mention of the war some 12 years earlier, but record K'awiil Chan
K'inich's 'scattering' ceremonies at both Seibal and Tamarindito in 746
and his overseeing of rituals performed by his Seibal vassals in 745 and
747.[19] The vanquished king Yich'aak B'alam is the most prominent of
these figures and he evidently survived his defeat to serve as a subject
lord. He dedicated the mortuary shrine of an ancestral predecessor, K'an
Mo' B'alam ('Precious Macaw Jaguar'), while on the same day a *ch'ok
ajaw* or 'young lord' was elevated to his position under the watchful eye
of the Dos Pilas king.

Overreach?

After 20 years exemplifying the king's role of both diplomat and warrior,
the fortunes of K'awiil Chan K'inich took a decisive turn for the worse in
761, with a series of events that are still poorly understood. A hieroglyphic stairway found at Tamarindito mentions his 'going out' – usually
a reference to enforced flight.[20] This was followed seven days later by an
'axe' attack against Tamarindito itself. Its perpetrator is now lost,
but K'awiil Chan K'inich is not heard of again and Dos Pilas was all but
abandoned at this time.

Just why its power dissolved so suddenly is difficult to assess. After a
century of expansion Dos Pilas exerted control over a large area and,
without a significant population at its core, it is likely that it had become
overly reliant on the loyalty of its vassal lords, the normal source of any
rebellion.[21] In earlier times it had benefited from its ties with a powerful
foreign patron in the shape of Calakmul, but the political landscape
of the lowlands was changing rapidly and by now these networks of
hierarchical support were all but extinct.

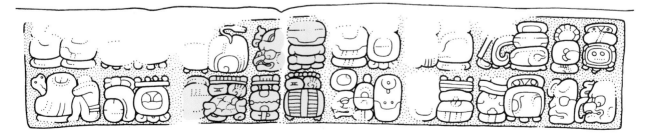

AT AGUATECA

Tan Te' K'inich
>770–802>

AT AGUAS CALIENTES

Chak Lakamtuun
>790>

AT SEIBAL

Ajaw B'ot
771–800>

AT LA AMELIA

Lachan K'awiil Ajaw B'ot
802–807>

TAN TE' K'INICH

Glyphic spelling	Accession
TAN? TE' K'INICH	8 February 770
Also known as	(9.16.19.0.14
Ruler 5	5 Ix 12 Pop
Birth	*Father*
22 January 748	Ucha'an K'an
(9.15.16.12.1	B'alam
12 Imix 14 Kumk'u	*Monuments*
	Aguateca Stelae 6,
	7, 12, 13 & 19

AJAW B'OT

Glyphic spelling	Accession
a-AJAW-b'o-to	20 January 771
K'UHUL-ITZ'A:T?-ta	(9.17.0.0.0
Also known as	13 Ajaw 18 Kumk'u)
Ah Ahpo Chuen	*Monuments*
	Seibal Stelae 5, 6 &
	7

RULE OF THE PETTY KINGS

With the fall of K'awiil Chan K'inich major changes took place in the Petexbatun-Pasión area and political authority rapidly splintered. When a new order emerged it was dominated by a range of local magnates, each of whom erected monuments and used the once restricted title 'divine lord of Mutal'.

Fortunes among the traditional centres varied. Tamarindito produced its account of the 761 war a year later, but this is the last we hear from either this site or Arroyo de Piedra. The former 'twin capital' of Aguateca survived and may have served as a refuge for the surviving Dos Pilas elite. Its rulers continued to exercise a kind of pre-eminence over the new landscape, though it was clearly of a low order. It is 770 before its next known king took office, as described on Stela 6.[22] His name is poorly preserved but its outlines are consistent with those of **Tan Te' K'inich**, a ruler known from several later monuments as well as more portable objects, such as a newly found section of human skull. The recently discovered Stela 19 at Aguateca tells of a battle he fought in 778 and reveals that he was a son of a hitherto unknown Aguateca king: Ucha'an K'an B'alam ('Master of Precious/Yellow Jaguar').[23]

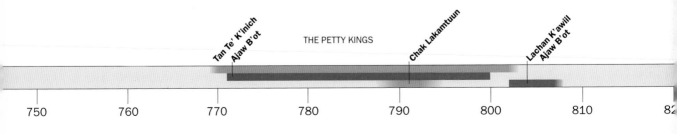

Tan Te' K'inich / Ajaw B'ot   THE PETTY KINGS   Chak Lakamtuun   Lachan K'awiil Ajaw B'ot

750   760   770   780   790   800   810   82

CHAK LAKAMTUUN	
Glyphic spelling CHAK-LAKAM[TU: N]-ni	*Monument* Aguas Calientes Stela 1

LACHAN K'AWIIL AJAW B'OT	
Glyphic spelling la-CHAN-K'AWI:L AJ- AJAW-b'o-to *Also known as* Ah Ahpo Chuen *Birth* 25 June 760 (9.16.9.4.19 13 Kawak 7 Mol)	*Accession* 1 May 802 (9.18.11.13.4 10 K'an 2 Xul) *Monuments* La Amelia Panels 1 & 2; Hieroglyphic Stairway 1

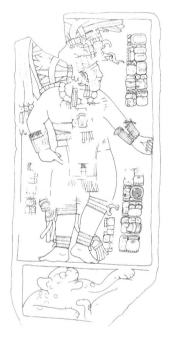

Lachan K'awiil Ajaw B'ot on La Amelia Panel 2, AD 804.

(*Below*) Storage vessels and a *metate* lie on the floor of an elite residence burned in the final assault on Aguateca.

Seibal, formerly ruled by its own dynasty under the overlordship of Dos Pilas, became the seat of another Mutal-titled king, **Ajaw B'ot**, a year later in 771. He carried the captor's epithet 'Master of He of Fire' and took office, unusually, on the K'atun-ending 9.17.0.0.0 – celebrating its anniversary 30 years later. Whether this was an entirely independent figure, or a lord under the nominal control of Aguateca is unclear (a damaged section of Seibal Stela 6 mentions Aguateca and interaction between the two). Chapayal, a site 9.3 miles (15 km) to the northeast of Seibal, also makes reference to Ajaw B'ot, probably a sign that he exercised his own sphere of influence.[24] Further kings sprang up at smaller sites close to the Pasión River: **Chak Lakamtuun** at Aguas Calientes, **Lachan K'awiil Ajaw B'ot** at La Amelia and others at El Caribe (though these last did not use the Mutal title).

Most seem to have ruled under the patronage of Aguateca. Tan Te' K'inich's final appearance in 802 was not at his capital but at La Amelia, where he presides over some ceremony performed by Lachan K'awiil Ajaw B'ot. This lord erects additional monuments at his site, but the last discernible date, from 807, represents the final appearance of the Mutal emblem and royal dynasty in the Petexbatun.

The collapse of Dos Pilas hegemony seems to have benefited a series of adjacent kingdoms and Itzan, Cancuen and Machaquila all show renewed vigour at this time.[25] As we have seen, in the Petexbatun itself the next half-century saw no single power rise to take its place; instead the proliferation and debasement of royal titles points to a devolved and much weakened landscape. Yet, dramatic as it may seem, this dissolution served merely as the prelude to the next phase: nothing less than the annihilation of organized society in the region.

THE FALL OF THE PETEXBATUN

No area better illustrates the chaos into which Classic society now descended than the Petexbatun. In this region we have clear evidence that six centuries of cultural florescence ended in warfare of unprecedented intensity.

At Aguateca extensive fortifications were built to augment its already impressive natural defences. Eventually, over 3 miles (4.8 km) of walls enclosed not only the city itself but sizeable areas of agricultural land and access to essential water supplies (p. 67). Surrounding hilltops and their hamlets were similarly encircled, perhaps as part of a strategic defence plan. Despite these preparations – which seem never to have been completed – excavations have shown that disaster was postponed rather than averted. Takeshi Inomata's excavations in the central core show it to have been destroyed by fire and its elite dwellings deserted in great haste, leaving jade and shell valuables scattered inside and many ceramics still in their original domestic positions, the first time that the abandonment of a Classic city has been documented in such detail.[26]

The abandoned main plaza of Dos Pilas was ultimately occupied by villagers who tore masonry from surrounding temples and palaces to engineer a double-lined defence of their community.

The original capital at Dos Pilas seems to have been abandoned after the events of 761, but in time its once sacred plaza became home to a simple squatter's village. Clearly fearing attack, these last inhabitants (as well as others at nearby El Duende) stripped the temples and palaces of their stone facings to construct the crude masonry foundations of two

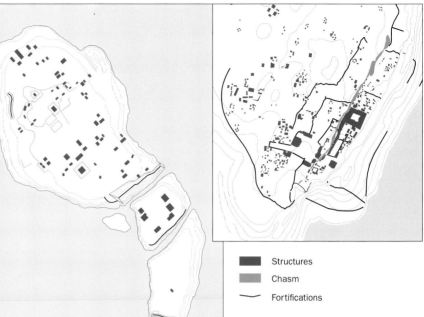

Structures

Chasm

Fortifications

Aguateca (*top right*) was protected by walls totalling over 3 miles (4.8 km) in length. The nearby peninsula of Punta de Chimino (*top left*, not to scale) was defended by a triple line of ditches and ramparts.

concentric walls, both topped by wooden palisades.[27] The sorry state of Dos Pilas today – its buildings reduced to shapeless mounds – is largely a consequence of this desperate robbery. It is unclear how long these defenders resisted their enemies, but recent discoveries of spearpoints in the 'killing alley' between the two walls and an associated pit of decapitated skulls by Arthur Demarest and his team suggest that they were eventually overwhelmed.[28] A date early in the 9th century, in line with other sites in the region, seems most likely.

A final refuge?

Nearby Punta de Chimino, a small site occupying a peninsula jutting into Lake Petexbatun, seems to have survived a little longer. Here the defences were truly monumental. Along its narrow landward approach, some 50,000 cu. yards (38,250 cu. m) of rock had been excavated to construct three sequential trenches; the displaced material used to build matching ramparts, the largest 30 ft (9 m) in height. The final, deepest ditch was flooded to create an island citadel. Although the original date of construction is unclear, it was obviously enhanced at this late date.[29]

The enemies who finally stormed the Petexbatun cities have left few if any clues to their identity, but the extreme fragmentation of authority in the region could easily cast vicious local feuding as the culprit. However, the involvement of incoming communities cannot be fully discounted. Certainly when some semblance of order returns to the region it is associated with a new ceramic type, Fine Orange.[30] Political authority arrived from the east, with a new elite group engendering a final Classic Maya resurgence in the Pasión region, reviving the Seibal kingdom after 830 (p. 227).

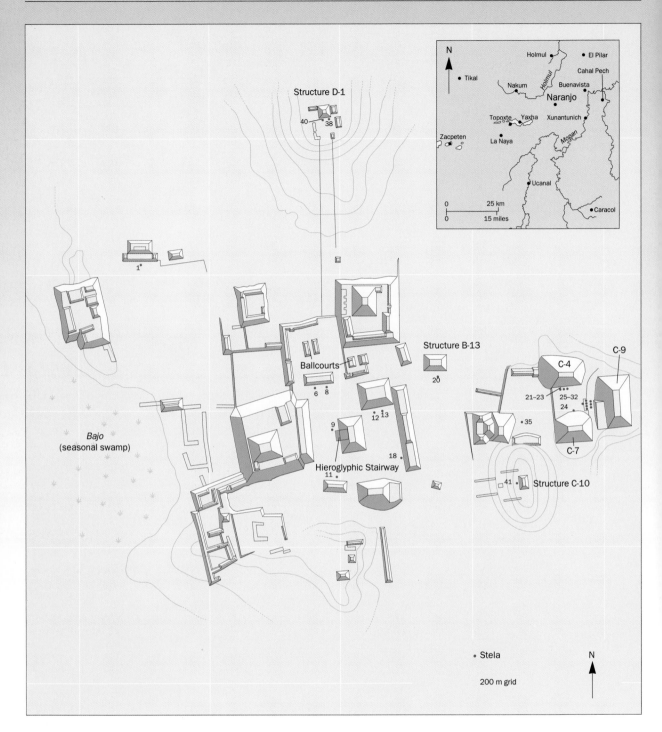

Structure D-1

40   38

1

Structure D-1

Bajo
(seasonal swamp)

Ballcourts

6   8

9

11

Hieroglyphic Stairway

Structure B-13

20

12 13

18

Structure C-10

41

C-4

21–23   25–32
          24

35

C-9

C-7

• Stela

200 m grid

N

N

Holmul   El Pilar

Tikal   Cahal Pech

Nakum   Buenavista

Naranjo

Topoxte Yaxha   Xunantunich

Zacpeten   Mopan

La Naya

Ucanal

Caracol

0   25 km

0   15 miles

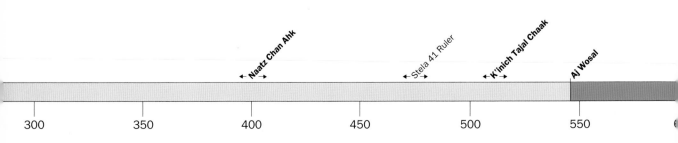

Naatz Chan Ahk

Stela 41 Ruler

K'inich Tajal Chaak

Aj Wosal

300   350   400   450   500   550

NARANJO

D ISCOVERED BY THE GREAT AUSTRIAN EXPLORER TEOBERT MALER in
1905, Naranjo is located midway between two major river
drainages, the Holmul and Mopan, with ready access to their fertile
valleys in modern-day Belize and the Caribbean coast beyond. Almost
no archaeological work has been conducted at the site, so little is known
of its origins or development. But a fine collection of stelae, covering at
least 345 years of its dynastic progress, has provided a reasonable picture
of its complex political affairs.

Occupying a key position between a number of the most belligerent
and powerful Classic kingdoms – Tikal, Caracol and Calakmul – Naranjo's
fortunes were always shaped by its performance in war. Its history
divides neatly into early, middle and late periods, each interspersed by
significant lacunae. These gaps followed defeats so serious that the
city fell under the domination of foreign powers, or even suffered the
extinction of its ruling line. Yet, amidst all this turmoil the Naranjo
kingdom – possibly known as Saal in ancient times – was also a place of
artistic accomplishment. The city and its surrounding region were
responsible for some of the finest painted ceramics produced in the
Maya world.

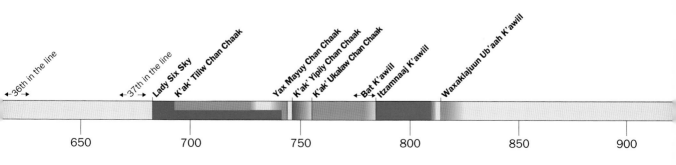

Naatz Chan Ahk
?

K'inich Tajal Chaak
?

Aj Wosal
Double Comb
546–615>

(*Right*) Crowned with a simple headband and diadem of the 'Jester God' *huunal*, we see Aj Wosal (perhaps Woosal) on the front of Stela 25. AD 615.

(*Below*) Decorated with the severed head of the Maize God (see p. 222), this plate belonged to the otherwise unknown Naranjo ruler K'inich Tajal Chaak.

THE EARLY PERIOD

The first enthronement recorded at Naranjo was not that of a mortal king, but of the kingdom's founding god, a character dubbed (a little inelegantly) the 'Square-nosed Beastie'. Our two sources for this event disagree on exactly how long ago this took place (one offers a date some 22,000 years in the past, the other surpasses 896,000!) but in both the intention was to place it deep in mythological time, perhaps as part of a cyclical history.[1]

The first historical rulers of Naranjo are, by contrast, little known. The earliest portrait we have appears on Stela 41, a celebration of the K'atun-ending of 9.2.0.0.0 in 475, where the king is depicted in the guise of a fire god holding a symbolic fire-drill, a popular theme at the city. Sadly, his name has not survived. A lidded ceramic vessel that can be style-dated to about 400 carries the name **Naatz Chan Ahk**, while a fine plate commissioned for **K'inich Tajal Chaak** is

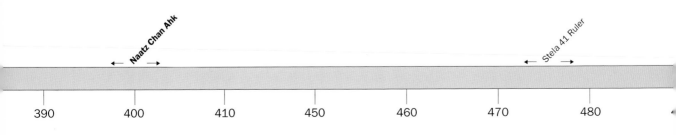

Naatz Chan Ahk

Stela 41 Ruler

390   400   410   450   460   470   480

NAATZ CHAN AHK	
Glyphic spelling na-tzu CHAN-a-ku	

K'INICH TAJAL CHAAK	
Glyphic spelling K'INICH[CHAN?] TAJAL-CHA:K? ('Great-Sun Torch Rain God')	*Mother* Lady Casper

AJ WOSAL	
Glyphic spelling AJ-wo-sa-la *Also known as* Ruler I, Double Comb *Dynastic title* 35th in the line *Accession* 5 May 546 (9.5.12.0.4 6 K'an 3 Sip)	*Father* Pik Chan Ahkul *Mother* Lady Stone-in-Hand Sky *Monuments* Stelae 15?, 16, 17, 25, 27 & 38; Altar 1

probably from the early 6th century. Instead of the local emblem glyph both are identified by another title, Sak 'Chuwen', that seems to be of greater antiquity but similarly restricted to Naranjo's high king.

AJ WOSAL

Naranjo's historical narrative really commences with the accession of Aj Wosal, who began one of the longest reigns of the Classic period in 546. No older than 12 years of age at the time, he went on to celebrate four K'atun-endings in power during a span of at least 69 years. His earliest monuments are poorly preserved and do not have legible dates, but Stela 38 is firmly fixed to the end of the 8th K'atun in 593, while the fragmentary Stela 27 includes a 5 K'atun Ajaw reference (indicating an age of 78 or over), placing it after 613. He commissioned Stela 25 to mark the 3½ K'atun-anniversary of his accession in 615.[2]

Aj Wosal's longest inscription is to be found on Altar 1, a small oval stone that once partnered Stela 38. Their original position was at the foot of Structure D-1, a small hilltop pyramid approached by a broad causeway that defined the northern limit of the site core. It begins with the accession

(Right) An unlikely survivor of the harsh sub-tropical environment, these finely incised glyphs come from Altar 1, which originally stood together with Stela 38 in front of the hilltop Structure D-1. AD 593.

(Below) This polychrome bowl names Aj Wosal in its rim text, while his 3 K'atun Ajaw title (marking his then current age between 39 and 59 years) indicates that the vessel was painted sometime in the late 6th century.

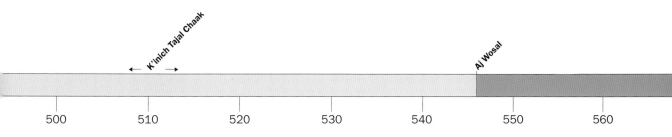

YAXHA: CITY ON THE LAKE

Less than a day's walk from Naranjo lies the expanse of Lake Yaxha and, on its northern shore, a great capital of the same name. To judge from its badly ruined corpus of early monuments, its heyday fell in the first centuries of the Classic era, when the city grew to an immense size (it is the third-biggest ruin in modern-day Guatemala after El Mirador and Tikal). This early history remains poorly known and the number of inscriptions for all periods extremely small. Although Naranjo enjoyed the upper hand for much of the Late Classic, it could never fully subdue its giant neighbour and they fought a series of wars. Yaxha's possession of one of the few twin-pyramid complexes outside Tikal is particularly interesting and may be a pointer to its later political affiliations. The city's other claim to fame is the survival of its name from ancient to modern times, its glyphic toponym reading *yaxa'* 'Green/Blue Water'.[3]

YAX-a

of the mythical founder, before recounting a now damaged event in 258 BC that took place at Maxam, a Naranjo place-name. This is followed by a pair of contemporary events (one a poorly understood burial rite) before naming Aj Wosal's parents: his mother Lady Stone-in-Hand Sky and father Pik Chan Ahkul – probably his predecessor. Aj Wosal is placed as the '35th in the line' of the kingdom's founding deity. Already impressed by his longevity, Altar 1 concludes by linking Aj Wosal to a prophetic completion of the 10th Bak'tun of the Long Count in AD 830.[4]

The sides of the aforementioned Stela 25 are largely filled with a litany of Aj Wosal's successive jubilees, but one clause offers important information about the wider political landscape of the Early Classic. His 546 accession is said to have taken place under the 'supervision' of the Calakmul king Tuun K'ab' Hix. We have here the earliest surviving example of this form of political patronage, where one king sanctions the rule of another, and the first sign of Calakmul's emerging power. Since this record appears at the very end of his long reign it is probably safe to assume that Aj Wosal remained a loyal client and ally throughout. His death, which probably fell not too long after 615, was to set Naranjo on a rather different, indeed disastrous, course.

THE FIRST HIATUS PERIOD: THE CARACOL AND CALAKMUL WARS

Between the reigns of Aj Wosal (the 35th in the line of the founding deity) and K'ak' Tiliw Chan Chaak (the 38th) two other kings held power at Naranjo. Their obscurity owes much to their failure in wars that pitted Naranjo against two powerful adversaries: Caracol, its regional rival to the south; and Calakmul, its former patron to the north. Neither of their personal names has survived and both are referred to only by the generic title of Naranjo kings, Sak Chuwen, in the records of their foes.[5]

The first of these conflicts began with engagements in May and August 626, in which Naranjo twice suffered defeats of the *jub'uy* 'brought down' type at the hands of the Caracol ruler K'an II.[6] The coup de grace, the 'star war' conquest of Naranjo itself, came on 24 December 631 and was delivered not by Caracol's forces, but by those of Calakmul. The dramatic reversal in Naranjo–Calakmul relations is a sure sign that Aj Wosal's political affiliations had been repudiated by his successor. Calakmul's wrath may be reflected in the unusual treatment meted out to the unfortunate 36th ruler, subject of the rarely seen verb, *k'uxaj*, 'tortured' or possibly 'eaten', presumably signalling his demise (p. 106).[7]

Aj Wosal

540   550   560   570   580   590   600

The conquest stairway

Much of this story is detailed on an extraordinary hieroglyphic stairway Maler discovered at the heart of the Naranjo capital. Commissioned by Caracol's K'an II to celebrate the 9.10.10.0.0 ending of 642, it records various details of his biography and part in the conflict, while giving special prominence to the final victory of Calakmul. Together with an isolated panel similarly devoted to K'an II (trimmed and re-used as a stairway block), its presence at Naranjo has long been seen as evidence for a lengthy period of Caracol domination. Yet the stairway was found reset and incomplete and it is far from clear that Naranjo was its original provenance. One of the missing blocks was later found by Ian Graham at the site of Ucanal, 20.5 miles (33 km) to the southeast, where it had been left in a ballcourt well after the city's ruin. Of even greater interest is a fragment of matching design, dimension and material recovered from fallen debris at Caracol – in many ways the most logical origin of this monument (p. 92).[8]

Our only reference to the 37th ruler comes from a fragmentary stucco text recently uncovered at Caracol.[9] Here a revitalized Naranjo, clearly free of foreign control, is said to have attacked Oxwitza' ('Three Hill Water'), the ancient name of Caracol, in February 680, inflicting a comparable 'star war' defeat (p. 95). Narratives of this kind, recorded by the losing party, usually recite defeat only to contrast it with ultimate victory and it is likely that a further, still to be excavated, section tells of Caracol's retribution. That such a sequence did indeed occur is suggested by the dynastic crisis that unfolded at Naranjo as not only its king, but its entire ruling line, promptly disappeared.

This photograph, taken by Teobert Maler, shows four of the blocks that make up the Naranjo Hieroglyphic Stairway together with three monstrous skulls (now lost).

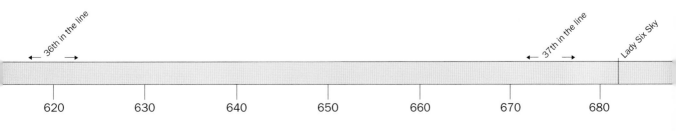

36th in the line

37th in the line

Lady Six Sky

620   630   640   650   660   670   680

Lady Six Sky
682–741

K'ak' Tiliw Chan Chaak
Smoking Squirrel
693–728>

In the very first appearance of a theme that would be repeated many times at Naranjo, Lady Six Sky stands triumphantly atop the contorted body of a vanquished enemy. Female portraits of this type are exceedingly rare in Maya art and otherwise only known from Calakmul. Stela 24, AD 702.

LADY SIX SKY	
Glyphic spelling IX-6 CHAN-?-AJAW ('Lady Six Sky-? Queen')	11 Chikchan/12 Kimi 8/9 Pop)
	Father
Also known as Lady Wac Chanil Ahau, Lady of Dos Pilas, Lady of Tikal	B'alaj Chan K'awiil of Dos Pilas
	Mother Lady B'ulu'
	Son K'ak' Tiliw Chan Chaak
Death 10 or 11 February 741 (9.15.9.11.5/6	*Monuments* Stelae 3, 18, 24, 29, 31

K'AK TILIW CHAN CHAAK	
Glyphic spelling K'AK'-TIL-wi CHAN-na-CHA:K ('Fire-burning Sky Rain God')	*Accession* 28 May 693 (9.13.1.3.19 5 Kawak 2 Yaxk'in)
	Wife Lady Une' B'alam of Tuub'al
Also known as Ruler II, Smoking Squirrel, Scroll Squirrel, Smoke Squirrel, Butz' Tiliw	*Mother* Lady Six Sky of Dos Pilas
Dynastic title 38th in the line	*Son* K'ak' Ukalaw Chan Chaak
Birth 3 January 688 (9.12.15.13.7 9 Manik' 0 K'ayab)	*Monuments* Stelae 1, 2, 21, 22, 23, 26, 28, 30 & 40?

LADY SIX SKY AND K'AK' TILIW CHAN CHAAK

Efforts to create a new royal line for Naranjo, or bolster the pedigree of a lesser local lineage in the wake of recent wars, first appear on 27 August 682. This day marks the 'arrival here' of a princess called **Lady Six Sky**, daughter of the Dos Pilas king B'alaj Chan K'awiil. As we have seen at Tikal, 'arrival' is imbued with the wider meaning of dynastic foundation or refoundation. Three days later she performs a formal ritual to this effect, visiting an important pyramid, probably to rededicate a dynastic shrine and restore the supernatural basis of the kingdom.[10]

Reign of the warrior queen

Although never invested as a Naranjo ruler (she always carries the *mutal* emblem of her native Dos Pilas), Lady Six Sky assumed every other prerogative of kingship, portraying herself on monuments and performing key calendrical rituals. This even extended to military symbolism: two stelae show her trampling captives in the manner of any warrior-king. It is clear that she assumed the role of queen regnant and effectively ruled, then perhaps co-ruled, for a substantial period.[11]

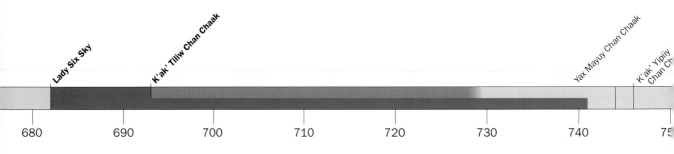

Lady Six Sky   K'ak' Tiliw Chan Chaak   Yax Mayuy Chan Chaak   K'ak' Yipiiy Chan Ch

680   690   700   710   720   730   740   75

Enthroned at only five years old, K'ak' Tiliw Chan Chaak was the cornerstone of Naranjo's revitalization during the late 7th century. In his early years the instrument of his mother and a Calakmul overlord, he later emerged as a successful ruler in his own right. Stela 30, AD 714.

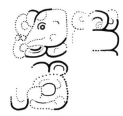

In this battered but crucial passage from Stela 1, K'ak' Tiliw Chan Chaak is described as the *yajaw* or 'vassal lord' of the powerful Yich'aak K'ak' of Calakmul.

One the finest of the so-called 'Holmul-dancer' vessels, this tall cylinder vase was excavated by Jennifer Taschek and Joseph Ball from an elite burial at Buenavista, a centre 9 miles (14.5 km) to the east of Naranjo. It shows two aspects of the Maize God, identified here as specific patrons of the Tikal and Calakmul kingdoms, in the refined pose of Maya dance. Its rim text names K'ak' Tiliw Chan Chaak as its original owner, probably indicating that the vase was a gift he presented to one of his provincial clients.

Five years after her arrival, in 688, the future king of Naranjo, K'ak' Tiliw Chan Chaak ('Chaak who fire-burns the sky'), was born. Although their relationship is never clearly specified, Lady Six Sky's exalted status and close association with the new heir has long convinced scholars that she was his mother.[12] Very pointedly, no mention is made of his father – clear evidence that there was to be no continuity with the old royal patriline. What references are made to Naranjo's past are to the reign of Aj Wosal, with whom Lady Six Sky directly compares her own ritual performances, as well as placing herself in an analogous position to Aj Wosal's mother, Lady Stone-in-Hand Sky.[13] To further emphasize their association, the new dynasts grouped their stelae together with those of their illustrious precursor – as if to form an indivisible whole.

A figurehead and vassal

In May 693 **K'ak' Tiliw Chan Chaak** became the 38th ruler to succeed the kingdom's mythical founder. Easily the best known of all Naranjo's kings, his renown stems from his fine corpus of monuments and the astounding list of military successes they recount. Yet two key factors lie behind his story. The first is his tender age at accession, an infant of barely five years; there can be no doubt that he was long simply a figurehead for the reign of Lady Six Sky and whatever faction supported her rule within the Naranjo nobility. The second emerges from the scarred remains of Stela 1. In a passage that links the birth of K'ak' Tiliw to his accession, where we would normally expect to see his name, we find instead: 'the lord of Yich'aak K'ak', Divine Lord of Calakmul'.[14] This

marks K'ak' Tiliw, like his grandfather before him, as a vassal of the powerful Calakmul kingdom, and must lead us to suspect that the whole process of dynastic renewal took place under their auspices (p. 110). For the remainder of the Classic era, Naranjo would be ruled by a lineage which traced its claims to kingship from the line of Tikal exiles supported by Calakmul.

Campaigns of the Middle period

With her son safely enthroned, Lady Six Sky moved with haste to commence war-making in his name, the first action following just 20 days after the ceremony. Two centres, B'ital (probably lying between Naranjo and Caracol) and Tuub'al (perhaps sited towards Lake Peten-Itza) were attacked and 'burned', while the lord K'inichil Kab' was 'brought down'.[15] Two years later, in 695, Naranjo battled its giant neighbour Tikal at a place called Yellow Rabbit, capturing a lord named Siyaj K'awiil ('K'awiil is born').[16] Most likely this was part of a wider campaign that culminated in Tikal's clash with Calakmul later the same year – a decisive defeat for Yich'aak K'ak'. One of the captives of this war carries the title aj sa(al), probably meaning 'He of Naranjo' and a sign that Lady Six Sky contributed warriors to the battle (pp. 44–5). Between 696 and 698 Naranjo records four more burnings, including a second and final defeat of K'inichil Kab' and, more importantly, the torching of the capital of Ucanal. This resulted in the capture of its king Itzamnaaj B'alam (a namesake of the better known Yaxchilan ruler), who appears as a kneeling prisoner on the face of Stela 30.[17]

As he reached maturity, K'ak' Tiliw opened his own account with a second wave of campaigning. In 706 he 'entered the city of Yootz (capital of a minor kingdom otherwise known from a pair of painted vessels)', and its ruler is shown battered and trampled on Stela 21.[18] In 710 a more impressive victory was achieved, the burning of Yaxha and the capture and sacrifice of its king. Related passages describe some of the aftermath: the exhumation of a recently deceased Yaxha ruler, Yax B'olon Chaak, and a 'scattering' (apparently of his bones) on an 'island' – perhaps Topoxte on Lake Yaxha.[19] Four years later Sakha', perhaps a site close to the modern-day Lake Saknab, adjoining Lake Yaxha, was similarly burned, while the same fate befell a now unidentifiable victim in 716.

A new realm

This heady sequence of early victories (Stela 22 alone reads like a conflagration of the eastern Peten) gives an impression of ruthless expansion. But with the exception of Ucanal and Tikal, none of the victims is identifiable and the campaigns seem aimed at modest centres within easy reach of Naranjo. Rather than expanding the city's traditional sphere, Lady Six Sky's focus may well have been reclaiming former possessions that resisted the new matriarchal regime, bringing her into conflict with neighbours who had broadened their influence at Naranjo's expense.

Part of Naranjo's attempts to retain control of its hard-won gains can be detected in a marriage alliance of K'ak' Tiliw's. Throughout Mesoamerica, victorious rulers consistently sought to cement their acquisitions by establishing a joint bloodline, marrying off children or taking wives from their new subjects. One of his wives, Lady Une' B'alam ('Baby Jaguar') seems to have been a prize of the war against Tuub'al since she was a royal woman from this site. Elsewhere, Naranjo's continued influence over its conquests is reflected in two ceremonies in 712. Though heavily damaged, both seem to describe the accession of new rulers, one at Ucanal, the other probably Yootz, under the supervision of the still teenaged Naranjo king.[20]

Naranjo's relationship with Calakmul after the death of Yich'aak K'ak' is still unclear. That K'ak' Tiliw recorded his fealty to the great king as late as 711 suggests that it was a source of continued pride. We have no record of K'ak' Tiliw's own death, though the 3 K'atun Ajaw title he bears on his son's Stela 13 shows that he endured until at least 728. Two broken monuments, Stelae 26 and 40 (the first bearing part of his name, the second carved in a style typical of this period) are candidates for the latter part of his reign. An important find at Lady Six Sky's birthplace of Dos Pilas was a reference which, although damaged, seems to indicate that she died in 741 (p. 62).[21]

(*Right*) Enthroned on a jaguar-skin cushion, this detail from Stela 22 shows a 14-year-old K'ak' Tiliw Chan Chaak. The complex headdress he wears is composed of elements that spell out his name.

(*Below*) The name of K'ak' Tiliw's wife Lady Une' B'alam or 'Baby Jaguar' appears in three different spellings. It was the last example, with its reclining jaguar in a classic pose of infancy, that provided the key to its meaning and a reading for her namesake, an early queen of Tikal (pp. 26–7).

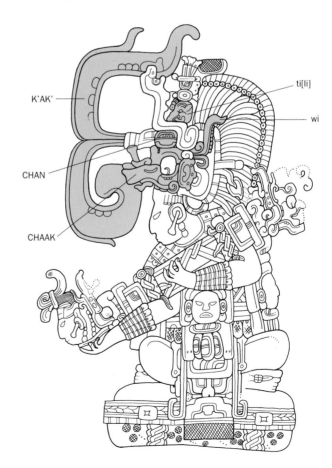

Yax Mayuy Chan Chaak

?–744

K'ak' Yipiiy Chan Chaak

746–?

The date of K'ak' Yipiiy Chan Chaak's inaugural monument, Stela 20, survives only as a Calendar Round position, making it difficult to place with certainty. But since all other alternatives fall during the reign of other kings, or are unacceptably early or late in terms of style, 15 August AD 746 emerges as the best candidate.

YAX MAYUY CHAN CHAAK	
Glyphic spelling	*Death*
YAX-ma-yu(-yu)	4 February 744?
[CHAN]CHA:K-ki	(9.15.12.11.13
	7 Ben 0 Pop)

K'AK' YIPIIY CHAN CHAAK	
Glyphic spelling	*Accession*
K'AK'-yi-pi-ya CHAN-	15 August 746
na-CHA:K	(9.15.15.3.16
Also known as	7 Kib 14 Yax)
Smoking New	*Monument*
Squirrel, Smoking	Stela 20
Bak'tun	

THE SECOND HIATUS PERIOD: THE TIKAL WAR

The glorious epoch of K'ak' Tiliw Chan Chaak and Lady Six Sky ended in another great silence, Naranjo's Second Hiatus period. At least two reigns spanned this era, whose cause, as with the first, can be laid at the door of military defeat. The earliest mention of **Yax Mayuy Chan Chaak** appears on Stela 18, the last monument of Naranjo's Middle period and dedicated to Lady Six Sky in 726.[22] There is some possibility that its finely incised rear face (quite unlike the relief carving of its side texts) was a later addition in which the new king sought to establish his long connection with Lady Six Sky and K'ak' Tiliw. We have no record of his inauguration, but he seems to have been K'ak' Tiliw's direct successor, presumably a son, who may have taken power only after the death of Lady Six Sky in 741. In any event, he was the incumbent in 744 when Naranjo was the target of a decisive assault at the hands of Tikal.

The fall of Wak Kab'nal

One of the great wooden lintels of Tikal Temple 4 is devoted to an account of this action, its surrounding prelude, aftermath and ritual commemoration. In February 744, Tikal launched a 'star war' attack against Wak Kab'nal

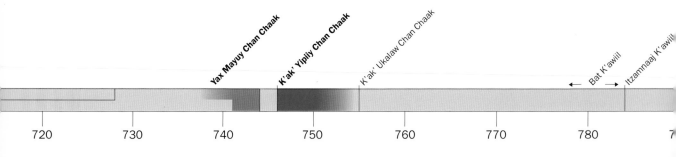

Yax Mayuy Chan Chaak   K'ak' Yipiiy Chan Chaak   K'ak' Ukalaw Chan Chaak   ← Bat K'awiil →   Itzamnaaj K'awiil

720   730   740   750   760   770   780   7

(*Above*) This passage describes Naranjo's conquest at the hands of Tikal in AD 744. Evidently a large ceremonial litter and god effigy were captured at the same time, seen here (*below*) etched as graffiti on a Tikal temple wall and again (*bottom left and right*) in the form of an intricately carved wooden lintel from Tikal Temple 4. Note the base with its pattern of Naranjo name glyphs, with the Tikal king triumphantly sitting in place of his vanquished rival.

('Six Earth Place'), described as the 'city of the Square-nosed Beastie' and presumably the Naranjo capital itself. Following passages recount the capture of Yax Mayuy Chan Chaak's personal god and a victory pageant involving the display of a giant palanquin or litter, shown in the accompanying scene. Emblazoned Naranjo name glyphs along its base, under the feet of the Tikal king, suggest that this is the seized throne described in the text, while at the same time they serve in place of the prostrate prisoner as a symbol of the kingdom's 'trampled' status. The consequences for the Naranjo king were suitably dire. On Tikal Stela 5, erected just 128 days after the battle, he is shown as a trussed captive at the feet of the Tikal king Yik'in Chan K'awiil, about to meet his death in ritual sacrifice (p. 49).[23]

A new king

The only monument that interrupts the Second Hiatus period, Stela 20, names the next known ruler, **K'ak' Yipiiy Chan Chaak**. Set in a rather isolated position in the eastern part of the site core, it shows him in the standard pose of Naranjo kings, brandishing a double-headed serpent bar and standing on a contorted captive. The date of his accession survives only as a Calendar Round notation, and a damaged one at that. Its most likely placement falls in 746, two years after the Tikal war.[24]

Despite this promising sign of renewed stability, it is 30 years before another Naranjo monument can be identified. This return to silence points to continued political upheaval that may well be linked to further conflict with Tikal. In 748 Tikal captured a high-ranking lord whose *wuk tzuk* 'Seven Provinces(?)' title links him to the Naranjo-Yaxha region – a triumph they celebrated on no fewer than three monuments, one the enormous Tikal Rock Sculpture (p. 50).[25]

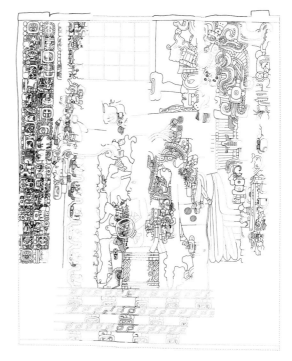

K'ak' Ukalaw Chan Chaak
Smoking Batab
755–780>

Bat K'awiil
?

Itzamnaaj K'awiil
Shield God K
784–810>

Waxaklajuun Ub'aah K'awiil
814–?

K'AK' UKALAW CHAN CHAAK	
Glyphic spelling	*Father*
K'AK'-(u)KAL(wa)	K'ak' Tiliw Chan
CHAN-na-CHA:K	Chaak
Also known as	*Mother*
Ruler IIIa, Smoking	Lady Une' B'alam of
Batab, Smoking	Tuub'al
Axe, Axe Blade	*Sons*
Accession	Itzamnaaj K'awiil,
8 November 755	Bat K'awiil
(9.16.4.10.18	*Monuments*
9 Etz'nab 11	Stelae 6, 11?, 13,
Muwan)	19, 33 & 36
Wife	
Lady Shell Star of	
Yaxha	

BAT K'AWIIL	
Glyphic spelling	*Brother*
k'e?-ji ?-le? K'AWIIL	Itzamnaaj K'awiil
Father	
K'ak' Ukalaw Chan	
Chaak	

K'AK' UKALAW CHAN CHAAK

A parentage statement on the rear face of Stela 13 shows that the next Naranjo king, K'ak' Ukalaw Chan Chaak, was a son of K'ak' Tiliw Chan Chaak and his queen Lady Une' B'alam. He acceded in November 755 and yet, most unusually, seems not to have documented the event in stone for a further 25 years. In fact, all five of his known stelae were erected together in celebration of the 9.17.10.0.0 ending of 780.[26] It is hard to conceive that an active and independent ruler would have left so long a period unmarked by vainglorious tributes to himself, or let important period-endings go unrecorded. More plausible is that K'ak' Ukalaw's earlier monuments were despoiled in some military reverse, or else that he was long under the circumscription of another kingdom, perhaps the now resurgent Tikal.

As usual, K'ak' Ukalaw is shown trampling vanquished foes, though few of the names incised on their twisted bodies are legible today. One military record given narrative treatment is the burning of B'ital in 775, the same site attacked by K'ak' Ukalaw's grandmother 82 years before. Stela 11, which seems to be another of his works, records a similar action, possibly dated to 777.

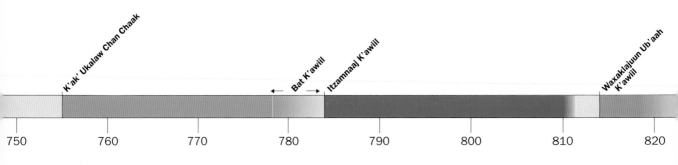

750   760   770   780   790   800   810   820

Stela 6, erected in AD 780, shows K'ak' Ukalaw at his inauguration in 755.

(*Opposite above*) Stela 13 provides this resolute portrait of K'ak' Ukalaw Chan Chaak in AD 780.

Rather confusingly, some K'ak' Ukalaw monuments refer to him by a quite different name 'He of Flint' (perhaps his childhood monicker). Nuptial ties make clear that we are dealing with one and the same character, married to a Lady Shell Star, a royal *ix ajaw* of Yaxha.[27] As with K'ak' Tiliw's union to a woman of Tuub'al, this marriage may have followed from its earlier conquest. Lady Shell Star provided him with his main inheritor, Itzamnaaj K'awiil.[28] What seems to be a second son appears on a plate excavated at the site of Holmul, north of Naranjo. Nicknamed **Bat K'awiil**, he carries a full emblem glyph and on this evidence may have been a short-reigning successor.

THE SPIRIT COMPANIONS

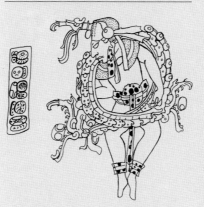

In addition to their shamanic powers as communicators with the gods, Maya kings were also ascribed mystical alter egos, 'spirit companions' or 'co-essences'. Known in Classic Mayan as their *way* (pronounced 'why'), these counterparts took the form of fantastical beasts, often combinations of two creatures, like the Old World griffin or satyr. Similar beliefs survive in some present-day Maya communities, where the companions are thought to reside within the body by day, but by night roam about causing mischief.[29]

The spirit companions of kings: (top) This 'unrolled' cylinder vase of K'ak' Tiliw Chan Chaak shows a crowded scene of spirit companions belonging to kings from, among others, Tikal, Calakmul and Caracol; (left) The 'White Bone House Centipede', the way of Palenque; (below) The sun-bellied jaguar way, one of several possessed by the kings of Calakmul.

For reasons that remain unclear, K'ak' Ukalaw made extensive use of an alternative name: 'He of Flint'.

ITZAMNAAJ K'AWIIL	
Glyphic spelling ITZAMNA:J-K'AWI:L *Also known as* Ruler IIIb, Shield *Birth* 13 March 771 (9.17.0.2.12 13 Eb 5 Sip) *Accession* 4 February 784 (9.17.13.4.3 5 Ak'bal 11 Pop)	*Wife* Lady Scroll of Yaxha? *Father* K'ak' Ukalaw Chan Chaak *Mother* Lady Shell Star of Yaxha *Brother* Bat K'awiil *Monuments* Stelae 7, 8, 10, 12, 14 & 35

(*Above*) The reign of Itzamnaaj K'awiil brought renewed stability and military success to the Naranjo kingdom. Stela 8, AD 800.

While mythic resonances are felt throughout Maya politics, rarely are they described so explicitly as in Naranjo's war against Yaxha. The supernatural episode in which a young god *puluy* 'burns' an aged jaguar deity is known from a painted vase (*far right*). The myth itself is first retold on Itzamnaaj K'awiil's Stela 35, then re-enacted on its front face (*right*), where, flaming torch in hands, the king threatens to immolate his prisoner K'inich Lakamtuun.

ITZAMNAAJ K'AWIIL

Fewer than four years after K'ak' Ukalaw's great display of 780, the king was dead and succeeded by his 13-year-old son Itzamnaaj K'awiil. His rule heralds a return to regular monumental activity, with six stelae erected between 790 and 810. Unfortunately, most are rather uninformative, dealing with his genealogical pedigree and the standard calendrical ceremonies.

Happily, Stelae 12 and 35 are more detailed than Itzamnaaj K'awiil's other monuments; they expand on military themes and the ruler's most important campaign, a new war against Yaxha. His strong kin ties with this city, as the son of a Yaxha queen, had clearly failed to unite the interests of these old adversaries (demonstrating the feeble nature of such bonds). Stela 12 begins with attacks against three locations – probably satellites of Yaxha – within a few days of each other in February 799, leading to assaults on the city itself in July and September. Tikal is mentioned twice during this narrative, although neither appearance is sufficiently well preserved to determine its role.

The final, decisive battle receives special treatment on Stela 35. This begins, rather unusually, with a mythological episode known from other sources, in which a reclining jaguar deity is 'burned' by a young god. Moving to contemporary events, we are told of the defeat of the Yaxha king K'inich Lakamtuun ('Great-Sun Banner Stone (Stela)'), expressed as the 'beheading' of his personal deity. Why did Itzamnaaj K'awiil choose to parallel these two events, which show no obvious connection? The answer is to be found on Yaxha Stela 31, commissioned by K'inich Lakamtuun just two years earlier in 797. Here one of his own war successes, a capture in 796, is credited to the same jaguar deity, identifying it as an important war patron of the Yaxha kingdom. The front face of Itzamnaaj K'awiil's Stela 35 shows a final playing out of the paradigm as, dressed as the victorious young god and holding a large flaming torch, the ruler re-enacts the myth with the bound Yaxha king as its victim.[30]

An intriguing denouement may be described in a passage on Stela 8, which was erected together with Stelae 12 and 35 in 800. On a day a few months after the battle, it mentions a woman whose title phrase concludes with the name K'inich Lakamtuun. Could this refer to Itzamnaaj K'awiil's marriage to the widow or another relative of the vanquished Yaxha king?

WAXAKLAJUUN UB'AAH K'AWIIL	
Glyphic spelling	Rabbit, 18 JOG
18-u-b'a(ah)	*Accession*
K'AWI:L-li	24 June 814
('18 images of	(9.19.4.1.1
K'awiil')	1 Imix 19 Mol)
Also known as	*Monument*
Ruler IIIc, 18	Stela 32

WAXAKLAJUUN UB'AAH K'AWIIL

Four years after the final reference to Itzamnaaj K'awiil in 810, Naranjo's last known ruler, Waxaklajuun Ub'aah K'awiil, took office. His Stela 32, erected in May 820, was one of the most exuberant sculptures produced at the site and showed the king seated on a ceremonial palanquin, swathed in billowing fire emerging from torch-pierced heads of *k'awiil* (its remains have since been destroyed by looters). This event took place in March 820, not, it seems, at Naranjo, but at the site of Ucanal. Some clues to its significance can be gleaned from a text incised on the steps leading to the king's throne, which describes the presentation of bundled tribute items on two occasions in 815 (whose contents are referred to metaphorically as *k'uk' b'alam* 'quetzals and jaguars'). Uniquely, the tribute items are specified as being in units of 40 and 100.[31]

Further activity is represented by the stylistically late Stela 9, whose multi-figure composition is typical of Cycle 10, that is, after 830. By now, stelae were also being erected at Xunantunich, a rapidly expanding site perched on a hilltop high above the Mopan River, 8 miles (13 km) to the southeast of Naranjo. It is unclear whether this had become a new, fortress-like retreat for the traditional dynasty (one of its texts may show a Naranjo emblem glyph), or whether a provincial lineage was now asserting its claim to kingship as central authority faltered. Its monuments are badly weathered, but surviving dates extend only as far as 830, suggesting that elite occupation here did not long outlast that at Naranjo itself.

The troubled Terminal Classic, a period of steep decline for most of the great cities, saw contrasting growth for some of their satellites. One of these was a site close to Naranjo called Xunantunich. Already set high on a defensible hilltop, it further dominated the landscape with a pyramid some 131 ft (40 m) in height, today known as the Castillo. The site has recently been the subject of excavations by Richard Leventhal and Wendy Ashmore.

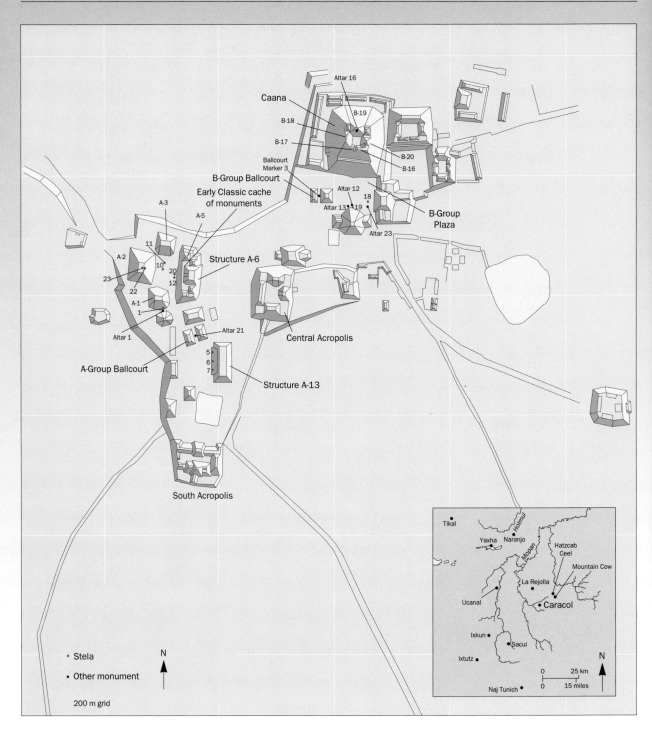

Caana

Altar 16

B-19

B-18

B-17

B-20

B-16

Ballcourt
Marker 3

B-Group Ballcourt

Early Classic cache
of monuments

Altar 12

Altar 13 19 18

Altar 23

B-Group
Plaza

A-3

A-5

Structure A-6

11
A-2
10
23
22
20
12

A-1
1

Altar 1

Altar 21

Central Acropolis

A-Group Ballcourt

5
6
7

Structure A-13

South Acropolis

• Stela

• Other monument

N

200 m grid

Tikal

Yaxha Naranjo

Holmul

Mopan

Hatzcab
Ceel

Mountain Cow

La Rejolla

Ucanal

Caracol

Ixkun

Sacul

Ixtutz

Naj Tunich

N

0   25 km

0   15 miles

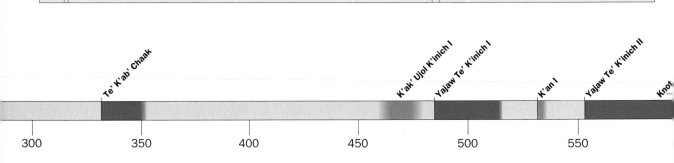

Te' K'ab' Chaak

K'ak' Ujol K'inich I

Yajaw Te' K'inich I

K'an I

Yajaw Te' K'inich II

Knot

300   350   400   450   500   550

CARACOL

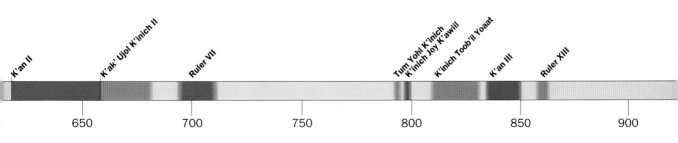

ONCE THOUGHT TO BE OF ONLY MODEST SIZE and something of a political backwater, discoveries in recent years have revolutionized our view of Caracol. Surveys beyond its relatively compact central core have revealed a densely settled hinterland, heavily modified by agricultural terracing. This peripheral area was linked to the seat of government by a wide-ranging network of raised roads built of rubble and compacted plaster. Epigraphic finds have had an equally important role in this re-assessment. Possessing strong links with the greatest Maya powers, Tikal and Calakmul, Caracol was a key player in the diplomatic and military manoeuvrings of the once obscure transition between the Early and Late Classic. A still mysterious setback led to a hiatus in building and monument dedications spanning a century or more of the latter, but the city revived itself to become one of the more vibrant centres of the twilight Terminal Classic. A full-scale investigation of the site and its environs began in 1985, conducted by the University of Central Florida's Arlen and Diane Chase.

K'an II

K'ak' Ujol K'inich II

Ruler VII

Tum Yohl K'inich
K'inich Joy K'awiil

K'inich Toob'il Yoaat

K'an III

Ruler XIII

650   700   750   800   850   900

Te' K'ab' Chaak
331–349>

K'ak' Ujol K'inich I
Ruler I

c. 470

Yajaw Te' K'inich I
484–514>

K'an I
Ruler II

531–534>

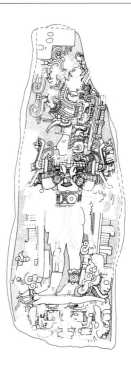

K'an I is shown holding the double-headed serpent bar, a royal sceptre involved in the conjuring of ancestral spirits. Stela 16, AD 534.

TE' K'AB' CHAAK	
Glyphic spelling TE'?-k'a[b'a]-cha-ki	('Tree Branch Rain God')

K'AK' UJOL K'INICH I	
Glyphic spelling K'AK'-(u)-JOL K'INICH ('Fire-headed Sun God') *Also known as* Ruler I, Smoking Skull I	*Wife* Lady Penis-head of Xultun? *Son* Yajaw Te' K'inich I?

YAJAW TE' K'INICH I	
Glyphic spelling ya-AJAW-TE' K'INICH ('Lord of the Lineage? Sun God') *Accession* 12 April 484 (9.2.9.0.16 10 Kib 4 Pop) *Father* K'ak' Ujol K'inich I?	*Mother* Lady Penis-head of Xultun *Son* K'an I *Monuments* Stelae 13 & 20?; Altar 4

EARLY KINGS OF CARACOL

The first royal name recorded at Caracol, **Te' K'ab' Chaak** ('Tree Branch Rain God'), appears in two Late Classic texts, one placing him in 331 the other 349. The first is poorly understood, the second largely illegible, but their antiquity and importance to later kings should point to Te' K'ab' Chaak as Caracol's dynastic progenitor.[1]

Information about Te' Kab' Chaak's immediate successors is sparse. A surviving section of Stela 23 supplies a date falling between 361 and 420. It includes the combination *yajaw te'* 'Lord of the Tree', very likely part of the name Yajaw Te' K'inich, one of several recurring royal forms at Caracol. No monuments are known from the reign of **K'ak' Ujol K'inich I** ('Fire-headed Sun God'), whose place in the chronology is still uncertain. His name appears in a genealogy from the 6th-century Stela 16 and again as a belt device shown on the later Stela 6.[2] Such ornaments often spell ancestral names such as this, though their precise relevance is obscure. Caracol history takes a more substantial form with the accession of **Yajaw Te' K'inich I** in 484. Stela 20, which seems to show him seated within an elaborate throne or cave, bears a date from 487 and was found at the base of the large A-6 temple. His Stela 13, celebrating

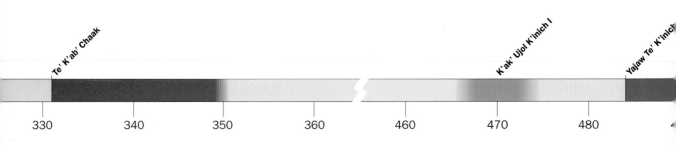

Te' K'ab' Chaak   K'ak' Ujol K'inich I   Yajaw Te' K'inich

330   340   350   360   460   470   480

ROYAL TITLES AT CARACOL

K'UHUL-K'AN-tu-ma-ki   *3-WITZ-AJAW*

Unlike most Classic kings, the rulers of Caracol did not use a conventional emblem glyph, the title based on the formulaic *k'uhul ajaw* 'divine lord'. In its place we find *k'uhul k'antumaak*, which includes the term *maak* 'person'. It seems to have been used more widely than orthodox emblems and defined a stratum of leading lords. Another royal title, *ox witz ajaw* 'Three Hills Lord' – especially popular in the Early Classic – was derived from the Caracol place-name Oxwitza'.[3]

Structure A-6 is the largest of four buildings set on a large platform overlooking the A-Group Plaza. Excavation of its successive construction phases has yielded radiocarbon dates reaching back as far as the 1st century AD. The great cache of buried monuments (Stelae 13, 14, 15 and 16, Altar 7) found close to the adjacent Structure A-5 and the early monuments set at its base (Stelae 12 and 20) are pointers to the special significance this area held throughout Caracol's history.

K'AN I	
Glyphic spelling	(9.4.16.13.3
?-O:L-K'INICH	4 Ak'bal 16 Pop)
('?-hearted Sun	*Wife*
God')	Lady K'al K'inich
Also known as	*Father*
Ruler II, Lord	Yajaw Te' K'inich I
Jaguar, Antenna	*Son*
Top I	Yajaw Te' K'inich II
Accession	*Monuments*
13 April 531	Stela 16; Altar 14

the end of the 4th K'atun in 514, establishes a model of upright and conservative royal portraiture that Caracol followed for the next century. Its incised text has weathered badly, but originally included a pedigree naming his parents and possibly grandparents as well.

K'AN I

Yajaw Te' K'inich's son, **K'an I**, seems to have succeeded him in 531. The two monuments that detail his reign were found buried in a special deposit close to A-6. Stela 15 was carved in slate, one of Caracol's favourite media, quarried from the nearby Maya Mountains. It is a good example both of this stone's fine-grained texture and its tendency to shatter into small fragments. Thus, only part of this long inscription can now be read. His presumed accession was 'supervised' by a higher authority, but it is unclear if this was a divine being or one of the region's dominant 'overkings'. The text goes on to describe an otherwise unknown *ch'ak* 'axe' attack against Oxwitza' ('Three Hill Water') – the ancient name of Caracol – and mentions lords from both Calakmul and Tikal. Given the retrospective nature of many Caracol texts, it is hard to be certain when, and under whose reign, these events occurred. K'an I's only K'atun-ending, 9.5.0.0.0 of 534, was celebrated on Stela 16. Much of its text is taken up by a list of other characters, including his parents, his grandfather K'ak' Ujol K'inich I and a royal woman from Xultun. Less explicable is the inclusion of Waterlily Jaguar, the current ruler of Copan, though he may have been another relative or political ally.[4]

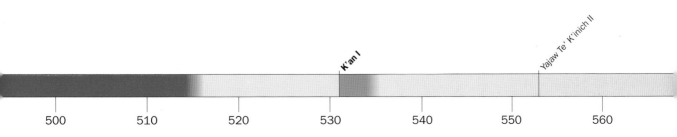

500   510   520   530   540   550   560

Yajaw Te' K'inich II
Ruler III
553–593>

Knot Ajaw
Ruler IV
599–613>

K'an II
Ruler V
618–658

This portrait of Yajaw Te' K'inich II appears on Stela 6, commissioned by his son Knot Ajaw in 603.

YAJAW TE' K'INICH II	
Glyphic spelling ya-AJAW-TE'- K'INICH[?] ('Lord of the Lineage? Sun God') *Also known as* Ruler III, Lord Water, Lord Muluc *Accession* 16 April 553 (9.5.19.1.2 9 Ik' 5 Wo)	*Wives* Lady 1, Lady Batz' Ek' *Father* K'an I *Mother* Lady K'al K'inich *Brother* Chekaj K'inich? *Sons* Knot Ajaw, K'an II *Monuments* Stelae 1, 4? & 14; Altars 1, 6, & 24

YAJAW TE' K'INICH II

With the accession of K'an I's son Yajaw Te' K'inich II in 553 we get a much clearer picture of Caracol's place in the political geography of the Early Classic. A period of diplomatic and military tumult in the first few years of his reign would see Caracol move from the orbit of one great power, Tikal, to that of its rival, Calakmul. The success of Yajaw Te' K'inich's stewardship can be measured in the century-long era of prosperity that followed, setting Caracol on the road from the minor capital he inherited to the metropolis it would ultimately become.

Yajaw Te' K'inich II's first monument, Stela 14, erected less than a year after his elevation, commemorates the 9.6.0.0.0 ending of 554. But the real story of his reign unfolds elsewhere, on Altar 21, an especially elaborate 'giant ajaw' stone commissioned by his son K'an II in 633 (see panel). Now splintered into many fragments and with much of its long text quite destroyed, it nonetheless ranks among the most important historical finds of recent years.[5]

Caracol as a client kingdom

Altar 21 is one of two later texts that add a detail about Yajaw Te'

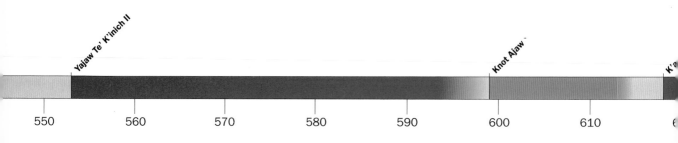

550   560   570   580   590   600   610

'Giant Ajaw' Altars

The completion of the 20-year K'atun cycle was marked by a variety of ceremonies. In addition to the erection of a stela there was usually the dedication of an accompanying altar. Caracol was one of the cities that produced a specially embellished form, the 'Giant Ajaw' altar, of which 18 have been discovered at the site thus far. Each is inscribed with a large glyph, the day on which the relevant K'atun ended (one of 13 possible positions from the 260-day Tzolk'in, all falling on the day Ajaw). The earliest, inscribed 2 Ajaw, corresponds to the 9.3.0.0.0 mark of 495; the last, with 7 Ajaw, the 10.0.0.0.0 ending of 830. This system of identifying individual K'atuns survived the 9th-century collapse to become the principal means of reckoning time in the Postclassic, as seen in the *Books of Chilam Balam*, native annals of the Colonial period. From these sources we know that K'atuns sharing the same ending day shared the same basic prophecies, part of the Maya's conception of cyclical history.

Altar 19, found in the A-Group Plaza, bears the day position 1 Ajaw, equivalent to 9.10.0.0.0 or 24 January 633.

Now badly smashed, Altar 21 was commissioned by K'an II to celebrate the 9.10.0.0.0 K'atun-ending of AD 633 and set in the central playing alley of the A-Group Ballcourt. The bulk of its text concerns the life of his father Yajaw Te' K'inich II and Caracol's 6th-century interactions with the dominant powers Tikal and Calakmul.

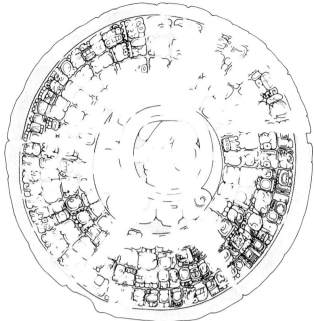

K'inich's inauguration that finds no mention on his own, contemporary Stela 14. Crucially, it reveals that the ceremony took place under the supervision and sponsorship of the Tikal king Wak Chan K'awiil (p. 39).[6] While the power of Early Classic Tikal has long been inferred from its huge size (it dwarfed every rival of the time), few signs of its political muscle can be detected in inscriptions. This rare instance is all the more valuable because it demonstrates that affiliate kings were able to suppress this kind of information on their own monuments. Yajaw Te' K'inich's subordination is revealed to us only as later kings sought to explain the turbulent course of events and the dramatic reversal in Caracol's alignment. Tikal–Caracol relations collapsed within three years, erupting into violence in April 556 when Tikal inflicted a *ch'ak* or 'axe' event, perhaps involving a lordly execution, on its erstwhile client.[7]

The breaking of Early Classic Tikal

In narrative terms, these episodes serve as a prologue to the climactic events of six years later. In April 562 Tikal's Wak Chan K'awiil fell victim to a 'star war' action – a defeat that would change the course of Early Classic history. Altar 21 once went on to give a detailed account of its aftermath, with further mention of the Tikal king as well as his counterpart from

K'ak' Ujol K'inich II

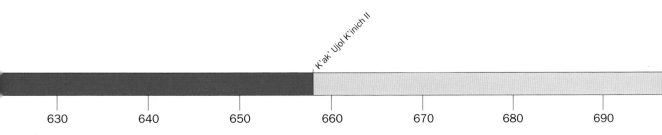

630   640   650   660   670   680   690

Calakmul, but now little more can be extracted from this badly damaged section. Such accounts usually concern the display and treatment of prisoners, a prelude to their sacrifice, increasing the likelihood that Wak Chan K'awiil did not long survive the encounter. Calakmul's involvement in the proceedings is highly significant and may resolve the biggest remaining question about the war – the identity of Tikal's conqueror.

While it is attractive to see a vengeful Caracol, smarting from its recent injury, as the assailant, there are problems with this David and Goliath scenario. When it comes to the victor's name, the surviving glyph outlines show no correspondence to the names or titles of Yajaw Te' K'inich. Instead, those that remain are fully consistent with the glyphs of Sky Witness, the current Calakmul king. Caracol provides other examples of crediting victory to a foreign power; it ascribes two later 'star war' triumphs to this same kingdom. While caution is still required, Calakmul emerges as much the better candidate for the stunning victory of 562. The impact of this reverse is reflected in the immediate onset of Tikal's 130-year silence, a period during which Caracol undoubtedly prospered, but Calakmul rose to regional supremacy (pp. 104–110).[8]

Later life

A broken section of Stela 4, probably from 583, shows that Yajaw Te' K'inich's new liaison with Calakmul continued and tells of its king Scroll Serpent supervising some now lost event. Yajaw Te' K'inich lived to see his third full K'atun ceremony as king, his last monuments, Stela 1 and Altar 1, marking the 9.8.0.0.0 ending of 593. He was succeeded by his 23-year-old son Knot Ajaw in June 599, but only after an intriguing reference to a *huun ajaw*, a 'royal headband' and soon after *ti yune* 'to his child'.[9] Four years later, the 9.8.10.0.0 ending of 603 is said to have been *ilaj* or 'seen' by Yajaw Te' K'inich – an expression rarely applied in 'beyond the grave' contexts. Conceivably, these are signs that the aged king adopted his son as co-ruler during his final years.[10]

KNOT AJAW

Although one of Caracol's lesser-known figures, Knot Ajaw's monumental legacy was once impressive, with a set of two, or more probably three, stelae forming a line to the west of Structure A-13. His first, Stela 6 erected in 603, is notable both for the length of its inscription (originally over 144 glyphs) and its unusual twin portraits, showing the king and his father on opposing faces. It includes two mentions of Chekaj K'inich, another lord to carry the Caracol emblem glyph. He is described as a *yitz'in* 'younger brother', apparently of Yajaw Te' K'inich, suggesting that he served as some kind of 'guardian uncle' to Knot Ajaw. Stela 5, which marks the end of the 9th K'atun in 613, shows Knot Ajaw in elaborate attire, holding his serpent-headed ceremonial bar horizontally across the chest in an archaic Early Classic style. On all sides he is surrounded by

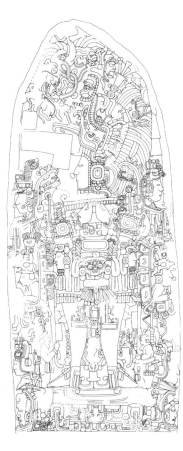

Deeply conservative in their sculptural style, retaining anachronistic details of costuming and pose superseded elsewhere, Caracol artisans produced this depiction of a richly attired Knot Ajaw on Stela 5 of AD 613.

KNOT AJAW	
Glyphic spelling	(9.8.5.16.12
?-?-HU:N?	5 Eb 5 Xul)
Also known as	*Father*
Ruler IV, Ahau	Yajaw Te' K'inich II
Serpent, Flaming	*Mother*
Ahau	Lady 1
Birth	*Brother*
28 November 575	K'an II
(9.7.2.0.3	*Monuments*
2 Ak'bal 16 Mak)	Stelae 5, 6 & 7?;
Accession	Altars 11? & 15
24 June 599	

K'AN II	
Glyphic spelling	*Death*
?-O:L-K'INICH SAK-	21 July 658
[b'a]WITZ-IL	(9.11.5.15.9
('?-hearted Sun	2 Muluk 7 Mol)
God, White Hilltop')	*Father*
Also known as	Yajaw Te' K'inich II
Ruler V, Lord Storm-	*Mother*
water Moon,	Lady Batz' Ek'
Antenna Top II	*Brother*
Birth	Knot Ajaw
18 April 588	*Monuments*
(9.7.14.10.8	Stelae 3 & 22;
3 Lamat 16 Wo)	Altars 2, 7, 17, 19
Accession	& 21; Naranjo
6 March 618	Hieroglyphic
(9.9.4.16.2	Stairway; Naranjo
10 Ik' 0 Pop)	Panel 1

Carved from slate, this so-called 'mace head' (an object of unknown function) pairs K'an II's regnal name of *? ohl k'inich* with his pre-inaugural *sak b'aah witzil* 'White Hilltop'.

K'an II's mother, Lady Batz' Ek', played a key role in his reign.

the open maws of serpents and other 'portal' openings to the supernatural realm of the dead, each of which disgorges an ancestor named by their (mostly illegible) glyphic headdresses. Originally, this scene portrayed a dynastic genealogy stretching back at least four generations.

K'AN II

Perhaps the most successful of all Caracol rulers, K'an II's 40-year reign saw a surge of growth at Oxwitza', with a burgeoning of the surrounding settlement and corresponding expansion of the road network. It is clear that this new wealth was not restricted to the leading elite, but spread among a much broader section of society. Even some distance outside the city centre, building quality is high and tombs well stocked with valuables.[11]

Born in 588, K'an II's boyhood name was *sak b'aah witzil* 'White Hilltop'. He took his grandfather's regnal name at his inauguration in 618 but, in a pattern seen elsewhere, he very often combined it with his original monicker so that the two might not be confused. He was the son of a junior wife of Yajaw Te' K'inich II and a half-brother of Knot Ajaw.[12] This slight deviation in the succession put him at some pains to stress his legitimacy and raise the profile of his mother. His most important monument, Stela 3, addresses both issues. It describes his ritual bloodletting under the direction of his father at the age of five, an ordeal always used as a claim to rightful inheritance. His father's reign is given a lengthy account on Altar 21, recalling each of his K'atun-endings (though the 9th K'atun presided over by his brother is omitted and K'an II ignores his rule entirely).

Caracol's queen mother

K'an II's mother, Lady Batz' Ek', 'arrived in the centre of Oxwitza' in September 584. By then she was 18 years of age, her husband – who had already been in power for 31 years – much her senior. The sons of junior wives often lavished attention on their maternal background, but her role as 'witness' to K'an II's accession and overall prominence (almost half of the Stela 3 text is devoted to her) suggests that she took an effective political role too.

In 1986 excavations within the B-19 pyramid, one of three on the massive Caana platform that dominates the centre of the city (pp. 92–3), encountered a major tomb. It proved to be that of an adult female, accompanied by rich offerings of jadeite jewelry and ceramics.[13] The north wall is painted with a Long Count date that seems to be 9.10.1.12.11, or 27 September 634, probably the day of her burial. This high-status location would certainly be appropriate for Lady Batz' Ek', who would have been 68 years old at the time.

Calakmul and the Naranjo wars

Caracol's links with the dynasty of Calakmul, developed during his father's reign, were of critical importance to K'an II and he detailed them

CARACOL'S ROAD NETWORK

One of Caracol's best-known features is the system of raised causeways that radiate from the city's central core to its outlying suburbs. Most of these stone-built roads, varying in width from narrow paths to broad avenues, terminate in compounds with large-scale architecture (some with their own monuments) which may have been administrative subcentres or the seats of particular lineages. A few extend beyond the city to more distant provinces: one leads 6 miles (10 km) northeast to the site of Cahal Pichik; another traverses 7.5 miles (12 km) towards La Rejolla. Smaller causeways called 'vias' branch from the major roads to reach individual residential groups.[14]

Showing the firm hand of central

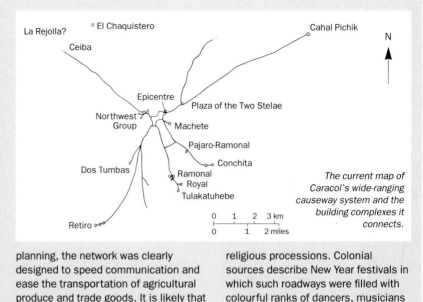

The current map of Caracol's wide-ranging causeway system and the building complexes it connects.

planning, the network was clearly designed to speed communication and ease the transportation of agricultural produce and trade goods. It is likely that the causeways also saw the passing of religious processions. Colonial sources describe New Year festivals in which such roadways were filled with colourful ranks of dancers, musicians and bearers carrying sacred images.

Found within a buried version of the B-19 pyramid on the Caana platform, this large chamber contained one of the most elaborate female burials yet found in the Maya region. Its back wall had been painted, in black on a red ground, with a Long Count date (now barely legible), presumably the occasion of her death or burial. Lady Batz' Ek' emerges as its most likely occupant.

at some length. They include some now lost event performed under the aegis of Yuknoom Chan (619); the accession of his successor Tajoom Uk'ab' K'ak' (622); a gift received from this king (627); and his later death (630); as well as two war successes of Yuknoom Head (631 and 636). Even the long-dead Sky Witness was recalled, perhaps a statement of his death in 572. These diplomatic contacts underpinned a military alliance, best seen in the coordinated campaign they conducted against the kingdom of Naranjo.

K'an II's contribution began with an attack against an unidentified location within Naranjo territory, dubbed 'Ko-Bent-Cauac', in May 626. The same site was attacked again 40 days later, while a battle in May the following year against a place called Tzam always appears as part of this series. There is no mention of Calakmul participation in these clashes, but the record of a ballgame event (often linked to prisoner sacrifice) by Tajoom Uk'ab' K'ak' on the day of the victory over Tzam is suggestive of some involvement. Certainly when the decisive assault on Naranjo took place in December 631 it was at the hands of Calakmul.[15]

K'an II's most elaborate record of the campaign took the form of a hieroglyphic stairway. Found at Naranjo, it has long been seen as a conquest monument erected by Caracol during an extended occupation; its final condition, incomplete and set in an illegible order, is taken as a sign that it was subsequently 'killed' by a revived Naranjo dynasty. But a small, matching fragment found in fallen rubble at Caracol now offers a real chance that this major work, that in every other way resembles a Caracol monument, once had its home at Caracol. In this scenario, it was torn from its original location during a later Naranjo assault and parts carried away as trophies (p. 73).

Caana or 'Sky Place' is the largest
structure at Caracol. Its form echoes
a Preclassic model, a platform
crowned by three pyramids arranged
around a central court.
Their sequential phases conceal a
number of wealthy, though
unidentified, tombs. Other parts
of the complex clearly served
residential, administrative
or religious functions.

K'ak' Ujol K'inich II

Ruler VI

658–680>

Ruler VII

>702>

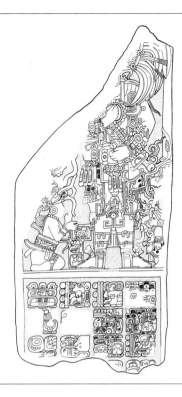

Carved from slate extracted from the nearby Maya Mountains, this stela fragment depicts a Caracol ruler whose name is now lost. He is shown with a dwarf and a kneeling captive. The latter is identified by caption as a *k'uhul ajaw* or 'divine lord', though it is too damaged to identify securely. Stela 21, AD 702.

K'AK' UJOL K'INICH II	
Glyphic spelling	*Accession*
K'AK'-u-JOL-K'INICH	22 June 658
('Fire-headed Sun	(9.11.5.14.0
God')	12 Ajaw 8 Xul)
Also known as	*Monuments*
Ruler VI, Smoking	Stucco texts from
Skull II	Structure B-16-sub
	and B-18; La Rejolla
	Stela 3

K'AK' UJOL K'INICH II

By the summer of 658, K'an II was in his 70th year and, we must suspect, in less than good health. In the normal course of events a Maya king would be firmly in his grave before another took his place, but here the convention was broken (as it may have been once before, p. 90) to allow the inauguration of a successor, K'ak' Ujol K'inich II, while the old king still lived. Whether designed to forestall a disputed succession or to meet some urgent political imperative, its precise circumstances are unknown. The lack of any parentage statement for K'ak' Ujol K'inich means we cannot even be sure that he was a son of K'an II. The ceremony took place on 22 June and was quickly followed by K'an II's death, their reigns overlapping by just 29 days.[16]

The fall of Oxwitza'

This transfer of power is described in a stucco band from the Caana platform, one of only two such records from K'ak' Ujol K'inich's reign to survive at Caracol itself. It appears midway between a recounting of K'an II's victories and something altogether less glorious. In February 680, during the king's 22nd regnal year, the Caracol capital Oxwitza' was the

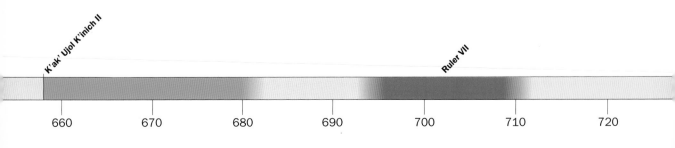

K'ak' Ujol K'inich II   Ruler VII

660   670   680   690   700   710   720

Seen here under excavation, this stucco band once ran along the buried façade of Structure B-16 on the summit of Caana. It recounts events in the life of K'ak' Ujol K'inich II, including the 'star war' attack Naranjo inflicted on Caracol in AD 680.

The caves at Naj Tunich were once painted with numerous texts and figured scenes (sadly since vandalized and destroyed). One phrase mentions a candidate for Ruler VII called Tz'ayaj K'ak'.

RULER VII	
Monument	
Stela 21	

victim of a 'star war' assault, its capture or ravishing at the hands of rival Naranjo (p. 73). Mention of this disaster is followed by the laconic '60 days later K'ak' Ujol K'inich arrived at Oxwitza''. Forced from his capital by the fighting, it seems to have been two months before he could safely return.

Where might the king have taken refuge? This cannot be answered with any certainty, but it is interesting that La Rejolla, an important satellite occupying a defensible hilltop close to the Chiquibul River 7.5 miles (12 km) to the northwest, contains the only known stela of K'ak' Ujol K'inich II. The stucco band continues, but has yet to be fully excavated. It seems likely that the text did not end with Caracol's humiliation but, in accordance with other narratives of this kind, went on to describe some subsequent vengeance over its old enemy.[17]

CARACOL'S HIATUS: AD 680–798

This is the last we hear of K'ak' Ujol K'inich II and the record at Caracol is severely disrupted for the next 118 years. Such hiatus periods are invariably a sign of political crisis and where, as here, they coincide with a halt in all major construction, the trauma was clearly profound and prolonged. Further defeats can be strongly suspected. It may well be significant that traditional enemies such as Tikal and Naranjo flourished for much this time, while Caracol's great ally Calakmul suffered defeat and decline.

Some fallen stucco hieroglyphs from structures on the Caana complex refer to this interval, but only one monument is known: a lower section of Stela 21 dated to the 9.13.10.0.0 ending of 702. Worked in fine-grained slate, this richly detailed piece shows a king accompanied by a dwarf and bound captive. There is an earlier date (perhaps from 687) but the name of its patron, dubbed **Ruler VII**, is entirely missing.

A candidate for this king comes from the painted cave of Naj Tunich, 29 miles (46 km) to the south of Caracol. Discovered only in 1979, a huge entrance leads to a series of passageways with walls once painted with finely rendered figures and inscriptions (p. 97). It was clearly an important site of pilgrimage and its texts record visits by the lords of both nearby and distant polities. Among them, in a passage dated to 692, appears a Caracol lord called Tz'ayaj K'ak'. He lacks the kingly 'divine' prefix to his emblem title and so his precise status remains uncertain.[18]

Tum Yohl K'inich   K'inich Joy K'awiil

740   750   760   770   780   790   800

Tum Yohl K'inich
Ruler VIII
>793?>

 K'inich Joy K'awiil
Ruler IX
>798>

 K'inich Toob'il Yoaat
Ruler X
>810–830>

 K'an III
Ruler XII
>835–849>

 Ruler XIII
>859>

TUM YOHL K'INICH	
Glyphic spelling tu-mu-O:L K'INICH ('?- hearted Sun God')	*Also known as* Ruler VIII

K'INICH JOY K'AWIIL	
Glyphic spelling K'INICH-JOY[K'AWI:L]-li ('Great-Sun Tied K'awiil') *Also known as* Ruler IX, Mahk'ina God K, K'inich Hok' K'awiil	*Monuments* Stelae 9? & 11; Altars 3 & 23; Ballcourt Markers 1, 2 & 3

TUM YOHL K'INICH AND K'INICH JOY K'AWIIL

The next character in Caracol history, **Tum Yohl K'inich**, is an elusive one. Despite his designation as Ruler VIII some doubt remains as to whether he was a true king, or even that all appearances of the name represent the same person. He first appears in the cave of Naj Tunich, though, as with Tz'ayaj K'ak', the lack of the 'divine' prefix to his title leaves his status in some doubt.[19] On a date that remains difficult to interpret, he is involved in a 'fire-bearing' ritual under the supervision of a lord or ruler of Ixkun, a kingdom 21.5 miles (35 km) to Caracol's south-west (this rare expression otherwise appears only at Ixkun itself, where it occurs in the midst of a war narrative).[20] A lord of Calakmul is involved in some related event. All other appearances of the Tum Yohl K'inich name are during the reigns of later Caracol kings.

A revival

It was not until the end of the 8th century that full royal traditions were restored to Caracol and its regional influence re-asserted. This late florescence began under a new ruler, **K'inich Joy K'awiil**.[21] He began a programme of new construction, one of his early commissions

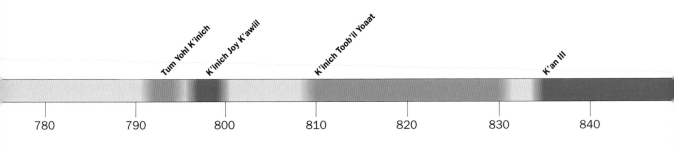

Tum Yohl K'inich   K'inich Joy K'awiil   K'inich Toob'il Yoaat   K'an III

780   790   800   810   820   830   840

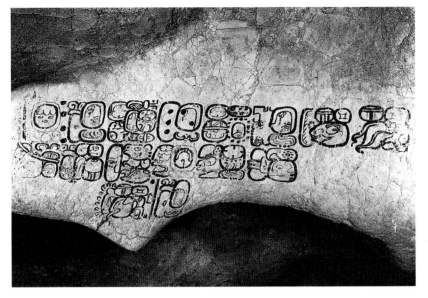

(*Above*) K'inich Joy K'awiil as seen on Stela 11, AD 800.

(*Right*) Deep in the cave of Naj Tunich, this fine example of painted calligraphy records a 'fire-bearing' conducted by Tum Yohl K'inich under the supervision of a lord of Ixkun. The text goes on to mention the Calakmul lord Yax Mo' Suutz' ('First Macaw Bat'). Drawing 82.

(*Below*) Altar 23 celebrates the capture of kings from B'ital and Ucanal, shown with hands bound behind their backs, seated on stone tables or altars. AD 800.

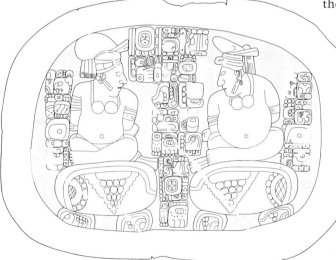

being the B-Group Ballcourt. Of the three carved markers set into its central playing alley, one provides the earliest date we have for his reign, 798, but otherwise traces back 467 years to the time of the 'founder' Te' K'ab' Chaak.

K'inich Joy Kawiil's fine Stela 11, erected in the A-Group Plaza in 800, mentions Tum Yohl K'inich in a way that might suggest the latter was the former's father. But this idea runs into difficulties with the most interesting of Joy K'awiil's monuments, Altar 23. Found in the B Plaza and also dated to 800, it shows two bound captives, rulers of Ucanal and B'ital. The important but little-known Ucanal kingdom was another to flourish during Caracol's Hiatus, while B'ital was a more minor polity only otherwise mentioned as a defeated foe of Naranjo.[22] The seizures themselves are credited to a Tum Yohl K'inich, who bears the same titles as the 'father' from Stela 11. Caracol rulers often devoted attention to their fathers' lives, but the phrasing here suggests that these are contemporary events under the direction of K'inich Joy K'awiil. The implication is that this particular Tum Yohl K'inich was a high-ranking lieutenant or living relative of the king.

K'INICH TOOB'IL YOAAT	
Glyphic spelling	*Accession*
K'INICH-to-b'i-li	6 March 804?
YOAAT?-ti	(9.18.13.10.19?
Also known as	9 Kawak? 7 Sip)
Ruler XI, Lord	*Monuments*
Quincunx	Stelae 8?, 18 & 19;
	Altars 12, 13, 16?
	& 22?; Mountain
	Cow Altar 2

K'INICH TOOB'IL YOAAT

We are given some lengthy name phrases for the next Caracol ruler, though most can be reduced to the key component of K'inich Toob'il Yoaat (or Yopaat).[23] The kingdom's Terminal Classic renaissance continues unabated, while stylistic changes typical of this period ('conversational' scenes and other thematic innovations) are felt for the first time. Five or six monuments can be attributed to Toob'il Yoaat, most of them sited in the B-Group Plaza. One of the earliest, Stela 18, bears a large and unconventional skeletal serpent or centipede; its text, recording the end of the 19th K'atun in 810, is inscribed along its curving body. Stela 19, of more orthodox design but great stature (over 11.5 ft or 3.5 m in height), followed in 820, a year which also saw the dedication of two altar stones.

(*Below*) Altar 12 was once associated with Stela 19 at the southern end of the B-Group Plaza, facing the Caana pyramid. K'inich Toob'il Yoaat (right) converses with his ally Papamalil of Ucanal, whose throne doubles as an identifying toponym for that city, an iconic spelling of *k'anwitznal* 'Yellow Hill Place'. The surrounding text gives further details of Caracol–Ucanal relations, possibly including the capture of the same Ucanal ruler seen on Altar 23 (see p. 97). AD 820.

(*Above*) Altar 13 conveys Caracol's close relationship with Ucanal during the reign of Toob'il Yoaat. The central scene shows the Caracol king and his Ucanal counterpart Papamalil presiding over a captive called Makal Te'. AD 820.

The two stones show Toob'il Yoaat in the company of a lord linked to Ucanal called Papamalil.[24] The precise relationship between the two kingdoms at this stage is unclear, but it was certainly very different from the hostility of Joy K'awiil's reign. They participated jointly in ceremonies undertaken at both cities and were allies in war, though their campaigns – among the very last recorded by the Classic Maya – are little understood. The larger Altar 12 includes a mention of Tum Yohl K'inich performing a 'throne' ceremony at Ucanal, perhaps in 793. It also names another holder of the Caracol emblem, a potential ruler called Ib'il Tz'aabil (possibly in some kind of mortuary rite).

Toob'il Yoaat's known building works are restricted to the Caana platform. Temple B-18, surmounting the westernmost pyramid, was remodelled and a series of stucco glyphic medallions set into its façade. Now fallen and shattered, surviving sections include prominent references to Papamalil. Finally, at the foot of adjacent B-19, it may have been Toob'il Yoaat who set the giant ajaw altar inscribed 7 Ajaw, recording the key Bak'tun-ending of 10.0.0.0.0 in March 830. In more than one sense this was the end of an era for Caracol.

K'AN III AND RULER XIII

Although Caracol had initially profited from the changing climate of the Terminal Classic, it could not long escape the crisis that had already brought many fellow kingdoms to their knees. Caracol's own descent spanned the reigns of two rulers, their monuments manifest examples of powerful trends afoot. While royal monuments were previously erected in the centre of the city, the year 849 saw Caracol's penultimate king, **K'an III**, set Stela 17 and its associated Altar 10 in an outlying residential group. Like Toob'il Yoaat before him, the king shares prominence on these monuments with other lords, leading nobles or outsiders. There is a strong sense that autocratic kingship is having to adapt to new circumstances, that kings now need to negotiate their position with magnates whose power matches or even exceeds their own. The earliest monument of his reign, dating to 835, was set up even further away, in the secondary site of Mountain Cow, close to Hatzcab Ceel. An important Early Classic centre, this was one of the local rivals Caracol absorbed as it rose to dominance in the region. The late strengthening of satellite communities, which show increasing activity throughout the lowlands, undoubtedly reflects this growing debilitation of centralized power.

The last known king of Caracol, **Ruler XIII** (whose name only partially survives), left the all-glyphic Stela 10, whose crudity of carving and abbreviated chronology distinguish it from true Classic traditions. Its final glyph, the day 4 Ajaw, would seem to mark the half-K'atun 10.1.10.0.0 of 859. There are no further signs of elite activity at Caracol and, even though some occupation continued amid the crumbling city, no later lord of Oxwitza' engraved his heroic deeds in stone.

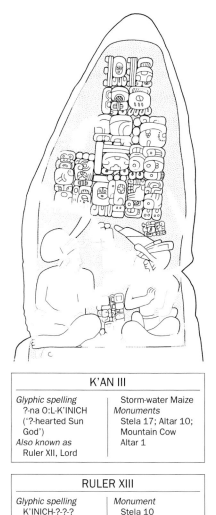

During the Terminal Classic, a significant number of Maya monuments begin to depict pairs of lords engaged in conversation or performing joint ceremonies. The centrality of the king as 'divine lord' and sole source of political authority seems critically undermined; a wider elite class must co-operate as never before to hold a strained society together. K'an III (left) faces a *ch'ok*-titled lord. Stela 17, AD 849.

K'AN III	
Glyphic spelling ?-na O:L-K'INICH ('?-hearted Sun God') *Also known as* Ruler XII, Lord	Storm-water Maize *Monuments* Stela 17; Altar 10; Mountain Cow Altar 1

RULER XIII	
Glyphic spelling K'INICH-?-?-? ('Great-Sun ?')	*Monument* Stela 10

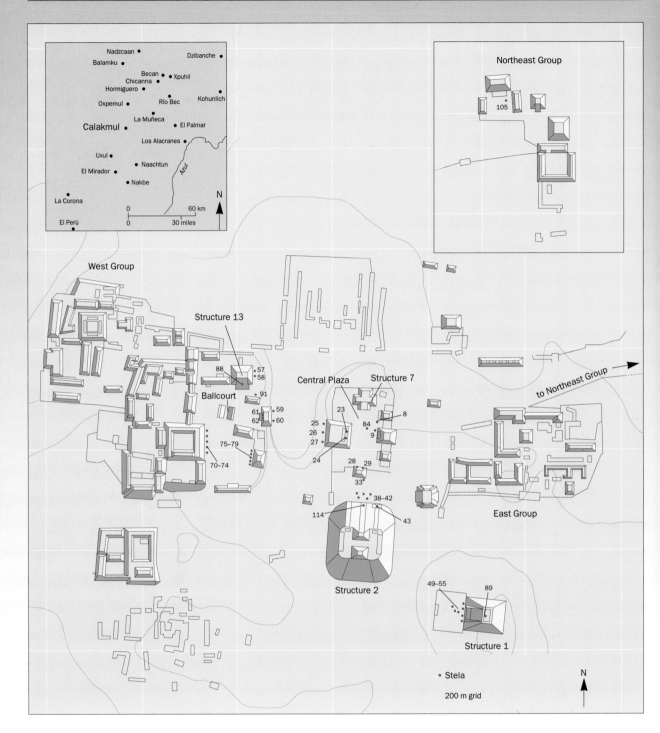

Nadzcaan

Balamku

Dzibanche

Becan · Xpuhil
Chicanna ·
Hormiguero ·

Oxpemul · · Río Bec

Kohunlich

La Muñeca ·

Calakmul · · El Palmar

Los Alacranes ·

Uxul ·

Naachtun ·

El Mirador · · Nakbe

La Corona ·

El Perú ·

Azul

N

0   60 km

0   30 miles

Northeast Group

105

West Group

Structure 13

88

57
58

Ballcourt

91

61   59
62   60

75–79

70–74

Central Plaza

Structure 7

23

8

25   84
26   9
27

24

28   29

33

38–42

114

43

to Northeast Group

East Group

49–55   89

Structure 2

Structure 1

· Stela

200 m grid

N

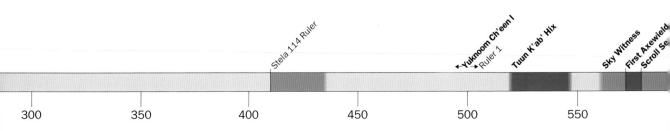

Stela 114 Ruler

◄ Yuknoom Ch'een I
► Ruler 1

Tuun K'ab' Hix

Sky Witness

First Axewield

Scroll Se

300   350   400   450   500   550

CALAKMUL

KAAN, THE KINGDOM OF THE 'SNAKE', was one of the most important and powerful of all Classic Maya kingdoms. During the 6th and 7th centuries it eclipsed its arch-rival Tikal and succeeded in building a widespread 'overkingship', whose influence was felt in the farthest corners of the Maya world (pp. 20–1). The correct identification of its capital has long been a perplexing problem, but the city of Calakmul can now be confirmed as its major seat of power.

Discovered only in 1931, both the remarkable size of Calakmul and its profusion of monuments immediately pointed to its significance. Probably the largest Classic city, it ranges over more than 11 sq. miles (30 sq. km) and boasts at least 117 monuments, by far the most numerous at any Maya site. But the chalky local limestone has proved all too vulnerable to the harsh tropical rains and on most little more than dates survive. In the light of this destruction it is unsurprising that it has taken time to penetrate Calakmul's history and assemble a king list of any length or detail. Although the kingdom still presents many puzzles, recent discoveries at Calakmul can be combined with a greater understanding of its numerous foreign mentions to lift the veil from this long-silent colossus. The ruins of Calakmul were investigated by William Folan between 1984 and 1994 and since 1994 by a large-scale project of the Mexican Instituto Nacional de Antropología e Historia (INAH) led by Ramón Carrasco.

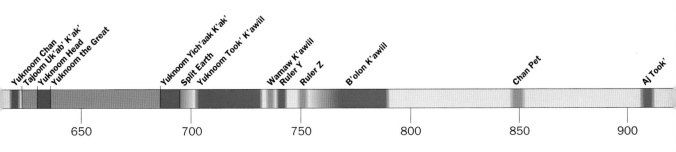

Yuknoom Ch'een I

?

Tuun K'ab' Hix

>520–546>

Sky Witness

>561–572

First Axewielder

572–579

A series of 11 painted vessels, dubbed the 'Dynastic Vases', describe the accessions of Kaan rulers. Although they include many historical names, this listing seems to be either ancestral or legendary.

YUKNOOM CH'EEN I	
Glyphic spelling	yu[ku]-no-ma[CH'E:N?]-na

THE FIRST SNAKE KINGS

While at least an outline history for Calakmul and the Kaan kingdom can be pieced together for the Late Classic, its earliest development remains stubbornly obscure. We do have a lengthy king list that traces its royal line back to a 'founder', but in many ways this document poses more questions than it answers. No fewer than 11 painted vases carry varying lengths of the same sequence, the longest charting the inaugurations of 19 kings, beginning with 'Skyraiser'. Unfortunately, their Calendar Round dates have no anchor in the Long Count and cannot be fixed in time. More problematically, while several names are familiar from monumental inscriptions, they do not follow the same order and their accession dates differ from their carved counterparts in all cases. Several important early kings are also missing from the list. Whether fact or fabrication, we seem to have a line reaching deep into an ancestral past. It may be significant that these 'codex-style' vessels were produced not at Calakmul itself but in the old heartland of the Preclassic, the El Mirador Basin and especially around the ancient city of Nakbe. They may link the Kaan state to a deeper history of political authority in the region (see p. 114).[1]

According to the 'Dynastic Vase' king list the founder of the Kaan polity was 'Skyraiser'.

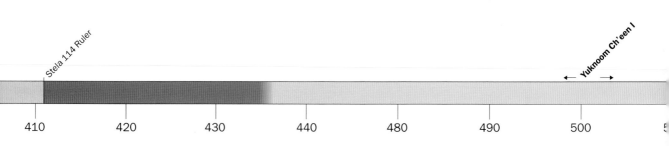

Stela 114 Ruler

Yuknoom Ch'een I

410   420   430   440   480   490   500

Seen here under excavation, Stela 114 was discovered, by William Folan and his team, set into a special niche close to the base of Structure 2. Dated to the B'aktun ending 9.0.0.0.0 in AD 435, the ruler's name is, unfortunately, too damaged to read.

Early Classic Calakmul

Calakmul was itself a Preclassic site of some magnitude which, like Tikal, survived the demise of fellow cities to prosper in the Early Classic. Among a number of early finds at Calakmul is Stela 114, reset into a niche at the base of Structure 2, the great temple platform that dominates the centre of the site (p. 107).[2] Dating to 435, much of its long text is opaque in meaning but concentrates on the K'atun-anniversary of an event in 411, probably a royal accession. Also found on Structure 2, set into a vaulted room, was Stela 43 from 514.[3] Damage prevents full sight of his name and titles, but this 'Ruler 1' does carry an early spelling of the *k'uhul chatan winik* epithet, normally the preserve of high-ranking, but non-royal, elites from the Calakmul region and adjacent El Mirador Basin. No clear Kaan title appears on these damaged stones and further insights are now thwarted by a gap in the city's monumental record lasting 109 years. This is puzzling since we know from a range of sources that this period saw a major flowering of Kaan power in the lowlands. We must conclude either that its stelae were subsequently buried or destroyed, or else that Calakmul did not host the ruling dynasty at this time.[4]

Northern traces

The first clear references to Kaan rulers come from well to the north of Calakmul. Excavations at the sizeable city of Dzibanche, under the direction of Enrique Nalda, have uncovered the constituent blocks of a remarkable 'captive stairway'. Its risers are carved with a series of bound and contorted prisoners, accompanied by the dates of their seizure, personal names and mention of the Kaan ruler **Yuknoom Ch'een I**.[5] Unfortunately, a single undeciphered term holds the key to whether these victims are captured vassals of the king, or seizures ascribed to him. The dates are uncertain too, but two might fall as early as the 5th century. Nearby El Resbalón has long texts in the form of hieroglyphic steps, though the

A significant discovery was made at Dzibanche (also spelt Tz'ibanche) in 1994 when a number of finely carved steps came to light. They show bound captives in a particularly early style, their names appearing as rear-belt ornaments. Texts describe the conquest of their towns (dates uncertain) and name the Kaan king Yuknoom Ch'een I.

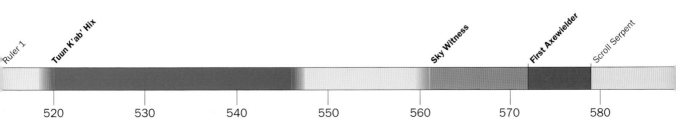

Ruler 1   Tuun K'ab' Hix   Sky Witness   First Axewielder   Scroll Serpent

520   530   540   550   560   570   580

IDENTIFYING THE SNAKE KINGDOM

From the first discovery of emblem glyphs it was clear that there was one important example – that based on a snake's head – which could not be assigned to a known site. Joyce Marcus first suggested Calakmul as its correct home in the 1970s, an idea confirmed in recent years with the identification of the two place-names it used in the Late Classic period (below). The first of these, Oxte'tuun ('Three Stones') probably refers to the city itself; the second, which can now be read as Chiik Naab' (whose meaning is still unclear), may specify a larger surrounding area.[6] Despite the severe weathering of its standing monuments, both place-names appear on Calakmul monuments and even some examples of the full emblem glyph *k'uhul kaanal ajaw* 'Divine Lord of the Snake [Kingdom]' can be made out.

3-TE-TU:N-ni   *chi[ku]-NA:B'*

Carved from slate and only about 6 in. (15 cm) in diameter, this mirror-back names First Axewielder as the Kaan king.

TUUN K'AB' HIX	
Glyphic spelling TU:N-K'AB'-HIX ('Stone Hand Jaguar')	*Also known as* Cu Ix, Ku Ix *Wife* Lady Ek' Naah ('Star House')

SKY WITNESS	
Glyphic spelling	(u)-?-[?-CHAN]

FIRST AXEWIELDER	
Glyphic spelling	YAX-YOAAT?

thorough jumbling and resetting of blocks in later times makes them difficult to understand today. Enough context survives to suggest that the local dynasty was under the direction of Kaan rulers, though their identities are hard to pin down and only one date, in 529, is really clear.[7]

THE RISE OF A SUPERPOWER

By the time it is first referred to by southern kingdoms in the mid-6th century, the Kaan dynasty is assembling a far-flung political network. Such activity would necessarily bring it into competition with Tikal and a struggle for dominance of the Central Area must now have been underway. The first concrete evidence of Kaan's widening power comes when the ruler **Tuun K'ab' Hix** ('Stone Hand Jaguar') presides over the accession of Naranjo's Aj Wosal in 546 (p. 72).[8] Tuun K'ab' Hix's activities had already reached as far south as the Usumacinta River, since one of his vassals (perhaps a woman) had fallen captive to Yaxchilan in 537 (p. 121).

We next pick up the story with the reign of **Sky Witness**. Until recently quite unknown, he can now be appreciated as one of the major players of Early Classic history. The year 561 saw him install a ruler at Los Alacranes, part of a region called B'uuk' in ancient times.[9] But his influence would soon come to encompass greater prizes, beginning with Naranjo's southern neighbour Caracol. This was achieved at the direct expense of Tikal, whose patronage he displaced. The precipitous decline in Tikal's fortunes culminated in its defeat and conquest in 562. Record of this vital conflict survives only at Caracol, where the name of the victor is now reduced to broken outlines. The degree to which these fit the name and title of Sky Witness, but not those of his counterpart at Caracol, makes him the likely culprit. The same text links Sky Witness, identified by a battered Kaan title, to other events on this day, probably concerning the sacrifice of the defeated Tikal ruler Wak Chan K'awiil (pp. 39, 89–90). The next Tikal king, Animal Skull, claims a quite different pedigree and there is every reason to believe that the existing line was liquidated at this time (pp. 40–1). However we ultimately understand the events of 562, it is clear that Tikal was left humbled and dispossessed. The ensuing 130-year gap in its monumental record mirrors with precision the period of Kaan's greatest strength and the two features are clearly linked.

Other mentions of Sky Witness appear far to the north on an isolated and undated stone at the site of Okop, and, for reasons that are still unclear, as the protagonist of an attack on westerly Palenque in 599 (though he was certainly dead by this time and this may be some narrative contrivance or a non-ruling namesake).[10] The final reference is at Caracol in 572 and, since he seems to have been succeeded within the year, this damaged phrase might once have recorded his death.

A different Kaan king appears on another new Dzibanche monument, where he celebrates the end of the 7th K'atun in 573. This appears to be the same character, **First Axewielder**, known from a small inscribed mirror-back. If so, he could only have reigned for about six years.

Scroll Serpent
579–611>

Yuknoom Chan
>619>

Tajoom Uk'ab' K'ak'
622–630

Yuknoom Head
630–636

SCROLL SERPENT	
Glyphic spelling u-[?]CHAN ('? of the Snake') *Also known as* Uneh Chan *Accession* 2 September 579	(9.7.5.14.17 11 Kaban 10 Ch'en) *Wife* Lady Scroll-in-hand? *Son* Yuknoom the Great?

SCROLL SERPENT

As the Early Classic draws to a close we have the reign of another major figure, Scroll Serpent, who took office in 579. His tenure saw major campaigns in the western Maya region, with attacks against Palenque in 599 and 611 (pp. 159–161). The second was the more decisive and in little over a year the two leading figures at this city were dead and its patriline broken. Both assaults took place in April, in the midst of the dry season, no doubt facilitating crossings of the major physical obstacle, the Usumacinta River. In a society where wars were generally waged between neighbours, these expeditions – the furthest yet known for the Maya – reveal the scale of the Kaan kingdom's ambition and organizational prowess in the years following the collapse of Tikal's power.[11]

Established relationships in the east were maintained. Scroll Serpent appears on the fragmentary Stela 4 from Caracol, apparently supervising some action of the Caracol king Yajaw Te' K'inich II before 583. As with all the Kaan kings of this era, not a single Scroll Serpent monument stands at Calakmul today. That this was also the case in the Late Classic can be inferred from the rather lengthy accounts of his reign made by two later kings. Both Stelae 8 and 33 recount his celebration of the 9.8.0.0.0

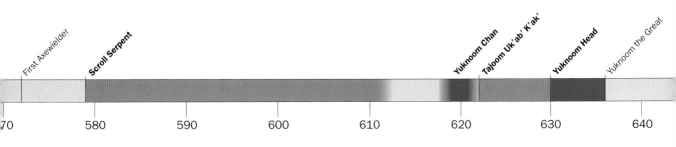

First Axewielder   Scroll Serpent   Yuknoom Chan   Tajoom Uk'ab' K'ak'   Yuknoom Head   Yuknoom the Great

70   580   590   600   610   620   630   640

WATER MANAGEMENT AT CALAKMUL

All the heavily populated cities of the lowlands faced pressure on their water supplies during the dry months of spring and early summer. Calakmul shows the most sophisticated management of its resources and the greatest investment in the necessary public works. There are at least five major reservoirs at the city, the largest a massive rectangle 794 x 695 ft (242 x 212 m), easily the biggest in the Maya world. Filled by a small river during the rainy season, it holds water to this day and is a mainstay of archaeological fieldwork at the site.[12]

The great reservoir at Calakmul, situated 1.2 miles (2 km) north of the city centre.

mark of 593, the former, interestingly, providing a particular location, either a portion of Calakmul or another site entirely.[13] The latter was erected by Yuknoom the Great in 657 and may well contain a reference to his birth in 600. If so, he must have been a son of Scroll Serpent, while intervening rulers could well represent more of his progeny.

FROM YUKNOOM CHAN TO YUKNOOM HEAD

A wealth of references at Caracol focuses our attention on events in the eastern Peten. A fleeting glimpse of the next Kaan dynasty, **Yuknoom Chan**, comes as he supervises the Caracol ruler K'an II in a now illegible event in 619. Three years later in 622, the much damaged Stela 22 reports the inauguration of his successor, **Tajoom Uk'ab' K'ak'** (p. 92).[14] The first Late Classic monuments at Calakmul – the royal couple depicted on Stelae 28 and 29 – were erected in 623, but neither preserves a legible example of the king's name nor sign of the snake emblem.[15]

At about this time the death of the long-reigning Aj Wosal of Naranjo coincides with a collapse in Kaan patronage of this major kingdom. The recent demise of Scroll Serpent may have been another contributory factor. In all hegemonic systems the transition of authority from an established figure to an untried successor is a period of uncertainty, a juncture at which old ties might be altered or repudiated entirely. A new Naranjo regime seems to have made the break by at least 626, the year it lost two battles to Caracol. Tajoom Uk'ab' K'ak' could well have been involved in a related clash the following year, but any attempt on his part to restore the status quo was cut short by his death in 630 (p. 92). It was left to his successor, **Yuknoom Head**, to re-assert Calakmul ascendancy by seizing Naranjo in a 'star war' attack in 631.[16] The Naranjo king met a very particular fate, *k'uxaj* 'tortured' or 'eaten', perhaps a special punishment for his secession (p. 72). We are told that this took place at Calakmul – anciently called Oxte'tuun or 'Three Stones' – on the very day of the battle and seemingly he was already a captive in their hands. Yuknoom Head went on to conduct a second conquest five years later, in March 636, though the target cannot now be identified. A stelae pair at Calakmul, 76 and 78 (the former dated to 9.10.0.0.0 in 633) should be his work, though as usual, erosion prevents further study. The first foreign references to Calakmul as a site come at virtually the same moment as public monuments return to the city and some special reconstitution of the kingdom may have taken place at this time.

YUKNOOM CHAN	
Glyphic spelling yu-ku-no-ma TI'?-CHAN-na	*Also known as* Chan

TAJOOM UK'AB' K'AK'	
Glyphic spelling ta-jo-ma u-K'AB'-K'AK' ('? Fiery Hand') *Also known as* Ta Batz'	*Accession* 28 March 622 (9.9.9.0.5 11 Chikchan 3 Wo) *Death* 1 October 630 (9.9.17.11.14 13 Ix 12 Sak)

YUKNOOM HEAD	
Glyphic spelling yu[ku](noom)-?-IL *Also known as* Cauac Head	*Monuments* Stelae 76 & 78

A liquid-spilling star over the name-glyph of Naranjo marks its conquest on 24 December AD 631. The text goes on to recount the grisly fate of its king and give the agent of both events as Yuknoom Head. Naranjo Hieroglyphic Stairway, AD 642.

(Left) From ground-level the scale of Structure 2 is imposing, even though its highest point remains well out of sight.

(Below) Structure 2 as it may have looked at the beginning of the Late Classic era, before the addition of a new 2B pyramid and further, overlying façades. A few traces of paint survive on fragments of plaster, but the scheme shown here is largely conjectural.

(Bottom) Recent excavations have revealed the remains of six enormous masks that once dominated Structure 2's façade.

2A

2B

2C

2D

Building containing Stela 43

Stela 114 set into a niche here

STRUCTURE 2:
A BEHEMOTH AT THE HEART OF CALAKMUL

Of all the great temple platforms within Classic Maya cities, the most massive was Calakmul's Structure 2. Measuring 394 ft (120 m) on each side of its base, and rising to a height of more than 148 ft (45 m), its scale alone invites comparison with Preclassic architecture – especially that of mighty El Mirador, whose highest mounds can be seen, if faintly, from its summit.

Indeed, at its core there is a Preclassic pyramid, now labelled 2A, that still represents its highest point. A long stucco-decorated building on its northern face was covered in the Early Classic by a huge extension supporting three new temples, 2B, C and D, each with its own access stairway. Ramón Carrasco has recently uncovered the six gigantic masks that dominated this façade. Some retain traces of their plaster coatings and once-brilliant paintwork. Buildings set along its base (each of which housed or entombed early stelae) came later, as did a southward expansion that squared the overall plan and provided room for two more upper structures.

The setting of Tomb 4 into the floor of 2B – the richest burial yet found at Calakmul (see p. 111) – spurred a particular remodelling in the early 8th century. 2B was buried beneath a sizeable temple pyramid and the great masks obscured by a new stepped frontage. Finally, in quite late times, this was overlaid by yet another façade, an ambitious project that may never have been completed.[17]

Yuknoom the Great
Yuknoom Ch'een II
636–686

Yuknoom Yich'aak K'ak'
Jaguar Paw Smoke
686–695?

Split Earth
695?>

The terrible erosion of monuments at Calakmul means that no portraits of Yuknoom the Great survive in good condition at the city itself. Fortunately, however, one small image is preserved on a lidded vase dated to 9.12.0.0.0, AD 672.

YUKNOOM THE GREAT	
Glyphic spelling	*Accession*
yu-ku-no-ma	28 April 636
CH'E:N?-na	(9.10.3.5.10
Also known as	8 Ok 18 Sip)
Yuknom Ch'en	*Father*
Birth	Scroll Serpent?
11 September 600	*Monuments*
(9.8.7.2.17	Stelae 9, 13, 30?,
8 Kaban 5 Yax)	31, 32?, 33, 34?,
	35, 36, 37?, 75,
	77?, 79, 85?, 86,
	87?, 93 & 94

YUKNOOM THE GREAT

The 'golden age' of Calakmul power continued with the 50-year reign of Yuknoom the Great. He was born in 600, adopting the name of the Early Classic king Yuknoom Ch'een on his accession in 636.[18] Calakmul's prodigious output of stelae really begins under his direction and as many as 18 were his personal commissions. It is also likely that he was responsible for many of the major building programmes at the city, especially among the palace complexes that dominate its core and seem to be a special signature of its political activities.[19]

In large measure the story of Yuknoom the Great's reign pivots on his struggle with a resurgent Tikal. This coincides with a split in the Tikal dynasty and the emergence of two implacably opposed factions, both headed by lords claiming to be 'divine lords' of Mutal. Calakmul took an active role in the affair, either by supporting an existing client or by taking the losing party under its protection. In either case, the exiled B'alaj Chan K'awiil proclaimed himself a vassal of Yuknoom the Great and joined him in campaigning against the Tikal incumbent Nuun Ujol Chaak. In the process, B'alaj Chan K'awiil established a new dynastic seat at Dos Pilas, in the Petexbatun region, where he ruled as a Tikal 'anti-king'.

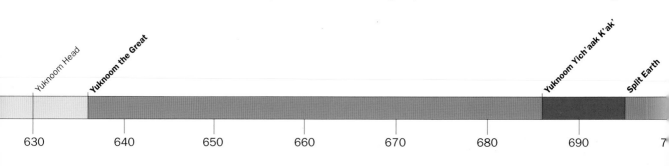

Yuknoom Head   Yuknoom the Great   Yuknoom Yich'aak K'ak'   Split Earth

630   640   650   660   670   680   690   7

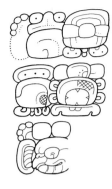

Yuknoom the Great's long tenure covered a period of particularly intense conflict between Calakmul and Tikal. This passage from Dos Pilas records a 'star war' attack he conducted against Tikal in January AD 657.

Presumably it was in support of these claims that Yuknoom the Great attacked Tikal in 657, the beginning of a complex series of wars (p. 42). Initially, Nuun Ujol Chaak was forced to flee Tikal, though eventually, probably by means of a campaign or campaigns now lost to us, he did manage to restore himself to his capital. By 672 Nuun Ujol Chaak had mustered sufficient strength to invade the Petexbatun, expelling his rival from Dos Pilas and setting a new round of conflict in motion. Calakmul came to Dos Pilas' aid once again and in 677 further triumphs over Tikal led directly to B'alaj Chan K'awiil's return to the Petexbatun. In all likelihood, it was a combined Calakmul-Dos Pilas force that gave B'alaj Chan K'awiil a significant victory over Nuun Ujol Chaak in 679 (pp. 42–3, 57).

King of kings

The intense strife of this time was not confined to the central Peten and Petexbatun regions but also gripped areas further east. A rejuvenated Naranjo succeeded in overrunning Caracol in 680. Yet the disappearance of the Naranjo dynasty within two years points to an unrecorded but devastating defeat of its own. Whoever inflicted the blow, there is every sign that Calakmul orchestrated its aftermath and a daughter of B'alaj Chan K'awiil was dispatched to Naranjo to initiate a new dynasty in 682 (p. 75).

The 'overkingship' of Yuknoom the Great is attested at a number of major sites, though surely only a sample of its full extent. On an unknown date he oversaw the inauguration of the El Perú ruler K'inich B'alam ('Great-Sun Jaguar'). This king was further bonded by marriage to an *ix kaanal ajaw*, a Calakmul princess. An impressive 152 miles (245 km) to the south of Calakmul, in the Pasión region, Yuknoom the Great was patron to the Cancuen kingdom through three generations of kings – installing at least two of them in 656 and 677.[20] In the lower reaches of the Usumacinta River, Yuknoom the Great or one of his emissaries was similarly involved in the accession of a king at Moral in 662. Further upstream Yuknoom the Great was able to influence the affairs of Piedras Negras, one of his lieutenants supervising some kind of ritual event there in 685 (p. 144).

Yuknoom the Great ended his reign as a venerable octogenarian, probably early in 686. At his passing Calakmul was still the pre-eminent power of the central lowlands, yet its failure in one key area, to fully subdue Tikal, would ultimately prove costly.

This fragmentary stucco text was once part of a jade mosaic mask found in Tomb 4 of Structure 2. The manner in which it names Yuknoom the Great suggests that it was a personal portrait, perhaps one used in ancestral impersonation.

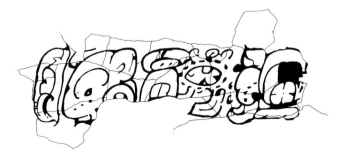

YUKNOOM YICH'AAK K'AK'	
Glyphic spelling yu[ku](noom)-[yi]ICH'A:K-ki-K'AK' ('? Fiery Claw') *Also known as* Jaguar Paw Smoke, Jaguar Paw *Birth* 6 October 649 (9.10.16.16.19 3 Kawak 2 Keh)	*Accession* 3 April 686 (9.12.13.17.7 6 Manik' 5 Sip) *Brother* U-Hand-K'inich *Monuments* Stelae 104, 105?, 115 & 116

SITE Q AND LA CORONA

As long as the home of the Kaan kingdom remained in doubt many researchers used the description 'Site Q' (from the Spanish *¿que?* meaning 'which?'). In fact, we now know that most of the looted monuments attributed to Site Q come not from Calakmul itself but from two or more unknown dependencies. A fresh candidate has recently emerged in the shape of La Corona, first pinpointed by a NASA satellite. An expedition headed by Ian Graham – the indefatigable forest explorer whose recording of Maya inscriptions has made a key contribution to the decipherment process – visited the site in 1997 and revealed La Corona's close ties with Calakmul. These included references to Yuknoom the Great's 1st K'atun-anniversary of rule in AD 656 and Yich'aak K'ak's celebration of the 13th K'atun in 692. Significantly, the name of the local ruler is given as Great Turkey, who is also mentioned in one of the Site Q texts. This tells of a ballgame rite he conducted at Calakmul, probably in 687.[21]

In this ballplaying scene we see (at right) Great Turkey, a vassal of Yich'aak K'ak' from La Corona. The associated caption most likely commemorates the date 9.12.15.0.0 of AD 687, and states that 'it happened at Oxte'tuun Chiik Naab', or Calakmul itself. Such records give some insight into the great gatherings of lords that took place on these occasions, as client nobility travelled to the capital to participate in solemn rituals, sumptuous feasts and great public spectacles. Site Q Ballplayer Panel 1.

YUKNOOM YICH'AAK K'AK'

Yich'aak K'ak' or 'Fiery Claw' – better known under the nickname Jaguar Paw Smoke – is the only Calakmul king to have achieved wide recognition until now. It is a great pity that our actual knowledge of him is rather limited. There are signs that he took a leading role in the kingdom well before his official assumption of power. He receives extraordinary prominence on Stela 9, a thin slate stone dating to 662, which carries an extended account of his birth in 649 and ascribes him a full royal title. Perhaps the aged Yuknoom the Great, ailing or infirm, passed the effective running of the state to the younger man, most likely his son. If so, Yich'aak K'ak' should be credited with a major hand in Calakmul's recent military and diplomatic successes.[22]

Yich'aak K'ak's formal enthronement in 686 was duly recorded by both El Perú and Dos Pilas, where he inherited the loyalty of K'inich B'alam and B'alaj Chan K'awiil respectively. The elevation of the five-year-old K'ak' Tiliw Chan Chaak at Naranjo in 693 brought him a new client, revealing the role Calakmul had played in installing his dynasty a decade or so earlier (p. 76). While Yich'aak K'ak's authority seems every bit as extensive as his predecessor's, we should not imagine that grand public histories convey the complex undercurrents that fill any political landscape; they always reflect the priorities of their authors. A glimmer of such complexity and partiality appears in a scene painted on a cylinder vase, presumably from Tikal. It shows an emissary of Yich'aak K'ak' kneeling and delivering tribute to an enthroned Tikal lord, probably its king, in 691.[23]

End of the 'golden age'

Contacts between the two states were decidedly different in August 695, when Yich'aak K'ak' led his forces into battle against the Tikal king Jasaw Chan K'awiil I (p. 45). This was one of the most influential clashes of the Classic era, though, as usual, the description of it lacks any real

Among the most poignant images of captives in Maya art are those of this lord from the site of Hixil ('Jaguar'). He is said to be the 'grandson' or 'grandfather' of an otherwise unknown 'divine lord' of Calakmul called Split Earth. A separate text (at right) seems to describe a battle in November AD 695, naming him victor.

SPLIT EARTH	
Glyphic spelling ?-ta	

colour or detail and we are limited to a terse 'Yich'aak K'ak's flint and shield were brought down'. We do know, however, that the humiliation was compounded by the capture of a prominent Calakmul deity called *yajaw maan* (it is unclear if the seizure of these effigy figures was commonplace or signals some kind of rout). While its political ambit was far from destroyed, this reverse did bring Calakmul's golden age to a close. Diplomatic interaction of all kinds fell away sharply in the years that followed, with the greatest effect on explicit statements of overlordship – only one or two such relationships can be identified after this. Hegemony of the kind exercised by Classic Maya powers relied heavily on their military prestige and defeat could quickly undermine their hold over clients and affiliates, provoking thoughts of secession.

Yich'aak K'ak's fate is uncertain. A stucco tableau within Tikal's royal palace shows a captive from the battle but, although the king is named in an accompanying caption, their linkage is far from certain (p. 45). No phalanx of monuments memorializes Yich'aak K'ak's reign at Calakmul and what standing stones do date to his tenure, like Stela 105 from 692, occur only in the isolated Northeast Group of the city. Two more, Stelae 115 and 116, were found broken and buried within Structure 2.[24] Here they might be linked to Tomb 4 and support the idea that this impressive burial belongs to Yich'aak K'ak' himself (see panel).[25]

A narrow glimpse of subsequent events comes from an enigmatic pair of bones found in the tomb of Jasaw Chan K'awiil. They describe a new Calakmul ruler, **Split Earth**, who seems to have been in power by November 695.[26] Whether this was a legitimate king, or simply some Tikal-sponsored pretender, is as yet unknown.

A NEW ROYAL TOMB

In 1997, excavations deep within the mighty Structure 2 uncovered a buried temple, now called 2B-sub. Beneath its floor was found the lavishly provisioned Tomb 4. It contained the skeleton of a man shrouded in textiles and jaguar skin, both partially preserved by an applied resin. Among the offerings were a jade mosaic mask; a pair of heirloom Early Classic jade ear ornaments; beads fashioned from bone, mother of pearl and spondylus shells; collections of spiny oyster shells; obsidian 'eccentrics'; and the fragmented remains of lacquered wooden objects. There were a number of fine ceramic vessels – one in codex-style – originally wrapped in loose-weave cloth. The most outstanding of these was a plate with an image of *huunal*, the so-called 'Jester God', a divine patron of kingship. The rim text explicitly names Yich'aak K'ak' as the plate's owner. Everything was originally held within an enclosed bier, an arched structure of wood carved with elaborate designs and hieroglyphs and painted in several colours. This wonderful object has now decayed entirely, leaving only a partial impression and a few flecks of paint on the hardened mud packed around it.[27]

Discovered in Tomb 4, deep within Structure 2B, this large serving dish bears the legend *u lak yuknoom yich'aak k'ak'* 'the plate of ?-Fiery Claw'.

Yuknoom Took' K'awiil
>702–731>

 Wamaw K'awiil
>736>

Ruler Y
>741>

 Ruler Z
>751>

 B'olon K'awiil
>771–789?>

 Chan Pet
>849>

 Aj Took'
>909?>

YUKNOOM TOOK' K'AWIIL	
Glyphic spelling	*Monuments*
yu[ku]-?-?-li-TO:K'-K'AWI:L-li ('? Flint K'awiil')	Stelae 1, 7?, 8, 23, 24, 38, 39?, 40, 41?, 42?, 51, 52, 53, 54, 55, 70, 71, 72, 73, 74 & 89
Also known as Ruler 5/6/7	
Wife Lady of Stela 54?	

YUKNOOM TOOK' K'AWIIL

Calakmul responded to its recent adversity with a new surge in monument carving and as many as seven stelae were erected at the next major calendrical juncture in 702. These were the work of a ruler using a confusing series of name variants and abbreviations, for which Yuknoom Took' K'awiil is no more than a partial reading. To compound the problem still further, outside Calakmul he is referred to by a quite different part of his name, Scroll-head K'awiil. It is with this designation that he appears at Dos Pilas in 702. Although the nature of this contact is now lost, we can take it as a sign that Calakmul maintained its relationship with the exiled Tikal dynasty. Similarly, the overlordship of El Perú was preserved and at some unknown date Took' K'awiil supervised the accession of a new ruler there.[28] Ties with Naranjo seem to have been maintained too: its king boasts of his one-time fealty to Yich'aak K'ak' as late as 711. In sum, Calakmul's political sphere shows some resilience at this point.

It seems to have been Took' K'awiil who erected a magnificent set of seven stelae to celebrate the end of the 15th K'atun in 731 (bringing his output to a possible 21 monoliths). Most were arranged at the base of

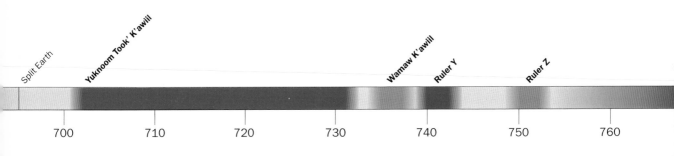

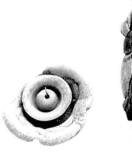

(*Above*) This naturalistic jade mask was discovered in a tomb at the summit of Structure 7, a temple pyramid occupying the northern side of the Central Plaza. Clearly a royal burial of the Late Classic, it is a great pity that no text identifies its owner.

(*Right*) Stela 54 depicts one of Took' K'awiil's wives. Her name does not survive. AD 731.

(*Left*) Showing a mature, full-bodied figure of Took' K'awiil with an unusual mane of curly hair, Stela 51 is the finest surviving monument from the city. AD 731.

Structure 1, a very large pyramid at the east of the central core. Hewn from a dense, durable limestone, presumably imported from some distance, they were once the best-preserved at the city (though their theft in the 1960s wrecked most of their inscriptions before they could be properly documented). While these stones are undoubtedly impressive, they should not be taken as a barometer of the wider health of the kingdom. An altar at Tikal, probably dedicated between 733 and 736, shows a bound Calakmul lord and points to a new defeat at the hands of this old enemy. The accompanying caption is damaged, but Took' K'awiil might be named there (pp. 48–9).[29]

on K'awiil

780   790   800   810   820   830   840

CODEX-STYLE CERAMICS

One of the major traditions of Late Classic painted ceramics, 'codex-style' is defined by a thin calligraphic line traced across a cream-coloured surface, thought to closely resemble the appearance of Classic Maya books or codices. Major advances in isolating the original production area of these artifacts have come from the archaeological work of Richard Hansen and stylistic and chemical 'fingerprinting' of Dorie Reents-Budet and Ronald Bishop. Though the texts on codex-style pottery place heavy emphasis on the kingdom of Kaan, they originate not at Calakmul but somewhat to the south, in the old Preclassic heartland around El Mirador and Nakbe.[30]

This codex-style pot was found in a burial on Structure 2.

This block recovered from Structure 13 describes B'olon K'awiil as the 'Lord of Chiik Naab'.

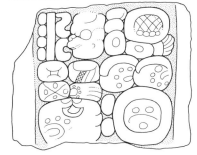

WAMAW K'AWIIL TO AJ TOOK'

What we know of Calakmul's later dynasty is meagre indeed. Compounding the perennial problem of eroded monuments at home is the kingdom's virtual disappearance from the 'international' scene, this once productive source having dried to the merest trickle. Accordingly, the sequence for this era is decidedly sketchy.

We learn of a new king from one surprising foreign source, Quirigua, in the far southeast. Calakmul's enthusiasm for distant involvements seems undiminished and in some ill-defined way it was connected with Quirigua's rebellion against its overlords at Copan (p. 219). Identified as a 'divine lord of Chiik Naab'' and dated to 736, his personal name is hard to make out but **Wamaw K'awiil** might be the form.[31]

A set of five particularly massive stelae were erected at Calakmul in 741. Unfortunately, the name of their commissioning king, **Ruler Y**, is damaged in all cases. Once again, this assertive display bears no relation to the wider political fortunes of the state, which continue to slide. Tikal's decisive victories over two of Calakmul's leading clients, El Perú in 743 and Naranjo in 744, reflect its powerlessness in the face of its rival's renewed expansion and constitute the final dismemberment of its one-time 'imperium'.

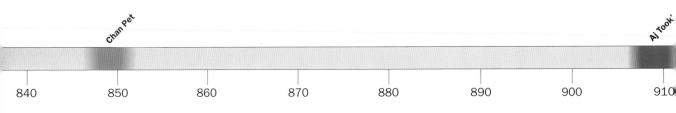

(*Above*) A telling reflection of Calakmul's decline are the crude, child-like carvings of its last monuments. Stela 50.

(*Opposite below*) The gently sloping stairway of Structure 13 is dominated by Stela 88 and its portrait of an unknown royal woman. The stair was completed late in Calakmul history and sealed many broken glyphic blocks.

WAMAW K'AWIIL	
Glyphic spelling	wa?-ma?-wi K'AWI:L

RULER Y	
Also known as Ruler 8, B'olon K'awiil I	*Monuments* Stelae 25, 26, 27, 59 & 60

RULER Z	
Glyphic spelling ?-?-? ?-?	*Monuments* Stelae 62 & 88
Also known as Ruler 8	

B'OLON K'AWIIL	
Glyphic spelling 9-K'AWI:L (Nine/Many K'awiils')	*Also known as* Ruler 9, B'olon K'awiil II *Monuments* Stelae 57 & 58

CHAN PET	
Glyphic spelling	4-PET-te

AJ TOOK'	
Glyphic spelling AJ-TO:K'-k'e? ('He of Flint')	*Monument* Stela 61

The end of the 16th K'atun in 751 was commemorated by the unfinished Stela 62, which features the damaged, but seemingly new name of **Ruler Z**. This stone might once have been paired with the similarly dated Stela 88, which carries the portrait of a queen. Her name is not preserved, but there seems to be a mention of another character called **B'olon K'awiil** ('Nine or Many K'awiils'). This name appears on a recently excavated block of hieroglyphic stairway, linked to a date shortly after 751. This should be the same B'olon K'awiil who was in power by 771 and erected a pair of tall stelae, 57 and 58, east of Structure 13 to mark the completion of 9.17.0.0.0.[32] A probable reference to him outside Calakmul comes from the far reaches of Chiapas, at the city of Tonina in 789 (p. 189).

Calakmul's waning influence over its northern possessions seems to be reflected in the rise of a new architectural style in these areas, the elaborate façades and 'false pyramids' of Río Bec. Related to the emerging Chenes and Puuc styles still further north, this takes shape at a number of flourishing sites, including Río Bec itself, Hormiguero, Chicanna, Xpujil and the moated city of Becan.

Final decline

A lone Calakmul monument was erected in 790, two in 800 and three in 810, though none preserves the name of its patron. As at Tikal, there was to be no commemoration of the key 10.0.0.0.0 Bak'tun-ending of 830 and central authority had apparently collapsed by that time. In another feature that mirrors Tikal, Calakmul's closest clients – sizeable cities in their own right – which erected few monuments during the height of its power, now show greater activity. At Oxpemul and the newly discovered giant of Nadzcaan they continue until at least 830, while at La Muñeca they extend to 889.[33] Both La Muñeca and Oxpemul certainly have even later carvings.

A final foreign reference to the Kaan kingdom appears in 849, when **Chan Pet** 'witnessed' the 10.1.0.0.0 K'atun-ending at Seibal. Though a broken pot found at Calakmul might be incised with this name, the lack of contemporary monuments should make us question whether the state still existed in any form worth the name (p. 227).

There was, however, one last rally at Calakmul, evident in the stunted form of Stela 61. Its portrait is largely gone but a name, **Aj Took'** 'He of Flint', and the snake emblem glyph do survive. Its date, as is typical of these late times, is expressed as a single day, distinguishable as either 12 or 13 Ajaw. The following 'scattering' ceremony points to a major calendrical juncture, with 899 or 909 the only likely placements (the latter, the full 10.4.0.0.0 ending is preferable).[34] To judge by their style, a few stones are even later and represent valiant, if rather pitiful, attempts by a remnant community to continue the Classic tradition. By the time of Stelae 84 and 91, inscriptions have been reduced to meaningless ciphers that seek only the illusion of writing, while Stela 50 is so crude and artless that it would seem to parody the works of greatness still standing around it.

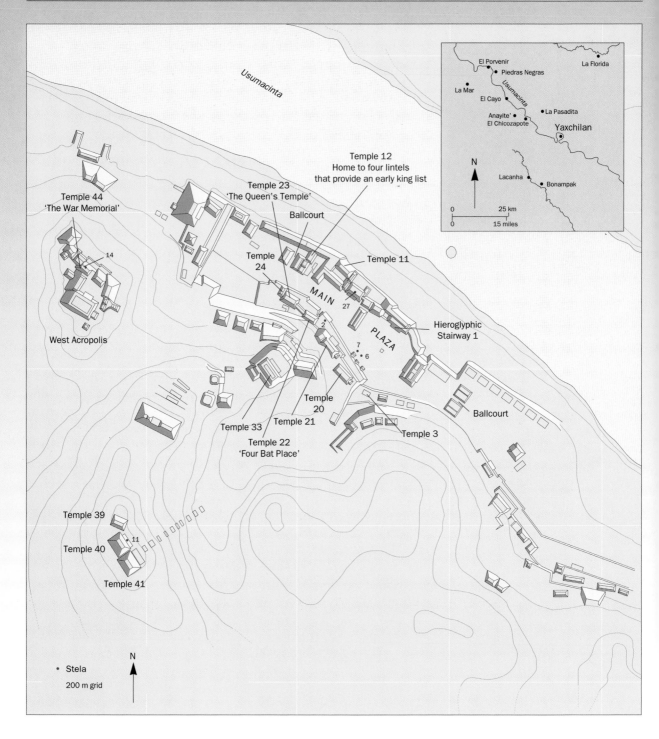

Temple 12
Home to four lintels
that provide an early king list

Temple 23
'The Queen's Temple'

Ballcourt

Temple 44
'The War Memorial'

14

Temple 11

Temple
24

MAIN

27

PLAZA

2

Hieroglyphic
Stairway 1

West Acropolis

7

6

Temple
20

Ballcourt

Temple 33

Temple 21

Temple 3

Temple 22
'Four Bat Place'

Temple 39

Temple 40

11

Temple 41

• Stela

N

200 m grid

Usumacinta

El Porvenir
Piedras Negras
La Florida

La Mar

El Cayo

Usumacinta

Anayite'
El Chicozapote

La Pasadita

Yaxchilan

N

Lacanha
Bonampak

0   25 km
0   15 miles

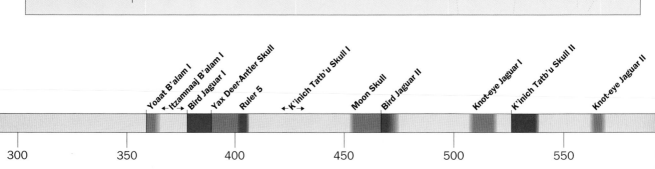

Yoaat B'alam I

Itzamnaaj B'alam I

Bird Jaguar I

Yax Deer-Antler Skull

Ruler 5

K'inich Tatb'u Skull I

Moon Skull

Bird Jaguar II

Knot-eye Jaguar I

K'inich Tatb'u Skull II

Knot-eye Jaguar II

300   350   400   450   500   550

YAXCHILAN

THE PASION AND SALINAS RIVERS converge to become the Usumacinta, the great water highway linking the Peten to the Gulf of Mexico. The city of Yaxchilan was set at the apex of a sweeping horseshoe bend and first seen by the pioneering English archaeologist Alfred Maudslay in 1882. The ceremonial heart of the city fills a narrow man-made terrace close to the river's southern bank, but with major structures perched on the slopes and summits of the karst hillscape at its back. Yaxchilan's dynasty describes an origin in the 4th century, but the city seen today is largely the creation of the two 8th-century kings that dominate its history: Itzamnaaj B'alam II and his son Bird Jaguar IV. Though Yaxchilan vigorously pursued monolithic stela-carving, its particular speciality was carved stone lintels, of which 58 span the doorways of major structures. Given the militaristic emphasis of its sculpture and texts, Yaxchilan has long been perceived as a regional capital and conquest state of some importance. Yet the greater understanding possible today gives a rather different view of its place in the region and its disjointed political development.

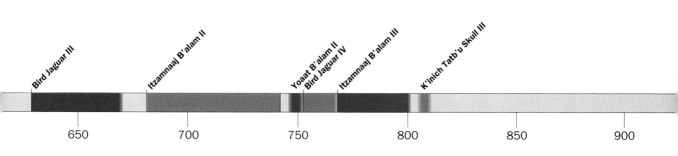

Bird Jaguar III   Itzamnaaj B'alam II   Yoaat B'alam II   Bird Jaguar IV   Itzamnaaj B'alam III   K'inich Tatb'u Skull III

650   700   750   800   850   900

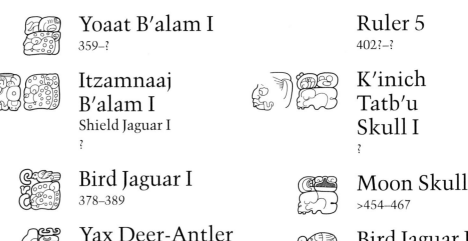

Yoaat B'alam I
359–?

Itzamnaaj B'alam I
Shield Jaguar I
?

Bird Jaguar I
378–389

Yax Deer-Antler Skull
389–402?

Ruler 5
402?–?

K'inich Tatb'u Skull I
?

Moon Skull
>454–467

Bird Jaguar II
467>

YOAAT B'ALAM I TO BIRD JAGUAR II

Almost nothing is known about the fabric of early Yaxchilan, which lies buried by later construction, but we have a reasonably complete knowledge of its dynastic sequence thanks to the survival of two later king lists. The earliest, divided among a set of four inscribed lintels, dates to the mid-6th century and enumerates the first through to the tenth rulers. The second, a hieroglyphic stairway created over 200 years later, is a longer and more detailed narrative; though its weather-worn condition means that only parts of it can be read today. The chronology of the earliest period is problematic, and the dates followed here are largely those of Peter Mathews, who has produced the most comprehensive analysis of Yaxchilan inscriptions thus far.[1]

History at Yaxchilan begins with the accession of its founder, **Yoaat** (or Yopaat) **B'alam I**, perhaps in 359, described as the *u naah tal chum ajaw* 'the first seated lord'.[2] All the listed kings, in both sources, are supplied with supplementary phrases naming lords from various foreign sites and kingdoms. Originally thought to be visitors to the Yaxchilan court, it is now clear that these are prisoners and represent a record of Early Classic warfare rare in its length and detail. Yoaat B'alam's victim is not

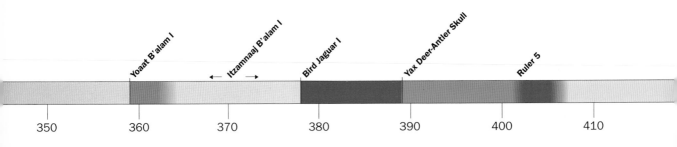

RULER 5	
Glyphic spelling	402?
?-B'ALAM	(8.18.6.5.13?
Accession	10 Ben? 11 Mol)
27 September	

K'INICH TATB'U SKULL I	
Glyphic spelling	*Also known as*
K'INICH ta²-b'u-	Mahk'ina Tah Skull I
JOLO:M?	

MOON SKULL	
Glyphic spelling	*Dynastic title*
ha-?-JOLO:M?	7th in the line

BIRD JAGUAR II	
Glyphic spelling	2 Lamat 1? Keh)
ya-?-B'ALAM	*Wife*
Also known as	Lady Chuwen
Yaxun Balam II	*Sons*
Accession	Knot-eye Jaguar I,
20 November 467?	K'inich Tatb'u
(9.1.12.7.8	Skull II

Lintel 11 begins a series of four listing the first ten kings of Yaxchilan and their most notable captives. *c.* AD 550.

given a royal title, though his name has some links with Piedras Negras.

The name of the second Yaxchilan king, **Itzamnaaj B'alam I**, combines the head of the sky deity *itzamnaaj* with the jaguar head read *b'alam*. The former appears in its avian version on the lintel listing, while the stairway provides the flowery jewel worn by the god preferred by later kings. We lack any dates for his reign, but he was succeeded by **Bird Jaguar I**, probably in 378. The fourth ruler, **Yax Deer-Antler Skull**, seems to have been inaugurated in 389. Unfortunately, the name of **Ruler 5** falls on a missing fragment of the lintel series and is badly eroded on the stairway blocks, though a jaguar head seems to be its major component. His successor **K'inich Tatb'u Skull I** is the earliest of three to share this name.[3] His war captive is the first of royal status, another Bird Jaguar, this one ruler of the nearby kingdom of Bonampak.

The seventh king, **Moon Skull**, came to power at some point before 454 (our first firm date in Yaxchilan chronology), when he dedicated a building called the 'Four Bat Place'.[4] Like many Maya buildings, it was later rebuilt on the same spot, rededicated in a 'seating' ceremony performed by Bird Jaguar IV 297 years later. Moon Skull's name, rather than a reference to the moon, is a spelling of the poorly understood Mayan word for 'spearthrower', the sling weapon the Aztecs called the *atlatl*. His reign saw a war against Piedras Negras, whose king, Ruler A, seems to have been captured. Moon Skull was succeeded by **Bird Jaguar II**, probably in 467.[5] Conflict with Piedras Negras continued and he is credited with seizing another of its lords, a *yajaw te'* (literally 'lord of the tree' but perhaps better understood as 'lord of the lineage'), a subordinate of its Ruler B, apparently in 478.

THE EMBLEMS OF YAXCHILAN

Yaxchilan is notable for its use of paired emblem glyphs – twin royal titles – an unusual feature whose significance is still unclear. Similar pairings between Bonampak and Lacanha, and Cancuen and Machaquila, represent some form of political union or joint rule of two kingdoms and a number of scholars have suggested similar origins for Yaxchilan. The more dominant of Yaxchilan's two forms was the 'split sky', seemingly read *siyaj chan* 'sky born'. Early variants show the sky glyph with a cut or torn edge, sometimes divided entirely in two; but by the Late Classic it had evolved into a simpler cleft design. The second emblem, of unknown reading, does not make a contemporary appearance until the reign of Itzamnaaj B'alam II (AD 681–742), though retrospective mentions link it even with the founder.

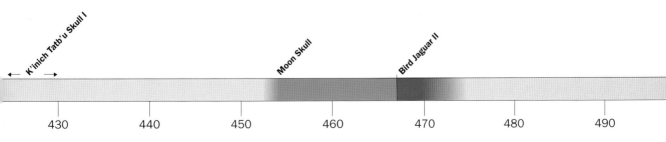

Knot-eye Jaguar I
>508–c. 518

 K'inich Tatb'u Skull II
526–537>

Knot-eye Jaguar II
>564>

The portrait of Knot-eye Jaguar I on Stela 27 is unique in showing evidence for Late Classic restoration of a damaged early monument. Re-carving affects the lower text panel, the king's hands, the 'scattering stream' and the bound altar it falls on to. AD 514.

KNOT-EYE JAGUAR I	
Glyphic spelling	*Brother*
JOY[B'ALAM]	K'inich Tatb'u
Father	Skull II
Bird Jaguar II	*Monument*
	Stela 27

K'INICH TATB'U SKULL II	
Glyphic spelling	*Father*
K'INICH-ta-(ta)-b'u-	Bird Jaguar II
JOLO:M?	*Mother*
Also known as	Lady Chuwen
Mak'ina Tah Skull II	*Brother*
Accession	Knot-eye Jaguar I
11 February 526	*Monuments*
(9.4.11.8.16	Lintels 11, 20?, 22,
2 Kib 19 Pax)	34, 35, 36?, 37,
	47, 48 & 49

KNOT-EYE JAGUAR II	
Glyphic spelling	
JOY[B'ALAM]	

KNOT-EYE JAGUAR I

The ninth Yaxchilan king was Knot-eye Jaguar I, probably to be read *joy b'alam* 'Tied Jaguar'.[6] His Stela 27 is the earliest known at the site and was commissioned to mark the 9.4.0.0.0 K'atun-ending of 514. Among the king's elaborate costume is a rear-facing belt ornament in the form of a human head which, at Yaxchilan, invariably represents a portrait of the wearer's father. In this case a jaguar headdress with a small bird perched on top identifies Bird Jaguar II.[7] Stela 27 is of particular interest since it was clearly damaged at some point and subsequently restored. Reworking is evident over much of the lower third of the stone and can be dated by style to the reign of Bird Jaguar IV (the crudity of the restored left hand led to this figure being nicknamed the 'wooden soldier').[8]

Knot-eye Jaguar was evidently a robust war leader, credited with capturing nobles from Bonampak, Piedras Negras and even, in 508, the great Tikal. However, Yaxchilan's long-running contest with rival Piedras Negras was eventually to claim him. Panel 12 at Piedras Negras shows a series of figures bound at the wrist and kneeling before the local king, one of whom is named in an accompanying caption as Knot-eye Jaguar (see p. 141).[9] No date for his capture is given, though the narrative

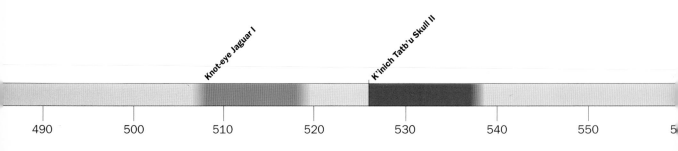

490   500   510   520   530   540   550   5

This example of 'full-figure' glyph-carving provides part of a Long Count date reading 9.4.11.8.16, corresponding to 11 February 526. This day marks the inauguration of K'inich Tatb'u Skull II.

The bound figure of Knot-eye Jaguar I as he appears at Piedras Negras as the prisoner of Ruler C. Piedras Negras Panel 12, c. AD 518.

implies that it occurred before 518. The next Yaxchilan monument, the shattered Stela 14, supplies a date in 521. Unfortunately, the name of its protagonist is entirely lost, though Bird Jaguar II is again named as the king's father. We might view this as a sign that Knot-eye Jaguar was seized after 521, but this stone may instead recount some pre-inaugural rite from the reign of his brother and successor.

K'INICH TATB'U SKULL II

It was 526 before another of Bird Jaguar II's sons, K'inich Tatb'u Skull II, assumed the Yaxchilan title. His place in the city's history is assured by the magnificent series of lintels he commissioned – most especially the four that constitute the king list so crucial to our understanding of the early period. Such lengthy retellings of royal lineage and past glories were often reactions to recent adversity; in this case his brother's defeat and capture would seem to provide the spur. Companion lintels record the king's accession and parentage; the highly elaborate 'full-figure' glyphs that open this text rank among the finest examples of Early Classic carving (p. 220). Yaxchilan may not have been especially large or impressive at this time, but it could certainly commission some of the best artisans of the age. The final lintel of the dynastic sequence is devoted to Tatb'u Skull's military career, which saw a considerable revival, describing his capture of lords from Lakamtuun, Bonampak and, in 537, Calakmul. Significantly, of all the captures detailed in the lintel series, only the successes against the great powers, Tikal and Calakmul, are given dates. The original location of these lintels is unknown, but they were ultimately reset in Structure 12 in the mid-8th century.

YAXCHILAN BETWEEN AD 537 AND 629

With the conclusion of the lintel king list we might hope to turn to the lengthier stairway text for at least some of the remaining Early Classic sequence. Unfortunately, the relevant section is almost completely effaced, leaving a significant gap in our knowledge (it contributes little of use until about 755). Of the four kings known to have reigned in the years between 537 and 629 only one can be firmly identified, **Knot-eye Jaguar II**.[10] Two later inscriptions describe a battle in 564 in which he captured a lord of Lacanha. A single monument, Stela 2, seems to come from this extended interval. It is badly weathered, but a date of 9.9.0.0.0, or 613, is likely.[11]

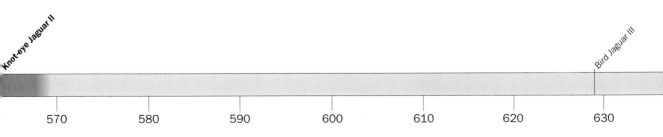

Knot-eye Jaguar II

Bird Jaguar III

570   580   590   600   610   620   630

Bird Jaguar III
629–669>

Itzamnaaj B'alam II
Shield Jaguar II
681–742

Yoaat B'alam II
>749>

Created by one of the great masters of
Classic Maya carving, Lintel 26 supplies
an idealized but deeply impressive
portrait of Itzamnaaj B'alam II. AD 726.

BIRD JAGUAR III	
Glyphic spelling AJ-6-TU:N-ni ya-?-B'ALAM-ma	(9.9.16.10.13 9 Ben 16 Yax)
Also known as 6-Tun Bird Jaguar, Bird Jaguar II, Yaxun Balam III	*Wife* Lady Pakal *Son* Itzamnaaj B'alam II
Dynastic title 15th in the line	*Monuments* Stelae 3/33 & 6; Throne 2 (all by Bird
Accession 15 September 629	Jaguar IV)

This elaborate 'full-figure' hieroglyph
spells the name of Bird Jaguar III.
Throne 2, *c.* AD 760.

BIRD JAGUAR III

The next Yaxchilan ruler, Bird Jaguar III, is known entirely from
retrospective mentions and 'recreated' monuments carved long after his
death. His accession can be calculated from subsequent K'atun-
anniversaries in 649 and 669, making for a date in 629 and ascribing him
a minimal reign of 40 years.[12] He is easily distinguished from his
namesakes by the additional name or title *aj waktuun* 'He of Six Stone'
and his particular captor's epithet of 'Master of Chakjal Te''. Usefully,
one text describes him as the '15th' in the line of the founder Yoaat
B'alam.[13] We are supplied with only one incident from his reign: the
capture in 646 or 647 of a lord from Hix Witz ('Jaguar Hill'), a still unidentified polity to the north of the Usumacinta River. On two occasions he
wears his father's portrait mounted as a belt ornament. Both are identified with the same skull and knot headdress, and this 'Knot Skull'
character may well have preceded him as ruler. Bird Jaguar III's wife, Lady
Pakal ('Shield'), is described as a woman of fortitude who lived to see her
6th K'atun, dying in 705 when at least 98 years of age. It was a son
produced at the very end of her child-bearing years, between 643 and 647,
who would ultimately inherit the crown.

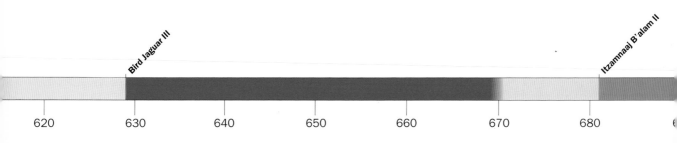

Bird Jaguar III   Itzamnaaj B'alam II

620   630   640   650   660   670   680

The need to recreate, or simply invent, a public record for Bird Jaguar III only serves to emphasize the disrupted character of Yaxchilan history up to this point. What we know of him has been tailored to suit a later rhetorical purpose and in large measure remains unsubstantiated (see p. 129). Piedras Negras' claim to one-time dominion over the upper Usumacinta – including Yaxchilan – together with its sharply contrasting evidence for political stability and large-scale construction, has led Mary Miller to suggest that Yaxchilan's missing history is the result of a lengthy period of subjugation to its larger neighbour (p. 144).[14] Yet we should also consider the role of the more distant Palenque and Tonina, both of whom seem to have exerted a powerful influence along the Usumacinta during Yaxchilan's vacant years (see pp. 170, 184).

ITZAMNAAJ B'ALAM II

Itzamnaaj B'alam the Great acceded in October 681 and was to remain in power for the next 60 years. The magnificent series of buildings he commissioned, richly endowed with lintels, inscribed steps and accompanying stelae, are a testament to his profound impact on the city. Yet these sparkling achievements become all the more remarkable when one considers that they were confined to the final third of his reign, when he is said to have been in his seventies, with little if any of them in place before 723. What had transformed Yaxchilan's fortunes so dramatically?

For an important clue we must look again to Piedras Negras, where Stela 8 records the capture of one of Itzamnaaj B'alam's lieutenants, a *sajal*, in 726. This close link between florescence and military action might indicate some new-found political liberty.[15] The retreat of once powerful foreign hegemonies may have left a vacuum and opportunity. If greater autonomy was reflected in greater revenue from the riverine traffic that made Yaxchilan's location so attractive, we would also have the means by which Itzamnaaj B'alam's explosive programme was possible.

The warrior king

Dedicated in 732 or shortly thereafter, Temple 44, part of the city's West Acropolis, is Itzamnaaj B'alam's famed 'war memorial'.[16] While it provides the usual boasting and self-aggrandizement of Classic kings, it is valuable as Yaxchilan's own account of its resurgence in the region. Each of its three doorways is furnished with a carved lintel and two

A triumphant Itzamnaaj B'alam II stands over his prisoner Aj Popol Chay, lord of Lacanha. Stela 18, after AD 723.

ITZAMNAAJ B'ALAM II	
Glyphic spelling	Lady Ik' Skull of
ITZAMNA:J-B'ALAM	Calakmul
Also known as	*Father*
Shield Jaguar the	Bird Jaguar III
Great, Shield Jaguar	*Mother*
I, Shield Jaguar II	Lady Pakal
Accession	*Son*
20 October 681	Bird Jaguar IV
(9.12.9.8.1	*Monuments*
5 Imix 4 Mak)	Stelae 13, 14, 15,
Death	16?, 17, 18, 19, 20
15 June 742	& 23; Lintels 4, 23,
(9.15.10.17.14	24, 25, 26, 44, 45,
6 Ix 12 Yaxk'in)	46 & 56;
Wives	Hieroglyphic
Lady K'ab'al Xook,	Stairway 3; Altars 7,
Lady Sak B'iyaan,	12 & 22

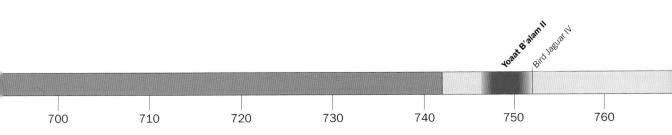

Lintel 45 shows the capture and submission of Aj Nik on 21 February 681. Grasped by the hair he almost seems to kiss the cotton shield of his captor Itzamnaaj B'alam. *c.* AD 731.

hieroglyphic steps. Their texts follow a sequence of Itzamnaaj B'alam's captures between 681 and 732, beginning with his pre-inaugural taking of Aj Nik. In standard practice, 'Master of Aj Nik' was hereafter fixed in his name phrase, to be repeated on some 32 different occasions. The captive himself was of no great standing, a sub-lord from a site called Maan or Namaan. After the capture of Aj Sak Ichiy Pat in 689 the story leaps to 713 with the seizure of Aj K'an Usja, an *ajaw* of the otherwise unknown site of B'uktuun. Two of the remaining conflicts are each paralleled with an analogous event from Yaxchilan's past. Thus the capture of the Lacanha lord Aj Popol Chay in 729 is compared to Knot-eye Jaguar II's exploits against this same kingdom 164 years earlier, while Itzamnaaj B'alam's seizing of a Hix Witz lord in 732 is compared to a matching triumph achieved by his father, Bird Jaguar III, 85 years before. By now Itzamnaaj B'alam was in his eighties and we can safely assume that he relied on his supporting group of *sajalob'* to do the actual fighting.

These same campaigns were detailed on a series of stelae he set in front of Temple 41, one of three major buildings crowning the highest vantage at the city. A tiny portion of stucco frieze may date its construction or renovation to the 3rd K'atun-anniversary of his rule in 740. The 726 defeat by Piedras Negras is, unsurprisingly, omitted both here and at Temple 44 – though it is important to note that he does not falsely claim victory.

These wars fit into a complex and dynamic picture of political hierarchy in the Usumacinta region which is far from completely understood. Itzamnaaj B'alam's realm encompassed the hilltop redoubt of La Pasadita, Yaxchilan's most important possession on the northern

A view of Temples 40 (left) and 39, two of three structures perched on a hilltop high above the city. Temple 40 was once decorated with vivid interior murals, now almost completely decayed.

RITUAL IN STONE:
MASTERPIECES OF THE QUEEN'S HOUSE

The most impressive sculptures at Yaxchilan, arguably the finest relief-carving to survive anywhere in the Maya region, are the three door lintels of Temple 23. This structure is said to be the *yotot*, 'the house of' Lady K'ab'al Xook, the principal wife of Itzamnaaj B'alam II, who features in all three scenes. Their narrative begins on Lintel 25, where the queen celebrates her husband's accession in 681 by the conjuring of a vision: a warrior masked as the Teotihuacan Storm God Tlaloc emerging from the jaws of a half-decayed Mexican-style part serpent, part centipede. The text tells us that this is the 'flint and shield' of the Yaxchilan patron god called Aj K'ak' O' Chaak. Most likely the warrior is a manifestation of the king

himself as defender of the city. On Lintel 24, dated to 709, Lady K'ab'al Xook pulls a thorn laden rope through her tongue, splattering blood on paper laid in a basket at her feet. The king illuminates the scene with a fiery torch or spear. Finally, on Lintel 26 she hands him a jaguar helmet for a still obscure rite that took place in 724.

Some of the carvings were commissioned as early as 723, although the formal dedication of the building – its 'entering with fire' – was not for three more years. Lintels 24 and 25 can now be seen in the British Museum, London; Lintel 26 in the Museo Nacional de Antropología, Mexico City.

The door lintels of Temple 23. (Above) Lintel 25, from the central door; (top left) Lintel 24, from the east door; (bottom left) Lintel 26, from the west door.

IX-k'a[b'a]-la XO:K?-ki
Lady K'ab'al Xook

IX-SAK-b'i-ya-ni
Lady Sak B'iyaan

IX-UH CHAN-na-?
Lady Ik' Skull

The name glyphs of three of Itzamnaaj B'alam's wives.

This carved bone was one of nine recovered from a burial within the floor of Lady K'ab'al Xook's Temple 23. Most were incised with her name, but this one is described as the bloodletter of her husband Itzamnaaj B'alam II.

side of the river, and the site of El Chicozapote, only 8.5 miles (14 km) from the Piedras Negras satellite of El Cayo. For certain periods he seems to have dominated the nearby Lacanha and Bonampak polities. This area was subject to Tonina overlordship around 715 (p. 184), though by 726 this role had been assumed by the polity of Sak Tz'i ('White Dog') (p. 146).

The wives of Itzamnaaj B'alam II

Itzamnaaj B'alam's principal queen, Lady K'ab'al Xook, enjoyed an exceptional status at the city. Temple 23 was dedicated to her in 726 and contained some truly spectacular examples of Maya stone carving (p. 125). Significantly, they were the work of imported masters, one a native of the unidentified Sak Ook. The main three-lintel programme of Temple 23 shows the queen performing an auto-sacrifice by pulling a thorned cord through her tongue, conjuring a warrior apparition (disgorged from the mouth of an envisioned serpent), and preparing her husband for some military ritual (handing him a jaguar helmet). Their deeply modelled relief and intricate detail – especially in the representation of textiles – have few rivals in the corpus of Maya art. An additional doorway at the side of the building features an all-glyphic lintel which includes a short genealogy for the queen's Xook ('Shark') lineage.[17] When we consider that this great edifice was the first of Itzamnaaj B'alam's major works – ahead of Temple 44 and its military boasting – his main priorities, the renewal of proper ritual and communion with tutelary gods through bloodletting and trance, become clear. As elsewhere, foundation, or in this case 'refoundation', is associated with overt Teotihuacan imagery, and the fabulous, half-skeletal serpent on Lintel 25 is of Mexican design.

Roberto Garcia Moll's excavations within Temple 23 revealed a series of burials in its floor and the richest, Tomb 2, placed behind the west door of the frontage, contained a mature woman accompanied by a large stock of pottery vessels and as many as 20,000 obsidian blades. It also included a set of nine carved bone bloodletters, six bearing Lady K'ab'al Xook's name. While this might point to the queen's grave, the adjacent, annex-like Temple 24 contains the record of her death in 749 and a fire ritual performed at her *muknal* 'burial place' – probably identifying this as her memorial shrine.

Temple 11, part of a small private compound close to the river, was built for another of Itzamnaaj B'alam's queens, Lady Sak B'iyaan (said to be an *ixik ch'ok* 'young woman') in 738. A third wife, Lady Ik' Skull (also known as Lady Eveningstar), a royal *ix ajaw* from Calakmul, was not mentioned during the king's lifetime.

In December 740 Itzamnaaj B'alam II celebrated his 3rd K'atun-anniversary of rule but was to live for only two years more, dying in June 742, when well into his nineties. Long-lived kings often outlive some, even many, of their heirs, bequeathing a complex and contested situation to their survivors. Subsequent events suggest that there were indeed rival claims to his inheritance.

The Yaxchilan 'interregnum' begins with the death of Itzamnaaj B'alam on 9.15.10.17.14, or 15 June 742. This phrase provides one of the standard metaphors: *k'a'ay u sak nik ik'il* 'his white flowery breath was extinguished'. Lintel 27, *c.* AD 755.

THE 'INTERREGNUM' OF AD 742–752

Ten years were to elapse between the death of Itzamnaaj B'alam II and the next inauguration documented at the site, that of his son Bird Jaguar IV in 752. This is the famed 'interregnum' for which Tatiana Proskouriakoff proposed a power struggle so intense that it kept any candidate from taking the throne.[18] Reconstructing the events of this era, from piecemeal and at times rather suspect information, has its difficulties but further insights do seem possible.

Lady K'ab'al Xook survived her husband by six years and appears to have remained a prestigious figure within the kingdom. An *ajaw* of her Xook lineage, probably a brother or nephew rather than her son, was captured in a clash with Dos Pilas in 745 (see p. 62) – though there is no clear sign that this had an impact on the succession.[19] Her high standing in the king's lifetime makes it likely that she had borne at least one male heir, for which there may now be some evidence.

The most important document of this era, probably the key to what understanding is now possible, appears not at Yaxchilan but at Piedras Negras. Here Panel 3 refers to a 'divine lord' of Yaxchilan who witnessed the K'atun-anniversary of Piedras Negras Ruler 4's reign in 749 (p. 149). He bears a variant of the founder's name and there seems little reason to doubt that this is a new king, **Yoaat B'alam II**, who ruled during part, if not all, of the 'interregnum' period. A party from Yaxchilan appear in the scene, where they are addressed by the enthroned Piedras Negras ruler, whose speech is incised between them. These difficult passages refer to the accession, under Piedras Negras tutelage, of a Bird Jaguar described as *amam* 'your grandfather/ancestor'.[20] This suggests a past event even though the associated date lacks a secure anchor and does not match anything in the known history of Yaxchilan. We must wonder what made this information of such significance to Piedras Negras. It is tempting to think that Piedras Negras is setting out information in direct contradiction of the records then extant at Yaxchilan (p. 149).[21]

This raises the wider issue of the reliability of Maya texts, about which questions have been raised in certain cases.[22] We know that where they can be tested archaeologically they have proved robust, not least at Copan, where recent excavations have produced excellent support for a long-doubted written record (pp. 192–3). If Maya kings commonly used deceit we would expect to see more contradictions in the record. It is significant, for example, that no two sides claim victory in the same battle (somewhat surprisingly, given the often inconclusive nature of war). Yet we must remain sensitive to the rhetorical purposes of the inscriptions, and it is necessary to assemble a wider regional and supra-regional context in which to judge the history of a particular kingdom.

The respectful presence of the new Yaxchilan king at Piedras Negras might suggest a period of ascendancy for this old foe. No evidence for Yoaat B'alam II's tenure survives at Yaxchilan and we may conclude that if he ever truly reigned at the city, he has been expunged from its record.

YOAAT B'ALAM II	
Glyphic spelling	SAK-? JUK'UB? YOA:T?[B'ALAM]-ma

Bird Jaguar IV
752–768

Bird Jaguar IV had a greater influence on the shape of his city than perhaps any other king of the Classic period. The dubious circumstances in which he rose to power inspired a prolific and historically rich output of at least 33 monuments and a dozen important structures. Lintel 17, British Museum.

BIRD JAGUAR IV	
Glyphic spelling ya-?-B'ALAM *Also known as* Bird Jaguar the Great, Bird Jaguar III, Yaxun Balam IV *Birth* 23 August 709 (9.13.17.12.10 8 Ok 13 Yax) *Accession* 29 April 752 (9.16.1.0.0 11 Ajaw 8 Sek) *Wives* Lady Great Skull, Lady Wak Tuun of Motul de San José, Lady Wak Jalam Chan Ajaw of Motul de San José, Lady	Mut B'alam of Hix Witz *Father* Itzamnaaj B'alam II *Mother* Lady Ik' Skull of Calakmul *Son* Itzamnaaj B'alam III *Monuments* Stelae 1, 3/33, 6, 9, 10, 11 & 35; Lintels 5, 6, 7, 8, 9, 16, 21, 27, 28, 29, 30, 31, 33, 38, 39, 40, 50? & 59; Temple 8 Tablet; Hieroglyphic Stairways 1, 3 & 4; Altars 1?, 3, 4 & 9

BIRD JAGUAR IV

Already 43 years of age when he came to power, Bird Jaguar IV was to prove one of the most energetic rulers of the entire Classic period, creating a profusion of public art and architecture during his 16-year reign. Throughout these efforts there runs a single, barely concealed agenda: the relentless promotion of his own legitimacy. More than any other Maya king, his every action betrays the heavy hand of the manipulator and propagandist.

The background to power

During the lifetime of Itzamnaaj B'alam, Bird Jaguar is unlikely to have been anything more than a junior claimant to the throne. He was born when his father was in his sixties, the son of a lesser queen, Lady Ik' Skull. It was not until 752 that Bird Jaguar was able to install himself as king (rather ostentatiously picking a 'round date' of 9.16.1.0.0 for the ceremony). He would now go to extraordinary lengths to justify his position, placing himself as Itzamnaaj B'alam's anointed successor and providing a history for the preceding 'interregnum' that placed him at the centre of affairs.[23]

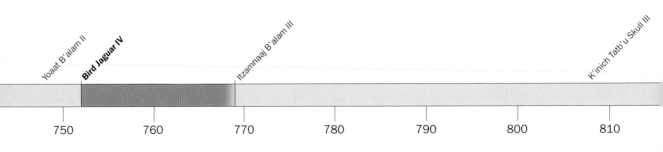

Yoaat B'alam II | **Bird Jaguar IV** | Itzamnaaj B'alam III | K'inich Tatb'u Skull III

750   760   770   780   790   800   810

Bird Jaguar IV here prepares for battle in the company of one of his wives, Lady Wak Jalam Chan Ajaw of the Motul de San José kingdom. His headdress includes a crest of the Teotihuacan Butterfly God (note the stylized proboscis). The battle, fought on 5 May 755, resulted in the capture of Jewelled Skull. Lintel 41, British Museum.

Two rituals were pivotal to Bird Jaguar's claim. Stela 11 (back) shows a dance ceremony conducted with his father in 741 – just a year before his death – in which they exchanged 'flap-staffs' (a kind of cloth banner). Five days later, Bird Jaguar, his mother Lady Ik' Skull and wife Lady Great Skull, drew blood and conducted visionary rites: conjuring double-headed serpents and centipedes which disgorged images of *k'awiil* (p. 179). His mother's bloodletting was documented, uniquely, on her own stela (Stela 35) with two scenes that replicate the sacrificial performance of Lady K'ab'al Xook some 30 years earlier. This was part of a broader effort by Bird Jaguar to raise the standing of his mother (who died in 751) from the obscurity she experienced in his father's time, and he went on to create other scenes showing her together with Itzamnaaj B'alam.

A new history for Yaxchilan

Bird Jaguar had a major hand in both of Yaxchilan's dynastic histories, resetting the lintels of the Early Classic king list into a new building and creating his own, much extended, version on the immense Hieroglyphic Stairway 1. This 480-glyph text places him at the conclusion of an uninterrupted narrative from the foundation of the dynasty. Yaxchilan's missing past was restored in other ways too. One early stela was repaired (p. 120), and at least two more and a sumptuous 'full-figure' hieroglyphic bench were produced as an entirely retrospective legacy for his grandfather Bird Jaguar III. In a similar vein, the author of the lintel king list, K'inich Tatb'u Skull II, received his own portrait on Lintel 50. Some of these activities included the obliteration of earlier texts. Stela 6, one of the tributes to his grandfather, is the remains of a monument whose front face had been entirely erased and re-carved, only a buried portion of

THE MYTH OF THE BALLGAME

When excavators cleared the front step of Temple 33 they uncovered a row of 13 carved blocks. The three finest, occupying the central axis, show Bird Jaguar IV, his father and grandfather playing with symbolic balls made, macabrely, from the bound bodies of their captives. Bird Jaguar's own panel is important because it contains the only surviving description of the myth of *ox ahal*, the 'Three Victories'. This story lay at the conceptual heart of the ballgame, giving its name to arenas and associated stairways as far apart as Tonina and Copan. It tells of the decapitation of three characters – probably Underworld gods – in the distant past. A form of the story survives in the 16th-century creation epic of the Quiche Maya, the Popol Vuh, where the Hero Twins compete with death gods in the ballcourt of the Underworld, the stage for the central struggle between life and death.[24]

Watched by two dwarves, Bird Jaguar prepares to receive a ball made from the body of a Lakamtuun lord. A panel with a miniature ballplaying scene (top left) shows the positioning of such panels at the top of staircases. Hieroglyphic Stairway 2, Step 7.

its base revealing its former self. The great hieroglyphic stairway was itself carved over an existing programme of figural and textual cartouches, whose outlines may once have been concealed with plaster.[25] One or both may be candidates for the works of the 'disappeared' king or kings of the 'interregnum'.

'He of 20 Captives'

Like many a Maya ruler, Bird Jaguar's mystique was closely bound to his image as an indomitable warrior. His favourite military titles, 'He of 20 Captives' and 'Master of Aj Uk', were seldom absent from his name phrase and much space was devoted to his various campaigns. Yet a modern understanding of these texts shows just how lowly most of these victims were. He made immense capital out of minor successes and Yaxchilan's reputation as a 'conquest state' only reflects how beguiling his efforts have proved.

Bird Jaguar's war records begin in 752, a few months before his accession, with the capture of a *sajal* from the otherwise unknown kingdom of Wak'ab'. In 755 he attacked the similarly obscure Sanab' Huk'ay and captured 'Jewelled Skull'. In this enterprise he was aided by K'an Tok Wayib', his *b'aah sajal* or leading noble, who shares three lintel scenes with the king. While joint portraits such as these were not an innovation, Bird Jaguar shared his monuments more widely than ever before and set them within the capital itself. It has been suggested that his rise to power relied on garnering support among the local nobility,

Bird Jaguar, wearing a 'cutaway' mask of the rain god *chaak*, presides over three unidentified prisoners. Stela 11, AD 752.

whose reward took the form of greater status and closer association with the king.[26] His last known capture took place in 759 and was assisted by another *sajal*, Tiloom, the ruler of La Pasadita. This conflict – given brief mention on Hieroglyphic Stairway 1 but a whole lintel at La Pasadita – is significant because the victim was a *k'inil ajaw* 'Sun Lord', the title closely associated with Piedras Negras.[27]

Bird Jaguar the builder

Bird Jaguar was responsible for a major architectural transformation of the site. The area of the Main Plaza, which had previously been riven by pronounced gullies dividing the core into distinct groups, was filled and levelled into a single broad expanse.[28] At least a dozen buildings were constructed or heavily modified during his reign. Some projects directly mirror the work of his father: his Temple 21 replicates the programme of Lady K'ab'al Xook's Temple 23, with closely matching scenes of bloodletting, visionary rites and militarism (though its quality does not bear comparison to the original). Only a few of Bird Jaguar's carvings show the deeply cut mastery of the sculptors in his father's employ and quantity generally triumphed over quality. Yet this should not distract us from the extraordinary vigour of these projects, which reflect Yaxchilan's considerable affluence at this time and freedom from foreign suzerainty.

BIRD JAGUAR'S QUEENS

Lady Mut B'alam of Hix Witz
[IX-MUT-tu B'ALAM]

Lady Wak Tuun of Motul de San José
[IX-6-TU:N-ni]

Lady Wak Jalam Chan Ajaw of Motul de San José
[IX-6 ja[la]-ma-CHAN-AJAW]

Lady Great Skull
[IX-CHAK-JOLO:M?-mi]

Direct references to marriage ceremonies and indeed to spouses in general – terms meaning 'his wife' or 'her husband' – are surprisingly rare in the inscriptions and it is usually only from parentage statements provided by the fruit of their unions that queens can be identified. Bird Jaguar is notable for the prominence he gives wives on his monuments, most likely because of the political ties they represented with neighbouring kingdoms. In a feature seen elsewhere in Mesoamerica, there is a recurring link between marriage and war, where brides are taken from defeated foes to cement a new relationship (see p. 77). Certainly Hix Witz, the home of one wife, was Yaxchilan's opponent in wars fought by Bird Jaguar's father and grandfather. Although these foreign wives enjoyed greater prestige during his reign, it was a local woman, Lady Great Skull who bore his son and successor Itzamnaaj B'alam III.

No doubt contemplating the unsavoury fate awaiting him, a *sajal* from the minor kingdom of Wak'ab bites his fingers in a gesture of submission and fear. Bird Jaguar made the capture in early AD 752, two months before his accession. Lintel 16, British Museum.

His final years

The last date associated with Bird Jaguar IV falls in June 768. The event, shown on Lintel 9, is significant, since it involves the king exchanging flap-staffs in a dance with his brother-in-law Great Skull, a previously unseen *sajal*. This mirrors Stela 11 and Bird Jaguar's claim to have received the sanction to rule from his father. Great Skull is described as the *yichaan ajaw* or 'uncle of the lord', a reference to Bird Jaguar's heir Chel Te' Chan K'inich.[29] Given the boy's youth, Great Skull could well have been bestowed with special powers to oversee his reign or act as regent.[30] Bird Jaguar died within a few months of the ceremony, just short of the 4 K'atun Ajaw status he would have reached in October 768.

Bird Jaguar's last monument shows him exchanging 'flap-staffs' with Great Skull. The ceremony may represent Great Skull's elevation to regent and guardian to the young heir Chel Te' Chan K'inich. Lintel 9, AD 768.

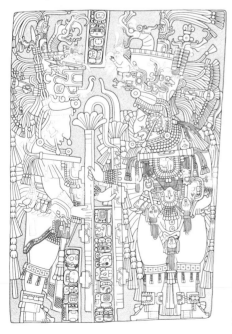

Temple 33, usually credited to Bird Jaguar, may well have been completed by his son as a tribute to his father. Each of its three lintels depicts Bird Jaguar engaged in a ritual dance. One shows Chel Te' Chan K'inich as a boy, but ascribed a series of royal titles, including a full emblem glyph; another provides the first depiction of Lady Great Skull, described as the 'mother of Itzamnaaj B'alam', the first use of his regnal name. Placed within the central chamber was a seated sculpture carved at over life-size. Now decapitated (its head still lies close by), it would seem to be a 'cult' statue that Bird Jaguar created for the veneration of his dead father (named by his headdress). A rich tomb found beneath Temple 33's forecourt remains unidentified.

Roofcomb

Façade sculpture
modelled in stucco

Full-figure
sculpture

Altar

Hieroglyphic
Stairway 2

Tomb
chamber

Altar

(*Above*) In this lintel from the central
doorway of Temple 33 we see the infant
Chel Te' Chan K'inich, the future
Itzamnaaj B'alam III, performing a
'bird-staff' dance with his father Bird
Jaguar IV in AD 757.

(*Top and left*) Temple 33, the
pinnacle of Yaxchilan's architectural
achievement, consists of a long three-
doored chamber, topped by a lofty crest
or 'roofcomb'. Like other major
buildings at the site it was originally
embellished with stucco ornament and
figures, now mostly lost. The colour-
scheme is speculative.

Itzamnaaj B'alam III

Shield Jaguar III

769–800>

K'inich Tatb'u Skull III

>808>

The last of Yaxchilan's major kings, Itzamnaaj B'alam III succeeded his father Bird Jaguar IV in AD 768 or 769. Lintel 58.

ITZAMNAAJ B'ALAM III	
Glyphic spelling ITZAMNA:J-B'ALAM che-le-TE' CHAN-K'INICH *Also known as* Shield Jaguar's Descendant, Shield Jaguar II, Shield Jaguar III *Birth* 14 February 752? (9.16.0.14.5 1 Chikchan? 13 Pop) *Wife* Lady Ch'ab Ajaw	*Father* Bird Jaguar IV *Mother* Lady Great Skull *Son* K'inich Tatb'u Skull III *Monuments* Stelae 5, 7, 20, 21, 22, 24 & 29; Lintels 1?, 2?, 3?, 12, 13, 14, 51, 52, 53, 54, 55?, 57 & 58; Hieroglyphic Stairway 5; Altar 10

ITZAMNAAJ B'ALAM III

Chel Te' Chan K'inich duly inherited the throne from his father, adopting the regnal name Itzamnaaj B'alam. Both appellatives were used throughout his reign, though he was often identified by a third, the captor's title 'Master of Torch Macaw'. His accession date has not survived, though he was in power by February 769, when he presided over a fire-making ritual at a provincial centre.

Itzamnaaj B'alam III's early reign saw the erection of monuments as fine as Stela 7, probably dating to 771, which is in the very best tradition of Yaxchilan's sculptural art. But over time there was a notable decline in standards and his output, though still considerable, does not compare with that of his prolific father. Major construction slowed too and he has only a handful of buildings to show for a reign twice the length of Bird Jaguar IV's.

Most of Itzamnaaj B'alam III's efforts were concentrated in extending the eastern edge of the ceremonial core, an area he linked with the central district with his main achievement, Temple 20. With its three carved lintels, four stelae (both original and reset) and a long hieroglyphic step, this is, to some extent, a remaking of his

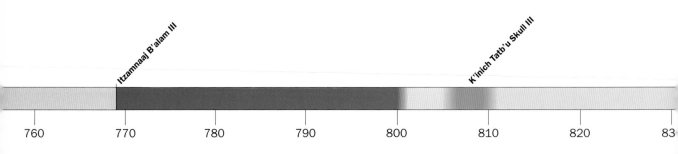

Itzamnaaj B'alam III

K'inich Tatb'u Skull III

760   770   780   790   800   810   820   83

grandfather's Temple 44. Its lintels focus on retrospective scenes surrounding the king's birth and the visionary rites of 741 that were so important to his father's claims to power. Historically, the most interesting document is the 182-glyph Hieroglyphic Stairway 5, a single step running almost the full length of the building's supporting platform. It supplies a lengthy sequence of captures up to the year 800, listing most, if not all, of the 15 prisoners he claims to have taken (he is posthumously ascribed a final total of 16). Indeed, much of his reign seems consumed by fighting. His victims include lords of Motul de San José, Lakamtuun, Namaan and Hix Witz. His leading supporter remained his uncle Great Skull, perhaps the regent of his early years, who was honoured by appearances on Lintels 14 and 58. His title *aj wuk b'aak* 'He of Seven Captives' suggests that he was a key military captain.

Yaxchilan's dependencies under Itzamnaaj B'alam III

Outside the city, Itzamnaaj B'alam III inherited his father's possessions, including the loyalty of Tiloom, the *sajal* of La Pasadita. The still unidentified Laxtunich has produced two fine panels: one shows the king together with a local *sajal* in 773, the second another lieutenant presenting him with three captives in 783. Yaxchilan's control of the Bonampak and Lacanha kingdoms was strong at this point, in a period that saw the distinction between these two fade with the emergence of a single paired emblem. A royal lady from Yaxchilan – probably the king's sister – was married to the Bonampak-Lacanha ruler Yajaw Chan Muwaan ('Lord of the Sky Hawk'), patron of its famous murals (p. 137).

This fine late work shows Itzamnaaj B'alam III inside a palace or pavilion (note the tied curtains above his head) and seated on a throne that bears his (reversed) name. He is receiving a group of three prisoners from one of his provincial lieutenants, Aj Chak Maax ('He of Great/Red Monkey'), who made the captures in 783. It comes from an unidentified site dubbed Laxtunich.

BONAMPAK: PAGEANT AND PATRONAGE

The site of Bonampak, 13 miles (21 km) from Yaxchilan, is home to the finest mural narrative to survive from Precolumbian America. Each of its three rooms is covered with vivid pageants of pomp and circumstance, framing a forest battle fought in the dying days of Classic civilization. The story begins with courtly scenes as three lords perform a dance to the accompaniment of musicians and a troupe of masked actors in fantastic costumes. Room 2 is dominated by a ferocious panorama of battle filling three walls, a dense melée of warriors, each bedecked in elaborate fighting finery. The remaining wall shows the presentation of captives. Miserable victims, tortured and bleeding, squat on a series of steps, while the victors pose above them. Room 3 returns to ceremonial, a twirling dance that fills the temple steps, and palace scenes where a group of royal ladies pierce their tongues, drawing sacrificial blood.

Itzamnaaj B'alam III was closely involved in the affairs of Bonampak and the central doorway of the mural building carries a lintel with his image. In the painted text within, the Yaxchilan king presides over the accession of a new Bonampak ruler. Traces of similar paintings at both Yaxchilan and La Pasadita show that they were once common in the region. The Bonampak murals themselves were never completed and were the last royal records at the site.[31]

(Above) Identified by his warrior title 'Master of Torch Macaw', this reference to Itzamnaaj B'alam III in the Bonampak murals concerns his 'overseeing' the accession of a local king.

(Top left) Though somewhat faded, this view of Room 1 still gives a good impression of the murals' original brilliance and power. (Top right) Trumpeters and masked actors (note the crayfish costume at right) perform a pageant in Room 1. (Left) This digitally restored scene of the Room 2 battle shows Yajaw Chan Muwaan seizing a victim by the hair.

His impressive series of monuments were carved, at least in part, by sculptors dispatched from Yaxchilan. In 787 the two kings campaigned against Sak Tz'i', and Bonampak Lintel 2 shows Itzamnaaj B'alam capturing a vassal of its ruler Yet K'inich. Itzamnaaj B'alam's supremacy is made plain when, in 790, he oversees the accession of a new Bonampak king.[32]

While he clearly lacked the momentum and resources of his father's time, Itzamnaaj B'alam III made strenuous efforts to maintain order and preserve Yaxchilan's political domain. It is to his credit that this was accomplished at a time when the mounting stresses of the Classic decline must already have been evident and the whole region was teetering on the edge of the abyss.

K'INICH TATB'U SKULL III

Shortly after 800 the reign of Itzamnaaj B'alam III gave way to that of his son, K'inich Tatb'u Skull III. His legacy is restricted to one rather crude lintel set within the small, single-doored Temple 3. Its style is so aberrant that early investigators thought it 'archaic' and one of the city's first monuments, instead of its very last. It describes the dedication of Temple 3, named as the *wayib'il* or 'sleeping house' of a list of patron deities, in 808. Throughout what is otherwise a war narrative, K'inich Tatb'u Skull III carries the warrior epithet 'Master of Turtleshell Macaw' and conducts the last recorded 'star war' and 'capture' events of the Classic period. The most interesting information comes from the final passage. Here the last king of Piedras Negras, Ruler 7, is named as the *b'aak* or 'captive' of K'inich Tatb'u Skull – evidence for one final, climactic clash between these age-old foes (p. 153).[33]

Yet such triumphs were hollow indeed, for this was the Classic order in its death-throes. Archaeological evidence suggests that large-scale occupation of Yaxchilan ceased soon after Temple 3's completion. Simple households appeared on the now redundant plazas, with broken monuments (such as Itzamnaaj B'alam III's Stela 24) incorporated into their rubble foundations. Some time after Yaxchilan's complete abandonment, the city became a place of pilgrimage for the Lacandon Maya, a remnant group formed from those driven into the forest by Spanish rule. The first modern visitors to the site were struck by the great number of simple Lacandon incense-burners or 'god pots' that crowded the floors of surviving buildings.

K'INICH TATB'U SKULL III	
Glyphic spelling	*Father*
[K'IN]chi-ni-ta-(ta)-	Itzamnaaj B'alam III
b'u-JOLO:M?	*Mother*
Also known as	Lady Ch'ab Ajaw
Mak'ina Tah Skull III	*Monument*
	Lintel 10

Cramped in style and poorly executed, Lintel 10 is the last of Yaxchilan's monuments and testimony to the declining standards of the Terminal Classic. It was commissioned by the city's last king, K'inich Tatb'u Skull III in AD 808.

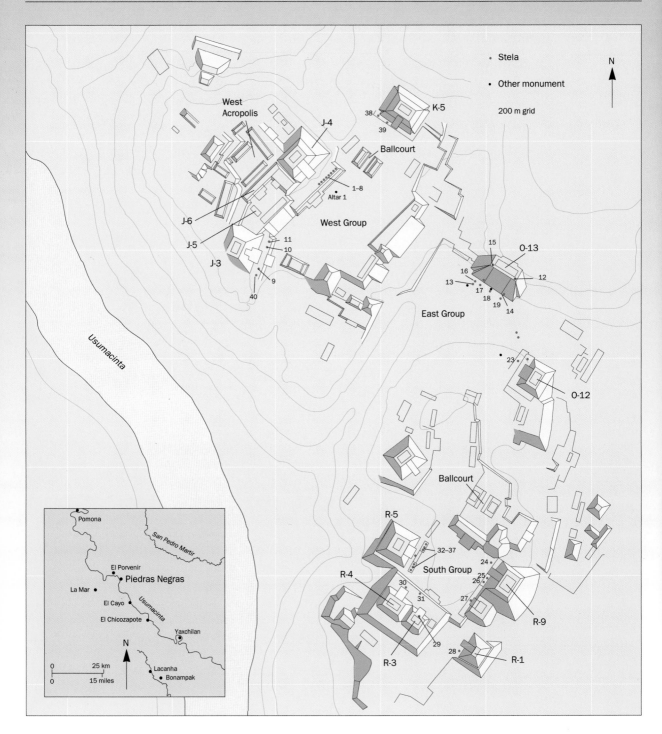

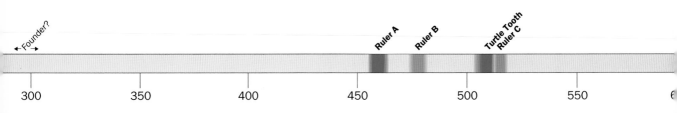

PIEDRAS NEGRAS

THE CITY OF PIEDRAS NEGRAS holds a special place in Maya studies. It was here that Tatiana Proskouriakoff succeeded in 'cracking' the historical content of the inscriptions, bringing Classic Maya kingship and politics into view for the first time. The largest of the sites along the Usumacinta, Piedras Negras fills a series of valleys set high above the river, some 25 miles (40 km) downstream from Yaxchilan. The ancient name of the city was Yokib', the 'entrance', inspired either by the steep canyons further downstream, or by the recently explored 100-m-wide sinkhole nearby, the kind of opening the Maya associated with portals into the Underworld.

In addition to a Late Classic stelae record of unusual continuity, Piedras Negras supplies important insights into the larger political community of the Classic Maya state. Its leading dependencies produced a series of fine monuments detailing relations between satellite and capital. Like all Maya kingdoms, Piedras Negras' wider authority waxed and waned, but at one time or another it counted a number of neighbouring kingdoms among its clients. Excavated by the University Museum, University of Pennsylvania, from 1931 to 1939, since 1997 the site has become the subject of a combined Guatemalan and American project led by Stephen Houston and Héctor Escobedo.

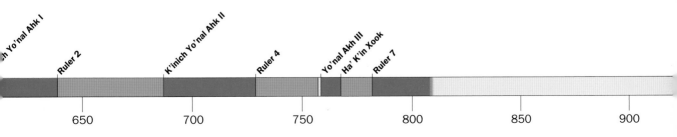

Ruler A
c. 460

 Ruler B
c. 478

Turtle Tooth
>510>

Ruler C
>514–518>

No monuments from the early period of Piedras Negras history have yet come to light, but the Late Classic Panel 2 seems to show a portrait of Turtle Tooth performing a ritual in AD 510.

RULER A	
Glyphic spelling ?[K'AN]-AHK ('? Precious/Yellow Turtle')	*Also known as* Turtleshell

RULER B	
Glyphic spelling ?[K'AN]-AHK ('? Precious/Yellow Turtle')	*Also known as* Turtleshell

TURTLE TOOTH	
Glyphic spelling ya-? a-ku ('Tooth? of the Turtle')	*Also known as* Ah Cauac Ah K'in

RULER C	
Accession 30 June 514? (9.3.19.12.12 9 Eb 10 Sek)	*Monument* Panel 12

EARLY PIEDRAS NEGRAS KINGS

Maya kingdoms were much concerned with establishing a mythic heritage that transcended normal time and space, and Piedras Negras was no exception. The Late Classic Altar 1 places the reign of its first king in the year 4691 BC – deep within the previous 'creation' – before linking another to the dawning of the current era in 3114 BC and a third to AD 297. Interestingly, this last date, the position 8.13.0.0.0, also appears in the texts of Pomona, Piedras Negras' downstream neighbour, and is close to the founding of dynastic rule at Yaxchilan. This may represent a more realistic starting-point for Classic-style government along the Usumacinta River, though Piedras Negras was still very small.

For clearer information about the city's early historical kings we must turn to Yaxchilan. Here the lintels of Structure 12 reveal unrelenting competition between the two polities, with a (one-sided) picture of Yaxchilan success. This might have begun as early as the 4th century when someone possessing a name with Piedras Negras connections was seized by the first Yaxchilan ruler. More certainly, a Piedras Negras king known as **Ruler A** fell victim to Moon Skull of Yaxchilan around 460. Ruler A's name, one of two that feature the word Ahk 'Turtle' and recur

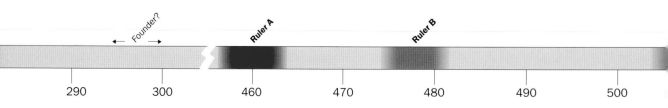

290   300   460   470   480   490   500

One of the most important royal names at Piedras Negras, recurring over many generations, was based on that of the aged earth deity known as God N. This Postclassic depiction shows him complete with his distinctive tied headdress and turtle carapace marked with the sign *k'an*, 'yellow/precious'. Dresden Codex p. 37.

Lintel 12 shows Ruler C in the company of four captives. The nearest of the three facing him is Knot-eye Jaguar I, king of Yaxchilan. Next kneels a lord of the Wa-Bird site, but the other two remain unidentified. Panel 12 was found broken and re-used in the masonry of the Late Classic temple O-13. *c.* AD 518.

throughout Piedras Negras history, is that of the aged earth deity, the turtleshell-clad God N. A later namesake **Ruler B** lost one of his sub-lords to Yaxchilan's Bird Jaguar II, most likely in 478. At some point before 508, another Piedras Negras lord, this time a vassal of the king **Turtle Tooth**, fell victim to Knot-eye Jaguar I (p. 120).[1]

Piedras Negras Panel 2, a much later monument, provides the only other details of Turtle Tooth's rule – his taking or receiving of a *ko'haw*, a plated helmet of Mexican design, in 510. In this he is overseen by a foreign king called Tajoom Uk'ab' Tuun, bearer of the prestigious title *ochk'in kaloomte'*. This term is associated with Mexican-derived legitimacy, especially that emanating from Teotihuacan, though, perhaps coincidentally, his personal name is similar to one used at Calakmul (p. 106). Turtle Tooth himself bears the *k'inil ajaw*, 'Sun Lord', epithet so closely associated with Piedras Negras that it virtually serves as a second emblem glyph.

Further evidence that Piedras Negras was subordinated to a greater power at this time comes from Panel 12, the earliest contemporary record at the site. Its landscape-format, multi-figure scene is one of a series at the city that share a thematic cord: dominion over its Usumacinta neighbours. Panel 12 marks the dedication of a temple honouring local deities in 518, though its narrative begins four years earlier, perhaps with the accession of a new king **Ruler C**. Three captured lords, each identified by a caption, face the monarch. One is the same Yaxchilan king, Knot-eye Jaguar I, who had enjoyed success against Turtle Tooth.[2] The 9.4.0.0.0 K'atun-ending of 514 is also recorded and, crucially, the appropriate 'scattering' ritual is performed by someone called simply the *yajaw* of the *ochk'in kaloomte'*, the vassal of a higher-ranking king.[3] This subordinate would need to be the Piedras Negras king himself, while his 'overking' is presumably the same *ochk'in kaloomte'* titled Tajoom Uk'ab' Tuun mentioned four years before.

Only two other Early Classic texts have been uncovered at the city, perhaps a sign of some 6th-century defeat and despoiling. Stela 30, placed in front of the R-4 pyramid of the South Group records the end of the 5th K'atun in 534, but only a tiny fragment of its patron's name survives. Stela 29, set on the summit of the adjacent R-3, carries the 9.5.5.0.0 mark just five years later and could be the work of this same ruler.

K'inich Yo'nal Ahk I
Ruler 1
603–639

Ruler 2
639–686

K'inich Yo'nal Ahk II
Ruler 3
687–729

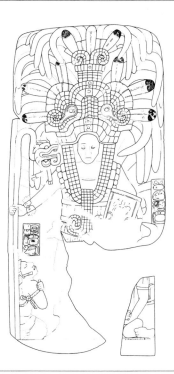

Enveloped by a huge headdress Karl Taube has identified as the Teotihuacan War Serpent, K'inich Yo'nal Ahk I poses with prisoners seized from Sak Tz'i' and Palenque. Stela 25, AD 628.

K'INICH YO'NAL AHK I	
Glyphic spelling	*Death*
K'INICH yo-o-NAL AHK	3 February 639
('Great-Sun ?-Turtle')	(9.10.6.2.1 5 Imix 19 K'ayab)
Also known as	*Wife*
Ruler 1	Lady Bird Headdress
Accession	*Son*
14 November 603	Ruler 2
(9.8.10.6.16 10 Kib 9 Mak)	*Monuments*
	Stelae 25, 26 & 31
	Burial
	R-5 pyramid?

K'INICH YO'NAL AHK I

The unusually complete sequence of Piedras Negras records begins with the accession of K'inich Yo'nal Ahk I in 603. The South Group continued as the ceremonial heart of the city, with a particular emphasis on the R-9 pyramid. The monuments that Yo'nal Ahk erected here proved especially influential and were emulated at the city for the next 150 years. His Stela 25 established an inaugural motif (the so-called 'niche' scene) showing the newly installed king seated high on a decorated scaffold or litter, elevated symbolically to the heavenly realm. A jaguar cushion atop a reed effigy caiman forms his throne, roofed by a canopy representing the sky and crowned by the great celestial bird, the avian aspect of the god Itzamnaaj. The seat itself was reached by a ladder, draped with a cloth marked by the king's bloody footprints, the contribution of a sacrificial victim slain at its base.[4]

Yo'nal Ahk's second motif was the 'warrior king', shown in frontal pose and garbed in a huge mosaic headdress of the Teotihuacan War Serpent.[5] Stela 26 (from 628) and Stela 31 (637) exemplify the form, the earlier stela charting wars Yo'nal Ahk fought against Palenque and Sak Tz'i' – capturing, respectively, an *aj k'uhuun* called Ch'ok B'alam

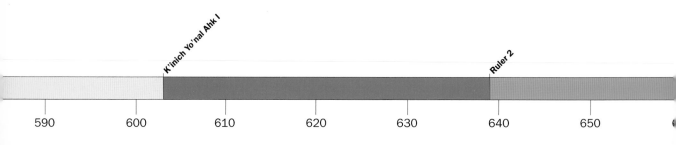

590   600   610   620   630   640   650

K'inich Yo'nal Ahk I

Ruler 2

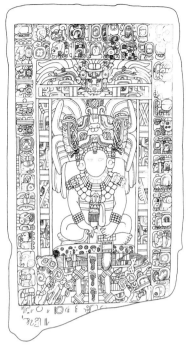

Stela 26, dated to 608, is the first monument at Piedras Negras to show the 'niche' accession motif. Here K'inich Yo'nal Ahk I is seated on an elevated throne reached by a lashed ladder marked with bloody footprints.

HISTORY REVEALED

Tatiana Proskouriakoff's revolutionary discovery of history in Maya inscriptions emerged from her meticulous observations of monuments and their chronological patterns. She noted that Piedras Negras stelae were arranged in groups and that the earliest in each usually showed a male figure seated in an elevated 'niche'. These scenes were associated with a particular hieroglyph – dubbed the 'toothache' sign – and a specific date. This was not the earliest date in each group, which was marked by another glyph – the 'up-ended frog' – which preceded the toothache event by anywhere between 12 and 31 years. The length of time covered in any one series of monuments did not exceed 64 years. She concluded that such groups reflect the lifetimes of individual rulers, with the up-ended frog denoting their birth or naming ceremony and the toothache their accessions. Modern phonetic readings confirm the hypothesis, translating the former as *siyaj*, 'born', and the latter *joyaj ti ajawlel*, 'bound into rulership'.

The up-ended frog (left) and the 'toothache' (right) glyphs.

('Young Jaguar') and an *ajaw* called K'ab' Chan Te' ('Hand Sky Tree').[6] Palenque was Piedras Negras' major rival for dominance over the lower reaches of the Usumacinta, while Sak Tz'i' was a lesser polity it seems to have controlled in later years (p. 146).

Yo'nal Ahk died in February 639, as recorded by his son and successor on Panel 4. This plaque details the dedication of his mortuary pyramid (or perhaps a tomb re-entry) in 658. Its placement inside the temple surmounting the R-5 pyramid should identify this as the memorial concerned.

RULER 2

Yo'nal Ahk I's 12-year-old son, known to us only as Ruler 2, succeeded him in April 639. His inaugural Stela 33 was the first of a series of at least six he erected at the base of the R-5 pyramid. His military adventures are recorded on the 'warrior'-style Stelae 35 and 37, detailing conquests in 662 and 669 – though only the first of these, against the lost Wa-Bird site, is now legible.

Easily the most interesting monument of this era is Panel 2. It commemorates the 1st K'atun-anniversary of Yo'nal Ahk I's death in 658 and Ruler 2's taking of a *ko'haw*, the Teotihuacanoid war helmet. The narrative then shifts back to the year 510 and the same action undertaken by Turtle Tooth in the presence of his foreign 'overseer'. The

RULER 2	
Glyphic spelling	*Wife*
? CHA:K ?-	Lady White Bird
[K'AN]AHK	*Father*
('? Rain God ?-	K'inich Yo'nal Ahk I
Precious?-Turtle')	*Mother*
Birth	Lady Bird
22 May 626	Headdress
(9.9.13.4.1	*Son*
6 Imix 19 Sotz')	K'inich Yo'nal Ahk II
Accession	*Monuments*
12 April 639	Stelae 33, 34, 35,
(9.10.6.5.9	36, 37, 38 & 39;
8 Muluk 2 Sip)	Panels 2, 4 & 7;
Death	Throne 2; Misc.
15 November 686	Stone 1?
(9.12.14.10.13	
11 Ben 11 K'ank'in)	

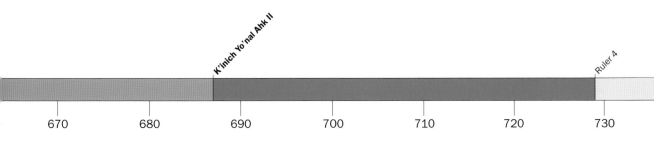

K'inich Yo'nal Ahk II

Ruler 4

| 670 | 680 | 690 | 700 | 710 | 720 | 730 |

Panel 2 shows a Piedras Negras king, probably the Early Classic Turtle Tooth, together with his heir receiving the submission of six fully armed youths, identified by their captions as lords from Lacanha, Bonampak and Yaxchilan. AD 667.

Ruler 2 was 36 years old when he triumphed over the Wa-Bird site in AD 662, recorded here on Stela 35. The now broken lower portion shows a resulting captive, possibly a high-ranking girl.

accompanying scene shows a ruler, together with his heir, Joy Chitam Ahk ('Tied Peccary Turtle'), receiving the submission of six kneeling youths of the *ajaw* rank, one each from Yaxchilan and Bonampak and four from Lacanha. But is the scene – and with it Piedras Negras' claim to dominion over the upper Usumacinta – from the early or contemporary era? The way that the feathers of the king's headdress reach up to touch Turtle Tooth's name phrase is probably significant and favours the earlier option. Nonetheless, a powerful analogy between the two periods may be the intention here. During the reign of Ruler 2 Yaxchilan is silent, with some suspicion that it languished under Piedras Negras control (see p. 123).

Ruler 2's later reign

There was now a switch in emphasis from the southern to the northern portion of the site, with the development of the K-5 pyramid and the setting of two stelae at its base. Panel 7 was found in debris at its summit and dates the work to 677 or thereabouts. It is a great pity that the stone is so badly smashed, since it once described relations with Hix Witz ('Jaguar Hill'), whose lords are shown delivering tribute, and mentions one or more brides from this polity.[7]

A panel from some unknown subsidiary provides a revealing episode from 685. It describes an 'adorning' with a *nuk* 'pelt' and a *ko'haw* 'helmet' belonging to Ruler 2. This was supervised by a lord carrying the title *aj b'aak* 'He of Captives', said to be in the service of the Calakmul ruler Yuknoom the Great.[8] This begs comparison with the aforementioned events in Turtle Tooth's reign and the foreign lord similarly involved there. This scrap of evidence, though still poorly understood, is enough to suggest that Piedras Negras was another kingdom embroiled in Calakmul's wide-ranging web of diplomacy and power politics.

(*Right*) Seen here as reconstructed in one of Tatiana Proskouriakoff's own watercolours of the city, K-5 was built or greatly expanded by Ruler 2 around 677. Stelae 38 and 39 can be seen at its base, a possible position for Panel 7 on its upper platform.

(*Below*) This delicate jadeite portrait of Yo'nal Ahk II was dredged from the bottom of Chichen Itza's great *cenote* or sacrificial well, 300 miles (483 km) to the north. Its text celebrates his 13th year in power in 699 and counts forward to his first K'atun-jubilee, still seven years in the future. His jaguar headdress makes for a play on his pre-inaugural name: the jaguar with a man in its mouth.

As the end of Ruler 2's life drew near, and probably in very poor health, he set a train of events in motion to ensure a proper succession. In November 686, he supervised some pre-nuptial rite for a 12-year-old princess called Lady K'atun Ajaw ('20-year Queen'), who was to be a bride for his son 'Jaguar Man'. The 61-year-old king died just two days later, probably during the night of 15/16 November.[9]

K'INICH YO'NAL AHK II

Just five days after the death of Ruler 2, and while preparations for his funeral were in progress, an 'adorning' event marks the union of his son Jaguar Man to Lady K'atun Ajaw, a princess of the little-known site of Namaan. If not exactly a 'skeleton at the feast', the unburied corpse of the king – perhaps in the form of a mummy bundle – could well have been its guest of honour. The interment of Ruler 2 took place four days later and the formal elevation of his son, now assuming the regnal name of his grandfather K'inich Yo'nal Ahk, followed within a few weeks in 687. His marriage is the most celebrated of any in Maya history, but its significance is not immediately clear. Lady K'atun Ajaw quickly rose to exalted status, sharing three monuments with her husband (her image adorning whole faces of Stelae 1, 2 and 3). We can well imagine that she was a forceful personality in her own right and that her prominence, like that of her contemporary Lady Six Sky of Naranjo, reflects some tangible political power.

The reign of Yo'nal Ahk II

Yo'nal Ahk completed the decisive shift away from the South Group begun by his father, with all future developments of note concentrated in the northwest of the city. All eight of his stelae were set in an orderly row

K'INICH YO'NAL AHK II	
Glyphic spelling ?-ji K'INICH-yo- o[AHK]-NAL ('Great-Sun Jaguar Man ?-Turtle') *Also known as* Ruler 3 *Birth* 29 December 664 (9.11.12.7.2 2 Ik' 10 Pax) *Accession* 2 January 687 (9.12.14.13.1 7 Imix 19 Pax)	*Wife* Lady K'atun Ajaw of Namaan *Father* Ruler 2 *Mother* Lady White Bird *Daughter* Lady Huntan Ahk *Monuments* Stelae 1, 2, 3, 4, 5, 6, 7, 8; Altar 1 *Burial* J-5 pyramid courtyard (Burial 5)

WHITE DOG

While the forests are peppered with ruined sites whose identities are unknown to us, the inscriptions present just the opposite problem: the names of many places whose locations are now lost. Somewhere in the Lacandon region lies Sak Tz'i' ('White Dog'), a polity mentioned by a number of other kingdoms. It was defeated by Piedras Negras in 628 and, to judge from its later involvement at El Cayo, was later closely integrated into the Piedras Negras realm (p. 151). It exerted a degree of overlordship in the Bonampak-Lacanha area around 726, but suffered defeats at the hands of combined forces from Yaxchilan and Bonampak in 787 (p. 137). At about this time it was overrun by Tonina and its ruler captured (pp. 188–9). Looted monuments record victories of its own against Bonampak and perhaps even Piedras Negras, though none can be dated with accuracy. Sak Tz'i' survived the collapse of all of its near neighbours and its last known mention – carved by a subject *sajal* – came in 864.

SAK-TZ'I'-AJAW   SAK-tz'i-i

(*Above right*) The expansive West Acropolis was home to Piedras Negras' royal court during the Late Classic. To the right can be seen Structure J-4 and the line of stelae erected by Yo'nal Ahk II.

beneath Structure J-4 of the expanding royal palace of the West Acropolis. They mark quarter-K'atun (five-year) intervals between 687 (9.12.15.0.0) and 726 (9.14.15.0.0), with the one exception of the 9.13.0.0.0 ending of 692, commemorated by Altar 1 in the plaza below.

In 706, Yo'nal Ahk conducted a *puluy utz'itil* rite, a kind of burning event, on the K'atun-anniversary of Ruler 2's burial. The precise nature of this ceremony, peculiar to Piedras Negras, is unknown.

Although Yo'nal Ahk's reign was lengthy, 42 years, it seems to have been a time of weakness and shrinking political control. By the turn of the 8th century, Palenque had expanded its sphere of influence to encompass a number of important sites on the Usumacinta, including, it seems, La Mar, just 10 miles (16 km) to the southwest of Piedras Negras (p. 170). The same region was later raided by Tonina (pp. 181–2). Interestingly, in 723 Yo'nal Ahk performs some event under the aegis of a foreign lord, but damage prevents us knowing more. Late in his reign he lost a *sajal* in an engagement with the Palenque captain Chak Suutz' (p. 172), perhaps part of the campaign in which the site of K'ina' ('Sun Water') was sacked in May 725.[10] A year later Yo'nal Ahk could claim some success against the newly resurgent Yaxchilan, with Stela 8 describing the seizure of a *sajal* in the service of Itzamnaaj B'alam II in 726.[11]

The succession

If Lady K'atun Ajaw's prominence is unusual, that bestowed on her daughter, Lady Huntan Ahk ('Cherished Turtle'), is unprecedented. Her birth in 708 is recorded on Stela 3, where she is shown as a diminutive three-year-old leaning on her mother's knee. Here, sculptors freed from

One of the largest monuments from Piedras Negras, Stela 8, shows Yo'nal Ahk II in full warrior garb presenting two bound captives. A minutely incised caption (detail) names the right-hand victim as a *sajal* of Yaxchilan's Itzamnaaj B'alam II. AD 726.

IX-?-AJAW
Lady K'atun Ajaw

IX-1-TAN-na-a-ku
Lady Huntan Ahk

(*Right*) A three-year-old Lady Huntan Ahk leans on the knee of her mother Lady K'atun Ajaw. Stela 3, AD 711.

the fixed postures of quasi-divine kings produced a rare trace of informality, the kind of naturalistic pose normally only encountered in figurines or on painted vessels. Did this mark the emergence of an assertive matriline under the influential queen, or had Yo'nal Ahk, by now 47 years old, simply despaired of producing a male heir? With the prospect of the succession passing through marriage to the female line there may have been a desire to secure her position with this singular honour. We have no evidence that Yo'nal Ahk II ever sired a son and the parentage of his successor is suitably murky. Although Ruler 4 wears a turtle-headdressed belt ornament on one occasion, suggesting an Ahk 'Turtle' name for his father, of the three references to his birth in 701 none goes on to provide his pedigree.

The last date of Yo'nal Ahk's reign falls in June 729, the occasion of what seems to be a further marriage, perhaps to a woman from Palenque. His death must have taken place shortly thereafter, since Ruler 4 was in place by November the same year. There is every reason to believe that Yo'nal Ahk II was laid to rest in Burial 5, an important tomb uncovered within the West Acropolis (*below*).

BURIAL 5

A depression in the courtyard facing Structure J-5, high in the West Acropolis, alerted archaeologists to the presence of a collapsed chamber beneath. Excavation revealed a vaulted tomb, Burial 5, the richest yet found at the city. It contained the body of a mature male accompanied by two juveniles. The lord's skull had been deliberately flattened during childhood (to produce the sloping forehead associated with the Maize God), but a better sign of his high status are the inlays of jade and pyrites drilled into 15 of his front teeth. Among the grave goods was a large quantity of jade, including finely worked bead necklaces and a figurine placed in his mouth. A hematite mirror – with 85 of its mosaic platelets still in place – was found set at an angle, positioned to reflect the king's image in death as it did in life. Among a haul of 213 cut and drilled shell plaques (once sewn onto some apparel) were four that shared a single text repeating the story of Lady K'atun Ajaw's betrothal and marriage to Yo'nal Ahk II. The king is named on each of four stingray-spine bloodletters in the tomb, and there is little reason to doubt, despite its unprepossessing location, that this is the tomb of the king himself.[12]

Ruler 4
729–757

Yo'nal Ahk III
Ruler 5
758–767

Ha' K'in Xook
767–781

Ruler 7
781–808?

Pictured at his accession in 729, Ruler 4 is enthroned and framed by a 'sky-band' of celestial emblems. Stela 11, AD 731.

RULER 4	
Glyphic spelling	*Death*
?-na-a-ku ?-HA'?	26 November 757
?[K'AN]AHK	(9.16.6.11.17
Birth	7 Kaban 0 Pax)
18 November 701	*Sons*
(9.13.9.14.15	Ha' K'in Xook?,
7 Men 18 K'ank'in)	Rabbit Hand?
Accession	*Monuments*
9 November 729	Stelae 9, 10, 11,
(9.14.18.3.13	22 & 40; Altar 2
7 Ben 16 K'ank'in)	*Burial*
	Courtyard of O-13
	(Burial 13)?

RULER 4

A 27-year-old Ruler 4 acceded to the Piedras Negras throne in November 729. Following local precedent he erected a stela every quarter-K'atun, with all but one arranged on a platform beneath West Acropolis' J-3 pyramid. A taste for innovation is evident on Stela 10, from 741, which shows the king seated on a giant jaguar litter (a theme best seen at Tikal, see p. 45). The lofty Stela 40 of 746 is even more unusual. It shows Ruler 4 scattering blood or incense into a 'psychoduct', a vent leading into a sub-plaza tomb (channels such as this have been found archaeologically at several sites). On a conceptual level, the connection between the living and the dead is manifested as a 'knotted cord' of breath which travels down to enter the nose of the deceased, whose crypt is shaped in the form of the quatrefoil cave. The body is dressed in Teotihuacano garb and seems to be described in the text as his mother. If Ruler 4 was not descended from Yo'nal Ahk II, such matrilineal connections may have had special importance for him. The date of this ceremony was exactly 83 Tzolk'in (about 59 years) after the death of Ruler 2, and here Ruler 4 seems to be making a special link with this prestigious precursor and partial namesake.

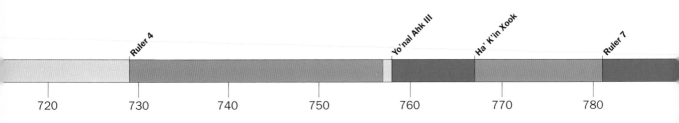

(*Left*) In this unusual scene Ruler 4 communes with a female ancestor, probably his mother, by scattering incense into her tomb. Note how the vault of the tomb doubles as the scalloped motif, in its full form the quatrefoil cave at the heart of the earth. Stela 40, AD 746.

(*Above*) Excavated from the fallen debris of O-13's upper sanctuary, Panel 3 has long been hailed as a masterpiece of Maya art. The scene is a retrospective narration of Ruler 4's 1st K'atun-anniversary of reign in 749, although it was created during the reign of Ruler 7, as late as AD 795.

The jubilee feast

One of the greatest celebrations of Ruler 4's reign was that marking his K'atun-jubilee in 749. This is described on the magnificent Panel 3, considered by many to be the finest composition in Maya art. As to its meaning, however, there is no real consensus, and even simple questions of where and when the pictured scene takes place are still debated. Like a scene 'rolled out' from a painted vessel, Panel 3 shows a palace chamber, the king presiding from a huge throne, flanked by an array of local nobles and honoured visitors. The former include the ranks of his *sajalob'*, some of whom are known from other texts (his *b'aah sajal* K'an Mo' Te' also served Yo'nal Ahk II). Of the guests, the most prestigious are a party from Yaxchilan. Although the caption naming the leading figure is mostly effaced, the main text tells us that the 'interregnum' ruler Yoaat B'alam II attended the jubilee. Ruler 4 addresses them with what seems to be a history lecture setting out their past subordination to Piedras Negras – though the dating remains problematic (see p. 127). The real festivities began two days later when Ruler 4 performed a 'descending macaw' dance, followed by a night-time feast in which fermented *kakaw* or cocoa beans – a highly prized beverage flavoured in various ways – was drunk.

SATELLITES OF PIEDRAS NEGRAS

Around each Maya city lay a series of subject towns, often ruled by lords holding the office of *sajal*. The outlying dependencies of Piedras Negras were unusually rich in sculpted panels detailing relations between province and central court. These ties are at their clearest when a king installs a local lord in office or when one of these potentates describes himself as 'owned' by the king – repeating, on a smaller scale, the relationships seen between greater and lesser kingdoms (p. 19). Most of the monuments concerned are memorial plaques that serve to dedicate tombs or mortuary shrines. Anciently known as Yax Niil, El Cayo is the best known of these satellites. In 1993 Peter Mathews and Mario Aliphat discovered a superb stone altar here in a near-perfect state of preservation.

Dated to 731 it depicts the 67-year-old *sajal* Aj Chak Wayib' K'utiim sitting cross-legged and scattering grains of incense onto an altar table facing an incense-burner filled with offerings.[13]

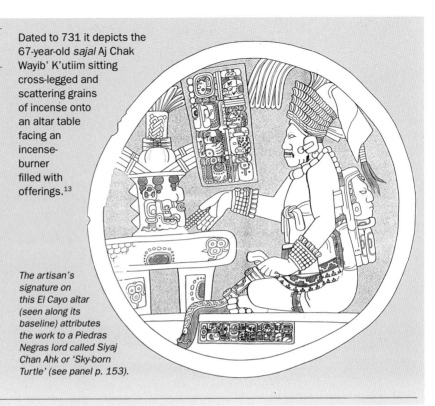

The artisan's signature on this El Cayo altar (seen along its baseline) attributes the work to a Piedras Negras lord called Siyaj Chan Ahk or 'Sky-born Turtle' (see panel p. 153).

The burial of Ruler 4

Panel 3, which was actually created in the reign of Ruler 7, goes on to describe the death of Ruler 4 on 26 November 757 and his burial three days later. This took place at the 'mountain' of *ho janaab' witz* – normally a mythological locale but here the name of his memorial temple.[14] Given the position of Panel 3 within the sanctuary of the O-13 pyramid, the most impressive at the city, this is surely the one described. The building became a special focus of dynastic commemoration from this point on, further reason to think that Ruler 4 introduced a new male line. Explorations beneath the plaza floor at the foot of O-13's frontal stair conducted by Héctor Escobedo led to the discovery of Burial 13 in 1997. Within were the remains of 3 individuals, an adult male and two adolescents, mirroring the provision of Burial 5 (p. 147). Among grave goods found scattered about its floor were over a 100 pieces of worked jade, once fine collar ornaments. One of the objects to carry text was a small pyrite disc showing the decapitated head of a Hix Witz lord. The tomb itself showed clear evidence of ancient disturbance. Many bones were missing and the remainder had been smoke-blackened and burnt long after decomposition had cleaned them of flesh. This ritual destruction seems to be described in the final passage of Panel 3, where Ruler 7 performs an *el naah umukil* 'house-burning at the burial' of Ruler 4 in 782.[15]

This small pyrite disc was found in Burial 13 directly in front of the O-13 pyramid, apparently the grave of Ruler 4. It depicts the severed head of a lord from the site of Hix Witz.

YO'NAL AHK III	
Glyphic spelling	*Accession*
IK'-NA:H-CHAK-? yo-	10 March 758
o[AHK]-NAL	(9.16.6.17.1
('Black House	7 Imix 19 Wo)
Red/Great	*Monuments*
?-Turtle')	Stelae 14 & 16

HA' K'IN XOOK	
Glyphic spelling	*Death*
HA'-K'IN-XO:K?-ki	24 March 780
('Water Sun	(9.17.9.5.11
Shark?')	10 Chuwen 19 Sip)?
Accession	*Father*
14 February 767	Ruler 4?
(9.16.16.0.4	*Monuments*
7 K'an 17 Pop)	Stelae 13, 18 & 23;
	El Porvenir Fragment

(*Below*) The finest of the 'niche' monuments is Stela 14, marking the accession of Yo'nal Ahk III. It was probably erected in AD 761. (*Below right*) Stela 13 shows Ha' K'in Xook scattering incense on 9.17.0.0.0, AD 771.

YO'NAL AHK III AND HA' K'IN XOOK

Relatively little is known of the next two Piedras Negras kings, though both were closely linked to Ruler 4. Undoubtedly the finest of the 'niche' scenes, Stela 14 signals the beginning of **Yo'nal Ahk III's** eight-year tenure in 758. Both this and his other monument, Stela 16, were set at the foot of the O-13 pyramid. Stela 16, erected in 766, is especially interesting since it records an accession ceremony in 763. Originally taken for the accession of a new Piedras Negras king (Ruler 6) this was, in fact, a subordinate *sajal* from Rabbit Stone, the nearby site of La Mar.[16] This unique honour shows just how important La Mar had become to the Piedras Negras dynasty, and one might even wonder whether Ruler 4 had some special connection with it. Another satellite, Yax Niil, known today as El Cayo, describes Yo'nal Ahk's involvement in ceremonies surrounding the burial of its ruling *sajal*, also in 763. Significantly, he did not install the *sajal*'s successor, a task performed two months later by Aj Sak Maax ('He of White Monkey'), the ruler of Sak Tz'i'. A similar sequence was repeated in later years, suggesting a formalized hierarchy of sites within the Piedras Negras hegemony at this time.[17] Piedras Negras' stormy relations with Yaxchilan resurfaced in the summer of 759, when a lord bearing the distinctive *k'inil ajaw* title fell captive to Yaxchilan forces under the bellicose Bird Jaguar IV.

Although the original Ruler 6 has been demoted to a mere *sajal*, there was a reign that filled this position in the sequence. Though its front is largely obliterated today, Stela 23 seems to have been another niche scene and its text records the accession of **Ha' K'in Xook** ('Water Sun Shark') in 767. His Stelae 13 (771) and 18 (775) were, once again, oriented to the O-13 pyramid and he seems to have been a son of Ruler 4 and brother of Yo'nal Ahk. The only real incident we have from Ha' K'in Xook's reign took place at El Cayo in 772, probably connected to the burial of another *sajal* there. The end of his life is described by the incoming Ruler 7 on the splendid Throne 1. The phrase *yaktaaj ajawlel* 'he abandoned/transferred rulership' marks the final handover of earthly power, placing his death or interment in March 780 (see p. 222). Subsequent rites performed by Ruler 7 may involve the installation of Ha' K'in Xook's bundled corpse and later some effigy at his mortuary shrine.

RULER 7	
Glyphic spelling AJ-1-?-na-ku K'INICH-ya-[?]AHK ('Great-Sun Tooth? of the Turtle-?') *Also known as* Ruler 6 *Birth* 7 April 750 (9.15.18.16.7 12 Manik' 5 Sotz')	*Accession* 31 May 781 (9.17.10.9.4 1 K'an 7 Yaxk'in) *Mother* Lady Bird *Monuments* Stelae 12 & 15; Altar 4; Throne 1; Panels 1? & 3

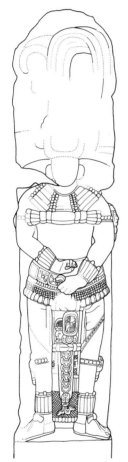

(*Above*) Stela 15 reflects the same bold three-dimensionality used in Panel 3. At this late stage in Piedras Negras history there is no hint of decadence or stagnation, indeed its continued innovation indicates quite the reverse.

(*Right*) The finest monumental seat known from the Classic period, Throne 1 is adorned with glyphic texts on its back, seat and both the front and sides of its legs. It was found, by University of Pennsylvania archaeologists, deliberately broken and scattered around the palace chamber of Structure J-6.

RULER 7

The next king at Piedras Negras, Ruler 7, was a namesake of the Early Classic Turtle Tooth, and took office in 781. His reign contrasts artistic triumph, presiding over the finest flowering of sculpture at the city, with military catastrophe, ending his life in defeat and captivity. The name of his father is now lost, but he shares the preoccupation with Ruler 4 shown by his two predecessors, and he was surely his descendant. His greatest tribute to Ruler 4 was the masterful Panel 3, set into a wall of O-13 to record the fire ritual at his tomb in 782 (performed a year to the day after the burial of Ha' K'in Xook) (p. 150). O-13 retained its pivotal role for the dynasty and both of Ruler 7's stelae were set high on its supporting platform. The first of these, Stela 15 from 785, marks an innovative move to nearly fully-rounded sculpture. Among his construction efforts were important additions to the West Acropolis, including the palace gallery J-6, in which Throne 1 was dedicated the same year. Built into a purpose-built niche, its legs and seat carry an elegantly carved text, while its back takes the form of a mask with busts of two figures, apparently the king's parents, set into its eyes like pupils.

The Pomona wars

Like several other kings on the eve of the collapse, Ruler 7 provides detailed descriptions of his military campaigns. These begin in August 787 with the capture of a sub-lord from the Wa-Bird site carrying the title *yajaw k'ak'* 'Lord of Fire'. The action moves to March 792 with a 'star war' attack on its western neighbour Pomona and a list of the resulting captives. This blow was less than decisive, however, and much the same events were repeated two years later (enumerated as the 'second star war'). Again a succession of prisoners were taken and it is a parade of these unfortunates that appears on the face of Stela 12, erected in 795.

(*Below*) Stela 12 celebrates Ruler 7's two triumphs over Pomona in 792 and 794, which he achieved in collaboration with his vassals from neighbouring La Mar.

(*Below right*) We learn of Ruler 7's ultimate fate in this short passage from Yaxchilan Lintel 10, where he is described as a captive of K'inich Tatb'u Skull III.

Stripped and bound, they cower beneath the imperious king and two of his lieutenants. Of these, the leading aide is Parrot Chaak, the ruler of Rabbit Stone/La Mar. Stelae at La Mar describe his elevation to lordship in 783 and record his own account of the Pomona triumph, including his seizure of two of the Stela 12 victims. Importantly, this text includes the name, now lost at Piedras Negras, of the defeated Pomona king 'Kuch' B'alam.[19] The importance of Parrot Chaak to Ruler 7 is emphasized by a mention on Throne 1 and another on Panel 3, where he is pictured as a child at the court of Ruler 4.

Defeat and capture

In the four-century-long rivalry between Piedras Negras and Yaxchilan, it was the latter who enjoyed the last word. A short passage on Yaxchilan's final monument, recently noted by David Stuart, describes Ruler 7 as the *b'aak* or 'captive' of its last king K'inich Tatb'u Skull III. This decisive clash apparently took place in 808.[20] The political message of Panel 3 seems a little clearer in light of this. Contemporary confrontations go unreported, but it harks back to a time when Yaxchilan paid proper respect to Piedras Negras. Ruler 4's puzzling speech may even seek to establish certain 'facts' distorted in Bird Jaguar IV's subsequent recreation of his city's history (p. 128).

The Piedras Negras dynasty seems to have survived the loss of Ruler 7, at least until 810 when the now much eroded Altar 3 may have been dedicated. Nonetheless, the end appears to have come violently. Recent excavations have detected burning in several locations, while Throne 1 was found willfully smashed and strewn about the chamber of the palace gallery J-6. This 1930s find did much to fuel the idea of a 'peasant's revolt' for the Classic collapse, though today we look to military attack as the normal cause of such desecration.

The collapse of kingly rule seems to have caused a rapid abandonment. This said, the Usumacinta remained a major trade route for at least a century and scatterings of the usual late ceramic styles reflect some sparse occupation throughout the Terminal Classic and Early Postclassic eras.

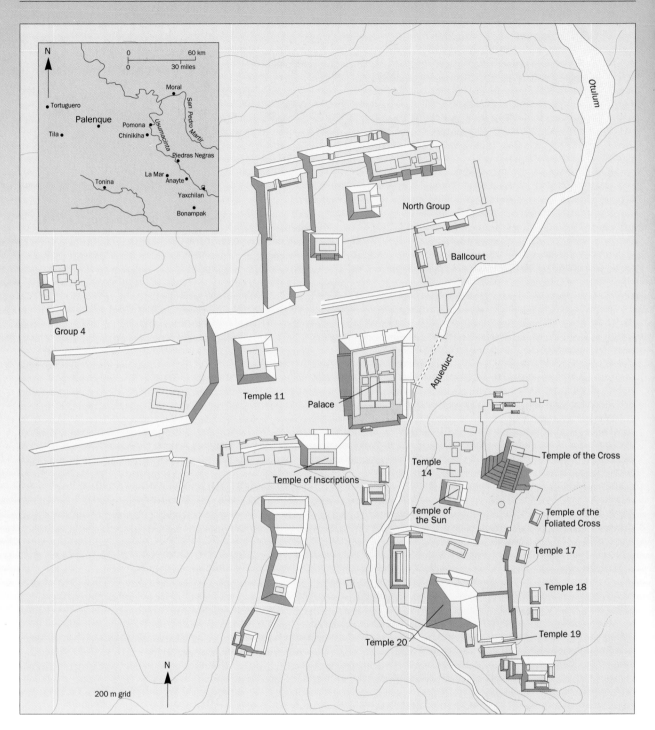

Palenque

Tortuguero
Moral
Tila
Pomona
Chinikiha
Usumacinta
San Pedro Martir
Piedras Negras
La Mar
Anayte
Tonina
Yaxchilan
Bonampak

0   60 km
0   30 miles

N

Otulum

North Group

Ballcourt

Group 4

Temple 11

Palace

Aqueduct

Temple of Inscriptions

Temple 14

Temple of
the Sun

Temple of the Cross

Temple of the
Foliated Cross

Temple 17

Temple 18

Temple 20

Temple 19

N

200 m grid

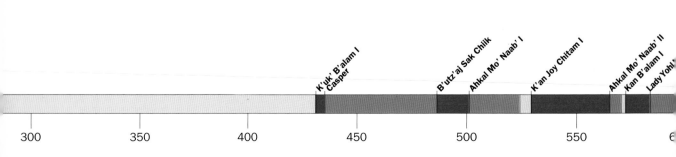

K'uk' B'alam I
Casper

B'utz'aj Sak Chiik

Ahkal Mo' Naab' I

K'an Joy Chitam I

Ahkal Mo' Naab' II
Kan B'alam I
Lady Yohl

300   350   400   450   500   550   6

PALENQUE

L YING AT THE NORTHERN EDGE OF THE CHIAPAS HIGHLANDS, Palenque straddles a limestone shelf overlooking the great plain stretching north to the Usumacinta River and beyond. It is famed for the sophistication of its sculptural style, the harmonious proportions of its architecture and, most of all, for the stupendous tomb of its 7th-century king K'inich Janaab' Pakal – a true wonder of ancient America. One of its peculiarities is the near absence of the monolithic stelae so popular elsewhere. Instead, comparable efforts were put into architectural sculpture, whether carved in its fine-grained limestone or modelled in stucco plaster. The blanched stonework seen today was once covered in extravagant figural and floral motifs, vibrantly painted in red, producing an almost baroque magnificence.

The history of the Palenque kingdom – anciently called B'aakal or 'Bone' – was as strife-torn as any of its contemporaries. Indeed, its greatest artworks and longest texts emerged as reactions to the defeat and breakdown of its royal line, as new dynasts strove to legitimize and consolidate their power. It had contacts with all the great Classic kingdoms, sharing co-operative relations with Tikal, but antagonistic ones with Calakmul, Tonina and Piedras Negras.

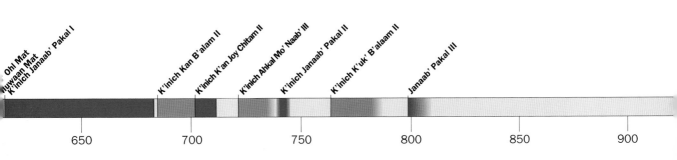

Ohl Mat
Muwaan Mat
K'inich Janaab' Pakal I
K'inich Kan B'alam II
K'inich K'an Joy Chitam II
K'inich Ahkal Mo' Naab' III
K'inich Janaab' Pakal II
K'inich K'uk' B'alaam II
Janaab' Pakal III

650   700   750   800   850   900

K'uk' B'alam I
431–435

Casper
435–487

B'utz'aj Sak Chiik
487–501

Ahkal Mo' Naab' I
501–524

K'UK' B'ALAM I	
Glyphic spelling	*Birth*
K'UK'[B'ALAM]	30 March 397
('Quetzal Jaguar')	(8.18.0.13.6
Also known as	5 Kimi 14 K'ayab)
Kuk, Bahlum K'uk'	*Accession*
	10 March 431
	(8.19.15.3.4
	1 K'an 2 K'ayab)

CASPER	
Glyphic spelling	*Accession*
ch'a-?	9 August 435
Birth	(8.19.19.11.17
8 August 422	2 Kaban 10 Xul)
(8.19.6.8.8	
11 Lamat 6 Xul)	

K'UK' B'ALAM I TO AHKAL MO' NAAB' I

Our knowledge of Palenque's early dynasty comes from a collection of retrospective texts produced at the end of the 7th century. They combine to trace its royal line through a list of historical kings and back to their mythical precursors. An archaeological understanding of Palenque's early development is, by contrast, extremely meagre. Important areas of the ruins are as yet untouched by excavation and several of its larger Late Classic structures conceal earlier phases.

The first ruler to occupy normal historical time and thus the founder of Palenque's Classic dynasty was **K'uk' B'alam I** ('Quetzal Jaguar'). Combining the two great emblems of Maya royalty, his name glyph consists of the head of the quetzal bird fixed with a jaguar's ear. He is consistently given the title 'Toktan Lord', a reference to an unknown location, presumably the original home of the dynasty. His reign began in 431, though it lasted a mere four years. This dates Palenque's genesis to the rule of Siyaj Chan K'awiil II at Tikal and Teotihuacan's greatest influence in the Peten. In fact, the name of Siyaj K'ak', leader of the Mexican *entrada*, appears on a 7th-century panel from the Palenque Palace and we might suspect that the dynasty's foundation was linked to these developments.[1]

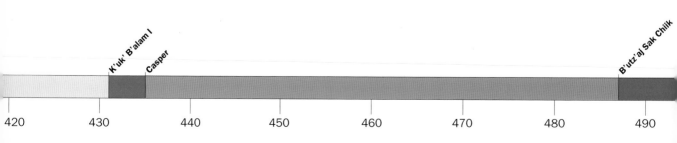

B'UTZ'AJ SAK CHIIK	
Glyphic spelling	*Birth*
b'u-tz'-a-ja-SAK-chi[ku]	14 November 459
('Smoking White/	(9.1.4.5.0
Resplendent	12 Ajaw 13 Sak)
Coati?')	*Accession*
Also known as	28 July 487
Manik	(9.2.12.6.18
	3 Etz'nab 11 Xul)
	Brother
	Ahkal Mo' Naab' I ?

AHKAL MO' NAAB' I	
Glyphic spelling	*Accession*
a-ku-AL MO' NA:B'	3 June 501
('Great-Sun Turtle	(9.3.6.7.17
Macaw Lake?')	5 Kaban 0 Sotz')
Also known as	*Death*
Chaacal I, Akul	29 November 524
Anab I	(9.4.10.4.17
Birth	5 Kaban 5 Mak)
5 July 465	*Brother*
(9.1.10.0.0	B'utz'aj Sak Chiik?
5 Ajaw 3 Sek)	

(*Opposite*) Our only contemporary portrait of an early Palenque king, this figure of Casper comes from a bowl carved from travertine, a soft calcite stone quarried from cave deposits. Dumbarton Oaks, Washington D.C.

(*Right*) A text on Casper's bowl reads: *yuch'ib ch'ok ch'a-? k'uhul b'aakal ajaw* or 'the drinking cup of the prince Casper, divine lord of Palenque'.

Many royal names at Palenque have yielded to decipherment, but that of **Casper**, K'uk' B'alam's successor, is not among them. Acceding in 435 at the age of 13, he would rule for half a century. A fine portrait of the king comes from an unprovenanced travertine bowl – a unique artifact since it is the one and only inscribed object we have from Palenque's Early Classic.[2] Its quality does much to counter the once widespread belief that Palenque's early rulers were lowly village chieftains magnified by their descendants.

Until recently, the only references we had to Palenque's third ruler, **B'utz'aj Sak Chiik**, were to his birth in 459 and accession in 487. In 1994, however, the excavation of Temple 17 uncovered a fine panel from the 7th century referring back to a date in 490 and to a poorly understood 'dedication' ritual performed by this king.[3] Its subject was Lakamha' ('Big Water'), the earliest mention of the site we know today as Palenque and the beginning of a shift in emphasis away from Toktan.[4] This may even constitute its historical founding.

The new panel from Temple 17 goes on to mention the likely brother of B'utz'aj Sak Chiik – here bearing the title *ch'ok* 'youth, prince' – who succeeded him as **Ahkal Mo' Naab' I** in 501.[5] This ruler was to receive a special, though still unexplained, prominence in the dynastic narratives of the great K'inich Janaab' Pakal I (615–683), where he heads all three of these important listings.

PLACE-NAMES AT PALENQUE

The name given to the city of Palenque itself – as opposed to the kingdom it controlled – was Lakamha' or 'Big Water'. Set on the very edge of the Chiapas highlands, where fast-flowing streams make spectacular cascades as they plummet to the plain below, it is easy to see why early inhabitants might have thought this an appropriate description. More specifically, it may have been the name of the Otulum, the stream that flows through the heart of the city, where it was channelled through a subterranean aqueduct. A second place-name, Toktan, is associated with Palenque's earliest periods and seems to have been a separate locale, the home of the dynastic founder and first capital.

LAKAM-HA'

to-ko-TAN-na

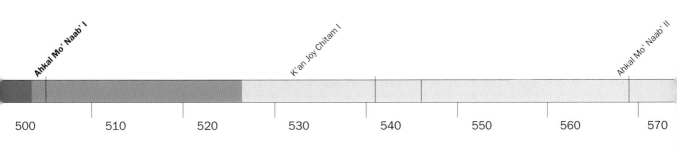

Ahkal Mo' Naab' I   K'an Joy Chitam I   Ahkal Mo' Naab' II

500   510   520   530   540   550   560   570

K'an Joy
Chitam I
529–565

 Ahkal Mo'
Naab' II
565–570

 Kan B'alam I
572–583

 Lady Yohl
Ik'nal
583–604

 Aj Ne' Ohl
Mat
605–612

 Muwaan Mat
612–615

An image of K'an Joy Chitam I, whose name can be made out in his headdress as well as in the adjacent glyphic caption, appears among a collection of ancestral rulers on the sarcophagus of K'inich Janaab' Pakal I (pp. 165–6).

K'AN JOY CHITAM I TO KAN B'ALAM I

Ahkal Mo' Naab' I died in 524 and some hint of difficulties at this juncture might be detected in the four-year gap before his successor **K'an Joy Chitam I** was crowned in 529. A single episode from this king's early life is placed in 496, his adoption of a junior title and presumed heir-apparency at the age of six. The ceremony took place at Toktan, suggesting that this was still the pre-eminent location at this time. His name is formed from three components: *k'an* 'precious' or 'yellow'; the head of a peccary (the American boar) which is *chitam* or *kitam* in most Mayan languages; and a 'toothache bundle' (tied around the peccary's head) that in other contexts seems to read *joy* 'to tie/tether'.[6] His reign of 36 years, remembered by more than one later ruler, endured until 565 when he died at the age of 74.

A second king with the name Ahkal Mo' Naab' – at times identified simply as the *mam* 'grandson' of Ahkal Mo' Naab' I – was inaugurated 85 days after K'an Joy Chitam's death.[7] **Ahkal Mo' Naab' II's** tenure was brief, barely five years, and he was succeeded by **Kan B'alam I** ('Snake Jaguar') in 572. Born just one year after his predecessor, we can presume that he was his younger brother. Kan B'alam I's reign lasted

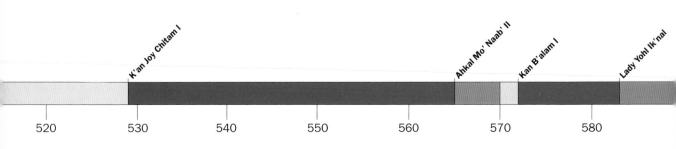

K'AN JOY CHITAM I	
Glyphic spelling K'AN-na-JOY[CHITAM]-ma ('Precious/Yellow Tied Peccary') *Also known as* Hok, Kan Xul I, K'an Hok' Chitam I *Birth* 3 May 490 (9.2.15.3.8 12 Lamat 6 Wo)	*Accession* 23 February 529 (9.4.14.10.4 5 K'an 12 K'ayab) *Death* 6 February 565 (9.6.11.0.16 7 Kib 4 K'ayab)

AHKAL MO' NAAB' II	
Glyphic spelling a-ku-AL MO'-na-b'i ('Great-Sun Turtle Macaw Lake?') *Also known as* Chacaal II, Akul Anab II *Birth* 3 September 523 (9.4.9.0.4 7 K'an 17 Mol)	*Accession* 2 May 565 (9.6.11.5.1 1 Imix 4 Sip) *Death* 21 July 570 (9.6.16.10.7 9 Manik' 5 Yaxk'in) *Brother* Kan B'alam I?

KAN B'ALAM I	
Glyphic spelling (K'INICH) KAN[B'ALAM]-ma ('Great-Sun Snake Jaguar') *Also known as* Chan Bahlum I *Birth* 18 September 524 (9.4.10.1.5 11 Chikchan 13 Ch'en)	*Accession* 6 April 572 (9.6.18.5.12 10 Eb 0 Wo) *Death* 1 February 583 (9.7.9.5.5 11 Chikchan 3 K'ayab) *Brother* Ahkal Mo' Naab' II?

THE MYTHIC ORIGINS OF THE PALENQUE DYNASTY

Classic Maya kingdoms traced their origins to both an historic 'founder' – the lord who established dynastic rule at a particular site – and to more esoteric sources: tutelary deities and heroes from mythological time and space. Palenque's rather complex supernatural history begins before the 'current creation' that started in 3114 BC. In the year 3309 BC a deity dubbed GI the Elder acceded to the rank of *ajaw* under the aegis of another god called Yax Naah Itzamnaaj. The hierarchical ranking of these two is analogous to that of mortal kings and we are reminded that earthly authority was seen to replicate a higher, divine order (p. 17).

A separate deity named, in part, Muwaan Mat was born seven years prior to the dawn of the new era, in 3121 BC. Over 18 days in 2360, at the age of 761, this character produced three children, the Palenque Triad of patron gods. They consist of a 'reborn' GI dubbed GI the Younger, an infantile K'awiil called GII and a local variant of the Jaguar Sun God called GIII.

Muwaan Mat was crowned as *ajaw* in 2305, taking the title *k'uhul matawiil ajaw*. Matawiil was the mythic location where these events took place and this epithet was subsequently used as a 'form of emblem glyph at Palenque. The last character to appear before the beginning of Palenque's mortal dynasty was called 'Bloodletter of the Snake'. His birth is recorded in 993 BC and his accession in 967. Placed in the epoch of the Maya's early mentors, the Olmecs, this legendary figure serves as a narrative bridge between the realms of history and myth.[8]

Muwaan Mat GI GII GIII

for a little under 11 years and he is the first Palenque king known to have used the *k'inich* name ('Great Sun', the principal appellative of the Sun God) that would be such a constant of later monarchs.

LADY YOHL IK'NAL TO MUWAAN MAT

The inscriptions provide greater detail about the next portion of Palenque's history, though its major themes, military defeat and dynastic turbulence, are resoundingly negative. Kan B'alam I died leaving no surviving male heir, and a sister, or more likely a daughter, **Lady Yohl Ik'nal**, became the first queen of Palenque in 583.[9] She was to remain in power for over 20 years, one of very few women in the Classic period to carry full royal titles and enjoy a full term.

The greatest setback of her career is detailed in a section of Palenque's only hieroglyphic stairway. Here, on a date best reckoned as 21 April 599,

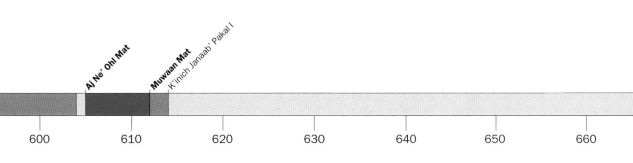

(*Above*) Beginning *ch'akaj lakamha'* 'Palenque was axed', this text from the East Panel of the Temple of Inscriptions marks the city's sacking at the hands of Calakmul's Scroll Serpent in April AD 611.

(*Right*) Accompanied by a caption giving her name and royal title, we see Lady Yohl Ik'nal as she appears on the sarcophagus of K'inich Janaab' Pakal I.

(*Below*) Palenque's rich collection of early dynastic records, first deciphered by Linda Schele, Peter Mathews and Floyd Lounsbury, serves to emphasize the importance of lineal descent and ancestral veneration to the Classic Maya. Here three rulers sprout from the earth in the form of fruit trees, a metaphor for resurrection and the afterlife. From left to right: Ahkal Mo' Naab' I (501–524), Kan B'alam I (572–583) and Lady Yohl Ik'nal (583–604). From the sarcophagus of K'inich Janaab' Pakal I, *c*. AD 683.

there is an 'axing' of Lakamha', an assault, apparently the sacking of the city.[10] While certain aspects of this phrase remain problematic, the perpetrator is clearly Calakmul. Launched from a great distance and including a crossing of the mighty Usumacinta River, this was an undertaking of considerable ambition and a clear measure of Calakmul's 'superpower' pretensions. The following phrase begins *yaleh*, which here translates as 'thrown down'. Its subject is the Palenque Triad of patron deities and represents either a metaphor for Palenque's defeat or, more likely, an actual despoiling of the kingdom's sacred idols (p. 105).[11]

A second defeat

Lady Yohl Ik'nal died in 604 and was succeeded by **Aj Ne' Ohl Mat** (spelling still rather unclear), probably her son. Another key figure of this

LADY YOHL IK'NAL

Glyphic spelling	Accession
IX-(Y)O:L-la IK'-NAL-la	21 December 583
('Lady Heart of the	(9.7.10.3.8
Wind Place')	9 Lamat 1 Muwan)
Also known as	*Death*
Lady Kan Ik, Lady	4 November 604
K'anal Ik'nal	(9.8.11.6.12
	2 Eb 20 Keh)
	Son
	Aj Ne' Ohl Mat?

AJ NE' OHL MAT

Glyphic spelling	Death
AJ-NE'?-O:L ma-ta	8 August 612
Also known as	(9.8.19.4.6
Ac Kan, Ah Lawal	2 Kimi 14 Mol)
Mat	*Mother*
Accession	Lady Yohl Ik'nal?
1 January 605	
(9.8.11.9.10	
8 Ok 18 Muwan)	

MUWAAN MAT

Glyphic spelling	Accession
?-[MUWA:N]MAT	19 October 612
Also known as	(9.8.19.7.18
Lady Sak K'uk',	9 Etz'nab 6 Keh)
Lady Beastie	

Lady Sak K'uk' presents her son K'inich Janaab' Pakal with the 'drum major' crown at his accession in 615.

era, Janaab' Pakal (not to be confused with the later K'inich Janaab' Pakal) is less easily fitted into the genealogy, and may have been either a second son or her husband. In later texts he is ascribed a full emblem glyph and, despite never taking the throne, wielded significant political power during the lifetime of the new king.

Aj Ne' Ohl Mat's eight-year rule was principally to be remembered for another military disaster. On 4 April 611, Lakamha' was penetrated and sacked for a second time, again at the hands of Calakmul, this time under the personal direction of their king Scroll Serpent.[12] The special emphasis this humiliation receives in the Temple of Inscriptions text (lacking any rhetoric of initial defeat contrasted with ultimate victory) suggests that it was essential to the understanding of subsequent events. Aj Ne' Ohl Mat clearly survived the encounter, but neither he nor Janaab' Pakal were to live for more than a year, dying in August and March of 612 respectively.

The narrative goes on to paint a vivid, though for us still rather confusing picture of the disarray that followed. A new ruler is said to have been installed a few months later, ascribed the name of **Muwaan Mat**, the ancestral deity and progenitor of Palenque's three supernatural patrons (p. 159). The next calendrical juncture, the end of the 9th K'atun in 613, is surrounded by some uniquely woeful language. First we have *satay k'uhul ixik, satay ajaw* 'lost is the divine lady, lost is the lord', before being told that certain key rituals were *not* performed.[13] One is left to wonder exactly who this ruler was and, indeed, if this was any kind of conventional reign at all. One idea has been that the god name served as a pseudonym for a new queen, a daughter of Janaab' Pakal called Lady Sak K'uk' ('Resplendent Quetzal').[14] With the patriline destroyed, a short-lived female regency could well have been necessary. But others have argued that the gender of the deity is male, weakening this hypothesis.[15] Interestingly, the god's accession in 3121 BC is described as *unaah tal* 'the first'. Whatever form the ruler elevated in 612 actually took, the shattered Palenque regime could well have viewed this as the summoned deity ruling for a second time.

This strange period lasted only three years, ending with the accession of the 12-year-old son of Lady Sak K'uk', K'inich Janaab' Pakal (Great-Sun ?Shield') in 615. His inauguration is graphically depicted on the Oval Palace Tablet, where his mother presents him with the 'drum major' crown. She was to live for a further 25 years, finally dying in 640, while her consort K'an Mo' Hix ('Precious Macaw Jaguar') survived her by two years. They probably retained much of the practical power while K'inich Janaab' Pakal was in his formative years.

K'inich Janaab' Pakal I

615–683

K'inich Kan B'alam II

684–702

K'inich K'an Joy Chitam II

702–711

The profile of a long-lived and much revered king, this stucco head of K'inich Janaab' Pakal was found in his tomb.

K'INICH JANAAB' PAKAL I	
Glyphic spelling K'INICH-JANA:B'-PAKAL-la ('Great-Sun ? Shield') *Also known as* Pacal, Pacal the Great. 8 Ahau, Sun Shield *Birth* 23 March 603 (9.8.9.13.0 8 Ajaw 13 Pop) *Accession* 26 July 615 (9.9.2.4.8 5 Lamat 1 Mol) *Death* 28 August 683 (9.12.11.5.18 6 Etz'nab 11 Yax)	*Wife* Lady Tz'akb'u Ajaw *Father* K'an Mo' Hix *Mother* Lady Sak K'uk' *Sons* Kan B'alam II, K'an Joy Chitam II, Batz Chan Mat? *Monuments* Oval Palace Tablet; Hieroglyphic Stairway; House C texts; Subterranean Thrones & Tableritos; Olvidado piers; sarcophagus texts *Burial* Temple of the Inscriptions

K'INICH JANAAB' PAKAL I

When the 12-year-old K'inich Janaab' Pakal took on the mantle of rulership, Palenque's fortunes were at a decidedly low ebb, battered by recent assaults and the deaths of several leading figures. Yet, despite this inauspicious start he is today the most famous of all Maya kings, even if this notoriety owes more to his astonishing burial than his long and productive life.

We know little about his early reign, though he took a wife, Lady Tz'akb'u Ajaw, apparently in 626, and subsequently had sons by her in 635 and 644 (both of whom would later succeed him). She seems to have come from Toktan, but also had ties with another important site called Oxte'k'uh 'Three Gods'. Janaab' Pakal's earliest inscription, from the Olvidado or 'Forgotten' Temple in the far west of the site, was not raised until 647, a few years after the death of both parents. In fact, this fine stucco text is the first contemporary record we have of any kind since the travertine bowl of Casper from some 160 years earlier. Palenque's missing record presumably lies buried within construction fill. Broken monuments from Janaab' Pakal's own reign (casually re-used in the masonry of the North Group complex) may represent only one of several episodes of monument destruction at the hands of conquerors. The only

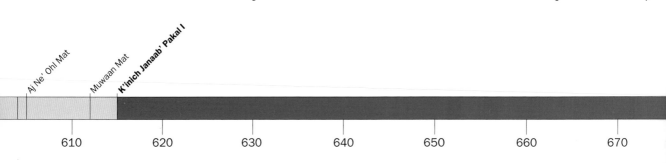

Among the great Classic capitals, Palenque stands alone in the pivotal position it gave to its royal court. Compact but well proportioned, the Palace of Palenque was set at the heart of this extensive city, able to monitor all movement within the central precinct and commanding views of the great plain that stretches all the way to the Gulf of Mexico.

conflict known from his early years took place shortly before 628, when a prominent noble, an *aj k'uhuun*, fell captive to Piedras Negras (p. 142).[16]

The Palace

The Olvidado was only one of numerous structures commissioned by Janaab' Pakal, with his greatest energies devoted to the unique Palace of Palenque (p. 164). He added a number of monuments to the last buildings of its original Early Classic level in 654, while laying a new higher platform across the central part of the complex. The first structure here, House E, was completed later the same year. Its name was *sak nuk naah*, the 'White Skin? House' (and indeed, this is the only structure in the palace painted white, the others being a uniform red). This became the setting for the Oval Palace Tablet depicting his own accession and a throne room that saw the inaugurations of at least three later kings. The adjacent House C was dedicated in 661 and, together with House B (added

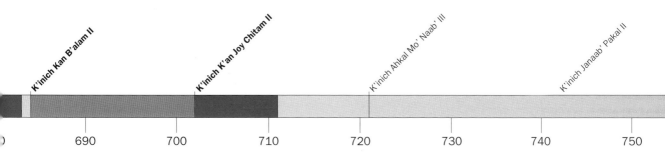

K'inich Kan B'alam II

K'inich K'an Joy Chitam II

K'inich Ahkal Mo' Naab' III

K'inich Janaab' Pakal II

690   700   710   720   730   740   750

THE PALACE OF PALENQUE

This maze of galleries, chambers, courtyards, stairways and tunnels constitutes the royal palace of Palenque, one of the most refined examples of Classic Maya architecture. Measuring 318 x 240 ft (97 x 73 m) at its base, it represents a century and a half of incremental growth atop even earlier buildings, now concealed within a 33-ft(10-m)-high platform.

Structurally, it is notable for its mastery of the corbelled vault or 'Maya arch'. Palenque's architects used a variety of weight-saving innovations to widen its span (sloping 'mansard' roofs and light lattice-built 'roofcombs'), producing spacious and well-lit interiors, quite unlike the narrow, gloomy chambers common elsewhere. Though the centuries have taken their toll, many traces of the Palace's once elaborate ornamentation still survive. Its buildings were embellished inside and out by heavy applications of modelled stucco, a cornucopia of supernatural motifs and figural scenes. The colour scheme was a dominant red with details picked out in green, yellow and blue.[17]

The complex served as the centre of government, the scene of official receptions and administration, but its role as a royal residence is clear from its well-planned personal facilities: its six latrines and two sweatbaths, which drain into a subterranean aqueduct. The earliest parts now visible, Houses B, C and E, date to the reign of K'inich Janaab' Pakal, with others, Houses A and D, that may be his later works or those of his son Kan B'alam II (684–702). K'an Joy Chitam II (702–c. 711) may have begun House A-D, while much of the southern portion and the idiosyncratic Tower were later, probably built by K'uk' B'alam II (764–783>).

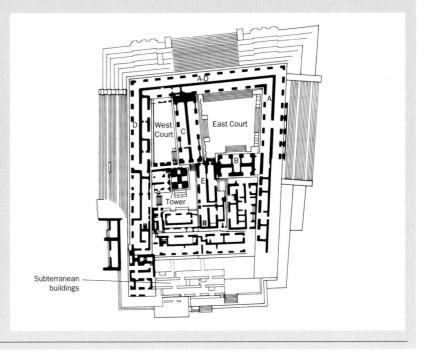

at about this time) and House A (after 668), defined a new East Court. Designed as a grand arena for presentation and reception, this spacious courtyard was suitably adorned with impressive images of humbled captives and texts lauding Janaab' Pakal's military achievements.

War and diplomacy

The eastern side of the court, the base of House A, was filled with an unusual cast of oversized prisoners. Those flanking the central stairway have texts on the loincloths that show that they were seized on successive days in 662. On the western side the steps leading up to House C carry an inscription that is one of the most interesting, and difficult, at Palenque. It is primarily a war narrative, dealing with the Calakmul attack of 599, before entering a poorly understood section naming an Itzamnaaj B'alam of Yaxchilan (who doesn't appear to be any of the known rulers of that name) and Janaab' Pakal's contemporary, Nuun Ujol Chaak of Tikal. The narrative culminates in 659 with what seems to be the capture of six lords, each of whom is shown along the base of House C offering gestures of submission. All are rather minor figures. One hailed

Ayiin Chan Ahk ('Caiman Sky Turtle') of Pipa' was one of six lords captured by Janaab' Pakal in AD 659.

THE KINGS OF TORTUGUERO

Palenque kings were not the only ones who claimed to be Divine Lords of B'aakal. Some 38 miles (61 km) to the west lies the smaller centre of Tortuguero, whose rulers carried the same title. We know little of its dynasty aside from one particularly prolific individual, a contemporary of K'inich Janaab' Pakal called B'alam Ajaw ('Jaguar Lord', AD 644–679). A vigorous warrior, B'alam Ajaw seems to have conquered the western Comalcalco kingdom in 649.[18] Though our evidence is limited, relations between the two B'aakal states might not have been friendly. In 644, and again in 655, B'alam Ajaw attacked Oxte'k'uh ('Three Gods'), an unknown site possessing consistent ties with Palenque.[19] For the origins of this shared B'aakal name we could look to the breakdown of the male line at Palenque and the crisis that accompanied its series of military failures. Internal disputes could easily have led to the foundation of a breakaway polity (as occurred between Tikal and Dos Pilas). Yet it is significant that when Tortuguero makes reference to its past it is to a lord called Ahkal K'uk' ('Turtle Quetzal') from the era of Ahkal Mo' Naab' I, the same ruler who begins all K'inich Janaab' Pakal's dynastic listings. This may be a sign that the B'aakal dynasty diverged at this early stage, around AD 510.

from Pipa', a location closely linked to the hilltop capital of Pomona due east of Palenque. The opposite side of House C, in the West Court, names a series of captives from the unidentified Wa-Bird site and describes the death of another Pipa' lord in 663.[20]

Janaab' Pakal's relationship with Nuun Ujol Chaak and distant Tikal is intriguing but still difficult to clarify. Six days after the stairway event Nuun Ujol Chaak 'arrived here' at Lakamha' in the company of the Palenque king.[21] For the Tikal monarch to stray so far from home at such a critical time (just two years earlier he had been driven from his capital by Calakmul) might well suggest that he was still in exile. Palenque, as its repeated maulings attest, was a bulwark against the spread of Calakmul ascendancy and it is unsurprising that she and Tikal should find common cause (p. 42).

Janaab' Pakal's long tenure ended in 683, during his 68th regnal year. If he had begun work on his own memorial, the Temple of Inscriptions, he did not live to see its completion and all its final texts and embellishments were overseen by his son and successor K'inich Kan B'alam II.

Discovery of the great tomb

In 1949, the great Mexican archaeologist Alberto Ruz Lhuillier was restoring the inner sanctuary of the Temple of Inscriptions when he noticed that one of the great slabs of its floor had an arrangement of 12 stone-plugged holes.[22] The plugs were removed and the holes used (as they had been intended) to lift the slab, revealing a rubble-packed shaft. This proved to be the mouth of a stairway leading deep into the heart of the pyramid. After four seasons of effort digging out the compacted fill, excavators had followed the steps 80 ft (25 m) down, negotiated a change of direction, and come to a short corridor. At its end was a stone box containing the disarticulated skeletons of five or six individuals and, to its left, a triangular stone door. The sealed doorway was first penetrated on 13 June 1952, when an intrusive flashlight revealed a sight that still has no equal in the Maya world.

Within the chamber

Behind lay a vaulted chamber 30 x 13 ft (9 x 4 m) dominated by a huge sarcophagus. Its elaborately worked lid is today the most famous of all Maya carvings, a sublime representation of the king's rebirth from the jaws of the Underworld (see also p. 122). Growing from the offering plate in which he lies is the 'world tree', the *axis mundi* of the Maya cosmos and the pathway by which he would ultimately reach the heavens. This is shown in the form of a 'sky band' framing the scene, studded with symbols representing the sun, moon and stars. The shorter sides of this frame give way to the names and portraits of the king's leading nobles: the *sajal* and *aj k'uhuun* who had key roles in his administration and perhaps in the design, organization of labour or even payment for the temple.

The coffin itself, hewn from a single great block of limestone, was carved on all four sides, showing ten figures emerging as trees sprouting

(*Above*) Janaab' Pakal's burial pyramid, the Temple of Inscriptions, was completed by his son Kan B'alam II around AD 690.

(*Below*) The king's body lay in a contoured cavity sealed by a closely fitting 'plug' of limestone covered by a huge stone lid.

from the earth. Each is identified by a caption: each of the parents of K'inich Janaab' Pakal appears twice, as does Lady Yohl Ik'nal, with single portraits of Janaab' Pakal, Ahkal Mo' Naab' I, K'an Joy Chitam I and Kan B'alam I. A text running around the lid rim records their death-dates together with that of the king. The massive block sits on squat feet decorated with additional portraits of his foremost nobles, this time fixed within glyphic stars. Between the first pair, on the chamber floor, were placed two stucco heads, one clearly a portrait of the king, the other most likely his wife Lady Tz'akb'u Ajaw. The walls of the tomb were adorned with nine life-size figures modelled in stucco. Some can be identified by name glyphs in their head-dresses and prove to be a procession of ancestors much like that of the sarcophagus sides.[23]

The body of the king

Draped across the great lid was the same kind of three-masked jade belt shown on many royal portraits. The lid was lifted to reveal a contoured cavity sealed by a tightly fitting plug. Within lay the body itself, bathed in bright red cinnabar (a toxic compound of mercury) and bedecked in copious amounts of jade jewelry. Apart from the multi-beaded collar and wristlets, there were jade rings on every finger, a jade cube clenched in one hand, a sphere in the other. His face was covered by a jade mosaic mask, his mouth framed by an ornament of red-painted pyrites.

Beyond the sarcophagus lay a stone track, clearly designed as a slide to accommodate the lid and expose the coffin beneath. This

INTO THE UNDERWORLD:
THE GREAT TOMB OF K'INICH JANAAB' PAKAL I

In all the Americas there is no burial more famous than that of K'inich Janaab' Pakal I. A veritable Tutankhamun of the New World, his is the most elaborate Maya tomb yet discovered. Its greatest wealth, far more valuable to scholars than its great trove of precious jade, is its pictorial imagery and glyphic texts, so rich and numerous they seem to crowd every available surface.

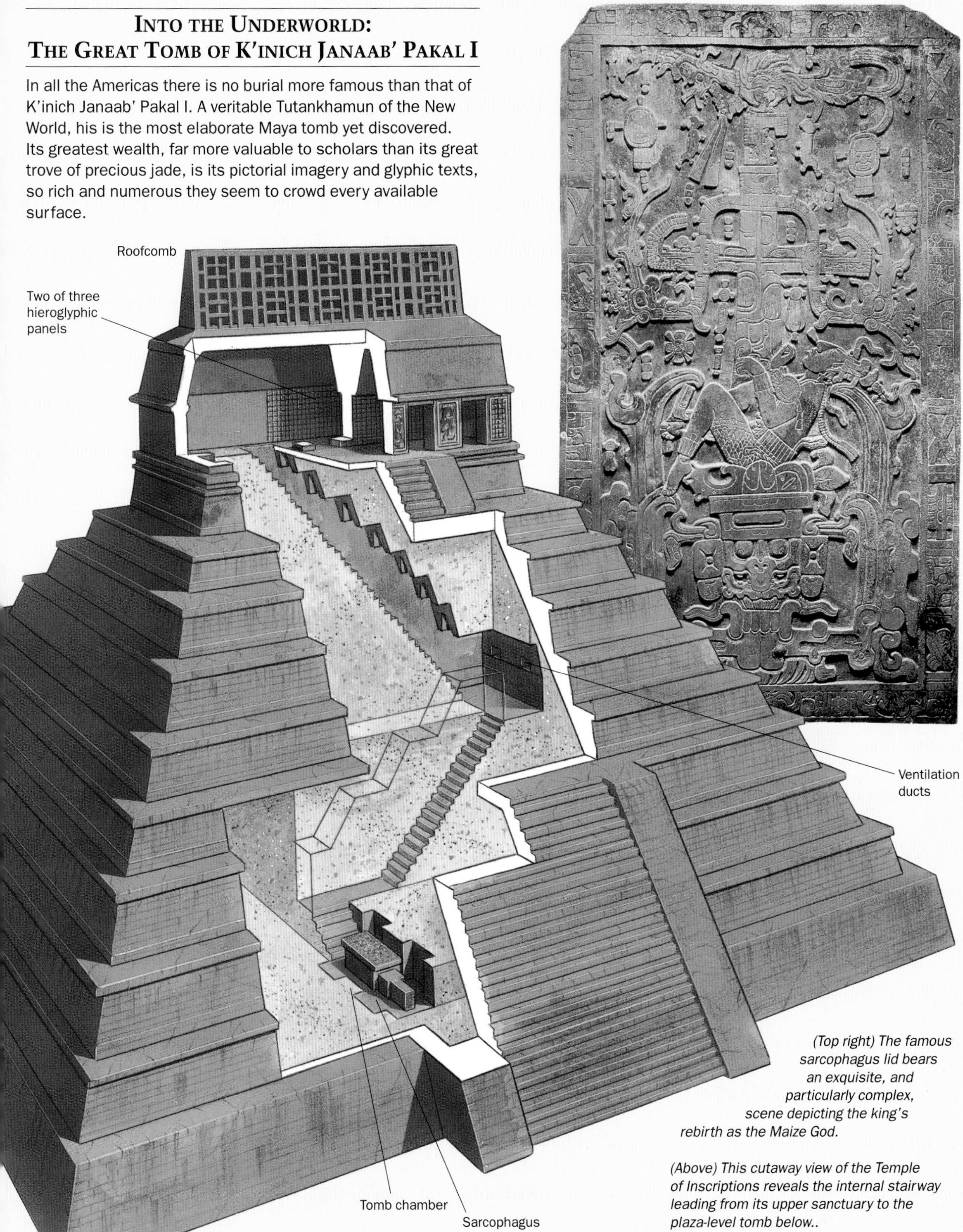

Roofcomb

Two of three hieroglyphic panels

Ventilation ducts

Tomb chamber

Sarcophagus

(Top right) The famous sarcophagus lid bears an exquisite, and particularly complex, scene depicting the king's rebirth as the Maize God.

(Above) This cutaway view of the Temple of Inscriptions reveals the internal stairway leading from its upper sanctuary to the plaza-level tomb below..

would have allowed Janaab' Pakal's burial to have taken place during, or even after, the temple's construction – but equally, would have allowed its re-entry, a common practice among the Classic Maya. On such occasions defleshed bones were removed, rearranged or, as might have been the case here, dusted with additional pigment. Similarly, while the descending stairway might have been designed to carry a funerary procession, the inclusion of two well-built tunnels leading to the west face of the pyramid – 'air-conditioning' for the stifling pit of the stairway – suggest that it had been planned for extended use, as a means by which to visit and communicate with the dead king. After the stairway was filled such contact was maintained by the addition of a limestone conduit, which was made to snake up the staircase, forming a 'psychoduct' connecting the sealed chamber to the outside world.

K'INICH KAN B'ALAM II

K'INICH KAN B'ALAM II	
Glyphic spelling K'INICH- KAN[B'ALAM]-ma ('Great-Sun Snake Jaguar') *Also known as* Chan Bahlum II *Dynastic title* 10th in the line *Birth* 20 May 635 (9.10.2.6.6 2 Kimi 19 Sotz') *Accession* 7 January 684 (9.12.11.12.10 8 Ok 3 K'ayab) *Death* 16 February 702 (9.13.10.1.5 6 Chikchan 3 Pop)	*Father* K'inich Janaab' Pakal I *Mother* Lady Tz'akb'u Ajaw *Brothers* K'an Joy Chitam II, Batz Chan Mat? *Monuments* Tablets and Alfardas of the Temples of the Cross, Sun and Foliated Cross; tablets and façade of the Temple of Inscriptions; Temple 17 Panel; Death's Head; Jonuta Panel; Temple of the Cross Stela.

The portraits of Kan B'alam II are among the most distinctive of any Maya king; whether carved in relief or modelled in the round, his imperious nose and full lower lip convey a striking realism. He was already 48 years old when he inherited the throne in 684 and, as if frustrated by so long a wait, was to spend the next 18 years creating some of Palenque's finest architecture and sculptural reliefs – if anything outdoing the achievements of his illustrious father.

Kan B'alam's first tasks were to preside over the entombment of K'inich Janaab' Pakal and to complete his mortuary temple. The three great hieroglyphic tablets housed in its upper sanctuary (at 617 glyph-blocks the second-longest body of Maya text) include Kan B'alam's accession and must have been finished under his supervision. Similarly, the four outer piers of the temple's façade, worked in stucco, were his commission and show standing figures cradling images of GII, the infant form of the serpent-footed deity *k'awiil* and one of the triad of local patrons. Part of what little text remains on this frontage describes him as the '10th in the line' (a count only possible if 'aberrant' reigns are excluded from the total).[24] By now, Kan B'alam had turned to creating his own architectural statement, an ambitious

Modelled in stucco plaster, this portrait of K'inich Kan (quite possibly Kaan) B'alam II comes from one of a series of life-size figures that once sat high in the roof ornamentation of Temple 14.

three-pyramid complex set on an artificial terrace overlooking the Temple of Inscriptions.

Group of the Cross

Dedicated together in 692, the Temples of the Cross, Sun and Foliated Cross form a coordinated programme of immense iconographic and textual complexity, blending the mythic and historical in a dizzying range of materials, formats and settings. In essence, Kan B'alam was providing a spiritual focus for each of the Palenque Triad of gods, as well as fixing his patriline within the great supernatural narrative of the kingdom's foundation. At the heart of each temple lies an inner sanctum of small, roofed chambers that represent symbolic 'sweat-baths', places of purification.[25] Each houses its own wall tablet bearing two images of Kan B'alam: one as a mature king, the other as a child, venerating the particular icon that gives each temple its modern name.[26] An event given special attention in the text marks a rare conjunction of Jupiter, Mars, Saturn and the moon that took place in July 690. It was marked by the burning of one temple, followed a day later by the dedication of another called the *k'inich k'uk' naah* or 'Great-Sun Quetzal House'. The same date was engraved on a large jade with the king's portrait, which ultimately found its way into the great well at Chichen Itza (p. 229).[27] To commemorate the end of the 13th K'atun in 692 Kan B'alam erected Palenque's only figural stela, a three-dimensional portrait, on an upper corner of the Temple of the Cross.

Each of Kan B'alam's three Cross Group temples features a carved panel housed in an enclosed shrine. That from the Temple of the Cross shows a flowering 'world tree' growing from a sacrificial bowl or brazier, flanked by the king first as a child and then a man. AD 692.

The esoteric themes of the Cross Group have long dominated our view of Kan B'alam, but recent evidence points to more of the pragmatic power that underpinned the city's wealth and confidence. He seems to have exercised an 'overkingship' that reached along much of the southern bank of the Usumacinta, encompassing sites such as La Mar and Anayte (pp. 181–2). To the south, he seems to have been in conflict with Palenque's major rival, the highland kingdom of Tonina. A small caption from the new Temple 17 panel describes Kan B'alam's attack on a Tonina location in September 687, just two years into his reign. The disappearance of Tonina's Ruler 2 at this point could be a sign that the encounter proved fatal for him (p. 181).

Kan B'alam II himself died on 16 February 702 and was buried the same day.[28] While his mortuary shrine has yet to be identified, most attention has focused on the Temple of the Cross, the largest of the group. In 1993 a consolidation programme by the Mexican Instituto Nacional de Antropología e Historia cleared its supporting pyramid for the first time, in the process revealing a great dedicatory cache of well over 100 ceramic effigy incense-burners spaced out around each tier of the modified hillside that forms its base. These evocative terracotta images of fire gods were a particular innovation of his reign. Although a number of intrusive burials were also uncovered in the pyramid, the main prize, the tomb of Kan B'alam himself, has thus far eluded investigators.

(*Above*) Distinctive to Palenque, these ceramic 'incense-burners' (in fact, supporting stands that held the actual burners), are modelled into the visages of fire gods, most often the aged anthropomorphic jaguar. A prodigious number were made during Kan B'alam's reign; a vast cache was placed around the tiers of the Temple of the Cross pyramid alone.

(*Right*) A view of the Cross Group; from left to right: the Temple of the Cross, the Temple of the Foliated Cross, Temple 14 and the Temple of the Sun.

This detail of the Palace Tablet shows Janaab' Pakal and his queen Lady Tz'akb'u Ajaw presenting the 'drum major' crown and 'flint and shield' war emblems to K'an Joy Chitam II.

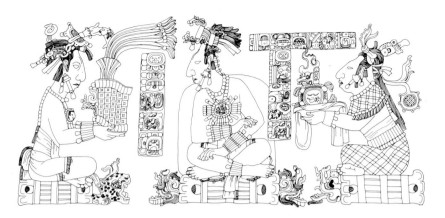

(*Bottom*) On this panel now in the Dumbarton Oaks collection, K'an Joy Chitam II is here seen performing a dance-ritual dressed as the axe-wielding Chaak, god of rain, lightning and thunder.

K'INICH K'AN JOY CHITAM II	
Glyphic spelling K'INICH-[K'AN]-JOY[CHITAM]-ma ('Precious/Yellow Tied Peccary') *Also known as* Kan Xul II, K'an Hok' Chitam II *Birth* 2 November 644 (9.10.11.17.0 11 Ajaw 8 Mak) *Accession* 30 May 702 (9.13.10.6.8 5 Lamat 6 Xul)	*Father* K'inich Janaab' Pakal I *Mother* Lady Tz'akb'u Ajaw *Brothers* Kan B'alam II, Batz Chan Mat? *Monuments* Palace Tablet; Del Río Throne?; Warrior Panel; Temple 14 Panel?; Dumbarton Oaks Panel.

K'INICH K'AN JOY CHITAM II

Kan B'alam either died without male issue or was predeceased by his heirs, since it was the second of K'inich Janaab' Pakal's sons, K'an Joy Chitam II, who replaced Kan B'alam as ruler in 702. In fact, his succession seems long anticipated since he took the title of *b'aah ch'ok* – 'head prince' or heir apparent – upon Kan B'alam's elevation in 684.[29] At 57, he was even older than his brother on taking power, but shared a similar desire to leave his mark in what years remained to him, beginning a vigorous programme of construction and monument dedication.

K'an Joy Chitam initiated work on the northern gallery of the Palace, linking Houses A and D to enclose the East and West Courts. A full complement of stucco reliefs and glyphic panels continued the decorative programmes of earlier Palace buildings. The most impressive of these, the Palace Tablet – which was set into the centre of the new gallery – is another of Palenque's puzzles. A monumental throne-back of great artistry (its anthropomorphic 'full-figure' glyphs are a particular highpoint), its long text puts K'an Joy Chitam within the dynastic progress of his father and elder brother, listing his various designation rites en route to ultimate power. Its scene shows K'an Joy Chitam receiving the key 'drum major' headdress from his father, probably in a childhood rite. It has recently been suggested that the subject of the accompanying caption is the headdress itself and the northern gallery, House A-D, was built to house this item of regalia in 720.[30] K'an Joy Chitam seems to supervise its dedication, but not, perhaps, in person. Behind this strange turn of events lies a dramatic return of Palenque's misfortunes.

In 711 a devastating retribution was wrought on the city by the forces of Tonina and the 66-year-old K'an Joy Chitam taken captive by his counterpart K'inich B'aaknal Chaak.[31] A solitary stone at Tonina shows the bound, but rather dignified Palenque ruler, still in possession of much of his royal finery (p. 183). Whether K'an Joy Chitam was killed immediately or held hostage is still unclear. In either case, the strange Palace Tablet seems to reflect special measures adopted by the Palenque nobility to preserve a symbolic kingship in the midst of renewed crisis. Parallels with the turmoil following the Calakmul attack appear strong.

K'inich Ahkal Mo' Naab' III

721–736>

K'inich Janaab' Pakal II

>742>

K'inich K'uk' B'alam II

764–783>

Janaab' Pakal III

799–?

K'INICH AHKAL MO' NAAB' III	
Glyphic spelling	*Father*
K'INICH-AHK-AL	'Batz' Chan Mat
MO'[NA:B]	*Mother*
('Great-Sun Turtle	Lady Kinuw
Macaw Lake?')	*Sons*
Also known as	K'inich Janaab'
Chaacal III, Akul	Pakal II?, K'inich
Anab III	K'uk' B'alam II
Birth	*Monuments*
13 September 678	Temple 18 texts,
(9.12.6.5.8	Temple 19 bench
3 Lamat 6 Sak)	and texts, Temple
Accession	21 texts; Tablets of
30 December 721	the Orator and
(9.14.10.4.2	Scribe; Bundle
9 Ik' 5 K'ayab)	Panel; House E
Wife	Painted text?
Lady Men Nik	

K'INICH JANAAB' PAKAL II	
Glyphic spelling	*Also known as*
u-PAKAL-la-K'INICH	Upakal K'inich
(K'INICH-) JANA:B'-	*Father*
pa-ka-la ('Shield of	K'inich Ahkal Mo'
the Sun God Great-	Naab' III?
Sun ?-Shield')	*Monuments*
	Bodega No. 1144

K'INICH AHKAL MO' NAAB' III

K'an Joy Chitam left no surviving heir and the next king, Ahkal Mo' Naab' III, represents something of a deviation in the line. We can take it that his father, Batz Chan Mat, had royal blood from his close association with Lady Tz'akb'u Ajaw and the fact that his burial in 680 was supervised by the great K'inich Janaab' Pakal. He was very likely a third son of this pair and elder brother to the two previous rulers.[32]

It was not until 721, ten years after his predecessor's capture, that Akhal Mo' Naab' assumed the throne. The prominence he would give to secondary nobles throughout his reign could well reflect their key role during this 'interregnum' and their part in restoring royal traditions to the kingdom.

The best known of these supporting lords was Chak Suutz' ('Great/Red Bat'), the king's military captain.[33] The Tablets of the Scribe and Orator show two views of his most prominent captive, a *sajal* of Piedras Negras ruler Yo'nal Ahk II (p. 146), perhaps taken in 725.[34] Excavation of Chak Suutz's palatial residence produced a fine panel listing more of his triumphs (see panel). Other subordinates appear on a small, and still rather mysterious panel fragment uncovered by

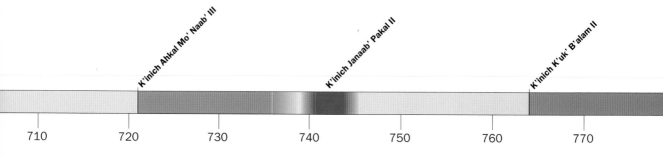

710   720   730   740   750   760   770

K'inich Ahkal Mo' Naab' III   K'inich Janaab' Pakal II   K'inich K'uk' B'alam II

CHAK SUUTZ': PALENQUE'S MILITARY COMMANDER

When Group 4, an elite residential compound close to the centre of Palenque, was excavated in 1950 its largest building was found to contain a sculpted wall panel in near pristine condition. Dubbed the Tablet of the Slaves, it shows Ahkal Mo' Naab' III sitting on the backs of two miserable prisoners and flanked by his parents, who present him with the 'drum major' crown and emblematic 'flint and shield'.[35] It was commissioned by his leading lieutenant, Chak Suutz' ('Great/Red Bat'), bearer of the high titles b'aah ajaw 'head lord', yajaw k'ak' 'lord of fire' and sajal. He had special responsibility for Palenque's military activities and is credited with a string of personal victories. They begin with the capture of three lords in AD 723, followed by attacks on what seems to have been a part of the Piedras Negras kingdom called K'ina' ('Sun Water') in 725, and two unknown locations, one a 'star war', in 729.[36] The panel concludes in 730 with the dedication of the building that houses it and celebration of his 3rd K'atun-birthday (59 years old) nine days later.

(Opposite) Ahkal Mo' Naab' III manipulates a large cloth bundle assisted by a group of secondary lords. AD 731.

K'INICH K'UK' B'ALAM II

Glyphic spelling K'INICH-K'UK'[B'ALAM]-ma ('Great-Sun Quetzal Jaguar') Also known as Bahlum K'uk' II, Mahk'ina Kuk Accession 4 March 764 (9.16.13.0.7 9 Manik' 15 Wo)	Father K'inich Ahkal Mo' Naab' III Mother Lady Men Nik Monuments Tablet of the 96 Glyphs; Creation Tablet; House B Mural?; Bodega No. 218

Arnoldo González which shows them manipulating a large cloth bundle together with the king in 731.

In 734 a lord holding the rank of yajaw k'ak' 'Lord of Fire' had Temple 19 dedicated in his honour within the narrow Otulum Valley, to the south of the Cross Group – an area that also saw the rebuilding of Temples 18, 18a, and 21 during Ahkal Mo' Naab's tenure. The recent excavation of Temple 19 has produced some truly remarkable monuments, with carving of such quality and refinement they might even be regarded as the pinnacle of Palenque's sculptural achievement. The most notable is a low slab-sided platform bearing ten seated figures, six of them leading nobles, and a 220-glyph text. An overt statement of renewal, it features a lengthy re-telling of Palenque's supernatural origins, centred on the accession of GI the Elder in 3309 BC. This is reflected in the pictured scene, which shows the king performing a re-enactment. Ahkal Mo' Naab' wears GI's 'heron and fish' insignia in his headdress, while a leading lord called Janaab' Ajaw (a grandson of K'inich Janaab' Pakal) impersonates the officiating god Yax Naah Itzamnaaj.[37]

Temple 18 remains one of the most interesting of Ahkal Mo' Naab's commissions. Its doorjamb panels describe the essentials of his birth and accession, linked to Muwaan Mat's enthronement 3,045 years earlier. The back wall of its sanctuary originally carried a stucco tableau. The scene (dated to 679 or 731) does not survive, but more than 125 fine modelled glyphs were recovered, most having fallen in a chaotic pile that can be reconstructed only in part. The text centres on the deaths of his father Batz Chan Mat and grandmother Lady Tz'akb'u Ajaw.[38] Three tombs were uncovered beneath the floor of Temple 18; one was looted in antiquity, and the contents of the other two were rich in jade artifacts but otherwise poorly preserved.

One of several sensational finds made by Alfonso Morales and his team in recent years has been this image of Ahkal Mo' Naab' III, part of a tall limestone pier in Temple 19.

This broken panel depicts the little-known K'inich Janaab' Pakal II, recently identified by Guillermo Bernal Romero. A number of joining fragments were found on the north side of the Palace.

K'INICH JANAAB' PAKAL II

Ahkal Mo' Naab' III was succeeded by his *b'aah ch'ok* 'head prince', presumably his son, named on a stucco-decorated pier from Temple 19 as Upakal K'inich or 'Shield of the Sun God'. On taking office the new king took the K'inich Janaab' Pakal name, though, doubtless to distinguish himself from his great predecessor, he always paired it with his pre-accession name.[39] Details of his reign are few, though portraits of him survive on the stucco pier and on a shattered panel found in debris on the north face of the Palace. The only date we have for him comes in 742, when he installed a secondary lord in some important office. It was at about this time that a Palenque princess, Lady Chak Nik Ye' Xook, was dispatched to distant Copan, later to become the mother of Yax Pasaj Chan Yoaat, its 16th ruler (p. 209) A Palenque king of similar, though not identical name to Upakal K'inich appears on a jade head found in Honduras, thought to be an item she took with her.[40] The little impression Janaab' Pakal II made on Palenque history points either to a short reign (followed by that of an even more obscure figure) or one beset by a new period of troubles. Records at Tonina do date a further Palenque defeat to about this time (p. 187).

K'INICH K'UK' B'ALAM II

The next ruler was a son of Ahkal Mo' Naab' III who took the name K'uk' B'alam II and became the last of Palenque's major rulers in 764. Knowledge of him is limited to a few broken monuments found in various parts of the Palace, all linked by a characteristic style of carved incision.[41] They include one truly remarkable piece. In 1935 a clearance of the debris lying between the Tower and House E uncovered the Tablet of the 96 Glyphs. Small by Palenque standards and now badly cracked (by the pickaxe of an injudicious workman), it is rightly regarded as the finest example of glyphic calligraphy to come down to us from the Classic period. Crisply incised, its beauty stems from the care with which every flourish of the painter's hand has been replicated in stone. In content, it recounts the dedication of the *sak nuk naah* (apparently House E of the Palace) by K'inich Janaab' Pakal in 654 and the subsequent accessions of K'an Joy Chitam II, Ahkal Mo' Naab' III and K'uk' B'alam II himself in this same building. The tablet was commissioned in celebration of K'uk' B'alam's 1st K'atun-anniversary of rule in 783.

Excavation in recent years has uncovered another of Palenque's characteristic portrait heads, though this time modelled in stone rather than in stucco. Its quetzal bird headdress and remnant jaguar ears identify it as K'uk' B'alam, while his naturalistic, rather paunchy features probably point to a likeness of the 8th-century king rather than his namesake, the 5th-century dynastic founder.

Identified by his quetzal headdress with (now damaged) jaguar ears, this stone portrait would seem to represent K'uk' B'alam II.

Widely acknowledged as the greatest masterpiece of Classic Maya calligraphy, the Tablet of the 96 Glyphs records a partial dynastic sequence running from K'inich Janaab' Pakal I to K'uk' B'alam II. AD 783.

This small incised vessel is the sole record of what may be Palenque's last king: Janaab' Pakal III.

JANAAB' PAKAL III	
Glyphic spelling 6-? ja-na-b'i pa-ka-la ('6 Death ? Shield') Also known as 6 Cimi Pakal	Accession 13 November 799 (9.18.9.4.4 7 K'an 17 Muwan)

JANAAB' PAKAL III

The last ruler known at Palenque, Wak Kimi Janaab' Pakal ('6 Death ? Shield'), or just Janaab' Pakal III, acceded in 799. This record comes from an incised blackware vessel found in a modest sub-floor burial in a residential quarter of the city. His use of the day name '6 Death' has been taken as a sign of growing Mexican influence (the taking of day names being a ubiquitous feature there), though, in truth, there had always been close contacts between the two cultures and this style has a lengthy history among the western Maya.

One last reference to the B'aakal kingdom appears on a clay brick from Comalcalco, far to the west of Palenque and at the very edge of the Maya world. Created around 814, it remains unclear if the B'aakal referred to here is Palenque itself or simply Comalcalco aspiring to its now faded glories.[42]

Palenque's collapse brings a by now familiar story: the sudden end of dynasty and history in the early 9th century, general depopulation and a final occupation by squatters. The great halls of the Palace – the majority of which stand to this day – must have provided shelter for itinerant travellers and hunters for close to a thousand years. Famously, when one was killed during the sudden collapse of a gallery, archaeologists found him where he died, no comrade or relative having retrieved the body for proper burial.

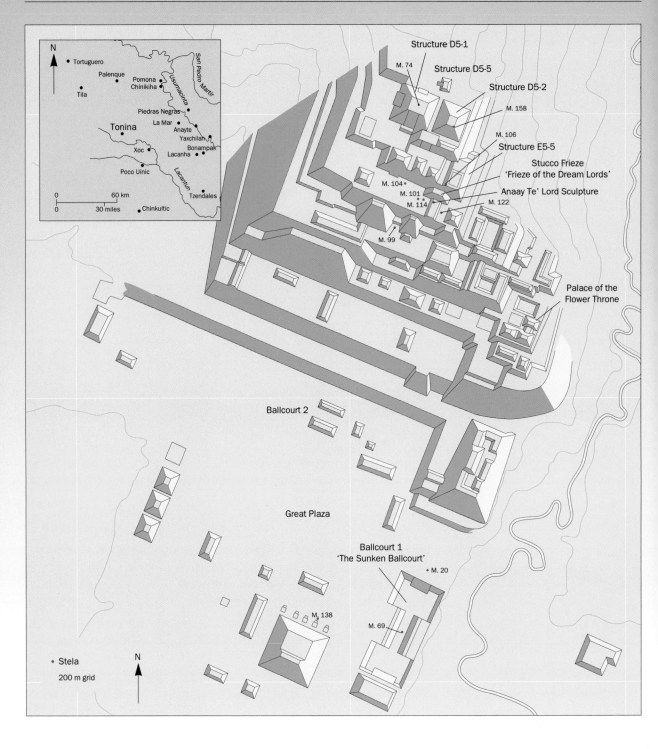

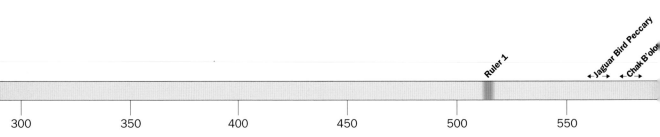

TONINA

CARVED INTO A STEEPLY RISING HILLSIDE in a sequence of seven terraces, the ceremonial core of Tonina boasts a unique and dramatic setting. From the plaza below, this Acropolis appears as a mountainous step pyramid crowded with temples or palaces at every level. Tonina lies in the Ocosingo Valley, surrounded not by the lush plains of the lowlands but by the peaks and pines of the Chiapas highlands. One of the few highland sites with a full Classic tradition, it kept in close contact with the cultural ferment of the heartland and may have taken a key trading role between the two zones.

Traditionally viewed as a rather dour and militaristic place, discoveries in recent years have revealed more of its artistic flair, most especially a virtuosity at stucco-modelling which equals that of its neighbour and great rival Palenque 40 miles (64.5 km) to the north. A distinctive regional style is apparent in its numerous sandstone stelae carved fully in-the-round. Tonina's solemn distinction is its possession of the very last Long Count date on a Maya monument, defining the end of Classic civilization in AD 909. Excavated by Pierre Becquelin and Claude Baudez of the French Archaeological Mission to Mexico from 1972 to 1980, Tonina is currently under investigation by the Mexican Instituto Nacional de Antropología e Historia under the direction of Juan Yadeun.

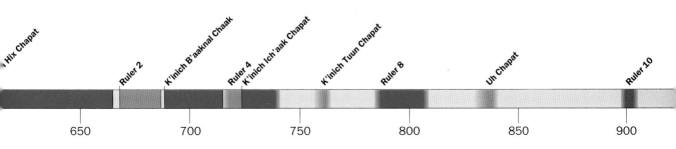

Hix Chapat · Ruler 2 · K'inich B'aaknal Chaak · Ruler 4 · K'inich Ich'aak Chapat · K'inich Tuun Chapat · Ruler 8 · Uh Chapat · Ruler 10

650   700   750   800   850   900

Ruler 1
>514>

Jaguar Bird Peccary
?

Chak B'olon Chaak
?

K'inich Hix Chapat
595?–665

This stela was discovered between the two temples which crown the Acropolis of Tonina and shows Jaguar Bird Peccary, an Early Classic ruler of the site.

RULER 1	
Glyphic spelling ITZAMNA:J-? *Also known as* Cabeza de Reptil	*Monument* 106, new altar

JAGUAR BIRD PECCARY	
Glyphic spelling B'ALAM ya-? AHK-AL ('Jaguar Bird Peccary')	*Also known as* Zots Choj *Monument* 177

CHAK B'OLON CHAAK	
Glyphic spelling CHAK-9-CHA:K	('Great/Red Nine / Many Rain God')

K'INICH HIX CHAPAT	
Glyphic spelling K'INICH HIX?[CHAPAT] ('Great-Sun Jaguar Centipede') *Also known as* Personage 2 *Accession* 14 February 595? (9.8.1.9.1	13 Imix 19 K'ayab) *Death* 5 February 665? (9.11.12.9.0 1 Ajaw 8 Kumk'u) *Monuments* 9?, 28, 125?, 154, 157; F.56, F.102?; Pestac Stela 1

EARLY TONINA

Surface remains at Tonina belong exclusively to the Late Classic period and as a result it was long thought to be one of the last major sites to take up the tradition of dynastic monuments. But with excavation now penetrating the superimposed layers of its hillside Acropolis, a vibrant Early Classic is slowly coming into view. In the future it may be possible to write an early history for the city, but for the moment our knowledge is restricted to a few sporadic finds.

Tonina certainly claims early origins – a text from the 8th century refers back to a king only identified by title in 217 – but the earliest known monuments are considerably later. The first of these is the fine, but now heavily broken, Monument 106. The pictured king, sitting on an iconic mountain described in the text, is **Ruler 1** in a sequence of ten Tonina kings compiled by Peter Mathews.[1] His personal name can be seen in a tiny medallion fixed to his forehead, where the god name Itzamnaaj is a major component. A better-preserved example appears on a remarkable altar recently uncovered by Juan Yadeun, dated to 514.[2] Another early stela, Monument 74, was found in a place of honour, reset in the sanctuary of Structure D5-1 at the very summit of the Acropolis. A memorial of the

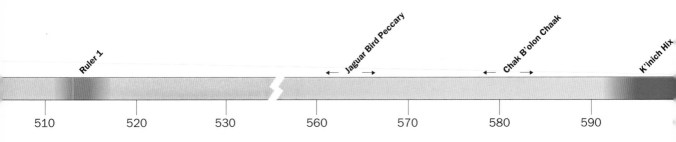

kind that was to prove so ubiquitous at the city, its date is unclear. It was once associated with the tomb of a king, here identified only as a 'Lord of Po(po')', the ancient name of the Tonina kingdom (see panel).

A pair of stelae, which can be dated by their glyph-style to the 6th century, introduce the city's trademark three-dimensional portraiture. The better preserved of the two, Monument 177 (also known as Zotz Choj) bears a ruler's name of **Jaguar Bird Peccary**. It includes his accession date, for which the year 568 is a good candidate. The second monument seems slightly later; its reference to a '12th in the line' might be this ruler's position in the local dynasty. The first foreign mention of Tonina appears on a throne from the site of Chinikiha on the Usumacinta River, about 45 miles (72 km) to the northeast. It describes the capture of a Tonina native in 573. A looted panel of unknown origin, now in the Tabascan town of Emiliano Zapata, describes a visit to the tomb of another Tonina king, **Chak B'olon Chaak**, which may have occurred in 589.

K'INICH HIX CHAPAT

As Tonina enters the Late Classic we catch sight of our first major figure. His name consists of the common *k'inich* or 'Great Sun' honorific followed by a jaguar head – normally read *b'alam* but perhaps *hix* in this case – wearing a headdress-like version of *chapat* 'centipede'. Bearing a closer resemblance to skeletal, buck-toothed snakes, centipedes in Maya art are pictured in a fantastic form appropriate to their supernatural status. They were associated with death and decomposition and seen as intermediaries with the Underworld. In fact, many of the so-called 'vision serpents' from which gods and the ancestral dead are disgorged are actually these mythic myriapods.[4]

The surviving two references to K'inich Hix Chapat's accession date are badly damaged, but the best reconstruction points to the year 595. His most important surviving text, Monument 154 of 633, describes the installation of subsidiary lords in the offices of *aj k'uhuun* and *nuun* (neither of which can be translated with confidence at present). Such cadres of supporting nobility vary in their prominence from one kingdom to another, though whether this reflects true differences in their importance is unclear. At Tonina they take an unusually high profile and show strong continuity between the reigns of different kings.

K'inich Hix Chapat's last mention is on a stela carrying a date in 665, found at Pestac, an outlying part of the city. It also recounts his birth and accession and bears all the hallmarks of a memorial stone.

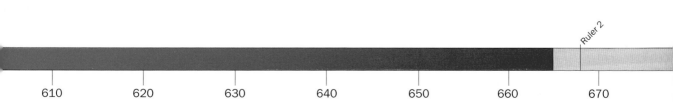

Ruler 2
668–687

K'inich B'aaknal Chaak
Ruler 3
688–715

Ruler 4
>717–723

The only complete portrait of Ruler 2 that survives today is Monument 26, a diminutive stela which shows him in standard pose, clutching a double-headed serpent bar. AD 672.

RULER 2	
Glyphic spelling YUKNOOM? ?-WAY *Also known as* Jaguar Casper *Accession* 20 August 668	(9.11.16.0.1 1 Imix 9 Mol) *Monuments* 8, 16, 17, 26, 85, 99 & 113

RULER 2

Three years separate the last date associated with K'inich Hix Chapat from the inauguration of Tonina's next king, currently known only as Ruler 2, in 668. His 19-year reign saw the city's sculptural repertoire concentrate on one of its most characteristic forms, the 'giant ajaw' altar, and most pervasive themes, the bound prisoner. The former, fashioned as large stone discs, were laid at each major calendrical ceremony and Tonina's enthusiasm for them was only exceeded by faraway Caracol (p. 89). The roped captive became a special fixation and the large number of these hapless victims has done much to give Tonina its militaristic reputation. Of particular interest are the two fragments that make up Monument 99, one of the few images in Maya art to show a female captive. More typical is Monument 8 from 682, a tall stela base, with its three naked captives bound at the arms, one a lord from an unknown site called Anaak'. The accompanying text lists the king's leading *aj k'uhuun*. One, K'el Ne' Hix, was to hold office for at least 34 years and serve under three successive monarchs.

Until recently, this was the last we knew of Ruler 2, but there is now some reason to think that his reign came to an inglorious end at the

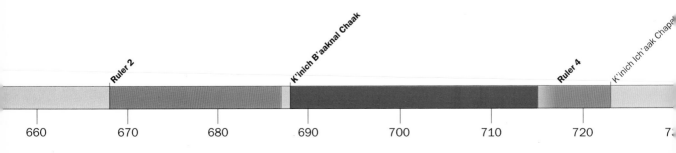

660   670   680   690   700   710   720   7.

Ruler 2   K'inich B'aaknal Chaak   Ruler 4   K'inich Ich'aak Chapa

This broken panel is one of the very few depictions of captive females in Maya art. Her dress or *huipil* has been cut to produce a series of holes and hanging flaps – a recurring symbol of defeat and humiliation. Monument 99.

This difficult passage from Palenque Temple 17 seems to refer to Ruler 2's defeat by Kan B'alam II in AD 687.

hands of Tonina's leading rival in the region, Palenque. This emerges from a small caption on a recently discovered panel from Palenque Temple 17. Rather cryptic in its phrasing, it describes the 'entering of his town'– a known euphemism for 'raid' or 'conquest' – in September 687. The defeated king has a damaged emblem but is called the 'Reed Throne-Spirit Companion'.[5] This is contrasted with the name of the victor, given as 'Bone-Spirit Companion', a form regularly used by the Palenque king Kan B'alam II. Whatever Reed Throne represents it is intimately associated with Tonina, twice appearing in the form of an emblem glyph carried by its kings. Most likely it is Ruler 2 himself who suffers the attack, while the fact that he was succeeded at Tonina within a year may indicate that he did not survive the clash.

K'INICH B'AAKNAL CHAAK

Tonina rebounded quickly from its defeat against Palenque and under the direction of its next king, K'inich B'aaknal Chaak ('Great-Sun Bone-Place Rain God') reached a highpoint of its political and military power. Long-range campaigns would take his influence to the northern limits of the Chiapas highlands and east into the heart of the Lacandon. B'aaknal Chaak was crowned in 688, inheriting the services of the two *aj k'uhuun* who served Ruler 2, but soon joined by another called Aj Ch'anaah. This character would later use the *yajaw k'ak'* 'Lord of Fire' title, probably denoting a key military position.

It is unsurprising that the principal theme of B'aaknal Chaak's 27-year reign was conflict with Palenque and the struggle for 'overkingship' of the region. Though the two antagonists lie barely 40 miles (64.5 km) apart, the mountainous terrain between them makes the effective distance much greater. As any topographic map makes clear, Tonina's primary access to the Classic heartland was not the rugged trek to the north, but through the river valleys that flow east to the Lacandon region and thence to the Usumacinta. It was here that B'aaknal Chaak began his challenge to Palenque's power, which must then have been close to its greatest extent.

Tonina victories of this era were once celebrated in several sculptural programmes, each of them arrays of resulting captives. Though all are fragmentary and dispersed today, their story can still be pieced together in large part. Ballcourt 1 seems to be the same arena dedicated by B'aaknal Chaak in 699 and the greatest of these triumphal statements (p.182). It was named, in part, *ox ahal* or 'three victories', a common epithet of ballcourts and their associated stairways and a reference to the mythical decapitations that underlay the ballgame as a paradigm of war and sacrifice (p.130).[6] It originally held six sculpted prisoners, each identified by name on a carved shield set beneath them. All surviving examples come from different locations and are said to be vassals of a Palenque ruler called simply *aj pitzal* 'ballplayer' — apparently an oblique reference to Kan B'alam. One of these vassals, Yax Ahk ('Green Turtle'), is already

THE SUNKEN BALLCOURT

The larger and much the more impressive of Tonina's two ballcourts is the sunken Ballcourt 1 found at the eastern edge of the Great Plaza. Remodelled on at least one occasion, it was paved with a mosaic of closely fitting stones, originally covered by a smooth layer of plaster. Its sloping side walls (an integral part of the playing area) featured the projecting torsos of as many as six sculpted captives, stretched over stone representations of feather-framed shields. It was probably dedicated in 699 to celebrate B'aaknal Chaak's successful campaigns in the Usumacinta region. All identifiable captives were vassals of arch-enemy Palenque. The renovation of the court took place after 776, the date of a memorial stone which was added as one of three markers along its central playing alley.[7]

The sunken form of Ballcourt 1 – here viewed from the north, looking out over the valley beyond – had a deep mythic significance, alluding directly to the place of Underworld sacrifice.

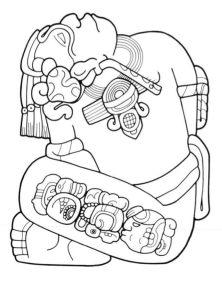

This twisted captive, Yax Ahk 'Green Turtle' of Anaay Te', is here dressed as a god in preparation for his sacrifice.

known from at least two carved panels, one of which tells us that he was an *ajaw* of Anaay Te'. Today, the place-name Anayte appears on the southern side of the Usumacinta, between Piedras Negras and Yaxchilan, where it describes a series of rapids, a lake and a major ruin.[8] The chances that it is ancient in origin are strong. Another of the ballcourt victims, who also appears on other sculptures at Tonina, was called Chan Maas and hailed from a site called Rabbit-e-Stone. This place-glyph finds mention in the inscriptions of Piedras Negras, where it probably represents a more complete spelling of that later identified as La Mar (p.151).[9] Parenthetically, this was not Tonina's only clash with Rabbit-e-Stone; on some unknown date it was conquered in a 'star war', with the defeat of a certain Nik Te' Mo' ('Flower Macaw'). While the ballcourt stones lack dates for these seizures, those on surviving panel blocks are expressed as single Tzolk'in positions — this incomplete form being a sure sign that they were closely spaced in time. This campaign may be related to the 'star war' B'aaknal Chaak conducted against lords beholden to *aj pitzal*, possibly dated to 692. Record of this appears on a shattered panel recently put on display at Tonina's fine new on-site museum, which shows a lord called K'awiil Mo' as the principal captive.[10]

With its temples and terraces once smoothly plastered and brightly painted, the man-modified mountain of the Tonina Acropolis would have been a dazzling sight right across the valley.

(*Right*) Monument 122 records the capture of K'an Joy Chitam II of Palenque, the greatest triumph of B'aaknal Chaak's reign. The explanatory text begins top right. The date is rather eroded, but 13 Ak'bal 16 Yax 9.13.19.13.3 – equivalent to 26 August 711 – is the only viable option. It then describes a 'star war' at the city of the Palenque king, whose name and title are inscribed on his leg in the form of a 'name-tag'.

Star over Palenque

B'aaknal Chaak's harrying of Palenque seems to have taken its toll and a resounding victory followed in 711. Here Tonina forces penetrated the Palenque capital in a new 'star war' and seized its king K'an Joy Chitam, the younger brother of Kan B'alam.[11] A sandstone panel at Tonina shows K'an Joy Chitam crouched and twisted, still wearing his jade jewelry but with his arms tied and paper strips inserted through his earlobes, the garb of the vanquished. His precise fate remains unclear, but the impact of his defeat is evident in the ensuing ten-year gap in Palenque's dynastic history (p. 171).[12]

K'INICH B'AAKNAL CHAAK	
Glyphic spelling	*Accession*
K'INICH-B'A:K-NAL-la CHA:K-ki ('Great-Sun Bone-place Rain God')	16 June 688 (9.12.16.3.12 5 Eb 0 Xul)
Also known as	*Monuments*
Ruler 3, Craneo de Serpiente, Kuk, Personage 3	3, 27, 29, 31, 52, 56, 63, 65, 72, 84, 111, 122, 134, 139, 140, 141,
Birth	143, 145, 161; F.3,
23 December 652 (9.11.0.3.13 7 Ben 1 Pax)	F.35?, F.88; COL. Altar 2?

(*Above*) This unprovenanced column altar provides evidence for Tonina's short-lived hegemony over the Lacandon region. Here a king of Bonampak, Etz'nab Jawbone, describes himself as the 'vassal lord' of B'aaknal Chaak in AD 715.

(*Right*) This fascinating panel shows a captive from Calakmul taken by Ruler 4 at some point between 716 and 723. A fragment from its left side mentions Pomoy, perhaps an ally Calakmul supported in one of its conflicts with Tonina. Monument 153.

RULER 4	
Glyphic spelling K'INICH-? K'AK' ('Great-Sun Jaguar God Fire')	(9.11.1.17.14 11 Ix 12 Sak) or 12 September 706 (9.13.14.12.14 11 Ix 12 Sak)
Also known as Dios Jaguar	*Monuments*
Birth 25 September 654	110, 136, 153, 165 & 170

By dint of his conquests and daunting reputation, B'aaknal Chaak had clearly established himself as an 'overking' with widespread authority. A valuable insight into its extent comes on an unusual column, originally from Bonampak, close to Yaxchilan. Here the local king describes himself as B'aaknal Chaak's vassal in 715.[13] Assuming that he was still alive at this point, Tonina's greatest warrior was now 63 and within a year of his death. One of the two 'giant ajaw' altars marking the 9.14.5.0.0 date of 716, Monument 165, names its celebrant as the *aj k'uhuun* K'el Ne' Hix, probably a sign that he served as a short-term regent.

RULER 4

The next Tonina king, Ruler 4, whose undeciphered name takes the form of a fiery jaguar god, was installed by at least 717. While we have a Calendar Round date for his birth, the lack of a Long Count anchor makes it impossible to decide between options in 654 and 706. He therefore acceded either as an old man, or one barely in his teenage years – in either case he was only in power for about five years.

Despite its short duration, Ruler 4's tenure was not without achievement and at least two sculptures depict bound captives he is credited with taking. One, named B'aah Tok' Xooy, cannot be linked to a known locality, but a second is called simply Aj Chiik Naab' or 'He of Calakmul'.[14] This find poses intriguing questions. Could there have been some direct, long-range engagement between the two kingdoms, or had Calakmul simply contributed warriors to an ally rather closer to hand? In this regard, it may be important that a broken portion of the

same stone mentions Pomoy, a kingdom that has yet to be identified archaeologically, but was a persistent foe of Tonina with probable later links with Calakmul (see p. 189).

We know that both K'el Ne' Hix and Aj Ch'anaah retained high office in the court of Ruler 4. Moreover, an altar unearthed in recent years records the death of a woman called Lady K'awiil Chan, apparently in 722. Unusually for a home reference she carries the queen's title *ix po(po)' ajaw*, perhaps a sign that she took a prominent role during Ruler 4's reign.

FRIEZE OF THE DREAM LORDS

In 1992 excavations at the eastern end of the fifth terrace produced easily the most spectacular find yet made at Tonina. A giant stucco mural, once brilliantly painted in red, blue and ochre, depicts the parallel universe of the *wayob'*, the 'spirit companions'. This bizarre dreamscape was populated by the alter egos of the Maya nobility, which take the form of fantastic, often ghoulish beasts (see p. 81). The complex frieze is divided into four by a feathered scaffold hung with the heads of sacrificial victims (a motif seen at Teotihuacan). The best-preserved section shows a skeletal figure called 'Turtle Foot Death' (note the turtleshells he wears on his feet), holding a decapitated human head. This seems to be the *way* of a Pipa' lord. Other figures include a small rodent carrying a bound jug or ball, a contorted acrobat smoking a cigar and the mythic hero Huun Ajaw, his hand newly severed by his nemesis, the great sky bird. The preponderance of burials on the fifth terrace makes it a fitting home for this 'otherworld' symbolism of darkness and transformation.

(Above right and below) *A wonderful example of Tonina's skill in stucco modelling, this great frieze has strong parallels to the mural paintings of Teotihuacan (above, detail from the Atelelco compound), where we see the same feathered frame and medallions with inverted figures, in this case birds.*

 K'inich
Ich'aak
Chapat
Ruler 5
723–739>

 Uh Chapat
Ruler 9
>837>

Ruler 10
>901>

 K'inich Tuun
Chapat
Ruler 6
>762

 Ruler 8
>787–806>

K'INICH ICH'AAK CHAPAT	
Glyphic spelling K'INICH ICH'A:K-CHAPAT ('Great-Sun Claw Centipede') *Also known as* Ruler 5, Garra de Jaguar *Birth* 20 March 696 (9.13.4.1.6 5 Kimi 14 Wo)	*Accession* 15 November 723 (9.14.12.2.7 5 Manik' 0 Muwan) *Mother* Lady Winik Timan K'awiil *Monuments* 7, 30, 135, 137, 138, 161, 164 & 174

K'INICH ICH'AAK CHAPAT

The next king, K'inich Ich'aak Chapat or 'Great-Sun Claw Centipede', acceded in 723. He shows special interest in his forebear, the great B'aaknal Chaak, and conducted a ritual 'fire-entering' into his tomb in June 730. At least one tomb at Tonina was found to contain urns holding crushed and burnt bones, probably the product of just this kind of ritual. The ceremony is recorded on Monument 161, a large circular altar dominated by the relevant day sign 5 Eb. The date of the ritual was carefully selected to exploit a calendrical conjunction of the kind Maya timekeepers delighted in, falling both 42 solar years and 59 Tzolk'in cycles after B'aaknal Chaak's accession in 688.

We might well surmise that Ich'aak Chapat was B'aaknal Chaak's son, but the only genealogical information he gives us relates to his mother, named on Monument 138 as Lady Winik Timan K'awiil. Parentage statements are so rare at Tonina that this must have special significance and serve either to boost the prestige of a minor queen, or hint at some deviation in the male line. Ich'aak Chapat produced quite a number of monuments, but the usual procession of war captives is strangely absent. He recorded the 5th and 13th Haab-anniversaries of his reign in

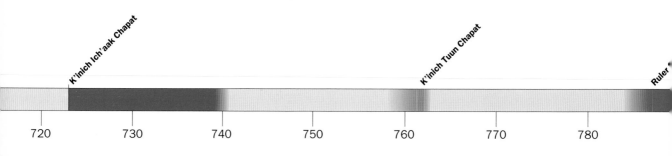

720   730   740   750   760   770   780

This magnificent circular stone is one of several 'memorial altars' describing the death, burial or subsequent tomb dedications of important members of the Tonina elite. This example features the over-sized glyph 5 Eb, the day on which the tomb of K'inich B'aaknal Chaak was 'entered with fire' in June 730, during the reign of K'inich Ich'aak Chapat.

729 and 736 and proved especially keen at commemorating the rarely observed eighth-of-a-K'atun which fell every two and a half years. Such an event in 739 is the last we hear from him, though the full extent of his tenure is currently unknown.

K'INICH TUUN CHAPAT

Whether a sign of political upheaval or simply an accident of preservation there are few records at Tonina for the next half-century. One of our few fixed points comes with Monument 47, a stela dating to 762. The king's name is almost certainly a variant of K'inich Tuun Chapat or 'Great-Sun Stone Centipede', a character long confused with the later Ruler 8. The recorded event is *och witz* 'entered the mountain', which could be a metaphorical reference to his death or burial in this case. A small stone box lid carries a clearer example of Tuun Chapat's name, although, perhaps because it has a missing base, its narrative and dating are obscure. Of greater interest is a panel fragment that links him to a new conflict with Palenque. The image of a bound prisoner is accompanied by a Palenque emblem glyph, though sadly the name of the king concerned falls on an adjoining, now missing, stone. Without the remainder of this text it is impossible to say if he is the prisoner himself, or simply his overlord.

Ballcourt 1 was remodelled at about this time and Monument 69 was added as one of three markers along its central playing alley. It records the death of a lord named Wak Chan K'ak' ('Six? Sky Fire') in 775 and his funerary rites the following year. Once thought to have been a king himself, he bears the descriptives *ch'ok*, 'youth, prince', and *b'aah al*, 'head child', and seems to have been an heir apparent who died before he could come to power.[15] We are almost certainly missing one or more rulers at this point. There are texts naming a Hix Chapat that look distinctly late in style, while someone with the name of Ruler 1 is mentioned during the reign of Ruler 8 (p. 188) – both could be namesakes of better-known precursors.

This unprovenanced stone box, allegedly found in a cave, dates to the reign of K'inich Tuun Chapat. The jade head is an ancient addition.

K'INICH TUUN CHAPAT	
Glyphic spelling	*Death*
K'INICH-TU:N-ni	9 February 762?
CHAPAT	(9.16.10.16.13
('Great-Sun Stone	9 Ben 11 Pop)
Centipede')	*Monuments*
Also known as	47, 107; Grolier 7
Ruler 6, Ruler 8	(Stone Box)

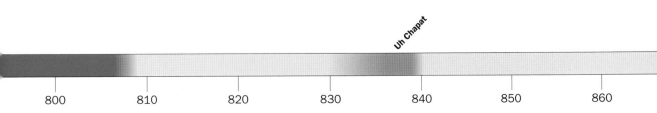

Uh Chapat

800   810   820   830   840   850   860

RULER 8	
Glyphic spelling K'INICH ?-?-CHAPAT ('Great-Sun ?- Centipede') *Birth* 6 July 756 (9.16.5.4.9 6 Muluk 17 Mol)	*Monuments* 1, 20, 34, 43, 83, 95, 114, 168?, 169, 171, 172, 175, Unnumbered Stela Base; Flower House Throne

RULER 8

Tonina enjoyed a final flowering under the last of its major kings, Ruler 8. He was born in 756, though nothing else about the first 30 years of his life, including his accession date, is known. He has been linked to a thorough reworking of the upper levels of the Acropolis, where both Structures E5-5 (6th-century in origin) and D5-2 (perhaps even older) were renovated and rich commemorative deposits set within them. When Stephens and Catherwood, the great early explorers of the Maya realm, visited Tonina in 1840 they found the interior walls of E5-5 covered with stucco-modelled figures, now lost. Just outside this temple, one of Ruler 1's stelae had been reset. The special interest Ruler 8 had for this king might be reflected in a memorial fire ritual he performed at his tomb in 799 (though it cannot be entirely ruled out that this was a more recent namesake, possibly even Ruler 8's father).

Ruler 8 contributed a number of new prisoner sculptures and, to further emphasize his military credentials, he styled himself *aj b'olon b'aak*, 'He of Many Captives'. One panel records his 'star war' conquest of Sak Tz'i' ('White Dog') and the capture of its ruler Stone-in-hand Star Jaguar. Sak Tz'i', though still unidentified, was an influential polity in

(*Above*) Recent excavations in the eastern part of the third terrace have unearthed Ruler 8's 'Flower House'. A bench within bears a text referring to his 'seating' in the building. Structurally, this throne room cuts through a much earlier building with an elaborate 'mountain monster' façade – hinting at Tonina's Early Classic splendour.

(*Right*) This panel begins with a tomb ritual, an 'entering with fire' that Ruler 8 conducted in AD 799. The subject has the same name as Ruler 1 and most likely the panel was a memorial to this long-dead king. The narrative then jumps back 10 years to the capture of Ucha'an Aj Chih, lord of Pomoy, who was Ruler 8's most prestigious victim.

Ruler 10

the Lacandon region (see p. 146), an area of one-time Tonina dominance. In 789, Ruler 8 led a new conflict against one of Tonina's frequent adversaries, the kingdom of Pomoy, and Monuments 169 and 175 depict a resulting captive called Ucha'an Aj Chih ('Master of He of Deer'). Interestingly, Monument 20 repeats the same information, but identifies this lord as the *uyajawte'*, or the vassal of a lord called B'olon K'awiil. His damaged title resembles a late form of the Kaan emblem and, given the potential link between Pomoy and Calakmul during the reign of Ruler 4, this could well be the same B'olon K'awiil who ruled Calakmul at about this time (see p. 115).

The year 794 saw Ruler 8 dedicate Monument 114, commemorating the death or tomb ritual of an important noble, seemingly some relative or vassal of Tuun Chapat. His last inscription, the stela base Monument 95, carries a date in 806, after which Tonina sinks into silence for the next 30 years.

LAST OF THE CLASSIC KINGS

Later monuments provide only momentary glimpses of a dynasty clinging to a fast-fading tradition. The city's relative isolation may well have been a factor in its longevity (its record currently outlasts that of Palenque by 110 years), but its record is very broken and it is by no means clear that its dynasty continued without interruption. Final collapse came at much the same time as the last lowland sites expired.

Missing the stela it once supported, a pedestal dedicated in 837 is the only clear record we have of Ruler 9 or **Uh Chapat**, perhaps 'Moon Centipede'.[16] A fine stucco frieze of captives on the south slope of D5-5 – pictured with garrottes at their throats, primed for torture or ready for execution – might date to 830 and be another of his works. By the time of the next known monument at Tonina, several decades later, artistic standards had deteriorated markedly. A half-sized stela and pedestal, the crude Monument 158, was set on the southeast corner of D5-2, the highest point of the Acropolis, by **Ruler 10** in 904. The text, while still literate, is so base in its style that the king's name is hard to isolate with confidence. Just five years later Tonina erected the fateful Monument 101, its last inscription and the last Long Count date in the entire Maya area, given as 10.4.0.0.0 or 15 January 909. Broken in two and with the king's name now lost, Tonina's record ends, as it began, in anonymity.

The usual scatterings of late ceramic types show that some occupation persisted for perhaps a century or more, but little is known about the governance of the valley until Dominican friars founded a church at Ocosingo, the modern town 8 miles (13 km) to the west of Tonina, in 1545. A rebellion of the native population of the valley in 1558 led to a forced resettlement at Ocosingo and the beginning of its role as the colonial capital of the region.

Monument 101, bearing the last Long Count date in Mesoamerica, was erected by an unknown Tonina king in AD 909.

UH CHAPAT	
Glyphic spelling	*Also known as*
UH-CHAPAT	Ruler 9
('Moon?	Monument
Centipede')	104

RULER 10	
Monument	
158 (stela and base)	

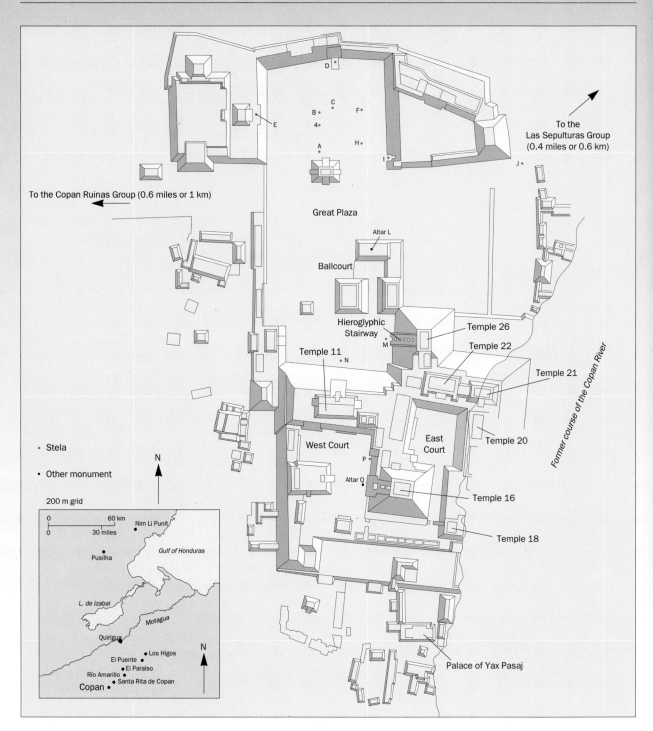

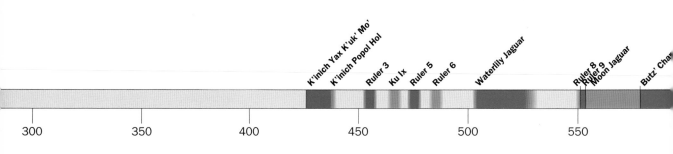

COPAN

THE SUBJECT of Stephens and Catherwood's first pioneering foray into the forest, Copan is one of the most closely investigated of all Maya cities. Its major claim to fame is the unsurpassed quality of its three-dimensional sculpture – a talent all the more remarkable for emerging not in the traditional core of Classic civilization, but in an enclosed valley at its eastern extremity. Yet today we are appreciating Copan for new reasons: as a unique source on the foundation of dynasties and of the complex relationship between the Maya and Teotihuacan.

Copan is dominated by a man-made hill at its heart – the Acropolis raised from the cumulative efforts of 16 kings, each building erected over the works of his predecessor. Over the past millennium the Copan River has cut a swathe from its eastern edge, destroying a series of important structures but exposing an invaluable 'cut' through its 400-year evolution. Now perforated by almost 2 miles (3 km) of excavated tunnels, this historical layer-cake has produced a vast amount of information and some of the most significant finds of recent years. Eminent archaeologists from varied institutions, working under the overall direction of William Fash since 1983, have investigated all parts of the city in search of a comprehensive picture of its ancient life.

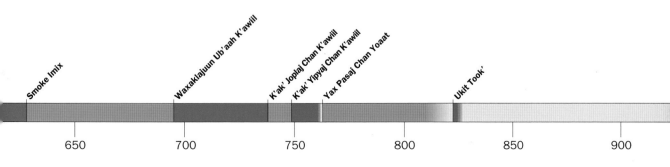

K'inich Yax K'uk' Mo'

Ruler 1

426–c. 437

K'inich Popol Hol

Ruler 2

>c. 437>

Ruler 3

c. 455

Ku Ix

Ruler 4

c. 465

Ruler 5

c. 475

Ruler 6

c. 485

K'INICH YAX K'UK' MO'	
Glyphic spelling K'INICH YAX-K'UK'[MO'] ('Great-Sun First Quetzal Macaw')	*Also known as* K'uk' Mo' *Son* K'inich Popol Hol *Burial* Temple 16 (Hunal)

K'INICH YAX K'UK' MO'

The founding father of Classic Copan was K'inich Yax K'uk' Mo' ('Great-Sun First Quetzal Macaw'). Until recently, what little we knew of him came entirely from retrospective Late Classic mentions, but probing of the city's deepest and earliest remains is now bringing his capital to light, taking us, it seems, to the very tomb of the founder himself.

Altar Q, carved some 350 years after his reign, is the definitive statement of Copan dynasty. Its four sides show each ruler in sequence seated on his name glyph.[1] On its western face, the encircling files of past and present meet and Yax K'uk' Mo' converses with the 16th king who commissioned the stone in 776 (p. 210). Its top surface recounts the story of Copan's inception. On 5 September 426 the founder – at first called simply K'uk' Mo' Ajaw 'Quetzal Macaw Lord' – took the snake-footed *k'awiil* sceptre and rose to kingly status. Three days later, a *taali* 'coming' event brought him (now bearing his regnal name) to the 'Foundation House' – perhaps the *wi te' naah* 'Root House'– a structure especially associated with dynastic genesis and seemingly of Mexican origin.[2] We now know that these ceremonies included the investiture of other lords in the region, specifically the first king of Quirigua (p. 216). While we are

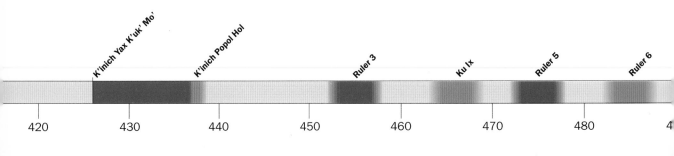

This portrait of K'inich Yax K'uk' Mo' comes from the inner shrine of the Late Classic Temple 16, *c.* AD 776.

COPAN BEFORE YAX K'UK' MO'

The Copan Valley, blessed with good soils and an abundant water supply, has attracted human settlement from ancient times. Excavations both in the district of Las Sepulturas (see p. 211) and elsewhere demonstrate that Preclassic Copan was a significant site well before Yax K'uk' Mo' brought the Classic revolution to the region. His *entrada* certainly displaced an existing elite, perhaps by force of arms. A few inscriptions provide hazy references to earlier times, though whether these concern dimly remembered history or newly manufactured myth is hard to say. One date falls in 321 BC, though no explanation accompanies it. The K'atun-ending 8.6.0.0.0 of AD 159 is recalled on more than one occasion, where it concerns a mysterious character named 'Foliated Ajaw' and a mythic event linked to monument dedication and sacrifice. He is also named on a carved peccary skull from Tomb 1, discovered in the 1920s, where he is said to 'wrap' a stela in AD 376.[3]

not told exactly where they took place, the location seems to have been a distant one. It was 152 days before Yax K'uk' Mo' and his party reached Copan itself (perhaps bearing a *k'awiil* god effigy), expressed as an 'arrival here' at Ox Witik, the most important place-name at Copan. Journeys of this kind, including the carrying of god images, are archetypal features of foundation stories throughout Mesoamerica.

The origins of Yax K'uk' Mo'

Who was Yax K'uk' Mo' and where did he come from? Late Classic portraits invariably show him wearing the 'goggle eye' ornaments of Teotihuacan origin, but our one near-contemporary depiction shows him, by contrast, in orthodox Maya garb (see p. 194). This eclectic mix of Maya and Mexican styles is evident in Yax K'uk' Mo's own time, in the architecture of his new city. His first structures, some built over the pre-existing adobe platforms of Preclassic Copan, established its basic layout and the two most important ritual locations, ultimately the sites of Temples 16 and 26. The former began its life with Hunal, a building in the *talud-tablero* style of Teotihuacan.[4] Though its superstructure was later demolished, traces of interior walls show that it was once enlivened with brightly coloured murals, just as at Teotihuacan itself. The latter, somewhat to the north, began with a platform nicknamed Yax. The style of this, with its inset-corner and apron mouldings, shows strong affinities with Tikal and the Peten.

The arrival story has clear parallels with the *entrada* of Siyaj K'ak' to Tikal in 378 and the introduction of the Teotihuacano New Order in the central Peten (see pp. 29–31).[5] The clear ties Yax K'uk' Mo' displays with both Mexican and Maya traditions strongly suggest that he was part of this New Order and, if not Mexican himself, then a Maya steeped in Mexican traditions (our earliest reference to him comes in 416 and suggests that he was already an important lord).[6] The inaugural ceremonies of 426 could have taken place in the Peten, or even distant Mexico.

The Hunal tomb

We lack a precise date for Yax K'uk' Mo's death, but he did not survive much beyond the turn of the 9th Bak'tun in 435 and was certainly dead by 437. In 1995 a team working on the early phases of Temple 16, led by Robert Sharer and David Sedat, found a vaulted crypt cut into the floor of Hunal. Within were the remains of an aged male, adorned with a suitably royal collection of jades, including a large bar pectoral, ear ornaments and tooth inlays. The skeleton showed evidence of several injuries consistent with battle wounds, including a broken right arm that had never properly healed. It has been noted that Yax K'uk' Mo's portrait on Altar Q shows a stunted right limb obscured by a small square shield, perhaps an accurate detail. Lying at the very core of the Acropolis, beneath a sequence of at least seven further buildings each dedicated to his enduring memory, this body seems certain to be that of the founder himself. Recent analysis of the bones shows none of the chemical signatures of a Copan native, identifying him as the foreigner the texts describe.[7]

Probably built by Popol Hol around AD 450, the Margarita temple, now deeply buried beneath Temple 16, was designed as a memorial shrine for Yax K'uk' Mo'. Entwined quetzals and macaws on its marvellously preserved stucco façade spell out *k'uk'* and *mo'*, while the yax emblems attached to their heads and tiny sun gods in their beaks complete these iconic spellings of the founder's name.

(*Below*) On the Motmot capstone, Yax K'uk' Mo' (left) and Popol Hol (right) face each other across a block of text. The quatrefoil frame and the particular locations named under their feet place them in supernatural space, the realm of the now deceased founder.

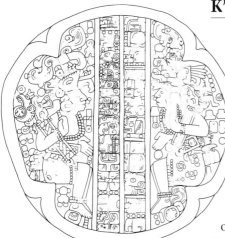

K'INICH POPOL HOL	
Glyphic spelling K'INICH[?] ('Great-Sun ?') *Also known as* Popol Hol K'inich, Mat Head, Tok'	*Father* K'inich Yax K'uk' Mo' *Monuments* Stelae 18 & 63; Motmot Capstone; Xukpi Stone

K'INICH POPOL HOL

At Yax K'uk' Mo's death in or around 437 the throne passed to his son, Popol Hol. Popol Hol is a modern nickname meaning 'Mat Head' in Mayan, derived from the braided designs that mark the curling headdress of his name glyph (a motif with Teotihuacan links). A particularly industrious figure, he quickly set about a major development of the site core and initiated a cult of veneration for his father that would endure for almost four centuries.

The Yax platform was replaced with the more elaborate, stucco-decorated Motmot. Set into the plaza floor, previously it was a circular capstone covering a most unusual grave. The disarticulated body of a woman was accompanied by a diverse collection of mercury, quartz, jade, numerous animal and bird bones, and three decapitated human heads (all male). Her identity remains a mystery but the style of this interment mirrors examples at Teotihuacan. The capstone itself was delicately carved with the opposed portraits of Popol Hol and Yax K'uk' Mo' divided by a stela-like text. It contains two dates, one the 9.0.0.0.0 mark of 435, another the stone's probable dedication in 441. The same 435 date was carved on the finely styled, all-glyphic Stela 63 – either a Popol Hol monument or one of Yax K'uk' Mo's to which he added his own side texts – which was set on the summit of the platform within

THE LADY IN RED

The Margarita tomb yielded the richest female burial yet discovered in the Maya area. Her remains, laid on a heavy stone table, were adorned with numerous jades (her anklets alone contained thousands of jade beads) and copiously covered with the red pigments hematite and cinnabar – hence her nickname 'The Lady in Red'. After her funeral, the Margarita temple above was partly demolished and replaced by a chamber connected to the crypt's access stairway. This was the scene for rites of remembrance and tomb re-entry that continued even after the building of yet another surmounting platform, Chilan. When eventually sealed, it received a trove of new offerings. The most impressive was the 'Dazzler', a lidded tripod vessel vividly painted in pure Teotihuacan style. No inscription reveals the queen's identity, but her extraordinary wealth and status have been seen to denote that she was the widow of the founder.

Ablaze with cinnabar and hematite, the remains of a woman – probably the wife of the founder – lies deep within the platform named Margarita.

The 'Dazzler' may show Yax K'uk' Mo' personified as his own memorial shrine.

a perishable building.[8] Two other Popol Hol monuments survive as fragments. One, Stela 18, is interesting since it includes the rare 'lashed ladder' sign *ehb'*, only otherwise used in the name of the Tikal founder Yax Ehb' Xook.

The founder's shrine

Popol Hol also built the first version of Copan's ballcourt. Like its successors, it was decorated with images of the mythic scarlet macaw, the ruling deity of a previous universe called Seven Macaw by later Maya.[9] However, the most intense activity of his reign was reserved for the Hunal structure and a construction sequence that would see three buildings quickly succeed each other on the same spot. After entombing his father in the floor of Hunal, he razed its superstructure and encased it within a platform dubbed Yehnal, re-aligning its northerly orientation to a westerly one. Unlike the Mexican style of Hunal, Yehnal was distinctly Maya in design: its 'apron-moulded' base bearing large red-painted masks of the sun god K'inich Tajal Wayib', closely akin to Peten buildings of the time. It was designed with an inbuilt burial chamber and access stairway, but before these could be used – probably within a decade – the whole structure was covered by a third platform, the much larger Margarita. The vibrantly painted stucco panels that flank its exterior stair (a major find of recent years) show macaws and quetzals entwined like giant 'monograms', iconic spellings of Yax K'uk' Mo's name.[10]

When the Margarita tomb was finally put to use it housed the remains of an elderly woman (see p. 195). Her fabulous wealth and prestigious treatment strongly suggest that she was Yax K'uk' Mo's widow and the mother of Popol Hol. Chemical analysis of her bones indicates that she was a local woman, probably a sign that the incomers cemented control by marrying into Copan's traditional elite.[11] The upper sanctuary of the Margarita was converted into an offerings chamber at this time and the perplexing 'Xukpi' stone – a dedication block stripped from either this building or Yehnal – re-used in its masonry. It gives a date in 437, refers to 'his skull/head', and names both Popol Hol and Yax K'uk' Mo', and perhaps even Siyaj K'ak'. Strange in style and phrasing, its full meaning is unclear.[12]

RULER 3 TO RULER 6

Little is known of the next four Copan kings. As elsewhere, early monuments were often broken up in later years and deposited, rather unceremoniously, into construction fill. From one such fragment we know that at least one of these kings was a son of Popol Hol.[13] **Ruler 3** is shown on Altar Q, but unfortunately his name-glyph 'throne' has largely broken away. Alongside him sits the fourth ruler, **Ku Ix**, the best known of the group. He either built or redeveloped the Papagayo building which replaced Motmot. Popol Hol's Stela 63 remained the focus of its inner sanctuary, but a new hieroglyphic step was added to its base. The extensive burning involved in the later 'killing' of this room severely damaged this block, but surviving sections show that it is one of the few inscriptions to quote a king directly. Passages (which include 'your gods' and 'your land') are *che'en* 'said' by Ku Ix and may well be addressed to Stela 63 and Yax K'uk' Mo' himself.[14] Two additional stela fragments carry Ku Ix's name, but not a single date helps us to place him in the chronology. The same fate is shared by **Ruler 5** and **Ruler 6**, who are known only from their listing on Altar Q.

RULER 3	
Glyphic spelling ya?-?	

KU IX	
Glyphic spelling TU:N?-K'AB'-HIX ('Stone Hand Jaguar')	Also known as Ruler 4, Cu-Ix *Monuments* Stela 34; Papagayo Step; CPN 584

RULER 5	
Glyphic spelling yu-?[ku?]-a	

RULER 6	
Glyphic spelling MUYAL?-JOL?	

This northern side of Altar Q shows (from right to left) the little-known Ruler 3, Ku Ix (Ruler 4), Ruler 5 and Ruler 6.

Waterlily Jaguar
Ruler 7
>504–524>

Ruler 8
>551

Ruler 9
551–553

Moon Jaguar
Ruler 10
553–578

Altar Q carries the sole surviving portrayal of Ruler 8.

WATERLILY JAGUAR	
Glyphic spelling	*Son*
B'ALAM-?-na	Moon Jaguar
Also known as	*Monuments*
Jaguar-Sun-God,	Stela 15; Altar Q'?;
Balam Nan	Ante Step?
Dynastic title	
7th in the line	

RULER 8	
Glyphic spelling	*Also known as*
b'u-?	Head-on-Earth

RULER 9	
Glyphic spelling	*Accession*
SAK-lu	28th December 551
	(9.5.17.13.7
	2 Manik' 0 Muwan)

WATERLILY JAGUAR TO RULER 9

Only slightly more in the way of contemporary evidence survives from the reign of **Waterlily Jaguar**, whose long name seems to read, in part, B'alam Nehn 'Jaguar Mirror'. He is the first Copan king to enumerate his dynastic position, stating that he is seventh in the line of Yax K'uk' Mo'. He seems to have been in office by 504, as recorded on the all-glyphic Stela 15 of 524. Waterlily Jaguar has the distinction of being the only Copan king to be mentioned outside the southeast region, appearing in a still uncertain context on Caracol Stela 16, dated to 534 (pp. 88–9). Archaeologically, he has been linked to a major expansion of the Acropolis complex, replacing an early palace (in the area later covered by the East Court) with a series of major structures, one of which, Ante, carries a dedication step dated to 542.[15] In later years he was memorialized on Stela E, probably a work of the 12th ruler, Smoke Imix. The text is damaged and confusing, but it may refer to rites communicating with the dead king.

Altar Q is the only evidence for the reign of **Ruler 8** and little more can be said for **Ruler 9**. His accession in 551 is chronicled on a block of Copan's Hieroglyphic Stairway, but he endured for less than two

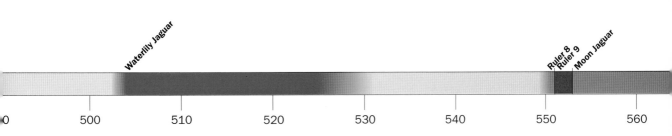

This eastern side of Altar Q shows (from right to left) Waterlily Jaguar, Ruler 8, Ruler 9 and Moon Jaguar.

years. One of these three rulers should be the occupant of the tomb called Sub-Jaguar, a fine royal burial uncovered under the East Court's Structure 25 and its later 'prancing jaguar' sculpture.[16]

Moon Jaguar

The next king, a son of Waterlily Jaguar known as Moon Jaguar, was crowned in May 553. Both his surviving monuments, Stela 17 of 554 and Stela 9 of 564, were found on the site of the present village of Copan Ruinas, once a major sub-complex 1 mile (1.6 km) to the west of the principal group. His most significant achievement came with the construction of Rosalila, a magnificent new shrine to the founder erected over the razed remains of five earlier temples.

What makes Rosalila so unique is its state of preservation. Ricardo Agurcia's tunnelling of Temple 16 discovered an entire building, from platform to roofcomb, carefully interred and virtually intact. The structure was still coated with its heavy stucco decoration and, beneath a final wash of white, brilliantly coloured in red, green and yellow. Its complex iconography sets Yax K'uk' Mo' in a grand cosmic scheme, fusing him in multiple images with the great sky deity Itzamnaaj in his avian aspect and a layered programme that includes personified mountains, as well as skeletal and crocodilian imagery. Rosalila's interior was blackened by well over a century of smoke and incense – rituals appropriate to its role at the heart of ancestral veneration – and

MOON JAGUAR	
Glyphic spelling tzi-B'ALAM-ma ('? Jaguar') *Also known as* Tzik B'alam, Cleft-Moon Leaf-Jaguar *Accession* 24 May 553 (9.5.19.3.0 8 Ajaw 3 Mak)	*Death* 24 October 578 (9.7.4.17.4 10 K'an 2 Keh) *Father* Waterlily Jaguar *Monuments* Stela 9 & 17; Rosalila Step

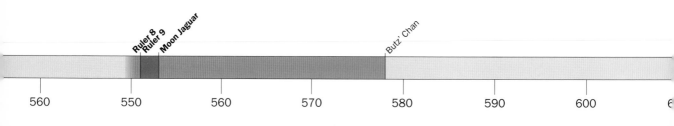

vents in its façade were designed so that billowing clouds would interact with the sculpture in an animated tableau.[17]

Rosalila was the last building at Copan to use stucco on such a lavish scale. With deforestation of the valley now well advanced, the great quantities of firewood needed to reduce limestone to plaster could no longer be afforded and all its successors show a move to stone-carved decoration. Less well preserved than Rosalila's exterior is its stone dedication step, though a date in 571 is just legible. The structure itself remains entombed within Temple 16, but a full-size replica has been built as the centrepiece of a new on-site museum, allowing this most perfect example of Early Classic architecture to be viewed from all sides and in all its multi-coloured glory.

Rosalila, the most perfectly preserved Early Classic building yet discovered, was a dynastic shrine constructed by Moon Jaguar over the deeply buried tomb of the founder. This full-size and meticulously detailed replica is the centrepiece of a new on-site museum.

Butz' Chan
Ruler 11
578–628

Smoke Imix
Ruler 12
628–695

Waxaklajuun Ub'aah K'awiil
Ruler 13
695–738

Copan's emerging interest in three-dimensional form is apparent in the works of Butz' Chan. Stela P, AD 623.

B'UTZ' CHAN	
Glyphic spelling K'AK'-?-wa CHAN-na-YOA:T? ('Fire-drinking? Sky Lightning God) *Also known as* Ruler 11, Smoking Heavens	*Accession* 17 November 578 (9.7.5.0.8 8 Lamat 6 Mak) *Death* 20 January 628 (9.9.14.16.9 3 Muluk 2 K'ayab) *Monuments* Stelae 7 & P; Altar Y? & X?

BUTZ' CHAN

The transition between the Early and Late Classic saw a steep rise in population throughout the Copan 'pocket' (the valley and its lesser branches), with homesteads and garden plots filling all the available level ground.[18] Copan's 11th ruler Butz' Chan acceded to the throne in the midst of this expansion, 24 days after the death of Moon Jaguar in 578. Two of his monuments have survived. Stela 7, which marks the K'atun-ending 9.9.0.0.0 of 613, was another found in the western outlier now covered by the modern village. The original location of Stela P, commissioned ten years later, is unknown, but it was found reset in the West Court of the Acropolis. These elegant, slightly tapered stones are the earliest monuments at the city to escape later breakage and burial. Their long texts are still somewhat elusive in their meaning, but seem to deal with ritual rather than historical information. Butz' Chan enjoyed a reign of 49 years, dying in 628. He was well remembered by his successors and is mentioned on no fewer than four later stelae. One, Stela A, describes some memorial rite from 730, a *susaj baak* 'slicing or peeling of bones', presumably involving relics drawn from his tomb.[19]

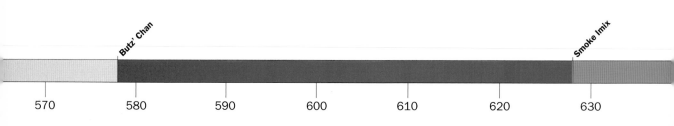

Butz' Chan   Smoke Imix

570   580   590   600   610   620   630

In a rather cryptic reference, Smoke Imix does not sit on his name glyph but on a title paying homage to his venerable age, a lord of 5 K'atuns (aged between 79 and 98 years). Altar Q, 776.

COPAN AND BELIZE

Two important cities in southern Belize, north of the Motagua region, show signs of contact with Copan. Kings at Pusilha took the names of both Butz' Chan and Smoke Imix shortly after their respective reigns, while one of its stelae chronicles the same AD 159 date and actor, Foliated Ajaw, so important to Copan. At Nim Li Punit kings wear the 'turban' headdress otherwise unique to Copan, while the ruler commemorated on the newly discovered Stela 16 (AD 790) carries the name Ox Witik K'awiil, seemingly a reference to the Copan place-name.[20] These features attest to some kind of cultural, or even political, sphere around Copan – perhaps of fluctuating intensity – encompassing a large part of the eastern borderlands.

SMOKE IMIX

SMOKE IMIX	
Glyphic spelling	*Death*
K'AK'-u-? HA'?-	15 June 695
K'AWI:L	(9.13.3.5.7
('Fire-drinking?	12 Manik' 0 Yaxk'in)
Water? K'awiil')	*Son*
Also known as	Waxaklajuun Ub'aah
Smoke Imix God K,	K'awiil?
Smoke-Jaguar Imix-	*Monuments*
Monster, Smoke	Stelae 1, 2, 3, 5, 6,
Jaguar, K'ak' Nab	10, 12, 13, 19, 23
K'awil	& E; Altars H', I', K
Dynastic title	& 5
12th in the line	*Burial*
Accession	Temple 26
5 February 628	(Chorcha)
(9.9.14.17.5	(Burial XXXVII–4)
6 Chikchan 18	
K'ayab)	

Copan's longest reigning monarch, Smoke Imix, assumed power 16 days after Butz' Chan's death on 5 February 628. Calculations drawn from his various K'atun-age statements place his birth in *c.* 612, making him about 15 when he took the throne. There is little if anything to show for his first 24 years in power, but in 652, on and around the ending 9.11.0.0.0, he produced an outpouring of at least seven monuments. Stelae 2 and 3 were erected in the city's Great Plaza, while the all-glyphic Stelae 10, 12, 13 and 19 were set in prominent positions across the valley. Over the years a number of theories have been offered to explain the arrangement of this last group: from territorial markers to solar sighting devices; from stations in a signal system to odes to mountain gods.[21] What is clear is that he strove to imprint his authority on the whole Copan landscape (perhaps in reaction to some impediment of his earlier reign). Their texts are extensive, but like those of Butz' Chan, rather jealous of their meaning. Further afield, Stela 23 was erected on the same 652 date at Santa Rita, a secondary site 7.5 miles (12 km) up the valley. Despite its peripheral location it dwells on one of the most fundamental of topics for the Maya, the founding of the 'current creation' in 3114 BC (p. 221).

One fascinating mention of Smoke Imix occurs on Quirigua Altar L, where he is named as the subject of a *tzak huul* event – perhaps meaning his 'conjured arrival here' – for this same 652 celebration (see p. 217). This might well be a sign that Quirigua remained in Copan's political orbit at this time and that the regional order established by K'inich Yax K'uk' Mo' 226 years earlier was essentially intact. Yet some caution is necessary – the only other example of this poorly understood event links sites which had recently been at war.[22]

Waxaklajuun Ub'aah K'awiil

| 650 | 660 | 670 | 680 | 690 | 700 | 710 |

THE CHORCHA TOMB

Deep beneath Temple 26 and its Hieroglyphic Stairway lies the buried pyramid called Chorcha. When its upper sanctuary was demolished in preparation for its successor, a large crypt (25 ft or 7.6 m long) was excavated in its floor and roofed with a series of 11 huge stone slabs. They covered one of Copan's most lavish interments, that of an adult male together with a child, presumably a sacrifice. The lord's body was wrapped in matting and adorned with a number of fine jades, among them a necklace of carved figures and heavy ear ornaments. Associated offerings included a total of 44 pottery vessels, scribal paraphernalia (ten paintpots and at least one decayed book), jaguar pelts, as well as rare spondylus and spiny oyster shells. Converging lines of evidence now suggest that the badly decayed skeleton is that of the great Smoke Imix. The fact that the stairway covering Chorcha is named as 'the steps of Smoke Imix' is especially significant.[23] Among a great haul of ceramic incense-burners left around the demolished Chorcha sanctuary were 12 whose lids were modelled in the form of human figures. The Teotihuacan-style 'goggle eyes' of one serves to identify him as K'inich Yax K'uk' Mo' and, by extension, the whole assembly as portraits of Smoke Imix and his 11 royal predecessors.[24]

Four of 12 royal effigies associated with the tomb. Note the goggle-eyes that identify one as Yax K'uk' Mo'.

(Above) Scattered debris inside the Chorcha tomb conceals the remains of a Copan king, almost certainly Smoke Imix himself.

(Right) This magnificent carving of a cormorant-crested Rain God is now thought to be from Smoke Imix's reign.

The 5-K'atun Lord

Over the remaining 42 years of his reign, Smoke Imix dedicated at least nine further monuments and was undoubtedly responsible for important additions to the city's architecture. Though few buildings can be directly attributed to him, he completed Structure 2, defining the northern boundary of the Great Plaza. The dissection of Temple 26 by William Fash and his team uncovered one of his most important works, the buried temple called Chorcha.[25] This began life with the ritual destruction of Ku Ix's Papagayo and its covering by the pyramid called Mascaron. At this time Stela 63 and its hieroglyphic step were broken, burnt, and ritually cached together with a set of stone macaw heads that seem to have been stripped from the first ballcourt. Chorcha was in essence a redevelopment of Mascaron, topped with a long gallery-like superstructure with seven doorways at front and back. The rich burial set into its floor is now thought to be Smoke

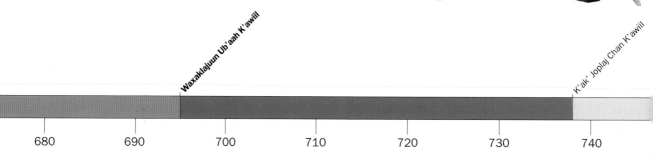

Waxaklajuun Ub'aah K'awiil

K'ak' Joplaj Chan K'awiil

680   690   700   710   720   730   740

This rendition of Waxaklajuun Ub'aah K'awiil's name illustrates the freedom that scribes possessed to combine signs for aesthetic or space-saving purposes. Here the gopher head read *b'aah* has been fused with the head of the deity *k'awiil*. Lesser elements (the possessive pronoun *u* in this case) were often omitted in well-known formulae such as these. Stela 4, AD 731.

Stela A, dedicated by Waxaklajuun Ub'aah K'awiil in AD 731.

Imix's own. He died on 15 June 695, after 67 years in power, and was interred just two days later (a sure sign that his tomb lay ready to receive him). He had recently entered his 5th K'atun – over 79 years old – an achievement so notable that this count alone serves as his identifying 'glyph throne' on Altar Q.

WAXAKLAJUUN UB'AAH K'AWIIL

The 13th ruler, Waxaklajuun Ub'aah K'awiil ('18 images of K'awiil'), acceded in July 695. In a reign of vivid contrasts, he presided over the very pinnacle of Copan's cultural and artistic achievement, before leading it to one of its greatest political disasters. In the creative sphere, the steady evolution of the city's three-dimensional carving broke into a revolution. Its 'organic' rendering of stone now matched stucco-modelling in its plasticity and control of volume, bringing a new sense of naturalism to public art at the city.

As ever, the role of art was to promote and sustain royal power. Like all his forebears at Copan, Waxaklajuun Ub'aah K'awiil eschewed the military triumphalism so common in more crowded and contested Maya regions, preferring to present awe-inspiring displays of his quasi-divine status and role as interface between the mortal and cosmic realms. Yet this rhetorical emphasis should not distract us from more pragmatic concerns. He certainly enjoyed control of the rich Motagua Valley, installing the Quirigua king K'ak' Tiliw Chan Yoaat in 724 – doubtless only one of many such relationships across the region (p. 218). But this ascendancy still had to be fought for. An unusual stone cylinder records Waxaklajuun Ub'aah K'awiil's burning in 718 of 'Xkuy', an as yet unidentified centre later subject to Quirigua.[26] His self-confidence and assertiveness is best seen on Stela A from 731, where he sets his kingly office in a symbolic, four-way orientation with those of Tikal, Calakmul and Palenque. Though still obscure in its details, the desire to fix Copan in the ranks of the mightiest Classic kingdoms is plain.[27]

A flowering of form

While Smoke Imix had distributed his monuments widely across the valley, Waxaklajuun Ub'aah K'awiil concentrated his efforts in the ceremonial core. His first work, Stela J from 702, stands at the eastern entrance to the city. Something of an oddity, it was crowned with a carved stone roof, making it a symbolic 'house'. The historical part of its inscription is woven into a mat design. A form of puzzle, unless the convoluted mesh is traced with precision the text is all but unintelligible. All his later works were grouped in the adjacent Great Plaza, which he remodelled by building the defining steps on its eastern and western flanks and platforms at its southern edge.

His Stelae C, F, 4, H, A, B and D, erected in that order between 711 and 736, represent one of the great legacies of the Classic era. For many, their fluidity and mastery of detail make them simply the highest

Portraits of Waxaklajuun Ub'aah K'awiil as they appear on (*from left to right*) Stelae C, A and B. As images of the impassive but all-powerful 'divine lord', fixed at the centre of his kingdom's spiritual universe, they are unequalled in the Maya world.

achievement of Maya sculpture. Each shows the king posed in ritual performance, clasping a double-headed centipede bar to his chest, but distinguished by the masks and regalia of various gods, among them the local patrons B'olon K'awiil, K'uy Nik Ajaw and Mo' Witz Ajaw.[28] Their texts record these impersonation rituals, shamanic transformations through which he invoked their power and secured their benediction. The stone assemblage was at once a pantheon of great variety and an emphatic repetition of the king's image.

A prolific builder

Waxaklajuun Ub'aah K'awiil made numerous additions to the fabric of the city. By 710 he had sealed Chorcha and the tomb of Smoke Imix within a new version of Temple 26 dubbed Esmeralda. This was fitted with the first version of Copan's Hieroglyphic Stairway, a lengthy dynastic chronicle (p. 208).[29] Judging by their style, he also built Temples 20 and 21 of the East Court (both fell into the Copan River early this century before its flow was diverted), while reverently encasing Rosalila within a new version of Temple 16 called Purpura.[30] As part of Rosalila's termination rites, a fine collection of 'eccentric' flints – chert expertly knapped into human and divine profiles – were wrapped in blue-dyed textiles and left as an offering.[31] Temple 22, erected to celebrate the 1st K'atun-anniversary of his reign in 715, is the best preserved of his projects. Its sculpture symbolically recreates the mountain where maize was born and rises out of the watery Underworld represented by the East Court.

WAXAKLAJUUN UB'AAH K'AWIIL	
Glyphic spelling 18-u-b'a-hi K'AWI: L-la ('18 images of K'awiil') *Also known as* 18 Rabbit, 18 JOG *Dynastic title* 13th in the line *Accession* 6 July 695 (9.13.3.6.8 7 Lamat 1 Mol)	*Death* 29 April 738 (9.15.6.14.6 6 Kimi 4 Sek) *Father* Smoke Imix? *Monuments* Stelae A, B, C, D, E, F, H, J, & 4; Altar S; Lower Hieroglyphic Stairway of Temple 26; Step of Temple 22; Ballcourt AIIb markers, Ballcourt A-III text & markers.

The final version of Copan's ballcourt was completed in AD 738, just a few months before Waxaklajuun Ub'aah K'awiil's unfortunate demise.

One of four separate references at Quirigua to the 'beheading' in 738 of Waxaklajuun Ub'aah K'awiil. Note the axe sign (tinted), reading *ch'ak* 'to chop'. Quirigua Stela J, AD 756.

Its interior step features the first-person quotation: 'I completed my K'atun'.[32]

Having remodelled an earlier version of the Ballcourt (A-IIb), Waxaklajuun Ub'aah K'awiil demolished it and constructed a new one further north, making this third and final version one of the largest and most elaborate of the Classic era. Like its predecessors, it was dedicated to the great macaw deity, the façades of its flanking buildings carrying no fewer than 16 mosaic sculptures of these fiercely taloned birds. The inclined slopes of the playing area carry a dedication text dating its completion to 6 January 738.[33]

Nemesis

The new ballcourt was less than four months old when the 43-year career of Waxaklajuun Ub'aah K'awiil, and with it Copan's golden age, came to a shattering conclusion. In April 738 he was seized by his vassal, the Quirigua king K'ak' Tiliw Chan Yoaat (p. 218). The initial incident is obscure – its only record, at Quirigua, describes some fire event involving two of his city's patron deities. Elsewhere we have seen how the capture or violation of god effigies was a recurring feature of Mesoamerican conflict (see pp. 45, 49, 79, 160). Whatever its significance, the decisive event took place six days later when the Copan king was 'beheaded'. Copan's own account of this humiliation, recorded some years later, puts a less embarrassing gloss on the episode: it talks about the king's demise by 'flint and shield' – a noble death in battle.

K'ak' Joplaj Chan K'awiil

Smoke Monkey
Ruler 14
738–749

K'ak' Yipyaj Chan K'awiil

Smoke Shell
Ruler 15
749–761>

Yax Pasaj Chan Yoaat

Ruler 16
763–810>

Ukit Took'

822

K'AK' JOPLAJ CHAN K'AWIIL	
Glyphic spelling	*Accession*
K'AK'-jo-po la-ja-	7 June 738
CHAN-na K'AWI:L	(9.15.6.16.5
('K'awiil that Stokes	6 Chikchan 18 K'ayab)
the Sky with Fire')	*Death*
Also known as	31 January 749
Smoke Monkey,	(9.15.17.12.16
Three Death	10 Kib 4 Wayeb)
Dynastic title	*Son*
14th in the line	K'ak' Yipyaj Chan
	K'awiil

K'AK' YIPYAJ CHAN K'AWIIL	
Glyphic spelling	(9.15.17.13.10
K'AK'-yi-pi ya-ja-	11 Ok 13 Pop)
CHAN-na K'AWI:L-la	*Father*
('K'awiil that Fills?	K'ak' Joplaj Chan
the Sky with Fire')	K'awiil
Also known as	*Monuments*
Smoke Shell,	Stelae M & N;
Smoking Squirrel,	Upper Hieroglyphic
Smoke Squirrel	Stairway of Temple
Dynastic title	26; Temple 26 text
15th in the line	*Burial*
Accession	Temple 11?
14 February 749	

K'AK' JOPLAJ CHAN K'AWIIL

The loss of Waxaklajuun Ub'aah K'awiil had profound consequences for Copan; no monuments were raised for the next 17 years and major construction seems to have come to a complete halt. One passage from the Hieroglyphic Stairway reads 'no altars, no pyramids...' and may be a description of, even a lament to, the troubles of this era.[34] Yet Copan's dynastic progress was not interrupted and we know that a new king, K'ak' Joplaj Chan K'awiil, was inaugurated just 39 days after his predecessor's execution. His name is that of another fiery sky god, in this case 'K'awiil that Stokes the Sky with Fire' – a close relative of the lightning deity recorded in modern times, Hopop Kaan Chaak, translated as 'Chaak that Sets Light to the Sky'. Given the absence of monuments it is unsurprising that his 11-year reign is little known. Weakened both psychologically and materially, Copan may even have been in some kind of subjection to its former vassal. The dismemberment of Copan's wider domain and loss of income from the Motagua trade route – whose value can be measured in the huge development of Quirigua – was a setback from which it seems never to have fully recovered.

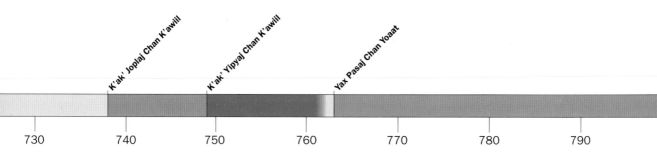

K'ak' Joplaj Chan K'awiil   K'ak' Yipyaj Chan K'awiil   Yax Pasaj Chan Yoaat

730   740   750   760   770   780   790

K'ak' Yipyaj Chan K'awiil, Altar Q, 776.

This view of the Copan Acropolis, looking southwest, shows its final form c. AD 800. Cutaway portions reveal earlier structures, while the 'cut' created by the Copan River, seen at left, is shown in its modern consolidated state.

K'AK' YIPYAJ CHAN K'AWIIL

K'ak' Joplaj Chan K'awiil died in January 749 and was succeeded by a son with the not dissimilar name K'ak' Yipyaj Chan K'awiil. His early reign lies within the Quirigua-induced hiatus, and even the major K'atun-ending 9.16.0.0.0 of 751 passed without lasting commemoration. Yet by this time plans must already have been taking shape for a determined programme of renewal, one which would soon return Copan to at least a semblance of its former glory.

Ancestor mountain

The greatest expression of this revitalization was a new version of the Temple 26 pyramid. The hieroglyphic stairway of Waxaklajuun Ub'aah K'awiil's Esmeralda was torn out and reset into a new flight, its text extended to double its original length, taking up Copan's history from where the original left off. A series of five fully rounded, life-size statues were spaced at intervals up the stair, each depicting an ancestral Copanec king in the guise of a Teotihuacan warrior. The set was completed by K'ak' Yipyaj's own portrait in the form of Stela M, erected at its foot on

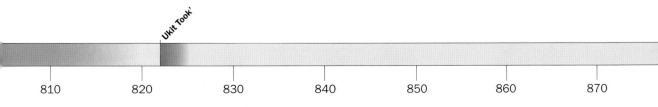

Ukit Took'

810   820   830   840   850   860   870

THE GREAT STAIRWAY

With as many as 2,200 individual glyphs, Copan's Hieroglyphic Stairway is the longest known Maya inscription, filling the entire 69 ft (21 m) staircase of Temple 26. The ancient collapse of the pyramid's frontage left over half its blocks in a chaotic heap at its foot. Reconstructing their original order is made doubly difficult by the condition of the stones, many of which are now badly weathered. The stair is really two monuments in one. Its lower reaches were commissioned by the 13th king, Waxaklajuun Ub'aah K'awiil in AD 710 and were later incorporated by the 15th, K'ak' Yipyaj Chan K'awiil, into a new stair in AD 755. A grand statement of continuity, it was a detailed dynastic chronicle first conceived at the highpoint of Copan's powers and extended as part of a conscious act of revitalization after Quirigua's rebellion of 738.

The grand hieroglyphic stair of Temple 26 was complemented by six life-size sculptures of former kings and K'ak' Yipyaj Chan K'awiil's own image on Stela M at its base.

9.16.5.0.0 in 756. Dedicated at the same time, Temple 26's now badly ruined upper sanctuary held a fascinating inscription. Composed entirely of full-figure hieroglyphs, it juxtaposed Maya script glyph-for-glyph with what David Stuart has aptly called a 'Teotihuacan font'. These spurious, Mexicanized glyphs are really a form of pseudo-writing, but successfully give the illusion of a bilingual text.[35]

Temple 26, an 'ancestor mountain' par excellence, presents us with the same political strategy used by Tikal a generation earlier. The once mighty, but now fallen Teotihuacan supplies the archetype and model around which a contemporary rejuvenation can be marshalled. More than a simple ideal, of course, the Mexican superpower was also the literal source to which both Copan and Tikal dynasties traced their ruling lines.

Another K'ak' Yipyaj Chan K'awiil monument, the fine Stela N, was set before the steps of Temple 11, adjacent to Temple 26, in 761. The king died within a year or so and there is good reason to believe his burial lies undisturbed within this voluminous pyramid. One Temple 11 text would appear to describe the dedication of his mortuary shrine and tomb-connected 'psychoduct' in 769. Indeed, a small tunnel found in Temple 11 leads down into the heart of the structure, though no excavation has yet traced its destination.[36]

(*Left*) The organic style of Copan's stone-carving continued in K'ak' Yipyaj Chan K'awiil's reign, here with Stela N from AD 761. This picture was one taken in 1885 by Alfred Maudslay. His photographic record of Maya monuments remains unsurpassed to this day.

(*Right*) A section of the full-figure texts from the sanctuary of Temple 26. Both columns spell the name of Waxaklajuun Ub'aah K'awiil: at right is the Maya form, at left its 'translation' into spurious Mexicanized glyphs.

YAX PASAJ CHAN YOAAT	
Glyphic spelling YAX-pa sa-ja-CHAN- na yo?-a-AT-ta ('First Dawned Sky Lightning God') *Also known as* Yax Pac, Madrugada, Rising Sun, New Sun-at- Horizon, Yax Sun-at- Horizon, New Dawn *Dynastic title* 16th in the line *Accession* 28 June 763 (9.16.12.5.17 6 Kaban 10 Mol) *Mother* Lady Chak Nik Ye' Xook of Palenque *Monuments* Stelae 8 & 29; Altars G1, G2, G3, Q, R, T, U, V, Z, B',	C', D', F', G', W', J''?, 41; CPN 19119, CPN 19222, CPN 19469, CPN 23748, CPN 2843; Temple 22a Stone, Temple 11 Wall Panels, Step & Reviewing Stand, Temple 18 Doorjamb and Wall Texts, Temple 21a Bench, 9N-82 Bench, Harvard Bench, Tegucigalpa Bench; CPN 157, 244, 26300; House Models from Structures 29 & 33; various incensarios. *Burial* Temple 18

YAX PASAJ CHAN YOAAT

Sixteenth in the line of Yax K'uk' Mo' was Yax Pasaj Chan Yoaat (or Yopaat) 'First Dawned Sky Lightning God', crowned as ruler in June 763. A boy-king, he could have been as little as nine years old at his accession. At the start of his reign Copan's reinvigoration was still in full flow; by its end, half a century later, both city and civilization were on the brink of total ruin.

Yax Pasaj's monumental programme was markedly different from that of his predecessors. He produced no figural stelae, concentrating instead on architectural texts and smaller altar-style monuments. Only one, rather unclear reference to his father is known, but his mother, a lady from distant Palenque, receives greater prominence and serves as his prime claim to royal descent. This apparent break in the male line did not prevent him honouring his predecessor K'ak' Yipyaj Chan K'awiil, and his first major work, the supporting platform of Temple 11 built in 769, probably caps his tomb. Temple 11's two-storey superstructure was completed in 773, its roof carrying a sculpted cosmos overlooking the city. At its northern corners two giant *pawahtuunob'* – 'sky bearers' who held the heavens above the earth – supported an entablature suitably fashioned as the celestial caiman.[37] Each of its four doorways was fitted with a pair of glyphic panels carved directly into the walls – half in the rare 'mirror writing', text written in reverse. An interior step once showed Yax Pasaj's accession, witnessed by ranks of local deities and ancestral kings seated on name-glyph thrones (among them Yax K'uk' Mo', Waterlily Jaguar, Butz' Chan and Smoke Imix).

(*Above*) This small but refined portrait of Yax Pasaj Chan Yoaat shows him with a sacrificial plate containing the head of *k'awiil*. Temple 11, *c.* AD 773.

(*Right*) The symbolic programme of Temple 11, examined in some detail by Mary Miller, embodies a multi-strata universe. Its lowest level, the stair of the Reviewing Stand seen here, looks out on the West Court and represents a descent into the watery Underworld.

Altar Q, a remarkable summary of the Copan dynasty, was dedicated by Yax Pasaj in AD 776. It shows the first 16 kings each seated on their name glyphs, with Yax Pasaj's accession date set between his own image and that of the founder Yax K'uk' Mo' (at left). Altar Q's top carries a text that sets out the key steps in the foundation of the kingdom in the years 426 and 427.

Yax Pasaj's other great creation was the final version of the founder's memorial, Temple 16, completed around 776. Barbara Fash and Karl Taube have recently reconstructed its sculptural programme, which has the anticipated emphasis on Mexican motifs and images of Yax K'uk' Mo'. At its base Yax Pasaj set Altar Q, the definitive statement of Copan's great cycle of royal lineage. An associated crypt held the bodies of 15 sacrificed jaguars, one for each of his royal predecessors.[38]

All the king's men?

Yax Pasaj Chan Yoaat is unique in having a group of named 'companions' that partner him on many monuments. These characters behave very much like kings themselves, they have 'seating' events, perform the 'scattering' rite and bear either full or modified emblem glyphs. Initially it was thought that these were siblings of the king and a sign that he was obliged to share power with an extended family, though more recent evidence suggests that they were companions of a more supernatural kind.[39]

Real evidence of growing status among the local nobility emerges from the Las Sepulturas and similar districts (p. 211). By 780 high-ranking lords were furnishing their palaces with hieroglyphic benches every bit as fine as the king's own commissions. At just this time, in 781, the ruler of the provincial seat of Los Higos erected his own stela (a rather conservative effort in the style of Smoke Imix), signalling a new assertiveness, even autonomy, among Copan's satellites. While the early years of Yax Pasaj's reign had seen large-scale building projects like those of Temples 11 and 16, there was now a corresponding downturn in his output. A victim of its own success, the Copan pocket was now straining under a population of 20,000 or more and living standards were deteriorating noticeably (see p. 213). It had

The name of Yax Pasaj Chan Yoaat shows an astounding variety in its spelling, exploiting a wide range of sign substitutions. This 'full-figure' form comes from a carved bench in the House of the Bakabs in the district of Las Sepulturas.

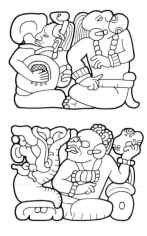

been a long time since the city could be fully supported by its immediate environs, and symptoms of distress reveal the decline of the state and its inability to draw essential goods from outside. In 802 Yax Pasaj celebrated his second K'atun in power, but record of his next major event, the 9.19.0.0.0 K'atun ending of 810, comes only from the former dominion of Quirigua (p. 224). With the stormclouds of the collapse gathering, this may be a sign that an embattled elite were attempting to bury old antagonisms and rally to their mutual support.[40]

LAS SEPULTURAS

Distributed across the Copan pocket are a range of residential wards and suburban subcentres of varying size and complexity. The most important of these has since disappeared beneath the modern village of Copan Ruinas, but the district of Las Sepulturas, close to the central core, has been the subject of thorough investigations, most recently those of William Sanders and David Webster. Its origins are apparently very ancient, with one house dating to Early Preclassic times, while as early as the Middle Preclassic it featured large cobble-built platforms and several very wealthy tombs. By the time it reached its final form around AD 800, it was composed of some 50 buildings arranged about seven major courtyards. Its centrepiece, the House of the Bakabs, was the palace of a high-ranking *aj k'uhuun*, boasting a finely sculpted exterior and an ornate hieroglyphic bench within. Interestingly, one portion of the Las Sepulturas complex proved to be a *barrio* or subdistrict for non-Maya peoples from central Honduras. Whether the *barrio* was an enclave of political clients or specialized merchants, its occupants were doubtless involved in the vibrant exchange network that brought polychrome vessels and other commodities from this eastern region.[41]

The most imposing building in the Las Sepulturas district is today called the House of the Bakabs. It was the palace of one of Yax Pasaj's leading vassals.

(*Above*) One of four interior columns in Temple 18 showing Yax Pasaj performing a war dance.

Demise of the dynasty

Yax Pasaj's straitened circumstances are no more evident than in his memorial shrine, the modest Temple 18. An access stairway led to a crypt below (anciently looted), while its upper sanctuary boasted four panels showing the king in the midst of war dances, brandishing spear and shield — just the kind of overt militarism otherwise so rare at Copan.

Stela 11 was found in two parts at the base of Temple 18. It was not a free-standing monument but part of a column that once supported its wide single doorway.[42] It depicts a bearded Yax Pasaj in the guise of the aged Maize God, the flaming torch of *k'awiil* fixed in his forehead and standing on the jawed entrance to the Underworld. Parallels with the famed sarcophagus lid of Palenque's K'inich Janaab' Pakal I are overt and unlikely to be coincidental given Yax Pasaj's close family ties to this western city (p. 165). The text of Stela 11 faced inwards and is best read as the continuation of an inscription carved on its interior walls. This opens with a date in 801, though little more can be made of it. Stela 11 seems to begin with the 'toppling of the Foundation House', which has been taken as a reference to the fall of the founder's line and even to the collapse itself.[43] The remaining text is more enigmatic still, but Yax Pasaj and Yax K'uk' Mo' conclude it as joint subjects.

As Yax Pasaj's last testament, Temple 18 certainly reflects, and may even respond to, its troubled, godforsaken times. Yet if it records the demise of the Copan dynasty, it may also be imbued with the belief that, just like the Maize God, it would enjoy future resurrection (p. 222).

DECLINE OF THE COPAN VALLEY

Research into the ancient ecology of Copan provides a vivid picture of human impact on the valley through four centuries of kingly rule and beyond it to the collapse. As early as the 6th century the population had exceeded its carrying capacity and would have relied on the importation of food and other essentials from outside. Pollen analysis demonstrates that the valley floor was by then denuded of tree cover, a process that ultimately saw even the pines of the uppermost peaks shorn for timber and firewood. The shortage of trees by the 7th century is reflected in the decline of stucco decoration (whose production consumes huge amounts of firewood) and its replacement by stone-carving. Deforestation would also have affected the micro-climate of the valley, reducing rainfall. The shortage of land took cultivation to ever steeper slopes, encouraging erosion and damaging the fertility of soils further down. Year-on-year yields would have fallen. Analysis of 8th-century burials reveals that malnourishment had become increasingly common and that infant mortality was rising steeply. Disease affected all social classes, the peasant and privileged alike, partly perhaps because epidemics would have spread even to the better fed. Burial offerings became progressively poorer and maintenance of ceremonial structures declined. With the 9th-century collapse of central authority the population dwindled to a fraction of its former strength. Postclassic villagers robbed stone from the great palaces and incorporated them into simple house platforms.[44]

UKIT TOOK'	
Glyphic spelling u-ki-ti to-TO:K' ('Patron? of Flint')	Accession 6 February 822 (9.19.11.14.5) Monument Altar L

(*Opposite*) Stela 11 was once a column in the doorway of Temple 18 and seems to form part of its interior text. Much of this narrative is now missing and by the time we reach Stela 11 any firm hold on the chronology is lost. On a date identified only as 8 Ajaw (linked by some to 9.19.10.0.0) we have the phrase *jomoy wiʔ teʼ naah*, the 'toppling/sinking of the Foundation House', followed by some reference to the Teotihuacan war serpent *waxaklajuun ubʼaah chan* before naming both Yax Pasaj and Yax Kʼukʼ Moʼ.

(*Right*) A final attempt to persevere with the Classic order came with the accession of Ukit Took' in AD 822. In an inaugural scene inspired by Altar Q, the new king (left) faces his predecessor Yax Pasaj Chan Yoaat – here in the position formerly given to Yax K'uk' Mo'. A further side of the stone was sketched out, but never completed.

UKIT TOOK' AND THE END OF KINGSHIP

By now exploitation of the valley had reached ruinous proportions and Copan's population were beset with shortage and disease. It was hardly an auspicious time to revive an institution in severe crisis throughout the Maya world, and it comes as little surprise that the last ruler of Copan, Ukit Took' ('Patron? of Flint') cuts an unfortunate figure. His Altar L mimics Altar Q in large degree, showing the new lord facing his predecessor Yax Pasaj Chan Yoaat, both seated on their name glyphs and holding batons of office. The text between them provides the date of his 'seating' in February 822. But the authority of Ukit Took' was fleeting. So fleeting, in fact, that it evaporated even before the monument could be completed. The enthronement scene was the only one of the stone's four sides to be finished, and just one other face was even begun.[45] For a city with such a passion for sculpture, it is poignant and fitting that this very moment of termination should be captured in stone. The valley had seen the last of its kings.

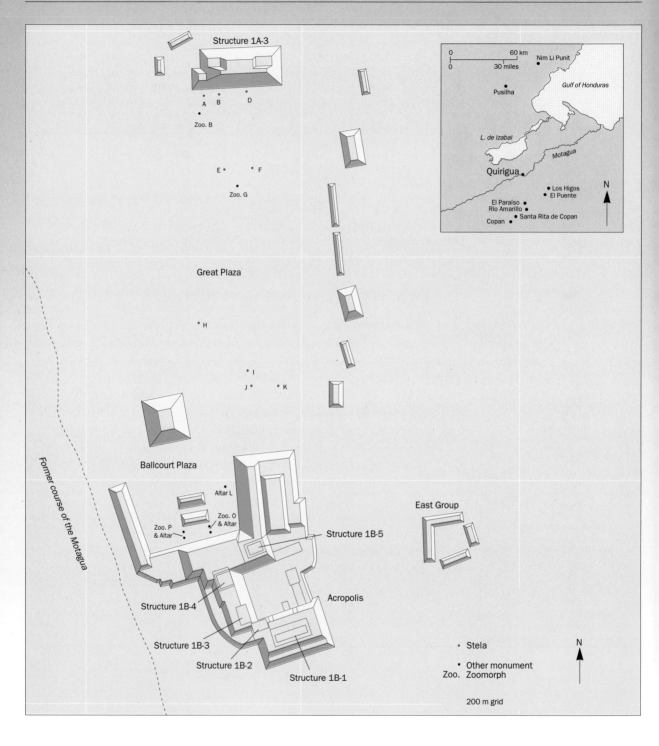

Structure 1A-3

A B D

Zoo. B

E F

Zoo. G

Great Plaza

H

I

J K

Ballcourt Plaza

Altar L

Zoo. O
& Altar

Zoo. P
& Altar

Structure 1B-5

Structure 1B-4

Acropolis

Structure 1B-3

Structure 1B-2

Structure 1B-1

East Group

Former course of the Motagua

Nim Li Punit

Gulf of Honduras

Pusilha

L. de Izabal

Motagua

Quirigua

Los Higos
El Puente

El Paraíso
Río Amarillo
Copan   Santa Rita de Copan

N

0   60 km
0   30 miles

• Stela

• Other monument
Zoo. Zoomorph

200 m grid

N

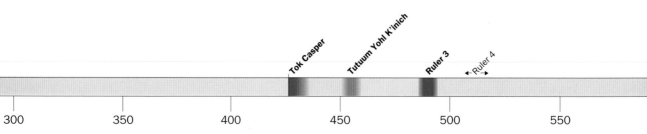

Tok Casper

Tutuum Yohl K'inich

Ruler 3

Ruler 4

300   350   400   450   500   550

QUIRIGUA

Situated in the steamy floodplain of the Motagua Valley, Quirigua had a key position on the major thoroughfare between the highlands and the Caribbean coast. For most of its life it was a modest, if not insignificant, site under the political thumb of Copan. But an 8th-century break in its traditional ties led to a transformation of unparalleled vigour, turning its heart into a ceremonial capital out of all proportion to its population and the setting for some of the largest monuments ever erected by the Maya.

From one perspective, Quirigua's emergence epitomizes the extraordinary vitality and organizational prowess of Late Classic civilization. From another, its emphasis on local rights and the breakdown of larger hegemonies can be seen as part of the decay in political authority that plagued the Classic's later stages. The site has received much attention since its rediscovery in the 19th century and from 1974 to 1980 the University of Pennsylvania, under the direction of Robert Sharer, conducted a significant programme of excavations both in the central core and the surrounding valley.

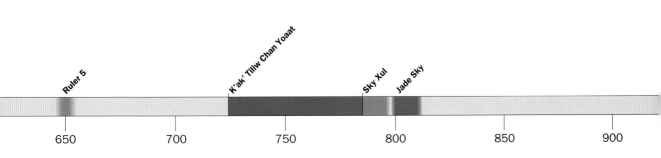

Ruler 5   K'ak' Tiliw Chan Yoaat   Sky Xul   Jade Sky

650   700   750   800   850   900

Tok Casper

426–?

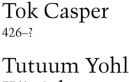

Tutuum Yohl K'inich

>455>

Ruler 3

>480>

Ruler 5

>652>

This early Quirigua king, whose identity is unclear, may have acceded in AD 493. Monument 26.

TOK CASPER	
Glyphic spelling to-ko ?	*Accession* 8 September 426 (8.19.10.11.0 8 Ajaw 18 Yax)

TUTUUM YOHL K'INICH	
Glyphic spelling tu-tu-ma yo-O:L K'INICH	('?-hearted Sun God')

RULER 3	
Glyphic spelling ?-AHK-? ITZ'A:T? ?	*Monument* Stela U (M.21)

RULER 5	
Glyphic spelling K'AWI:L-la ?-?-ti	*Monument* Altar L (M.12)

EARLY QUIRIGUA

Our knowledge of Quirigua's origins relies, as is so often the case elsewhere, on much later accounts. Its official history, as set out in the 8th century, begins in 426 with a *taali* 'coming' to the 'Foundation House' – a focus for dynastic rites and of apparent Mexican inspiration (p. 192). From a text at Copan that deals with these same events we know that this marks an office-taking by Yax K'uk' Mo', founder of Copan's royal lineage. Three days later a stela (as yet unknown) was erected and Quirigua's first king, nicknamed **Tok Casper**, was crowned 'under the supervision' of Yax K'uk' Mo'. The Quirigua kingdom was thus, from its very inception, part of a regional plan that put the Motagua Valley and its control of highlands–Caribbean trade within a Copan hegemony.[1] There are strong echoes here of Siyaj K'ak's New Order and the installation of a new political elite at a number of centres in the Peten (pp. 29–31).

Little is known of the next three centuries of Quirigua's existence. Ceremonial architecture of this period was rather dispersed, divided between a hilltop complex known as Group A and a broad earthen platform on the valley floor labelled 3C-1. Another late text supplies the next Quirigua king, **Tutuum Yohl K'inich**, who is said to have erected a stela

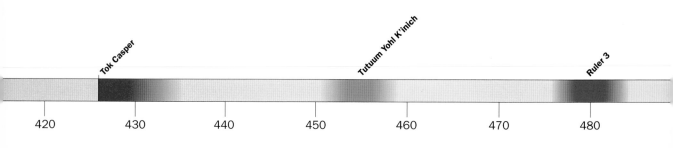

This passage from Copan's great Hieroglyphic Stairway may describe the accession of the first Quirigua king, Tok Casper, in AD 426. Note the Quirigua emblem second from right.

at 9.1.0.0.0 in 455 (though this too has yet to be found). The earliest known monument, Stela U, comes from the heart of Group A. Its much eroded portrait is executed in so-called 'wrap-around' style (where the king and his splayed regalia extend over three sides of a squared column). The form first emerged a generation earlier at Tikal (where Stelae 1, 2 and 28 are all examples) and would seem to signal ongoing contacts with the central Peten.[2] It carries a truncated reference to the 9.2.5.0.0 ending of 480, and describes some kind of dedication rite that took place a few months later. Damage obscures the identity of this **Ruler 3**, but the event took place 'under the supervision' of an *ochk'in kaloomte'*. This title was reserved for the highest rank of Maya kings and in this region only carried by the rulers of Copan. Thirteen years later Monument 26, another wrap-around stela, was erected close to 3C-1. A long text on its back dates it to 493 and mentions both a 'third' and a 'fourth king', but breaks in critical parts make their identification less than straightforward.

A new Quirigua

Sometime in the 6th or early 7th century some natural disaster, perhaps a volcanic eruption or severe hurricane, led to a devastating flood of the valley that buried the whole Early Classic surface beneath a deep layer of river silt. The unscathed Group A remained in use, as did those portions of 3C-1 that still stood above the new landscape, but it was one of the site's lesser complexes that was now developed into a new ceremonial core and river-port, the Quirigua we know today.[3]

The first monument here, Altar L, was a 'Giant Ajaw' altar dated to the 9.11.0.0.0 ending of 652 (see p. 89). As is usual in this form, the monument features a large day sign, though here in a rather clever play, the day Ajaw 'lord, ruler' is spelt by the portrait of the cross-legged figure of the king himself. A caption supplies the name of **Ruler 5** – of which only the god name *k'awiil* is really clear – as well as providing our first sight of the Quirigua royal title. It further describes a dance performance that took place 231 days later. Of particular interest is the surrounding text, which mentions Copan's 12th king, Smoke Imix. The event concerned, *tzak huul*, may refer to some evocation of the great lord for the K'atun-ending ceremony, but is not well understood and other interpretations are possible (p. 20). Despite its formal ingenuity, Altar L it is crudely executed, showing the work of local artisans unschooled in the sophistication of Copan sculpture.

Quirigua Altar L celebrated the K'atun-ending of 9.11.0.0.0 in 652, showing Ruler 5 as the day name Ajaw. The surrounding text, at left, mentions the Copan king Smoke Imix.

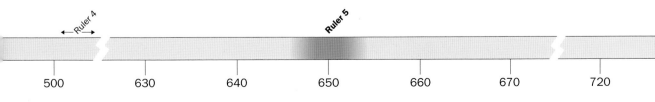

Ruler 4

Ruler 5

500   630   640   650   660   670   720

K'ak' Tiliw Chan Yoaat
Cauac Sky
724–785

Sky Xul
785–795>

Jade Sky
>800–810>

Bearded portraits in Maya art, such as this one of K'ak' Tiliw, serve to emphasize the prestigious age of the subject. Stela E, AD 771.

K'AK' TILIW CHAN YOAAT	
Glyphic spelling K'AK'-TIL-li-wi CHAN-na-yo?-A:T-ti ('Fire-burning Sky Lightning God') *Also known as* Cauac Sky, Kawak Sky, Two-Legged Sky, Two-Armed Sky, Butz' Tiliw, Ruler I, Ruler IV *Dynastic title* 14th in the line *Accession* 29 December 724	(9.14.13.4.17 12 Kaban 5 K'ayab) *Death* 27 July 785 (9.17.14.13.2 11 Ik' 5 Yax) *Monuments* Stelae A (M.1), C (M.3), D (M.4), E (M.5), F (M.6), H (M.8), J (M.10), S (M.19); Altar M (M.13); Zoomorph B (M.2)

K'AK' TILIW CHAN YOAAT

Rarely is the fate of a city so linked to the career of a single individual as Quirigua is with that of K'ak' Tiliw Chan Yoaat/Yopaat ('Fire-burning Sky Lightning God'). He came to the throne in 724, already a mature figure in his late twenties or early thirties. One of the four references to this accession includes the key addenda that the ceremony took place 'under the supervision' of Waxaklajuun Ub'aah K'awiil, the current ruler of Copan (p. 203).[4] He thus began his reign, like the first Quirigua king almost 300 years earlier, as one of Copan's provincial clients.

The rebellion

Political stability was an elusive ideal in the Classic Maya world, and a continual tension reigned between vassals and their overlords. For the suitably ambitious, rebellion offered an opportunity to escape their burdens and carve out their own realm – the course Quirigua now followed. All of the monuments that bear witness to K'ak' Tiliw's accession go on to recount the most decisive event in the life of both king and kingdom. In 738, his 14th regnal year, he performed the ultimate betrayal, seizing his lord Waxaklajuun Ub'aah K'awiil and decapitating

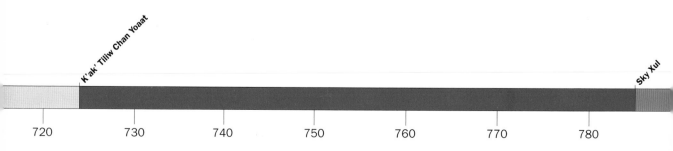

720   730   740   750   760   770   780

K'ak' Tiliw's initial subordination to Copan is made clear at his accession in AD 724. This passage – reading *uch'am k'awiil k'ak' tiliw chan yoaat ch'ahoom, ukab'jiiy waxaklajuun ub'aah k'awiil* 'Copan' *ajaw* – describes K'ak' Tiliw's receiving of the royal K'awiil sceptre under the supervision of the Copan king Waxaklajuun Ub'aah K'awiil. Quirigua Stela E, AD 761.

A buried version of Structure 1B-3 features a series of portraits of the squint-eyed Sun God K'inich that once overlooked the Motagua River.

him.[5] Just how the Copan king came to such an ignominious end is unclear. It may be significant that none of the Quirigua accounts uses a recognized term for war and this may hint that more duplicitous means were employed.

For Copan this was a real calamity, reflected in the 17-year silence into which it now sinks. Indeed, K'ak' Tiliw may have succeeded in imposing some authority over his former masters, at least for a time. His subsequent use of a '14th in the line' epithet could represent a genuine count at Quirigua, but looks suspiciously like a claim to succeed Waxaklajuun Ub'aah K'awiil, the 13th Copan king.[6] His use of Copan royal titles and god names, each prefixed by 'black' might predate the rebellion and represent a legacy from Copan's old regional order.

How had little Quirigua managed to overturn this age-old order of the southeast? The details of political treachery are hardly the stuff of public inscriptions, but we do receive a tantalizing glimpse of contact with the distant Peten. One later text describes a stela erection by K'ak' Tiliw in 736, just two years before the revolt. As noted by Matthew Looper, a still undeciphered term links this event to a 'divine lord of Chiik Naab'', presumably a ruler of Calakmul (p. 114). Given the context of this text (which concerns itself with otherwise unmentioned details of the rebellion) this cannot be coincidental. Quirigua seems to be claiming some kind of support in its secession from Copan – conceivably having transferred its allegiance to a more agreeable patron.[7]

The fruits of victory

While K'ak' Tiliw's bid for independence and glory was far from unique, it can be viewed as uniquely successful. In every way Quirigua's fortunes were transformed. Full command of the wealthy Motagua trade route would now fund a complete makeover of the site and a series of astounding monuments. Population levels, not only at the capital but at other sites throughout the valley, rose rapidly. Some of this rise may reflect immigration, incomers drawn to the realm of a successful and charismatic new leader. This said, we should bear in mind that the 'urban' population of Quirigua never exceeded a few thousand souls, a paltry figure when compared with crowded Copan or, even more so, the great metropolises of the Peten.

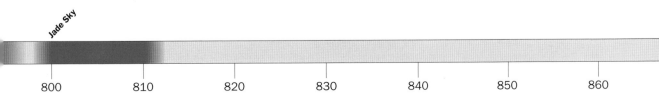

FULL-FIGURE WRITING

For the Maya both time and writing had an animate dimension; they were in some sense burdens carried by a succession of supernatural characters. This is most clearly seen in writing's 'full-figure' form, where the standard inventory of hieroglyphs are transformed into whole-bodied gods and beasts, often intertwined in designs of fiendish complexity. Waxaklajuun Ub'aah K'awiil's last monument, Copan Stela D from 736, was a full-figure tour de force but, typically, Quirigua now sought to compete in this area, successfully creating some of the most involved of all such inscriptions. It is hard to imagine that such virtuosity could have sprung into being, fully formed so to speak, from the rustic surroundings of Quirigua. These masters of their craft would have found their training elsewhere before being drawn to the employ of a prestigious and wealthy new patron.

Two full-figure glyphs, part of an Initial Series date. Stela D, Quirigua, AD 766.

One of the great figures of Maya research, Sylvanus Morley, poses alongside the sandstone mass of Stela F. Erected in AD 761, it reaches a height of 24 ft (7.25 m) above ground, only bettered by Stela E ten years later.

More than simply asserting his newly found autonomy, K'ak' Tiliw sought every opportunity to outdo Copan. Architectural imitation of its one-time master is evident throughout the city. The early Quirigua acropolis – really just a residential quadrangle – was rebuilt in much grander style. A new western façade, overlooking the river, was embellished with busts of the Sun God *k'inich*, fashioned in the stone mosaic technique pioneered at Copan. An early ballcourt was demolished and a new one sited just north of the Acropolis. Beyond it a grand ceremonial plaza was laid out – at 1,066 ft (325 m) long the largest in the entire Maya area. Both features reflect the layout of Copan.

The rest of K'ak' Tiliw's life was spent gracing his new arena with monuments of comparable magnitude. His earliest surviving work, Stela S,

Here 'unwrapped' from the north face of Stela F, we see K'ak' Tiliw bearing a *k'awiil* sceptre and small round shield. AD 761.

marked the 9.15.15.0.0 ending of 746 and thereafter he erected a monolith every five years. Stela H from 751 (its diagonal text a pale imitation of the mat-patterned Stela J from Copan) and Stela J from 756 show an ongoing development of the Early Classic 'wrap-around' style. The casting of the king's image into truly gigantic proportions came with the completion of the plaza's northern platform and its broad cobble-built terrace. This was the stage for the twin-sided portraits of Stelae F (761), D (766) and E (771), three of the tallest ever erected by the Maya – the last soaring 24 ft (7.25 m) above ground and tipping the scales at some 30 tons. Their awe-inspiring scale was designed to impress and intimidate; to stand before one was to be in the presence of a superman.

We should not, however, mistake this grandiloquence for simple egomania. Quirigua's physical transformation was essentially functional, as it remodelled itself into a capital worthy of commanding its own hegemony and assuming the ceremonial role once performed by Copan. Among Quirigua's clients only one is singled out for mention, 'Xkuy', an unidentified site that Copan had attacked and burned some years earlier (p. 203). In 762 K'ak' Tiliw oversaw the accession of its king 'Sunraiser Jaguar' and the repeated references he receives mark him as a loyal and valued ally.

Refounding the cosmos

Integral to this programme was the creation of a supernatural underpinning of Quirigua's new status. Great kings had special access to the divine realm and special responsibilities to intercede on behalf of their subjects. K'ak' Tiliw's stelae draw symmetries between contemporary time and the domain of 'deep time', the completion of huge calendrical cycles, measured in units of millions, even billions of years. These unworldly events take place in specific locations and his portraits show him standing on their iconic names. No simple re-enactment, the king had been transported through time and space to relive them.[9] Quirigua itself claimed special affinity with the Underworld entryways of the 'black hole' and the 'black body of water', whose names it seems to have adopted.[10]

(*Above*) A pivotal moment in Maya religion, the rebirth of the Maize God, is captured on this fine codex-style plate.

(*Top right*) His face emerging from the snarling gape of a giant jaguar, Zoomorph G is K'ak' Tiliw's memorial stone, created by his successor Sky Xul. After AD 785.

These themes find further expression on Stela C, dedicated together with Stela A in 775. It provides the most detailed account we have of the 'Maya Creation' – the founding of the current universe in 3114 BC (p. 221). The parallel drawn between this moment of genesis and Quirigua's own rebirth is hard to avoid.

With the last monument of his reign, K'ak' Tiliw developed another Copan form, the altar-like beasts called 'zoomorphs', inflating them to gargantuan size. His Zoomorph B was a multi-ton boulder hewn into the shape of a composite creature: part mountain, part cosmic crocodile. Dedicated in 780, its text consists entirely of the ornamental full-figure hieroglyphs (p. 220).

The king's death

The 60-year reign of K'ak' Tiliw came to an end on 27 July 785. His death and burial are described in uncommon detail on Zoomorph G, the first commission of his successor Sky Xul. His soul, expressed as the standard metaphor of 'white flowery breath', is said to have 'entered the road'. This marks the beginning of its journey through the darkness of death and towards ultimate rebirth, retracing the steps of the primeval Maize God. The following 'into the turtle stone' may refer to a physical sculpture, but conceptually charts the soul's entry into the heart of the earth, which the Maya conceived of as a giant turtle floating in a cosmic sea (see panel). An obscure passage follows, charting an event to which Sunraiser Jaguar was a witness. Ten days later (an exceptionally long time in a tropical climate, suggesting elaborate preparation of the body) K'ak' Tiliw was *mukaj* 'buried' at the '13 Kawak House', a structure that has yet to be identified. The accompanying phrase *yaktaaj ajawlel*, 'the leaving/transferring of kingship', marks the final passing of the ruler's burden (see also p. 151).

SKY XUL	

Glyphic spelling
  ?[CHAN] YOA:T?
Also known as
  Ruler II
Accession
  11 October 785
  (9.17.14.16.18
  9 Etz'nab 1
  K'ank'in)
	Monuments
	  Zoomorphs G (M.7),
	  O (M.15) and P
	  (M.16); Altar of
	  Zoomorph O (M.23),
	  Altar of Zoomorph P
	  (M.24)

SKY XUL

The king charged with the awesome task of succeeding a legend is known to us today as Sky Xul. He came to power in 785 and although his reign was relatively short, 10 to 15 years, it showed considerable energy and the city resounded with the hammering of masons at work for much of the time. Spurning the stela form, Sky Xul concentrated all his efforts on monolithic zoomorphs, and his three great boulder sculptures, two partnered by 'altars' of comparable quality, are marvels of Maya stoneworking.

The first, Zoomorph G from 785, was a homage to his predecessor. Modelled in the form of a crouching jaguar, the likeness of a bearded king – presumably K'ak' Tiliw himself – emerges from its gaping mouth. The sculpture is named, in part, the 'Jaguar Throne Stone' and is thus an analogue of one of the 'creation' thrones set down in 3114 BC (p. 221).[12] From here on, Sky Xul switched his attention from the Great Plaza to the smaller Ballcourt Plaza, where he dedicated two more crocodile-mountain hybrids, Zoomorphs O and P, in 790 and 795. It is the second of these, weighing as many as 20 tons, that represents the peak of his achievements. It is hard to overstate the complexity of its design or skill in execution. Every inch of the great beast is crowded with an exotic tangle of leafy scrolls and serpents, animated deities and glyphic panels. Its huge fanged jaws disgorge a figure of the king, seated in a cross-legged pose and carrying shield and *k'awiil* sceptre – the very model of royal deportment.

The accompanying altars of Zoomorphs O and P are scarcely less impressive. The altar of Zoomorph O shows a lightning god enveloped in cloud scrolls, floating above the earth. Its companion from Zoomorph P shows the crack in the earth that he has opened with his flaming axe and springing from it a fabulous, but unidentified, deity whose mouth emits snakes.

Two views of Sky Xul's masterpiece, Zoomorph P from AD 795. The north side (*left*) shows the twice life-size king seated in the jaws of a huge monster. Its southeastern flank (*right*) displays scroll-work so intertwined with glyphic motifs and deity portraits that it challenges the eyes of even those long-experienced in reading Maya art.

Text on the five monoliths totals almost 900 glyphs; although the 'face-up' exposure of the altars has blunted their legibility, hardly helped by a lazy stle at odds with the rest of the carving. Recognizable sections include events from the mythic past, the foundation of Quirigua, a number of rituals for the dead and several references to Copan. There is a continued emphasis on the doings of Sunraiser Jaguar and the site of Xkuy. On the quarter-Katun ending 9.18.5.0.0 in 795, Sky Xul 'scattered droplets' at the '13 Kawak House' – the burial site and memorial shrine of K'ak' Tiliw Chan Yoaat – and followed this by 'dancing' at a comparable memorial for the vanquished Waxaklajuun Ub'aah K'awiil. It is tempting to think that these are altar stones much like the undated Altars R and S, which each show a seated lord in the heart of a primordial cave. It should be noted that all of Sky Xul's works were achieved when most of the great Maya cities were in steep decline – making the extravagance of this display all the more remarkable.

A rather stunted portrait of Jade Sky, Quirigua's last known king, appears on Stela K in AD 805.

JADE SKY

Sky Xul died between 795 and 800 and was succeeded by Quirigua's 16th king, long known as Jade Sky. The monuments traditionally linked to his reign, spanning only ten years, show slightly different versions of the name, with unexplained changes in phonetic complements and verbal suffixes. These are either a product of late glyphic conventions or, it has been suggested, because we actually have more than one ruler here.[13] While the issue remains unresolved, it seems best to keep with the long-standing single ruler interpretation at present.

Our knowledge of Jade Sky's rule is restricted to a pair of stelae and two architectural texts. While his stela commissions mark a return to the traditions of K'ak' Tiliw, their stunted dimensions (and almost comically condensed portraits) are evidence enough that the regime could no longer muster the titanic resources of only a few years earlier. Stela I was dedicated in 800 and continued the preoccupation with K'ak' Tiliw's memory and the triumph over Copan (it supplies the only mentions of its opening event six days before the execution and contacts with Calakmul).[14] Stela K from 805 is much less forthcoming, restricting itself to chronological information of the most formulaic kind. While the scale of these stones is disappointing, Jade Sky invested greater energies in construction projects, erecting the two largest buildings of the Acropolis complex: 1B-5 and 1B-1.

The final chapter

The southernmost building, Structure 1B-1, contains the last date at Quirigua, 9.19.0.0.0, falling in June 810. This appears on a lengthy façade text (of which only a small portion survives), as well as on three benches running through its interior rooms. Interestingly, this returns to the recurring topic of Copan, describing the K'atun-ending celebration of his counterpart Yax Pasaj Chan Yoaat. The purpose

Structure 1B-1, here seen under restoration in the background is a large palace building with three distinct rooms. Each contains an inscribed bench that together form a continuous text. It records, among other things, the scattering rites of both Jade Sky (here spelt K'ak' Jolow Chan Yoaat) and the Copan king Yax Pasaj Chan Yoaat in celebration of the 19th K'atun-ending in AD 810.

behind this unusual reference remains unclear. It does not say that the two rulers conducted a joint ceremony, but probably does signal some late rapprochement between the two rivals – motivated by the common interests of an elite fraternity rapidly losing control over their world.[15] If so, it was already far too late. Quirigua was deserted within a few years, with severe decline or abandonment affecting sites throughout the valley.

But this was not quite the end for Quirigua and after a short period of dereliction it was re-occupied, albeit briefly, by a new group of settlers. Enthusiastic builders, they made some substantial additions to the Acropolis complex. Associated finds of the glossy-surfaced plumbate-ware and, especially, a reclining chacmool sculpture, point to distant origins, probably from Yucatan. No inscriptions record their history, but they seem certain to have been a merchant elite exploiting the power vacuum to take control of the Motagua trade route. The river continued as a major artery of commerce throughout the Postclassic, in later times controlled from the downstream site of Nito.[16]

JADE SKY	
Glyphic spellings	*Also known as*
K'AK'-jo-li-CHAN-na-ni yo-YOA:T?-it	Ruler V
(K'AK'-jo[lo]-ya-CHAN-na yo-YOA:T?-ti)	*Dynastic title* 16th in the line
(K'AK'-jo-[lo]-wo CHAN-na-YOA:T?-ti)	*Monuments* Stelae I (M.9) & K (M.11); benches and façade of Structure 1B-1

EPILOGUE: FALL OF THE DIVINE KINGS

By the dawn of the 10th century a political system that had thrived for many centuries, spawning one of the region's – indeed the world's – great cultural traditions, had perished entirely. The reasons behind this spectacular demise continue to fascinate the public and scholars alike. Theories have always been plentiful, facts rather harder to come by.

What we do know is that the final decades of the Late Classic saw the highest populations ever experienced in the Maya area and that the transition to the Terminal Classic (AD 800–909) marked the beginning of a dramatic decline. Within a few generations the Central Area, a landscape where millions once thronged, lay desolate and largely deserted.[1] While the precise numbers remain contentious, at their peak they were certainly large enough to have placed a significant strain on the environment. Sediments drawn from ancient lake beds have pointed to widespread deforestation and to eroded and exhausted soils.[2] Similar studies have found evidence for a prolonged drought that peaked in the mid-9th century, exacerbating the problem at a crucial time.[3]

To many, these are the hallmarks of 'overshoot', as a highly successful system reached, and then exceeded, its ecological limits.[4] A burgeoning population would need to intensify farming, but while this produces high yields in the short term, it cannot be sustained in the poor soils of the Maya region and the whole system becomes increasingly vulnerable to the vagaries of climate and plant disease. Poor nutrition would quickly promote human disease and infant mortality. Once failure had set in, even those areas that remained viable would have been swept away by the tide of social disintegration.[5] Competition for scarce resources provides a rationale for what signs we have of escalating conflict. The divided, highly localized nature of political authority would only have intensified the difficulties. Regimes whose power rested in their ability to control and redistribute wealth might maintain themselves only by stepping up predations on their neighbours, creating spirals of feud and retaliation that would destabilize an already fragile situation. Hegemonies extended by the most powerful states had produced some order in earlier times, but they could not be consolidated into more stable entities and evaporated quickly as the crisis mounted.

Since the collapse represents an end of those institutions that made public writing, few if any texts address the process directly. Instead, we can usefully trace patterns, changes in theme and emphasis that point to underlying trends. Although the Classic–Postclassic transition continues to present perplexing questions, we can chart much of its chronology.

The Terminal Classic

During the last decades of the Late Classic period the lowlands of the Central Area show a distinct rise in smaller sites erecting monuments, often using new or previously unseen emblem glyphs. In 790 more sites erected stelae than at any other time.[6] Diplomatic and genealogical information in the texts decline, increasing the relative prominence of warfare, a topic that only came to the fore in the Late Classic.[7] Beginning

Terminal Classic Seibal gives notice of mounting Mexican influence in the troubled Maya region. A Mexican-style, square day-sign cartouche can be seen in the top left corner. Stela 13, after AD 889.

SEIBAL: A LAST GASP OF CLASSIC KINGSHIP

Occupying a small crest of hills above the Pasión River, Seibal was first settled in Middle Preclassic times, with a Classic dynasty said to be in place by at least AD 415. It suffered major decline or even abandonment during the Early Classic, before a new occupation with Tikal links revived it in the Late Classic.[8] Its conquest by Dos Pilas in 735 reduced it to client status and its identity was further submerged when it hosted one of the rival Petexbatun kings from 771 to 800 or slightly after. The fall of these petty states left a vacuum filled by a newly resurgent Seibal. Although long ascribed to an intrusion by westerners, a different picture is now emerging from the inscriptions.

As first noted by Linda Schele, Stela 11 records the 'arrival at Seibal' of Aj B'olon Haab'tal on the last but one day of Cycle 9, 9.19.19.17.19, falling in March 830. This dynastic refoundation was 'supervised' by Chan Ek' Hopet, whose title aj k'anwitznal shows him to be a native of Ucanal, a city to the east.[9] The new regime was clearly intent on preserving the Classic ideal and establishing a powerbase in troubled times. Aj B'olon Haabtal (now boasting a lengthy regnal name) celebrated the 10.1.0.0.0 ending of 849 with five stelae set in and around his radial A-3 temple. His portraits vividly contrast classical Maya profiles on some, with more Mexican, moustachioed faces on others. Once again, we see a complex interplay between Maya and Mexican identities in pursuit of a once vital, though now obscure, political message.

Seibal's claim to wide political ascendancy can be found on Stela 10, where the 849 ceremony is said to have been 'witnessed' by the kings of Calakmul, Tikal and Motul de San José.[10] But by now these kingdoms were mere shadows of their former selves and the lofty titles probably mask little more than pretenders to fragmented realms.

shortly after 800, a wave of major abandonments took place and by 830 most of the major dynasties had fallen. In this sense the collapse was a rapid one. Some larger centres did persevere for a time, while at others the rulers of former satellites assumed royal titles and took up the old traditions.[11] Where inscriptions still appear, they are short, seldom providing more than dates, rituals and the names of presiding lords.

By 850 a number of these survivors begin to show a rise in Mexican traits. These are not the Teotihuacan-style revivals of earlier times but new forms: long 'bar' nose ornaments on royal portraits and square-framed day names in texts.[12] Maya kings seem to have been reaching out to models in contemporary Mexico. The Maya's relationship with their western cousins was complex and far from one-directional – as the handiwork of Maya artisans at Cacaxtla and Xochicalco, in central Mexico, attests. A few sites profited from these difficult times, at least for a while. A regime established at Seibal in 830 shows great energy in the midst of general calamity, erecting 17 stelae by 889 (see panel). Several of its undated monuments are even later, though they show an ever weakening grasp of Classic art and writing, and more aberrant forms and Mexican influences begin to predominate. By the early 10th century even Seibal was virtually deserted.

In the Northern Area the limited number and often poor preservation of inscriptions mean that we know little about the important Classic cities of Coba, Dzibilchaltun, Izamal, Edzna, Ek Balam, Oxkintok or Xcalumkin. But at the same time as the great crisis was sweeping further south, these were joined by a group of newly flourishing centres in the Puuc region on the western side of the peninsula, including Uxmal, Kabah, Sayil and Labna. Their distinctive architecture is characterized by complex, finely wrought façades with stacked masks of gods, clearly related to the Chenes and Río Bec styles further south. Uxmal represents the pinnacle of Puuc style and was the seat of a dynasty modelled fully in the Classic tradition. But this renaissance lasted little more than a century and Uxmal's last date, associated with the ruler Lord Chaak, falls in 907.[13]

Chichen Itza, set more centrally in the region, was the most complex city in the north. A rich body of Colonial sources paint it as a power with wide dominion, but one that saw successive takeovers by outsiders introducing Mexican influence (p. 229). The name of the city, meaning 'Mouth of the Well of the Itza', derives from the most prominent of these groups. The Itza, a term that appears in texts in the Early Classic Peten, might appear in the form hitza' ajaw on a stone disc from Chichen's circular Caracol or 'observatory', dated to 906.[14] Most Chichen inscriptions are earlier and found in Puuc-style buildings, many associated with the rule of K'ak'upakal K'awiil or 'Fire is the Shield of K'awiil' (c. 869–881). Occupation at the site continued into the Late Postclassic, though the exact date of its abandonment is unknown. Its great natural well or cenote remained a focus for pilgrimage and continued to receive offerings long after the Spanish Conquest.

(*Above*) The last city to claim any wide dominion over the Northern Area was Mayapan. Its major temples are little more than shrunken copies of those at Chichen Itza.

(*Below*) Mayapan's attempt to revive Classic tradition can be seen in its return to stela-carving. The blank glyph-blocks once carried a painted text. Stela 1.

The Postclassic

By the early 10th century the demographic collapse of the Central Area was well advanced, leaving Maya settlement concentrated in the north in the present-day Mexican states of Yucatan, Campeche and Quintana Roo, in the Guatemalan highlands to the south and parts of Belize. Although hieroglyphic writing remained in use (the four known Maya books all date to this era), very few inscriptions were now committed to stone, none at all in the highland area.

The chronology of the highlands – a region which saw little of the Classic period splendours – is poorly understood. The decline of Kaminaljuyu was followed by an intrusion of new communities from the west who displaced or absorbed the native population. These changes find some record in the annals of the best known of these groups, the Quiche Maya. By the mid-15th century the Quiche had subjugated their fellow incomers, including the Cakchiquel, Tzutujil, Mam and Kekchi, to master a great dominion from their capital at Utatlan. A description of their 'installation' of subject rulers suggests a hegemony very much like those of the Classic era.[15] Their grip was decisively weakened around 1470, however, when the Cakchiquel threw off Quiche control and began their own political expansion from a capital founded at Iximche.

In the north, the decline of Chichen Itza was followed by the rise of a new power in the shape of Mayapan. A densely settled, fortified citadel, its ceremonial heart was modelled, if poorly, on the great Itza city. In imitation of the Classic system, there was even a return to the carving of stone stelae. Colonial sources describe a dominant lineage, the Kokoom, who supplied its supreme ruler and required subject lords to live in the city, supported by tribute sent from their native towns. The Kokoom also appear in 9th-century inscriptions at Chichen, suggesting a long history of power in the region. The hegemony of Mayapan (whose true extent is unknown) was broken around 1441, when a rival lineage in the city, the Xiw, orchestrated a massacre of the Kokoom. The city was abandoned and its constituent polities, several establishing new capitals, re-asserted their autonomy. It was this landscape of fractious statelets that would be encountered by the first Spanish explorers to reach the Yucatan in 1517.

The Spanish Conquest

Following their comprehensive triumph over the Aztec Empire of Mexico in 1521, and subsequent subjugation of the Zapotec and Mixtec peoples of Oaxaca, the Spanish *conquistadores* turned their sights to the Maya. Here again, the superiority of European arms and use of cavalry were to be decisive factors in their victory, but so too was the tactic that had succeeded so well in Mexico – the recruiting of allies among the disparate kingdoms and the exploitation of age-old antagonisms. Thus it was with the aid of the Cakchiquel that Pedro de Alvarado, with some ruthlessness, overcame first the Quiche and then the Tzutujil in 1524. When the reality of life under the Spanish yoke became clear, the Cakchiquel rebelled and led a coalition against the

CHICHEN ITZA AND THE TOLTEC QUESTION

The spectacular ruins of Chichen Itza boast some of the most famous and photogenic examples of Maya architecture. The four-stairwayed El Castillo pyramid, circular Caracol 'observatory' and Great Ballcourt (the largest in Mesoamerica), have become icons of a culture. Yet there is real irony here, since Chichen is the most atypical of all Maya cities and its history an enduring enigma.

Chichen's reclining Chacmool sculptures, feathered serpents, *tzompantli* or carved 'skull rack', standard bearers and 'atlantean' throne supports, are all derived from the Toltec civilization, successor to Teotihuacan as the power of central Mexico. Yet the city also boasts much architecture in the northern Maya style of the Puuc. This has traditionally been interpreted in sequence: an 'Old Chichen' of the Terminal

Classic seized by outsiders and transformed into a Mexicanized 'New Chichen' of the Postclassic. But this has been challenged, increasingly so in recent years, by those who argue that the two styles are contemporary and Terminal Classic in date. It has become popular to see Chichen as the cosmopolitan champion of a new 'international style', a political and cultural response to the crisis further south.[16]

But several features of the old model remain persuasive. The only securely dated example of 'Toltec' carving, at the High Priest's Grave, falls in 998, more than a century after those associated with the Puuc style.[17] Oft-cited examples of ethnic conflict at Chichen are hard to dismiss entirely: embossed gold discs dredged from the famous well or *cenote* at the city show warriors in Toltec uniform spearing others in Maya dress. Finally, native histories explicitly link developments at Chichen with Mexican intrusions. What we seem to have is an uncanny echo of earlier developments in the Peten and the *entrada* of the Teotihuacanos. In the midst of the collapse, history may well have repeated itself and opened the Maya region to fresh penetrations by Mexican militarists.

(Left) A series of hammered gold discs show scenes of battle and heart sacrifice between warriors of contrasting Mexican and Maya garb.

(Below) Executed in pure Puuc style, the Iglesia is evidence of Chichen's vibrant Terminal Classic.

(Bottom) Viewed across the vast plazas of the city, the four-stairwayed Castillo pyramid has become an icon of Maya culture.

The Dresden Codex is one of only four Postclassic books to have escaped both the ravages of time and the fires of the Spanish priests.

This Late Postclassic stela was found beneath the church of Flores, the modern town built on the site of Noj Peten.

invaders, but the tide could not be turned and by 1527 all effective opposition in the highlands had been crushed.

A separate campaign to conquer the Yucatan Peninsula, led by a father and son both called Francisco de Montejo, was more protracted. Forced to abandon the attempt in 1528 and again in 1535, the son finally secured the submission of the powerful Xiw of Mani in 1542, leading to a general capitulation of the western polities. Those in the east continued the fight and, although they suffered a decisive defeat in 1546, resistance to Spanish, and later Mexican rule continued here well into the 20th century.

The last Maya kingdoms

The Peten, heartland of the Classic period, was never entirely abandoned and the Postclassic saw remnant communities and migrants from the north calling themselves Itza form some disparate polities around the chain of lakes at its core. Remote from Spanish settlement and surrounded by a dense rejuvenated forest, these vestiges of Maya independence survived until the very end of the 17th century. Chief among them was the island of Noj Peten, better known as Tayasal, on Lake Peten-Itza. Several attempts to subdue its rulers and convert them to Christianity were made over the years, but all proved fruitless (in 1623 a party of some 13 Spaniards and 80 native porters were allowed to visit the island, but were duplicitously seized and massacred). A final·effort at peaceful conversion was made in 1696, but its failure led to a determined military expedition the following year. On 13 March 1697, a force of 108 Spanish troops crossed the lake in a purpose-built galley, defeated a canoe-borne Maya army and stormed Noj Peten. Fatalities among the defenders were heavy, but not one of the latter-day *conquistadores* was lost. The modern-day town of Flores, now in Guatemala, was established on the site.

European colonization, as throughout the Americas, brought diseases that decimated the native population. Enforced Christianization soon eradicated most traces of elite learning among the survivors. A few bands did retreat to more remote corners of the forest, and today the tiny Lacandon community is the last of these pagan groups. The impoverished and downtrodden conditions of the Maya from the conquest to the present day have fostered a series of rebellions and revolutionary movements. One revolt in 1847 almost succeeded in seizing the entire Yucatan Peninsula, part of a sporadic conflict that only really ended with a treaty signed in Quintana Roo in 1936. There have been repeated conflicts in the highlands of Chiapas, of which the *zapatista* uprising of 1994 is only the most recent. The civil war that raged in Guatemala for many years – during which the Maya suffered horribly – was concluded by a peace accord at the end of 1996. The traditional resilience of the Maya people, who number today as many as eight million, has been joined in recent years by a new mood of cultural revival. The Maya are now engaged in a determined political struggle to gain an equitable place in the modern states that cover their ancient homeland.

NOTES AND BIBLIOGRAPHY

Notes

MAYA WRITING AND CALENDARS

1 See Kelley 1976; Schele 1982; Houston 1989; M.D. Coe 1999a; M.D. Coe & Van Stone 2001. **2** See Houston et al. 1998; Houston et al. 2000. **3** D. Stuart 1987; M.D. Coe & Kerr 1998. **4** See Thompson 1950. **5** Thompson 1927. **6** Lounsbury 1978.

THE ROYAL CULTURE OF THE MAYA

1 Taube 1985; Freidel et al. 1993. **2** Although this has been translated as *uchanul* 'his guardian' (Houston 1993) an alternative is A. Lacadena's suggestion of *ucha'an* 'his master', pers. comm. 1997. **3** Freidel 1990; Fields 1991. **4** Schele 1982; Schele & J. Miller 1983; Schele & M.E. Miller 1986. **5** Grube 1990c; D. Stuart & Houston 1994; D. Stuart 1996b; 1988. **6** Houston & D. Stuart 1996. **7** Grube 1992. **8** Schele & M.E. Miller 1986; D. Stuart 1988. **9** Tedlock 1985; Schele & M.E. Miller 1986; Freidel et al. 1993. **10** Kerr 1989–; Reents-Budet 1994. **11** V. Miller 1985. **12** M.D. Coe 1988; Grube & Schele 1993; Quenon & Le Fort 1997; Houston et al. 1998; Schele & Mathews 1998; D. Stuart 1998; Eberl 1999.

CLASSIC MAYA POLITICS

1 Freidel & Schele 1988; Hansen 1992. **2** Mathews 1975; Riese 1984; Grube 1988; Schele 1992; D. Stuart 2000. **3** Berlin 1958; Mathews 1991. **4** D. Stuart, Grube & Schele 1989. **5** Barthel 1968. **6** Marcus 1973; 1976; 1993. **7** Adams & R. Jones 1981; Adams 1986; see also Flannery 1972. **8** Mathews & Justeson 1984; Ringle 1988. **9** Mathews 1985; 1991. **10** Sabloff 1986; Freidel 1986. **11** See Hammond 1991; Demarest 1992; Houston 1993. **12** Martin & Grube 1994; 1995; Grube & Martin 1998; 'Overking': Higham 1995. **13** Mathews & Justeson 1984; D. Stuart 1984. **14** Houston & Mathews 1985; Bricker 1986. **15** S. Houston first proposed *chab* 'to supervise' in 1996, though we prefer the cognate *kab* on substitution grounds. **16** Hammond 1991; Lacadena & Ciudad Ruz 1998. **17** See Hassig 1985 and Berdan et al. 1996 for 'hegemonic' styles of control in Mexico.

TIKAL

Dynastic Bibliography: Coggins 1975; Jones 1977, 1987, 1991; Jones & Satterthwaite 1982; Fahsen 1986, 1988; Grube 1988, 1990a, 1998a; Schele & Freidel 1990; Schele 1992; Schele & Grube 1994a; Proskouriakoff 1993; Martin 1996a, 1998a, 1998b, 1999a, 1999b, 1999c; D. Stuart 1999a, 2000.

1 W.R. Coe 1990; C. Jones 1991. **2** Grube 1988; Schele 1992; Ehb': D. Stuart 1999a. **3** Grube 1998a. **4** Mathews 1985; Fahsen 1986. **5** Martin 1998a. **6** Grube 1998a; Martin 1999b. **7** D. Stuart in Schele & Grube 1994a. **8** C. Jones & Orrego 1987; Martin 1998a, 1999c. **9** D. Stuart 2000. **10** Laporte & Fialko 1990. **11** Harrison 1970, 1999. **12** Laporte & Fialko 1995. **13** Proskouriakoff 1993; Coggins 1975; 1983; D. Stuart 2000. **14** D. Stuart 2000. **15** Deciphered independently in 1992 by C. Prager & D. Stuart. **16** Martin 1998a. **17** See Adams 1998: fig.63. **18** Naachtun as Maasal: Grube in Martin 1998b. **19** Valdés 1996. **20** Laporte & Vega de Zea 1987. **21** Independently concluded by D. Stuart & S. Martin. **22** Martin 1999b. **23** As Nuun Yax Ayiin: D. Stuart pers. comm. 1993. Yax Nuun Ayiin: S. Guenter & M. Zender pers. comm. 2000. **24** Fahsen 2000; Martin 1998a. **25** Coggins 1975; W.R. Coe 1990. **26** Siyah Chan K'awiil: D. Stuart in Houston & D. Stuart 1996. **27** Grube 1998a, Martin

1998a. **28** Martin 1999b. **29** See also Schele et al. 1992. **30** Martin 1998a. **31** Coggins 1975; death date: Valdés, Fahsen & Muñoz Cosme 1997. **32** W.R. Coe 1990. **33** Valdés, Fahsen, Muñoz Cosme 1997. **34** Houston & D. Stuart: 1996. **35** Death date: D. Stuart pers. comm. 1999. **36** Martin 1998b; 1999a; 1999c. **37** A candidate for his accession might be 9.3.16.15.14 AD 511. **38** C. Jones 1991. **39** Martin 1998b; 1999c. **40** Houston 1987a, 1991. **41** Proskouriakoff 1950; Willey 1974. **42** C. Jones 1991. **43** Compare K772 with K4672 in Kerr 1989–. **44** Excavated by R. Larios & J. Guillemin (W.R. Coe 1990). **45** D. Stuart in Houston et al. 1992. **46** Puleston & Callender 1967. **47** For 'star war' Houston 1993; tribute formulae of this kind: D. Stuart 1995, 1998. **48** For exile: Grube & Nahm in Schele & Grube 1994c; at Palenque: Schele 1994. **49** Schele 1994. **50** Interment at Dos Pilas: S. Houston pers. comm. 1992; Burial 23: Coggins 1975. **51** J. Miller 1974; Schele & Freidel 1990. **52** Martin 1996a. **53** Schele & Freidel 1990; Martin 1996c. **54** e.g. Coggins 1975; Stone 1989; Haviland 1992. **55** Proskouriakoff 1993. **56** Martin & Grube 1994. **57** Grube & Schele 1994; D. Stuart 1998. **58** C. Jones pers. comm. 1996. **59** Coggins 1975. **60** W.R. Coe 1990. **61** C. Jones 1987. **62** C. Jones 1991, pers. comm 1996. **63** Martin 1994; 1995; 1996a. **64** Martin 1995, 1999c. **65** D. Stuart 1998. **66** C. Jones 1977. **67** C. Jones 1991; D. Stuart & Houston 1994; Sanchez et al. 1995. **68** See Larios & Orrego 1983. **69** Rice, Rice & Pugh 1998. **70** Marcus 1976; Schele & Grube 1994a. **71** W. Nahm in Schele & Grube 1994a.

DOS PILAS

Dynastic Bibliography: Houston & Mathews 1985; Johnston 1985; Houston 1987, 1993; Schele & Freidel 1990; Mathews & Willey 1991.

1 Houston 1993. There is some similarity to the name of Tikal's Animal Skull (Houston et al. 1992). However, according to his K'atun-age statement in 593 this king would have been minimally 72 years old at the birth of B'alaj Chan K'awiil in 625. We suspect that this is a different ruler, perhaps a namesake of K'inch Muwaan Jol. **2** Houston et al. 1992; Martin & Grube 1994. **3** Wars: Houston et al. 1992; Houston 1993; exile: W. Nahm & N. Grube in Schele & Grube 1994. **4** Houston 1993, Martin 1997. **5** Houston 1993. **6** W. Nahm in Schele & Grube 1994c. **7** Houston 1993. **8** D. Stuart & Houston 1994. **9** Houston & Mathews 1985. **10** Proskouriakoff 1973. **11** Mathews 1979a. **12** Demarest 1993; 1997. **13** Houston 1993. **14** Houston 1993. **15** Houston 1987b. **16** Houston 1993. **17** Houston 1993. **18** Houston 1993; Motul de San José mention and its date deciphered by H. Escobedo. **19** D. Stuart & Houston 1994. **20** N. Grube & A. Lacadena in Schele & Grube 1994c. **21** Johnston 1985. **22** Houston 1993. **23** Inomata 1997. T. Inomata & M. Eberl pers. comm. 1999. **24** Houston & Mathews 1985. **25** Mathews & Willey 1991. **26** Inomata 1997. **27** Houston 1987b. **28** Demarest et al. 1997. **29** Demarest et al 1997. **30** Foias & Bishop 1997.

NARANJO

Dynastic Bibliography: Berlin 1973; Gaida 1983; Closs 1984, 1985, 1989; Schele & Freidel 1990; Martin 1996a.

1 Dates: P. Mathews & D. Stuart in Martin 1996a. **2** Closs 1984. **3** D. Stuart 1985a. **4** Riese 1982; Grube & Schele 1993. **5** Probable king on vase K4958, Kerr 1989–1997 (Vol. 4). **6** Stone, Reents & Coffman 1985; *hub/jub*': Grube 1990a. **7** D. Stuart 1987. **8** Caracol origin: Martin 1998a. **9** Grube 1995; Stelae 34 and 37 might date to this era. **10** Schele & Freidel 1990. **11** Closs 1985. **12** Closs 1985; Proskouriakoff 1993. **13** Closs 1985. **14** Martin & Grube 1994. **15** *Pul* 'to burn': D. Stuart 1995. **16** Schele & Freidel 1990. **17** Houston 1983a. **18** Yo:tz name: Boot 1999. **19** Schele & Grube 1994c; Grube 1999. **20** See Stela 2. **21** Houston 1993: fig.4–9. **22** Martin 1996a. **23** Martin 1996a. **24** Closs 1989. **25** Martin 1995; 1999c. **26** Closs 1989. **27** Closs 1989. **28** Late spellings of K'awiil change from -AL to -IL suffixes and may reflect a shortened vowel. See Houston et al.

1998 **29** Houston & D. Stuart 1989; Grube & Nahm 1994; Calvin 1997. **30** Myth: D. Stuart 1995; Yaxha patron: Grube 1999. **31** LeFort & Wald 1995.

CARACOL

Dynastic Bibliography: Beetz & Sattertwaite 1981; Stone, Reents & Coffmann 1985; Houston 1987a; Chase, Grube & Chase 1991; Grube 1994.

1 Chase, Grube & Chase 1991. **2** Houston 1987a; Houston & D. Stuart 1997. **3** Beetz & Satterthwaite 1981; D. Stuart & Houston 1994. **4** Grube 1990b. **5** Houston 1987a, 1991. **6** Grube 1994. **7** Grube 1994. **8** Tikal Hiatus: Houston 1987a. **9** S. Houston pers. comm. 1993. **10** His K'atun-age statements also switch from 3 to 4 at this point. **11** Chase & Chase 1996a. **12** Grube 1994. **13** Chase & Chase 1987. **14** Jaeger 1994; Chase & Chase 1996b. **15** 'Star war': Sosa & Reents 1980; Stone, Reents & Coffmann 1985; Martin & Grube 1994. **16** Grube 1994. **17** Grube 1995. **18** Caracol glyph: S. Houston pers. comm. 1992. **19** Caracol glyph: S. Houston pers. comm. 1992. **20** Stone 1995; Colas 1998. **21** *Hoy/joy*: D. Stuart pers. comm. 1997. **22** *B'ital* reading: S. Houston pers. comm. 1992; Chase, Grube & Chase 1991. **23** *Yopaat*: D. Stuart pers. comm. 1999. **24** Grube 1994.

CALAKMUL

Dynastic Bibliography: Ruppert & Denison 1943; Miller 1974; Mathews 1979b; Marcus 1987; Schele & Freidel 1990; Martin 1993, 1996c, 1996d, 1997, 2000a, in press a; Marcus & Folan 1994; Pincemin et. al. 1998.

1 Martin 1997. **2** Pincemin et al. 1998. **3** For this 'Ruler 1' see Marcus 1987. **4** Martin 2000a. **5** Signs for no and CH'E:N: D. Stuart pers. comm.1998. **6** Emblem: Marcus 1973; Oxte'tun: D. Stuart & Houston 1994; Chik Nab: Martin 1997. **7** Carrasco & Boucher 1987. **8** Schele & Freidel 1990. **9** Sprajc 1997; Martin in press a. **10** Martin 1997. **11** Martin 1995, 1997. **12** Folan et al. 1995. **13** Martin 1996. **14** Martin 2000a. **15** Marcus 1987. **16** Martin & Grube 1994. **17** Folan & Morales 1996; Carrasco pers. comm. 1996; Carrasco 2000. **18** Accession date: D. Stuart in Graham 1997; Martin 2000a. **19** Martin in press b. **20** Martin & Grube 1994; 1995. **21** Mathews 1979b; Graham et al. 1975–; Graham 1997; D. Stuart in Graham 1997. **22** J. Miller 1974; birth: Mathews 1979b; Marcus & Folan 1994; Martin 2000a. **23** Houston & Mathews 1985. **24** Marcus & Folan 1994. **25** Carrasco et al. 1999. **26** Schele & Freidel 1990. **27** Carrasco et al. 1999; García-Morena & Granados 2000. **28** Martin & Grube 1994. **29** C. Jones & Satterthwaite 1982; Martin 1994; 1996. **30** Hansen et al. 1991; Reents-Budet et al. 1997. **31** Looper 1999. **32** Martin 2000a. **33** Flannery 1972; Marcus 1976; Carrasco & Wolf 1996. **34** Martin 2000a.

YAXCHILAN

Dynastic Bibliography: Proskouriakoff 1960; 1963-64; Mathews 1975, 1997[1985]; Schele & Freidel 1990; Tate 1990; Nahm 1997.

1 Mathews 1975; 1997[1985]; earlier dates: Nahm 1997. **2** *Yopaat*: D. Stuart pers. comm. 1999. **3** *Tatb'u Joloom*: D. Stuart pers. comm. 1999. **4** D. Stuart 1998. **5** See YAX HS.1 Step II 59–63 for this revision. **6** *Hoy/joy*: D. Stuart pers. comm. 1999. **7** Belt names: D. Stuart in Schele & M.E. Miller 1986; Stela 27: L. Schele pers. comm. 1991. **8** Martin 1998a. **9** M.E. Miller 1991; Schele & Mathews 1991. **10** Tate 1992. **11** Mathews 1997[1985]. **12** Mathews 1997[1985]. **13** Alternatively Itzamnaaj Balam II is 15th, D. Stuart pers. comm. 1998. **14** M.E. Miller 1991. **15** Grube 1998b. **16** M.E. Miller 1991. **17** T. Jones et al. 1990; Schele & Freidel 1990. The Xook term is still debated, but see T. Jones 1996. **18** Proskouriakoff 1963, 1964. **19** K. Josserand & N. Hopkins pers. comm. 1993. **20** 2nd pers. text: D. Stuart pers. comm. 1996. **21** Usually thought to be the accession of Bird Jaguar IV under Ruler 4 in 757, but could refer to an earlier pairing of these recurring names at the two cities. **22** See Marcus 1992.

23 Schele & Freidel 1990; Noble Bardsley 1994; Mathews 1997[1985]. 24 Tedlock 1985; Freidel et al. 1993. 25 Mathews 1997[1985]. 26 Schele & Freidel 1990. 27 Nahm 1997. 28 Carrasco 1991. 29 D. Stuart 1997. 30 Schele & Freidel 1990. 31 M.E. Miller 1986b; 1995. 32 Mathews 1980; Houston in M.E. Miller 1995. 33 D. Stuart in Houston et al.1999.

PIEDRAS NEGRAS

Dynastic Bibliography: Proskouriakoff 1960; Houston 1983b; Stuart 1985b; Johnston 1989; Schele 1991a; Schele & Mathews 1991.

1 Johnston 1989; Schele 1991a. 2 M.E. Miller 1991; Schele & Mathews 1991. 3 Martin 1996c; 1997. 4 Taube 1988. 5 Stone 1989; Taube 1992. 6 M.E. Miller 1991. 7 Houston et al. 1998. 8 Grube 1996. 9 D. Stuart 1985b; Grube in Mayer 1987. 10 Schele 1991b; This war and K'ina' tie noted independently by Guenter & Zender 1999. 11 Grube 1998b. 12 W.R. Coe 1959. 13 Mathews 1998. 14 Mathews 1979a; D. Stuart & Houston 1994. 15 Houston et al. 1998. 16 Houston 1983b; Rabbit Stone as La Mar: Schele & Grube 1994b. 17 Yo'nal Ahk III also appears on a provincial panel, now in the Kurt Stavenhagen Collection, in 760. 18 D. Stuart 1986. 19 Schele & Grube 1994b. 20 D. Stuart in Houston et al. 1999.

PALENQUE

Dynastic Bibliography: Berlin 1968; Mathews & Schele 1974; Schele & Freidel 1990; Schele 1991a, 1994; Grube 1996.

1 Martin 1999c. 2 D. Stuart in Kerr 1989– (Vol. 3). 3 González Cruz 1994. 4 D. Stuart & Houston 1994. 5 Name: D. Stuart 1999b. 6 Hoy/Joy: D. Stuart pers. comm. 1998. 7 Mam: D. Stuart pers. comm. 1999. 8 Berlin 1963; Lounsbury 1980; Schele & Freidel 1990; D. Stuart 1999b. 9 Yohl: Bernal Romero 1999. 10 Date proposed by F. Lounsbury; Palenque location: Martin 1995. 11 Grube 1996. 12 Attack: Looper & Schele 1991; by Calakmul: Martin 1995. 13 Grube 1996. 14 Schele & Freidel 1990; Bassie-Sweet 1991. 15 D. Stuart 1999b; hermaphroditism might be considered. 16 Grube 1996; a further defeat by Bonampak occurred in 603 or 655. 17 Greene Robertson 1985. 18 P. Mathews pers. comm. 1992. 19 D. Stuart 1999b. 20 Schele 1994. 21 Schele 1994. 22 Ruz 1973. 23 Schele & Mathews 1998. 24 W. Nahm pers. comm. 1996. 25 Houston 1996. 26 Bassie-Sweet 1991 (also F. Lounsbury). 27 Conjunction: Dütting 1982; Jade: Proskouriakoff 1974. 28 S. Houston pers. comm. 1996. 29 Houston & D. Stuart 1997. 30 K. Bassie-Sweet, N. Hopkins & K. Josscrand pers. comm. 1999. 31 Schele & Mathews 1991. 32 Bassie-Sweet 1991; Ringle 1996. 33 Schele 1991b. 34 Identified independently by Guenter & Zender 1999. 35 King's portrait: R. Wald pers. comm. 1998. 36 Star war: A. Herring pers. comm. 1996. 37 Morales 1999; D. Stuart 1999b. 38 Ringle 1996. 39 Upakal K'inich as heir: Martin in PARI Newsletter 26, 1998; Janaab' Pakal identification: Bernal Romero 1999. 40 Schele & M.E. Miller 1986. 41 Porter 1994. 42 Hoppan 1996.

TONINA

Dynastic Bibliography: Becquelin & Baudez 1979-82; Mathews 1979c; Ayala 1995, 1997; Yadeun 1992, 1993.

1 Mathews 1979c. 2 Date: P. Mathews & M. Quenon pers. comm. 1998. 3 Ayala 1995; 1997. 4 Chapat: Grube & Nahm 1994; iconography: K. Taube pers. comm. 1996; At Tonina: Boot 1998. In Western Ch'olan it seems to have a short vowel: cha-pa-ta, in Eastern long vowel CHAPA:T-tu. 5 Puh as 'reed': D. Stuart 2000. 6 Freidel et al. 1993. 7 Baudez & Mathews 1979; Becquelin & Baudez 1979–82. 8 Mathews in Ayala 1995. 9 The spelling ?-e-TU:N-ni appears on PNG P.4 (H1); Martin 2000b. 10 See also TNA M.27. 11 Schele & Mathews 1991. 12 Schele 1991a. 13 Houston & Mathews 1985; Martin & Grube 1994. 14 D. Stuart pers. comm. 1997. 15 D. Stuart 1997. 16 Uh: D. Stuart & Houston 1994.

COPAN

Dynastic Bibliography: Riese 1971, 1988, 1992; Marcus 1976; Pahl 1976; Schele & Freidel 1990; Fash 1991; Fash & Stuart 1991; Schele 1992; Stuart 1992; Schele & Looper 1996; Sharer et al. 1999.

1 King list: Marcus 1976; chronology & founder: D. Stuart & Schele 1986; Grube 1988; Schele 1992. 2 K. Taube pers.comm. 1997; D. Stuart pers. comm. 1999, 2000. 3 Schele & Freidel 1990; Fash 1991. 4 Sharer et al. 1999. 5 D. Stuart 2000. 6 As Tikal's K'uk' Mo': Schele et al. 1993. 7 Buikstra 1997; Sharer et al. 1999. 8 Stela 63: D. Stuart et al. 1989; excavation: Fash et al. 1992. 9 Kowalski & Fash 1991; Fash et al. 1992; Williamson 1996. 10 Sharer et al. 1999. 11 Buikstra 1997; Sharer 1997. Sharer et al. 1999. 12 Sedat & Sharer 1994; Schele et al. 1994. 13 Schele & Grube 1990. 14 Fash et al. 1992; Grube & Schele 1988; Grube 1998c. 15 Morales et al. 1990. Sharer et al. 1999. 16 G. Stuart 1997; Sharer et al. 1999. 17 R. Agurcia pers. comm. 1996; and in G. Stuart 1997. 18 Fash 1991. 19 Grube in Freidel et al. 1993. 20 D. Stuart & Grube 1999. 21 See Fash 1991. 22 Fash & D. Stuart 1991; for another tzak huul see Yaxchilan HS.3 Step V D7. 23 D. Stuart 2000. 24 Agurcia & Fash 1989; Fash 1991. 25 Fash 1991. 26 Schele 1987; Looper 1999. 27 Berlin 1958; Barthel 1968; Marcus 1973. 28 Centipedes: Taube pers. comm. 1996. 29 D. Stuart 1994. 30 R. Argurcia pers. comm. 1996. 31 Agurcia & Fash 1991. 32 Symbolism: Schele & M.E. Miller 1986. Text: D. Stuart 1992. 33 Grube et al. 1989. 34 D. Stuart pers. comm. 1997. 35 D. Stuart 1994; 2000. 36 Schele & Grube 1991. 37 M.E. Miller 1986a. 38 Fash 1991. 39 D. Stuart pers. comm. 1997. 40 Kelley 1962; Riese 1986; Schele & Freidel 1990. 41 Sanders 1986; Gerstle 1987; Webster 1989; Fash 1991. 42 For T.18 & St.11: Baudez 1983; Baudez & Dowd 1983. 43 Schele & Freidel 1990; Collapse: Stuart 1993; S. Guenter first raised the issue of St.11's incomplete text. 44 Abrams & Rue 1989; Webster & Freter 1989; Fash 1991; Storey 1992; Manaham 1999. 45 Morley 1920; B. Fash in Grube & Schele 1987; Fash 1991.

QUIRIGUA

Dynastic Bibliography: Kelley 1962; Sharer 1978, 1988; Riese 1986; Grube et al. 1991; Schele & Looper 1996; Looper 1999.

1 Stone 1983; Schele 1989; Grube et al. 1991; Looper 1999. 2 Sharer 1988. 3 Sharer 1988. 4 D. Stuart 1992. 5 War: Marcus 1976. 6 Riese 1984a. 7 Looper 1999. 8 MacLeod 1991; pers. comm. 1999; Freidel, Schele & Parker. 1993; D. Stuart 1996b. 9 Schele & Looper 1996. 10 Grube et al. 1991. 11 Taube 1985; Freidel et al. 1993; Quenon & LeFort 1997. 12 Looper 1999. 13 D. Stuart pers. comm. 1997. 14 Grube et al. 1991. 15 Schele & Freidel 1990. 16 Sharer 1988.

EPILOGUE

1 See Culbert & Rice 1990. 2 Rice et al. 1985; Wiseman 1985; Abrams & Rue 1989. 3 Curtis et al.1996. 4 Culbert 1973 (ed.); 1988. 5 Demarest 1997. 6 Morley 1937-8. 7 D. Stuart 1993. 8 Sabloff 1975. 9 Schele & Mathews 1998. 10 D. Stuart 1993. 11 Marcus 1976. 12 Proskouriakoff 1950; 1993; Chase 1985. 13 Kowalski 1985. 14 Noted by L. Schele & N. Grube. 15 Las Casas 1909; Martin & Grube 1994. 16 E.g. Lincoln 1986; Schele & Freidel 1990; Schele & Mathews 1998. 17 Graña-Behrens et al. 1999 have confirmed J.E.S. Thompson's original dating.

Bibliography

Titles highlighted with an asterisk (*) are particularly useful for the general reader.

ABBREVIATIONS
AA American Antiquity
AM Ancient Mesoamerica
CIW Carnegie Institution of Washington
CN Copan Notes (Unpublished)
DOS Dumbarton Oaks Studies in Pre-Columbian Art and Archaeology
ECM Estudios de Cultura Maya
IMS Institute for Mesoamerican Studies, State University of New York at Albany
INAH Instituto Nacional de Antropología e Historia (Mexico)
LAA Latin American Antiquity
MARI Middle American Research Institute, Tulane University
MVB The Maya Vase Book, see Kerr 1989–
NG National Geographic
PARI Pre-Columbian Art Research Institute
PMM Peabody Museum Memoirs
PRT Palenque Round Table or Mesa Redonda de Palenque, gen. ed. M. Greene Robertson
RRAMW Research Reports on Ancient Maya Writing
TN Texas Notes on Precolumbian Art, Writing, and Culture (Unpublished)
TR Tikal Report, University Museum
UMM University Museum Monograph, University of Pennsylvania
UT University of Texas

Abrams, E. & D. Rue, 1989, 'The Causes and Consequences of Deforestation among the Prehistoric Maya', in Human Ecology 16:377-395.
Adams, R., 1986, 'Río Azul: Lost City of the Maya', NG 169(4): 420–451.
— 1998, Río Azul: A Classic Maya City, Norman.
*Adams, R. (ed.), 1977, The Origins of Maya Civilization, Albuquerque.
Adams, R., & R. Jones, 1981, 'Spatial Patterns and Regional Growth Among Classic Maya Cities', AA 46(2): 301–322.
Agurcia, R., & W. Fash, 1989, 'Copan: A Royal Maya Tomb Discovered', NG 176(4): 480–487.
— 1991, 'Maya Artistry Unearthed', NG 180(3): 94–105.
*Agurcia, R., & J.A. Valdés, 1994, Copan & Tikal: Secrets of Two Maya Cities, San José.
*Andrews, G., 1975, Maya Cities: Placemaking and Urbanization, Norman.
Ayala, M., 1995, 'The History of Tonina According to its Inscriptions', Ph.D. dissertation, UT Austin.
— 1997, 'Who Were the People of Toniná?', in The Language of Maya Hieroglyphs, eds. M. Macri & A. Ford, 69–75, PARI, San Francisco.
Ball, J., & J. Taschek, 1991, 'Late Classic Lowland Maya Political Organization and Central-Place Analysis' AM 2(2): 149–165.
Barthel, T., 1968, 'El complejo "emblema"', ECM 7: 159–193.
Bassie-Sweet, K., 1991, From the Mouth of the Dark Cave, Norman.
Baudez, C. (ed.), 1983, Introducción a la arqueología de Copán, 3 Vols., Tegucigalpa.
Baudez, C., & A. Dowd, 1983, 'La decoración del templo (10L-18)', in Introducción a la arqueología de Copán, ed. C. Baudez, Vol. 2: 447–473, Tegucigalpa.
Baudez, C., & P. Mathews, 1979, 'Capture and Sacrifice at Palenque', 3rd PRT: 31–40, San Francisco.
Becquelin, P., & C. Baudez, 1979–1982, Tonina, Une Cité Maya du Chiapas, 3 Vols., Paris.
Beetz, C., & L. Satterthwaite, 1981, The Monuments and Inscriptions of Caracol, Belize, UMM 45, Philadelphia.
Berdan, F., R. Blanton, E. Hill Boone, M. Hodge, M. Smith & E. Umberger, 1996, Aztec Imperial Strategies, Dumbarton Oaks, Washington D.C.
Berlin, H., 1958, 'El glifo "emblema" en las inscripciones mayas', Journal de la Société des Americanistes, n.s. 47: 111–119.
— 1959, 'Glifos nominales en el sarcófago de

Palenque', *Humanidades* 2(10): 1–8.
— 1963, 'The Palenque Triad', *Journal de la Société des Americanistes*, n.s. 52: 91–99.
— 1968, *The Tablet of the 96 Glyphs at Palenque, Chiapas, Mexico*, MARI 26: 135–150.
— 1973, 'Beiträge zum Verständnis der Inschriften von Naranjo', *Bulletin de la Société Suisse des Americanistes* 37: 7–14.
Bernal Romero, G., 1999, 'Análisis epigráfico del Tablero de K'an Tok, Palenque, Chiapas', paper presented at the PRT 1999.
Boot, E., 1998, 'Centipedes and Fire Serpents at Chichen Itza', paper presented at the 3rd European Maya Conference, Hamburg.
— 1999, 'A New Naranjo Area Toponym: Yo:tz', *Mexicon*, Vol. 21 (2): 39–42.
Bricker, V., 1986, *A Grammar of Mayan Hieroglyphs*, MARI 56, New Orleans.
Buikstra, J., 1997, *The Bones Speak: High-tech Approach to the Study of Our Ancestors*, lecture presented for the Loren Eisley Associates, Univ. of Pennsylvania Museum, Philadelphia.
Calvin, I., 1997, 'Where the Wayob Live', in *MVB* 5:868-883, New York.
Carrasco, R., 1991, 'The Structure 8 Tablet and Development of the Great Plaza at Yaxchilan', *6th PRT*: 110–117, Norman.
— 1996, 'Proyecto Arqueológico de la Biosfera de Calakmul, Temporada 1993–94', unpublished INAH report.
— 2000, 'El cuchcabal de la Cabeza de Serpiente'. *Arqueología Mexicana*, 7(42): 12–19.
Carrasco, R., & S. Boucher, 1987, 'Las escaleras jeroglíficas del Resbalón, Quintana Roo', in *Primer simposio mundial sobre epigrafia maya*, 1–21, Guatemala.
Carrasco, R., S. Boucher, P. Alvarez, V. Tiesler Blos, V. Garcia Vierna, R. Garcia Moreno & J. Vazquez Negrete, 1999, 'A Dynastic Tomb from Campeche, Mexico: New Evidence on Jaguar Paw, A Ruler of Calakmul', *LAA* 10(1): 47–58.
Carrasco, R., & M. Wolf, 1996, 'Nadzca'an: Una antigua ciudad en el suroeste de Campeche, México', in *Mexicon* Vol. 18(4): 70–74.
Chase, A., 1985, 'Troubled Times: The Archaeology and Iconography of the Terminal Classic Southern Lowland Maya', *5th PRT*: 103–114, San Francisco.
Chase, A., & D. Chase, 1987, *Investigations at the Classic Maya City of Caracol, Belize: 1985–1987*, PARI Monograph 3, San Francisco.
— 1996a, 'A Mighty Maya Nation: How Caracol Built an Empire by Cultivating its "Middle Class"', *Archaeology* 49(5): 66–72.
— 1996b, 'The Causeways of Caracol', *Belize Today* 10(3/4): 31–32.
Chase, A., N. Grube & D. Chase, 1991, 'Three Terminal Classic Monuments from Caracol, Belize', *RRAMW* 36, Washington D.C.
Closs, M.D., 1984, 'The Dynastic History of Naranjo: The Early Period', *ECM* 15: 77–96.
— 1985, 'The Dynastic History of Naranjo: The Middle Period', *4th PRT*: 65–78, San Francisco.
— 1989, 'The Dynastic History of Naranjo: The Late Period', in *Word and Image in Maya Culture*, eds. W.F. Hanks & D.S. Rice, 244–254, Salt Lake City.
Coe, M.D., 1988, 'Ideology of the Maya Tomb', in *Maya Iconography*, eds. E.P. Benson & G. Griffin, 222–235, Princeton.
*— 1999a *Breaking the Maya Code*, 2nd edn, London & New York.
*— 1999b, *The Maya*, 6th edn, London & New York.
*Coe, M.D., & J. Kerr, 1998, *The Art of the Maya Scribe*, London & New York.
*Coe, M.D. & M. Van Stone, 2001, *How to Read Maya Glyphs*, London & New York.

Coe, W.R., 1959, *Piedras Negras Archaeology: Artifacts, Caches, and Burials*, UMM 18, Philadelphia.
*— 1967, *Tikal: A Handbook of the Ancient Maya Ruins*, Philadelphia.
— 1990, *Excavations in the Great Plaza, North Terrace, and North Acropolis of Tikal*, 6 Vols., TR 14, UMM 61, Philadelphia.
Coggins, C., 1975, 'Painting and Drawing Styles at Tikal', Ph.D. dissertation, Harvard University.
*— 1983, 'The Age of Teotihuacan and its Mission Abroad', in *Teotihuacan: Art from the City of the Gods*, eds. K. Berrin & E. Pasztory, 141-155. London.
Colas, P. R., 1998, 'Caves of Blood and War', paper presented at the 3rd European Maya Conference, University of Hamburg.
*Culbert, T.P. (ed.), 1973, *The Classic Maya Collapse*, Alburquerque.
— 1988, 'The Collapse of Classic Maya Civilization', in *The Collapse of Ancient States and Civilizations*, eds. N. Yoffee & G. Cowgill, 69–101, Tucson.
*— 1991, *Classic Maya Political History. Epigraphic and Archaeological Evidence*, Cambridge.
*— 1993, *Maya Civilization*, Montreal.
Culbert, T.P., & D.S. Rice (eds.), 1990, *Precolumbian Population History in the Maya Lowlands*, Albuquerque.
Curtis, J., D. Hodell, & M. Brenner, 1996, 'Climate variability on the Yucatan Peninsula (Mexico) during the 3500 years, and implications for Maya cultural evolution', *Quaternary Research* 46:37-47.
Demarest, A., 1992, 'Ideology in Ancient Maya Cultural Evolution: The Dynamics of Galactic Polities', in *Ideology and Pre-Columbian Civilizations*, eds. A. Demarest & G. Conrad, 135–157, Santa Fe.
— 1993, 'The Violent Saga of a Maya Kingdom', *NG* 183(2): 94–111.
— 1997, 'The Vanderbilt Petexbatun Regional Archaeological Project 1989–1994', *AM* 8(2): 209–227.
Demarest, A., M. O'Mansky, C. Wolley, D. Van Turenhout, T. Inomata, J. Palka & H. Escobedo, 1997, 'Classic Maya Defensive Systems and Warfare in the Petexbatun Region', *AM* 8(2): 229–253.
*Drew, D., 1999, *Lost Chronicles of the Maya Kings*, London.
Dütting, D., 1982, 'The 2 Cib 14 Mol Event in the Inscriptions of Palenque, Chiapas, Mexico', *Zeitschrift für Ethnologie* 107: 233–258.
Eberl, M., 1999, 'Tod und Begräbnis in der klassischen Maya-Kultur', Masters thesis, University of Bonn.
Fahsen, F., 1986, 'Algunos aspectos sobre el texto de la Estela 31 de Tikal', *Mesoamerica* 11: 135–154.
— 1988, 'A New Early Classic Text from Tikal', *RRAMW* 17, Washington D.C.
*Fash, W., 1991, *Scribes, Warriors and Kings. The City of Copan and the Ancient Maya*, London & New York.
Fash, W., & D. Stuart, 1991, 'Dynastic History and Cultural Evolution at Copan, Honduras', in *Classic Maya Political History*, ed. T.P. Culbert, 147–179, Cambridge.
Fash, W., R. Williamson, C. R. Larios & J. Palka, 1992, 'The Hieroglyphic Stairway and its Ancestors: Investigations of Copan Structure 10-L26', *AM* 3: 105–115.
Fields, V., 1991, 'The Iconographic Heritage of the Maya Jester God', *6th PRT*: 167–174, Norman.
Flannery, K., 1972, 'The cultural evolution of civilizations', *Annual Review of Ecology and Systematics* 3: 399–426.
Foias, A., & R. Bishop, 1997, 'Changing Ceramic

Production and Exchange in the Petexbatun Region, Guatemala', *AM* 8(2): 275–291.
Folan, W., J. Marcus, S. Pincemin, M. Carrasco, L. Fletcher & A. Morales, 1995, 'Calakmul: New Data from an Ancient Maya Capital in Campeche, Mexico', *LAA* 6: 310–334.
Folan, W., & A. Morales L., 1996, 'La estructura II-H, sus entierros y otras funciones ceremoniales y habitacionales', *Revista Española de Antropologia Americana*, 9–28.
Freidel, D., 1986, 'Maya Warfare: An Example of Peer-Polity Interaction', in *Peer-Polity Interaction and Socio-political Change*, eds. C. Renfrew & J.F. Cherry, 93–108, Cambridge.
— 1990, 'The Jester God: The Beginning and End of a Maya Royal Symbol', in *Vision and Revision in Maya Studies*, eds. F.S. Clancy & P.D. Harrison, 67–78, Albuquerque.
Freidel, D., & L. Schele, 1988, 'Kingship and the Late Preclassic Maya Lowlands – The Instruments and Places of Ritual Power', *American Anthropologist* 90(3): 547–567.
*Freidel, D., L. Schele & J. Parker, 1993, *Maya Cosmos: Three Thousand Years on the Shaman's Path*, New York.
Gaida, M., 1983, 'Die Inschriften von Naranjo (Peten, Guatemala)', *Beiträge zur mittelamerikanischen Völkerkunde*, Hamburg.
García Moll, R., 1996, 'Yaxchilán, Chiapas', *Arqueología Mexicana*, 4 (22): 36–45.
García-Morena, R., & J. Granados, 2000, 'Tumbas reales de Calakmul', *Arqueología Mexicana*, 7(42): 28–33.
Gerstle, A., 1987, 'Ethnic Diversity and Interaction at Copan, Honduras', in *Interaction on the Southeast Mesoamerican Frontier*, ed. E. Robinson, 328–356, BAR International Series 327, Oxford.
González Cruz, A., 1994, 'Trabajos Recientes en Palenque', *Arqueologia Mexicana* 2(10): 39–45.
Graham, I., 1997, 'Mission to La Corona', *Archaeology* 50(5): 46.
Graham, I., E. Von Euw & P. Mathews, 1975–, *Corpus of Maya Hieroglyphic Inscriptions*, Vols. 1–8, Peabody Museum, Cambridge (Mass.).
Graña-Behrens, D., C. Prager & E. Wagner, 1999, 'The Hieroglyphic Inscription of the "High Priest's Grave" at Chichen Itza, Yucatan, Mexico', *Mexicon* 21 (3): 61–66.
Greene Robertson, M., 1985, *The Sculpture of Palenque*, Vol. 3: *The Late Buildings of the Palace*, Princeton.
Grube, N., 1986, 'Untersuchungen zur dynastischen Geschichte von Naranjo, El Peten, Guatemala', *Zeitschrift für Ethnologie* 111: 47–118.
— 1988, 'Städtegründer und "Erste Herrscher" in Hieroglyphentexten des Klassischen Mayakultur', *Archiv für Völkerkunde* 42: 69–90.
— 1990a 'Caracol's impact on the Tikal hiatus', paper presented at the 6th Texas Symposium, Univ. of Texas, Austin.
— 1990b, 'A Reference to Water-Lily Jaguar on Caracol Stela 16', CN 68.
— 1990c, 'Die Errichtung von Stelen: Entzifferung einer Verbhieroglyphe auf Monumenten der Klassischen Mayakultur', in *Circumpacifica*, eds. B. Illius & M. Laubscher, 189–215, Frankfurt.
— 1991, 'Die Entwicklung der Mayaschrift', *Acta Mesoamericana* 3, Berlin.
— 1992, 'Classic Maya Dance', *AM* 3(2): 201–218.
— 1994, 'Epigraphic Research at Caracol, Belize', in *Studies in the Archaeology of Caracol, Belize*, eds. A. & D. Chase, 83–122, PARI, San Francisco.
— 1995 'Epigraphic Research at Caracol, Belize: An Update', manuscript.

*— (ed.), 1995, *The Emergence of Lowland Maya Civilization*, Möckmühl.
— 1996, 'Palenque in the Maya World', *8th PRT*: 1–13, San Francisco.
— 1998a, 'Una nueva interpretación de la secuencia dinástica de Tikal en el Clasico Temprano', paper presented at 4o Congress Internacional de Mayistas, Antigua, Guatemala.
— 1998b, 'Observations on the Late Classic Interregnum at Yaxchilan', in *The Archaeology of Mesoamerica*, eds. W. Bray & L. Manzanilla, 116–127, London.
— 1998c, 'Speaking Through Stones: A Quotative Particle in Maya Hieroglyphic Writing', in *50 Años de Estudios Americanistas en la Universidad de Bonn*, eds. S. Dedebach-Salazar et al., 543–558, Möckmühl.
— 1999, 'Monumentos esculpidos e inscripciones jeroglíficas en el Triángulo Yaxhá-Nakum-Naranjo, Región Noreste del Peten, Guatemala', manuscript.
Grube, N., & S. Martin, 1998, 'Política clásica maya dentro de una tradición mesoamericana: un modelo epigráfico de organización política "hegemónica"', in *Modelos de entidades políticas mayas*, ed. S. Trejo, 131–146, Mexico.
Grube, N., & W. Nahm, 1994, 'A Census of Xibalba: A Complete Inventory of "way" Characters on Maya Ceramics', *MVB* 4: 686–715, New York.
Grube, N., & L. Schele, 1987, 'U-Cit-Tok, the Last King of Copan', CN 21.
— 1988, 'Cu-Ix, the Fourth Ruler of Copan and His Monuments', CN 40.
— 1993, 'Naranjo Altar 1 and Ritual of Death and Burial', TN 54.
— 1994, 'Tikal Altar 5', TN 66.
Grube, N., L. Schele & F. Fahsen, 1991, 'Odds and Ends from the Inscriptions of Quirigua', *Mexicon* 13(6): 106–112.
Grube, N., L. Schele, D. Stuart & W. Fash, 1989, 'The Date of Dedication of Ballcourt III', CN 59.
Guenter, S.P., & M. Zender, 1999, 'Palenque and Yaxchilan's War against Piedras Negras', manuscript.
*Hammond, N., 1982, *Ancient Maya Civilization*, Cambridge & New Brunswick.
— 1991, 'Inside the Black Box: Defining the Maya Polity', in *Classic Maya Political History*, ed. T.P. Culbert, 253–284, Cambridge.
Hansen, R., 1992, 'The Archaeology of Ideology: A Study of Maya Preclassic Architectural Sculpture at Nakbe, Peten, Guatemala', Ph.D. dissertation, University of California.
Hansen, R., R. Bishop & F. Fahsen, 1991, 'Notes on Maya Codex Style Ceramics from Nakbe, Peten, Guatemala', *AM* 2(2): 225–243.
Harrison, P.D., 1970, 'The Central Acropolis, Tikal, Guatemala: A Preliminary Study of the Functions of its Structural Components During the Late Classic Period', Ph.D. dissertation, Univ. of Pennsylvania.
*— 1999, *The Lords of Tikal*, London & New York.
Hassig, R., 1985, *Trade, Tribute and Transportation: The Sixteenth-century Political Economy of the Valley of Mexico*, Norman.
Haviland, W.A., 1992, 'From Double-Bird to Ah Cacaw: Dynastic Troubles and the Cycle of the Katuns at Tikal, Guatemala', in *New Theories on the Ancient Maya*, eds. E.C. Danien & R. Sharer, 71–80, UMM 77, Philadelphia.
Higham, N.J., 1995, *An English Empire*, Manchester.
Hohmann, H., & A. Vogrin, 1982, *Die Architektur von Copan*, Graz.
Hoppan, J.-M., 1996, 'Nuevos datos sobre las inscripciones de Comalcalco', in *8th PRT*: 153-

158. San Francisco.
Houston, S., 1983a, 'Warfare between Naranjo and Ucanal', in *Contributions to Maya Hieroglyphic Decipherment* 1: 31–39.
— 1983b, 'On Ruler 6 at Piedras Negras, Guatemala', *Mexicon* 5(5): 84–86.
— 1987a, 'Notes on Caracol Epigraphy and Its Significance', in *Investigations at the Classic Maya City of Caracol, Belize 1985–1987*, eds. A. & D. Chase, 85–100, PARI Monograph 3, San Francisco.
— 1987b, 'The Inscriptions and Monumental Art of Dos Pilas, Guatemala: A Study of Classic Maya History and Politics', Ph.D. dissertation, Yale University.
*— 1989, *Maya Glyphs*, London.
— 1991, 'Appendix: Caracol Altar 21', *6th PRT*: 38–42, Norman.
*— 1993, *Hieroglyphs and History at Dos Pilas. Dynastic Politics of the Classic Maya*, Austin.
— 1996, 'Symbolic Sweatbaths of the Maya: Architectural Meaning in the Cross Group at Palenque, Mexico', *LAA* 7(2): 132–151.
Houston, S., H. Escobedo, D. Forsyth, P. Hardin, D. Webster & L. Wright, 1998, 'On the River of Ruins: Explorations at Piedras Negras, Guatemala', *Mexicon* 20(1): 16–22.
Houston, S., H. Escobedo, P. Hardin, R. Terry, D. Webster, M. Child, C. Golden, K. Emery & D. Stuart, 1999, 'Between Mountain and Sea: Investigations at Piedras Negras, Guatemala', *Mexicon* 21(1): 10–17.
Houston, S., & P. Mathews, 1985, *The Dynastic Sequence of Dos Pilas*, PARI Monograph 1, San Francisco.
Houston, S., J. Robertson & D. Stuart, 2000, 'The Language of Classic Maya Inscriptions', *Current Anthropology* 41(3).
Houston, S., & D. Stuart, 1989, 'The Way Glyph: Evidence for Co-essences among the Classic Maya', *RRAMW* 30.
— 1996, 'Of Gods, Glyphs and Kings: Divinity and Rulership Among the Classic Maya', *Antiquity* 70: 289–312.
— 1997, 'The Ancient Maya Self: Personhood and Portraiture in the Classic Period', *RES* 33: 73–102.
Houston, S., D. Stuart & J. Robertson, 1998, 'Disharmony in Maya Hieroglyphic Writing: Linguistic Change and Continuity in Classic Society', in *Anatomia de una civilizacion*, ed. A. Ciudad Ruiz et al., 275–296, Madrid.
Houston, S., S. Symonds, D. Stuart, & A. Demarest, 1992, 'A Civil War of the Late Classic Period: Evidence from Hieroglyphic Stairway 4', manuscript.
Inomata, T., 1997, 'The Last Day of a Fortified Classic Maya Center: Archaeological Investigations at Aguateca, Guatemala', *AM* 8(2): 337–351.
Jaeger, S., 1994, 'The Conchita Causeway Settlement Subprogram', in *Studies in the Archaeology of Caracol, Belize*, eds. A. & D. Chase, 47–63, PARI Monograph 7, San Francisco.
Johnston, K., 1985, 'Maya Dynastic Territorial Expansion', *5th PRT*: 49–56, San Francisco.
— 1989, 'A commentary on the hieroglyphic inscriptions of Piedras Negras, Guatemala', manuscript.
Jones, C., 1977, 'Inauguration Dates of Three Late Classic Rulers of Tikal, Guatemala', *AA* 42: 28–60.
— 1987, 'The Life and Times of Ah Cacau, Ruler of Tikal', in *Primer simposio mundial sobre epigrafia maya*, 107–120, Guatemala.
— 1991, 'Cycles of Growth at Tikal', in *Classic Maya Political History*, ed. T.P. Culbert, 102–127, Cambridge.
Jones, C., & M. Orrego, 1987, 'Corosal Stela 1 and Tikal Miscellaneous Stone 167: Two New

Monuments from the Tikal Vicinity, Guatemala', *Mexicon* 9(6): 129–133.
Jones, C., & L. Satterthwaite, 1982, *The Monuments and Inscriptions of Tikal: The Carved Monuments*, TR 33a, UMM 44, Philadelphia.
Jones, T., 1996, 'Polyvalency in the 'Xok' Glyph: Phonetic u and a Morphemic Patronym', *8th PRT*: 325–342.
Jones, T., C. Jones & R. Marhenke, 1990, 'Blood Cousins: The Xok-Balam Connection at Yaxchilan', in *U Mut Maya* 3, eds. T. & C. Jones, Arcata.
Kelley, D., 1962, 'Glyphic Evidence for a Dynastic Sequence at Quirigua, Guatemala', *AA* 27: 323–335.
*— 1976, *Deciphering the Maya Script*, Austin.
*Kerr, J., 1989–, *The Maya Vase Book: A corpus of rollout photographs of Maya vases*, Vols. 1–5, eds. B. Kerr & J. Kerr, New York.
Kowalski, J., 1985, 'A Historical Interpretation of the Inscriptions of Uxmal', *5th PRT*: 235–247.
Kowalski, J., & W. Fash, 1991, 'Symbolism of the Maya Ball Game at Copan: Synthesis and New Aspects', *6th PRT*: 59–67.
Lacadena, A., & A. Ciudad, 1998, 'Reflexiones sobre la estructura política maya clasica', in *Anatomía de una civilización*, eds. A. Ciudad Ruiz et al., 31–64, Madrid.
Laporte, J.P., & V. Fialko, 1990, 'New Perspectives on Old Problems: Dynastic References for the Early Classic at Tikal', in *Vision and Revision in Maya Studies*, eds. F.S. Clancy & P.D. Harrison, 33–66, Albuquerque.
— 1995, 'Un reencuentro con Mundo Perdido, Tikal, Guatemala', *AM* 6: 41–94.
Laporte, J.P., & L. Vega de Zea, 1987, 'Aspectos dinásticos para el clásico temprano de Mundo Perdido, Tikal', in *Primer simposio mundial sobre epigrafia maya*, 127–140, Guatemala.
Las Casas, B., 1909, *Apologética historia de las Indias. Nueva Biblioteca de Autores Españoles*, Vol. 13, Madrid.
LeFort, G., & R. Wald, 1995, 'Large Numbers on Naranjo Stela 32', *Mexicon* 17(6): 112–114.
Lincoln, C., 1986, 'The Chronology of Chichén Itzá: A Review of the Literature', in *Late Lowland Maya Civilization: Classic to Postclassic*, eds. J. Sabloff & E.W. Andrews V, 141–196, Albuquerque.
Looper, M., 1999, 'New Perspectives on the Late Classic Political History of Quirigua', Guatemala, *AM* 10:263-280.
Looper, M., & L. Schele, 1991, 'A War at Palenque During the Reign of Ah-K'an', TN 25.
Lounsbury, F., 1978, 'Maya Numeration, Computation and Calendrical Astronomy', in *Dictionary of Scientific Biography* 15: Supplement 1, ed. C.C. Gillespie, 759–818, New York.
— 1980, 'Some Problems in the Interpretation of the Mythological Portion of the Hieroglyphic Text of the Temple of the Cross at Palenque', *3rd PRT*, Part 2: 99–115, Austin.
*McAnany, P. 1995, *Living with the Ancestors. Kinship and Kingship in Ancient Maya Society*, Austin.
MacLeod, B., 1991, 'Maya Genesis: The First Steps', manuscript.
Manaham, K., 1999, 'Reevaluating the Classic Maya Collapse at Copan: New Data and Socioeconomic Implications', paper presented at the PRT 1999.
Marcus, J., 1973, 'Territorial Organization of the Lowland Classic Maya', *Science* 180: 911–916.
— 1976, *Emblem and State in the Classic Maya Lowlands*, Washington D.C.
— 1987, *The Inscriptions of Calakmul*, Univ. of Michigan Technical Report 21, Ann Arbor.
*— 1992, *Mesoamerican Writing Systems*, Princeton.

— 1993, 'Ancient Maya Political Organization', in *Lowland Maya Civilization in the Eighth Century AD*, eds. J. Sabloff & J. Henderson, 111–171, Dumbarton Oaks, Washington D.C.

Marcus, J., & W. Folan, 1994, 'Una estela más del siglo V y nueva informacion sobre Pata de Jaguar, gobernante de Calakmul, Campeche, en el siglo VII', Gaceta Universitria Ano IV No. 15–16, Campeche.

Martin, S., 1993, '"Site Q": The Case for a Classic Maya Super-polity', manuscript.

— 1994, 'Warfare and Political Organization in the Late Classic Central Southern Lowlands', paper presented at the 10th Texas Symposium, Austin.

— 1995, 'New Epigraphic Data on Maya Warfare', paper presented at the Primera Mesa Redonda de Palenque, Nueva Epoca, 1995, Palenque.

— 1996a, 'Tikal's "Star War" against Naranjo', *8th PRT*: 223–235, San Francisco.

— 1996b, 'Lords and Overlords: Decoding Political Hierarchy at Piedras Negras, Guatemala', paper presented at 'Maya Kings and Warfare in the Usumacinta Basin', British Museum, London.

— 1996c, 'Calakmul en el registro epigráfico', in 'Proyecto Arqueológico de la Biosfera de Calakmul, Temporada 1993–94', ed. R. Carrasco, unpublished INAH report.

— 1996d, 'Calakmul y el enigma del glifo Cabeza de Serpiente', *Arqueología Mexicana* 3(18): 42–45.

— 1997, 'The Painted King List: A Commentary on Codex-Style Dynastic Vases', *MVB* 5: 846–867.

— 1998a, 'At the Periphery: Early Monuments in the Environs of Tikal', paper presented at the 3rd European Maya Conference, University of Hamburg.

— 1998b, 'Middle Classic Tikal: Kings, Queens and Consorts', manuscript, London.

— 1998c, 'Report on Epigraphic Fieldwork at Calakmul: 1995–1998, 'Proyecto Arqueológico de la Biosfera de Calakmul, Temporada 1995–', ed. R. Carrasco, unpublished INAH report.

— 1999a, 'The Queen of Middle Classic Tikal', *PARI Newsletter*, March 1999: 4–5.

— 1999b, 'The Baby Jaguar: Dynastic Legitimation and Matrilineal Descent at Early Classic Tikal', paper presented at the PRT 1999.

— 1999c 'Thematic Issues in the Epigraphy of Tikal', paper presented at the School of American Research Advanced Seminar 1999.

— 2000a, 'Los Señores de Calakmul', *Arqueologia Mexicana*, 7(42): 40–45.

— 2000b, 'Tonina's External Relations', manuscript, London.

— in press a, 'A Preliminary Report on Epigraphic Fieldwork at Calakmul, Campeche', *Mexicon*.

— in press b, 'Court and Realm, Architectural Signatures in the Classic Maya Southern Lowlands', in *Royal Courts of the Ancient Maya*, eds. T. Inomata & S. Houston, Boulder.

Martin, S., & N. Grube, 1994, 'Evidence for Macro-Political Organization Amongst Classic Maya Lowland States', manuscript, London/Bonn.

*— 1995, 'Maya Superstates', *Archaeology* 48(6): 41–46.

Mathews, P., 1975, 'The Lintels of Structure 12, Yaxchilan, Chiapas, Mexico', paper presented at the Annual Conference of the Northeastern Anthropological Association, Wesleyan University.

— 1979a, 'The Inscription on the Back of Stela 8, Dos Pilas, Guatemala', manuscript, Calgary.

— 1979b, 'Notes on the Inscriptions of "Site Q"', manuscript, Calgary.

— 1979c, 'Souverains', in *Tonina, une cité Maya du Chiapas*, eds. P. Becquelin & C. Baudez,

Vol. 3: 1381–1383, Paris.

— 1980, 'Notes on the Dynastic Sequence of Bonampak, Part 1', *3rd PRT* Part 2: 60–73, Austin.

— 1985, 'Early Classic Monuments and Inscriptions', in *A Consideration of the Early Classic Period in the Maya Lowlands*, ed. G.R. Willey & P. Mathews: 5–55, IMS 10, Albany.

— 1991, 'Classic Maya Emblem Glyphs', in *Classic Maya Political History*, ed. T.P. Culbert, 19–29, Cambridge.

— 1997[1985], *La escultura de Yaxchilan*, INAH Mexico.

— 1998, 'Una lectura de un nuevo monumento de El Cayo, Chiapas, y sus implicaciones políticas', in *Modelos de entidades políticas mayas*, ed. S. Trejo, 113–129, Mexico.

Mathews, P., & J. Justeson, 1984, 'Patterns of Sign Substitution in Maya Hieroglyphic Writing: "The Affix Cluster"', in *Phoneticism in Maya Hieroglyphic Writing*, ed. J. Justeson & L. Campbell, 185–231, IMS 9, Albany.

Mathews, P., & L. Schele, 1974, 'Lords of Palenque: The Glyphic Evidence', *1st PRT*: 63–75, Pebble Beach.

Mathews, P., & J. Willey, 1991, 'Prehistoric Polities of the Pasion Region', in *Classic Maya Political History: Hieroglyphic and Archaeological Evidence*, ed. T.P. Culbert, 30–71, Cambridge.

Mayer, K.H., 1987, *Maya Monuments: Sculptures of Unknown Provenance*, Supplement 1, Berlin.

Miller, J., 1974, 'Notes on a Stelae Pair Probably from Calakmul, Campeche, Mexico', *1st PRT*: 149–162, San Francisco.

Miller, M.E., 1986a, 'Copan: Conference with a Perished City', in *City States of the Maya, Art and Architecture*, ed. E. Benson, 72–109, Denver.

— 1986b, *The Murals of Bonampak*, Princeton.

— 1991, 'Some observations on the relationship between Yaxchilan and Piedras Negras'. Paper presented at the 7th Texas Symposium, Austin.

*— 1995, 'Maya Masterpiece Revealed at Bonampak', *NG* 187(2): 50–69.

*— 1999, *Maya Art and Architecture*, London & New York.

*Miller, M.E., & K. Taube, 1993, *The Gods and Symbols of Ancient Mexico and the Maya*, London & New York.

Miller, V., 1985, 'The Dwarf Motif in Classic Maya Art', *4th PRT*, New York.

Morales, A., 1999, 'New Discoveries in Temple XIX and Temple XX, Palenque', paper presented at the PRT 1999.

Morales, A., J. Miller & L. Schele, 1990, 'The Dedication Stair of "Ante" Structure', *CN 76*.

Morley, S., 1920, *The Inscriptions at Copan*, CIW Publication 9, Washington D.C.

— 1937–1938, *Inscriptions of the Peten*, CIW Publication 437, Washington D.C.

Nahm, W., 1997, 'Hieroglyphic Stairway 1 at Yaxchilan', *Mexicon* 19(4): 65–69.

Noble Bardslay, S., 1994, 'Rewriting History at Yaxchilan: Inaugural Art of Bird Jaguar IV', *7th PRT*: 87–94.

Pahl, G., 1976, 'Maya Hieroglhic Inscriptions of Copan', Ph.D. dissertation, Univ. of California.

Pincemin, S., J. Marcus, L. Folan, W. Folan, M. Carrasco & A. Morales Lopez, 1998, 'Extending the Calakmul Dynasty Back in Time: A New Stela From a Maya Capital in Campeche, Mexico', *LAA* 9(4): 310–327.

Porter, J.B., 1994, 'The Palace Intaglios: A Composite Stairway Throne at Palenque', *7th PRT*: 11–18.

Proskouriakoff, T., 1950, *A Study of Classic Maya Sculpture*, CIW Publication 593, Washington D.C.

— 1960, 'Historical Implications of a Pattern of Dates at Piedras Negras, Guatemala', *AA* 25: 454–475.

— 1963–1964, 'Historical Data in the Inscriptions of Yaxchilan, Parts 1 & 2', *ECM* 3: 149–167 & 4: 177–201.

— 1973, 'The Hand-grasping-fish and Associated Glyphs on Classic Maya Monuments', in *Mesoamerican Writing Systems*, ed. E. Benson, 165–178, Washington D.C.

— 1974, *Jades from the Cenote of Sacrifice, Chichen Itza, Yucatan*, Cambridge.

*— 1976, *An Album of Maya Architecture*, Norman.

*— 1993, *Maya History*, Austin.

Puleston, D.E., & D.W. Callender, 1967, 'Defensive Earthworks at Tikal', *Expedition* 9(3): 40–48.

Quenon, M., & G. LeFort, 1997, 'Rebirth and Resurrection in Maize God Iconography', *MVB* 5: 884–902.

*Reents-Budet, D., 1994, *Painting the Maya Universe*, Durham.

— in press, 'Classic Maya Conceptualizations of the Royal Court', in *Royal Courts of the Ancient Maya*, eds. T. Inomata & S. Houston, Boulder.

Reents-Budet, D., S. Martin, R. Hansen & R. Bishop, 1997, 'Codex-Style Pottery: Recovering Context and Concept', paper presented at the Maya Meetings at Texas, UT Austin.

Rice, D., P. Rice & E. Deevey Jr., 1985, 'Paradise Lost: Classic Maya Impact on a Lacustrine Environment' in *Prehistoric Lowland Maya Environment and Subsistence Economy*, ed. M. Pohl, Peabody Museum Papers 77: 91–105.

Rice, D., P. Rice & T. Pugh, 1998, 'Settlement Continuity and Change in the Central Peten Lakes Region: The Case of Zacpeten', in *Anatomia de una Civilización*, eds. A. Ciudad et al., 207–252, Madrid.

Riese, B., 1971, *Grundlagen zur Entzifferung der Maya Hieroglyphen. Beiträge zur mittelamerikanischen Völkerkunde 11*, Hamburg.

— 1982, 'Die Popol Vuh Peten Platte (Naranjo Altar 1)', *Indiana* 7: 143–157.

— 1984a, 'Hel Hieroglyphs', in *Phoneticism in Maya Hieroglyphic Writing*, eds. J. Justeson & L. Campbell, 263–286, IMS 9, Albany.

— 1984b, 'Kriegsberichte der Klassischen Maya', *Baessler Archiv* 30(2): 255–321.

— 1986, 'Late Classic Relationship between Copan and Quirigua: Some Epigraphic Evidence', in *The Southeast Maya Periphery*, eds. P. Urban & E. Schortman, 94–101, Austin.

— 1988, 'Epigraphy of the Southeast Zone in Relation to Other Parts of Mesoamerica', in *The Southeast Classic Maya Zone*, eds. E. Boone & G. Willey, 67–94, Washington D.C.

— 1992, 'The Copan Dynasty', in *Handbook of Middle American Indians*, Supplement 5: 128–153, Austin.

Ringle, W., 1988, 'Of Mice and Monkeys: The Value and Meaning of T1016, the God C Hieroglyph', *RRAMW* 18.

— 1996, 'Birds of a Feather: The Fallen Stucco Inscription of Temple XVIII, Palenque, Chiapas', *8th PRT*: 45–61, San Francisco.

Ruppert, K., & J. Denison Jr., 1943, *Archaeological Reconnaissance in Campeche, Quintana Roo, and Peten*, CIW Publication 543, Washington D.C.

Ruz Lhuillier, A., 1973, *El Templo de las Inscripciones*, Mexico.

Sabloff, J.A., 1975, *Excavations at Seibal: The Ceramics*, PMM 13(2), Cambridge, MA.

— 1986, 'Interaction Among Maya Polities: A Preliminary Examination', in *Peer Polity Interaction and Socio-political Change*, eds. C. Renfrew & J.F. Cherry, 109–116, Cambridge.

Sabloff, J.A., & J.S. Henderson (eds), 1993, *Lowland Maya Civilization in the Eighth Century AD*, Washington D.C.

Sanchez, R., D. Rice, P. Rice, A. McNair, T. Pugh & G. Jones, 1995, 'La investigacion de la geografia politica del siglo XVII en Peten Central: La primera temporada', in *VIII Simposio de Investigaciones. Arqueologicas en Guatemala, 1994*, ed. J.P. Laporte & H. L. Escobedo, 707–720, Guatemala.

Sanders, W.T., 1986, *Excavaciones en el area urbana de Copan*, Vol. 1, Tegucigalpa.

Schele, L., 1982, *Maya Glyphs: The Verbs*, Austin.

— 1987, 'A Brief Commentary on a Hieroglyphic Cylinder from Copan', CN 27.

— 1989, 'Some Further Thoughts on the Copan-Quirigua Connection', CN 67.

— 1991a, 'An Epigraphic History of the Western Maya Region', in *Classic Maya Political History*, ed. T.P. Culbert, 72–101, Cambridge.

— 1991b, 'The Demotion of Chak-Zutz': Lineage Compounds and Subsidiary Lords', in *6th PRT*: 6–11, Norman.

— 1992, 'The Founders of Lineages at Copan and Other Maya Sites', *AM* 3: 135–145.

— 1994, 'Some Thoughts on the Inscriptions of House C', *7th PRT*: 1–10.

Schele, L., F. Fahsen & N. Grube, 1992, 'El Zapote and the Dynasty of Tikal', TN 34.

*Schele, L., & D. Freidel, 1990, *A Forest of Kings: The Untold Story of the Ancient Maya*, New York.

Schele, L., & N. Grube, 1987, 'The Brother of Yax Pac', CN 20.

— 1988, 'The Father of Smoke-Shell', CN 39.

— 1990, 'Two Early Monuments from Copan', CN 82.

— 1991, 'Speculations on Who Built the Temple under 11', CN 102.

— 1994a, 'Some Revisions to Tikal's Dynasty of Kings', TN 67.

— 1994b, 'Notes on the Chronology of Piedras Negras Stela 12', TN 70.

— 1994c, 'The Workbook for the XVIIIth Maya Hieroglyphic Workshop at Texas'.

— 1994d, 'Who Was Popol-K'inich? A Re-evaluation of the Second Successor in the Line of Yax-K'uk'-Mo' in Light of New Archaeological Evidence', CN 116.

Schele, L., N. Grube & F. Fahsen, 1993, 'The Tikal Copan Connection', 3 Parts, CN 121–123.

— 1994, 'The Xukpi Stone: A Newly Discovered Early Classic Inscription from the Copan Acropolis', CN 114.

Schele, L., & M. Looper, 1996, 'The Workbook for the XXth Maya Hieroglyphic Workshop at Texas'.

Schele, L., & P. Mathews, 1991, 'Royal Visits and Other Intersite Relationships Among the Classic Maya', in *Classic Maya Political History*, ed. T.P. Culbert, 226–252, Cambridge.

*— 1998, *The Code of Kings*, New York.

Schele, L., P. Mathews, & F. Lounsbury, 1983, 'Parentage Expressions From Classic Maya Inscriptions', manuscript.

Schele, L., & J.H. Miller, 1983, *The Mirror, the Rabbit, and the Bundle*, DOS 25, Washington D.C.

*Schele, L., & M.E. Miller, 1986, *The Blood of Kings: Dynasty and Ritual in Maya Art*, New York & London.

*Schmidt, P., M. de la Garza & E. Nalda, 1998, *Maya Civilization*, London.

Sedat, D., & R.J. Sharer, 1994, 'The Xukpi Stone: A Newly Discovered Early Classic Inscription from the Copan Acropolis. Part I: The Archaeology', CN 113.

Sharer, R.J., 1978, 'Archaeology and History of Quirigua, Guatemala', *Journal of Field Archaeology* 5: 51–70.

— 1988, 'Quirigua as a Classic Maya Center' in *The Southeast Classic Maya Zone*, eds. E.Hill Boone & G.R. Willey, 31–65, Washington D.C.

*— 1994, *The Ancient Maya* (5th edn.), Stanford.

— 1997, 'Yax K'uk' Mo' and Copan's Early External Connections, Early Copan Acropolis Paper 11, University of Pennsylvania.

Sharer, R., L. Traxler, D. Sedat, E. Bell, M. Canuto, & C. Powell, 1999, 'Early Classic Architecture beneath the Copan Acropolis'. *AM* 10:3-23.

Sosa, J.R. & D.J. Reents, 1980, 'Glyphic Evidence for Classic Maya Militarism', *Belizean Studies* 8(3): 2–11.

Sprajc, I., F. García Cruz & H. Ojeda Mas, 1997, 'Reconocimiento arqueologico en el sureste de Campeche, Mexico. Informe preliminar', *Mexicon* 19(1): 5–12.

*Stephens, J.L., 1841, *Incidents of Travel in Central America, Chiapas and Yucatan*, 2 vols, New York.

Stone, A., 1983, 'The Zoomorphs of Quirigua', Ph.D. dissertation, UT Austin.

— 1989, 'Disconnection, Foreign Insignia and Political Expansion: Teotihuacan and the Warrior Stelae of Piedras Negras', in *Mesoamerica after the Decline of Teotihuacan AD 700–900*, eds. R.A. Diehl & J.C. Berlo, 153–172, Washington D.C.

— 1995, *Images from the Underworld. Naj Tunich and the Tradition of Maya Cave Painting*, Austin.

Stone, A., D. Reents, & R. Coffman, 1985, 'Genealogical Documentation of the Middle Classic Dynasty of Caracol, El Cayo, Belize', *4th PRT*: 267–276, San Francisco.

Storey, R., 1992, 'The Children of Copan: Issues of paleopathology and paleodemography', *AM* 3: 161–167.

Stuart, D., 1984, 'Epigraphic Evidence of Political Organization in the Usumacinta Drainage', manuscript.

— 1985a, 'The Yaxha Emblem Glyph as Yax-ha', *RRAMW* 1, Washington D.C.

— 1985b, 'The Inscription on Four Shell Plaques from Piedras Negras, Guatemala', *4th PRT*: 175–184, San Francisco.

— 1986, 'The 'lu-bat' Glyph and its Bearing on the Primary Standard Sequence', paper presented at the Primer Simposio Mundial sobre Epigrafía Maya, Guatemala.

— 1987, 'Ten Phonetic Syllables', *RRAMW* 14, Washington D.C.

— 1988, 'Blood Symbolism in Maya Iconography', in *Maya Iconography*, eds. E.P. Benson & G. Griffin, 175–221, Princeton.

— 1992, 'Hieroglyphs and Archaeology at Copan', *AM* 3: 169–184.

— 1993, 'Historical Inscriptions and the Maya Collapse', in *Lowland Maya Civilization in the Eighth Century AD*, eds. J.A. Sabloff & J.S. Henderson, 321–354, Washington D.C.

— 1994, 'The Texts of Temple 26: The Presentation of History at a Maya Dynastic Shrine', paper presented at the School of American Research Advanced Seminar 'Copan: The Rise and Fall of a Classic Maya Kingdom', Santa Fe.

— 1995, 'A Study of Maya Inscriptions', Ph.D dissertation, Vanderbilt University.

— 1996, 'Kings of Stone: A Consideration of Stelae in Maya Ritual and Representation', *RES* 29/30: 149–171.

— 1997, 'Kinship Terms in Maya Inscriptions', in *The Language of Maya Hieroglyphs*, eds. M.J. Macri & A. Ford, 1–11, PARI, San Francisco.

— 1998, '"The Fire Enters His House"', in *Function and Meaning in Maya Architecture*, ed. S.D. Houston, Washington D.C.

— 1999a, 'The Founder of Tikal', manuscript.

— 1999b, 'The New Inscriptions of Temple XIX', paper presented at the PRT 1999.

*— 2000 '"The Arrival of Strangers": Teotihuacan and Tollan in Classic Maya History', in, *Mesoamerica's Classic Heritage*, eds. D. Carrasco, L. Jones & S. Sessions, 465–513, Boulder.

Stuart, D., & N. Grube, 1999, 'A New Stela from Nim Li Punit, Toledo, Belize', manuscript.

Stuart, D., N. Grube & L. Schele, 1989, 'A Substitution Set for the "Macuch/Batab"', CN 58.

Stuart, D., N. Grube, L. Schele & F. Lounsbury, 1989, 'Stela 63: A New Monument from Copan', CN 56.

*Stuart, D., & S. Houston, 1994, *Classic Maya Place Names*, DOS 33, Washington D.C.

Stuart, D., & L. Schele, 1986, 'Yax-K'uk'-Mo', the Founder of the Lineage of Copan', CN 6.

*Stuart, G., 1997, 'The Royal Crypts of Copan', *NG* 192(6): 68–93.

*Stuart, G.S., & G.E. Stuart, 1993, *Lost Kingdoms of the Maya*, Washington D.C.

Taschek, J.T., & J.W. Ball, 1991, 'Lord Smoke-Squirrel's Cacao Cup: The Archaeological Context and Socio-historical Significance of the Buenavista "Jauncy Vase"', *MVB* 3: 490–497, New York.

*Tate, C., 1992, *Yaxchilan: The Design of a Maya Ceremonial City*, Austin.

Taube, K., 1985, 'The Classic Maya Maize God: A Reappraisal', *5th PRT*: 171–181, San Francisco.

— 1988, 'Classic Maya Scaffold Sacrifice', in *Maya Iconography*, eds. E. Benson & G. Griffin, 331–351, Princeton.

— 1992, 'The Temple of Quetzalcoatl and the Cult of Sacred War at Teotihuacan, *RES* 21:53–87.

*— 1993, *Aztec and Maya Myths*, London.

*Tedlock, D., 1985, *Popol Vuh*, New York.

Thompson, J.E.S., 1927, 'A Correlation of the Mayan and European Calendars', *Field Museum Series* 17: 1–22, Chicago.

— 1950, *Maya Hieroglyphic Writing: An Introduction*, Washington D.C.

— 1962, *A Catalog of Maya Hieroglyphs*, Norman.

Valdés, J.A., 1986, 'Uaxactun: Recientes Investigaciones', *Mexicon* 6(6): 125–128.

Valdés, J.A., F. Fahsen & G. Muñoz Cosme, 1997, *Estela 40 de Tikal: Hallazgo y Lectura*, Guatemala.

Webster, D. (ed.), 1989, *The House of the Bacabs*, DOS 29, Washington D.C.

Webster, D., & A. Freter, 1989, 'Settlement History and the Classic Collapse at Copan: A Redefined Chronological Perspective', *LAA* 1: 66–85.

Willey, G.R., 1974, 'The Classic Maya Hiatus; A Rehearsal for the Collapse?', in *Mesoamerican Archaeology: New Approaches*, ed. N. Hammond, 417–430, Austin.

Williamson, R., 1996, 'Excavations, Interpretations, and Implications of the Earliest Structures beneath Structure 10L-26 at Copan, Honduras', *8th PRT*: 169–175, San Francisco.

Wiseman, F., 1985, 'Agriculture and Vegetation Dynamics of the Maya Collapse on Central Peten, Guatemala', in *Prehistoric Lowland Maya Environment and Subsistence Economy*, ed. M. Pohl, Peabody Museum Papers 77: 63–71.

Wren, L., & P. Schmidt, 1991, 'Elite interaction during the Terminal Classic period: new evidence from Chichen Itza', in *Classic Maya Political History*, ed. T.P. Culbert, 199–225, Cambridge.

Yadeun, J., 1992, 'Toniná, El laberinto del inframundo', Gobierno del Estado Chiapas, Mexico.

— 1993, *Toniná*. México.

ACKNOWLEDGMENTS AND ILLUSTRATION CREDITS

The authors would like to thank the following for their generous help: Ricardo Agurcia, Anthony Aveni, Ed Barnhart, Clara Bezanilla, Sylviane Boucher, Ramón Carrasco, Cristin Cash, Arlen & Diana Chase, Bunny Coates, Michael Coe, Lori Conley, Arthur Demarest, Federico Fahsen, Barbara and William Fash, Ian Graham, Norman Hammond, Peter Harrison, Adam Herring, Stephen Houston, Takeshi Inomata, Christopher Jones, Justin Kerr, Mathew Looper, Colin McEwan, Peter Mathews, Arthur Miller, Mary Miller, John Montgomery, Enrique Nalda, Sandra Noble, Jorge Pérez de Lara, Lewis Ranieri, Dorie Reents-Budet, David Schele, Massimo Steffani, Yann Secouet, David Sedat, Robert Sharer, Loa Traxler, Mark Van Stone, Monica del Villar. Simon Martin would like to thank Jeffrey Quilter, the Senior Fellows, and staff of Dumbarton Oaks, Washington D.C. for an invaluable Research Fellowship for the year 1996-7.

Abbreviations: a – above, b – below, c – centre, l – left, r – right, t – top. AWS Archivio Whitestar, Italy; BM © British Museum; BF Barbara Fash; IG Ian Graham (CMHI – Corpus of Maya Hieroglyphic Inscriptions, Harvard University); JK © Justin Kerr, plus file #; JM John Montgomery; LS Linda Schele; MEM Mary Ellen Miller; MGR © Merle Greene Robertson, 1976; MZ Michel Zabé; NG Nikolai Grube; NGS National Geographic Society, Image Collection; PMHU Peabody Museum of Archaeology and Ethnology, © President and Fellows of Harvard College, Harvard University; PW Philip Winton; RD Rafael Doniz; RJMA Rautenstrauch-Joest-Museum of Anthropology, Cologne; RS Robert Sharer; SH Stephen Houston; SM Simon Martin; TP Tatiana Proskouriakoff; TW Tracy Wellman; UPM University of Pennsylvania Museum, Philadelphia; WRC William R. Coe.

All glyph drawings are by NG and SM; **Jacket (front)** l, r Dumbarton Oaks Collection, photos SM; c Museo Nacional de Arqueología y Etnología, Guatemala, photo E. Thiem/Lotos-Film; **Half-title** SM; **Frontis.** MZ; **5 from top** PMHU, JK 2885, PMHU, RS; **6** TP; **7t** John Bigelow Taylor; **b** JK 4889; **8** Michael D. Coe; **9** SM; **10** PW; **14** Dallas Museum of Art, photo SM; **15** JK 1453; **16** JK 2206; **18l** PW after Michael Adams; **r** PW after Peter Mathews; **21** SM (with Yann Secouet); **24** PW after Carr & Hazard; **25l** MEM; **c** UPM; **r** JK 2695; **27t** UPM, Neg. # 62-4-972; **b** UPM, Neg. # 59-4-481, photo WRC; **28l** John Bigelow Taylor; **b** TW; **29** Drawing by WRC, courtesy of Tikal Project, UPM; **30** From *The Ancient Maya*, 3rd ed. by Morley & Brainerd, 1956; **31tl** JK 7528; **tr** JK 5742; **b** SM; **32** MEM; **33t** Arthur Miller; **b** JK 4884; **34l** UPM, Neg. # 60-4-204, photo WRC; **b** Gerald Berjonneau; **35l,c,r** drawings after Jones & Satterthwaite, 1982; **36t** UPM; **c** PW after SM; **b** UPM, Neg. # 68-4-805; **37** Daniel Chauche; **38** SM; **39** SM; **40** JK 1261; **41t** JK 4679; **b** © G. Dagli Orti, Paris; **43** PW after SM; **44** UPM Neg. # 69-5-55; **45** Collection Museum der Kulturen, Basel, photo Peter Horner; **45t** UPM, Neg. # 63-4-1536, photo WRC; **c** UPM, Neg. # 74-4-192. Photo WRC; **b** UPM Neg. # 63-5-87. Photo WRC; **47t** Jorge Pérez de Lara; **b** MEM; **48** JK 4887; **49** Collection Museum der Kulturen, Basel, photo Peter Horner; **50** NG; **51t** Martin Lubikowski after WRC; **c** NG; **b** JK 2695; **52** UPM; **53** Russell Hoover; **54** PW after SH; **55l** SH; **c** JK 1599; **r** Michael D. Coe; **56** LS; **57** American Museum of Natural History, N.Y.; **58** SH; **59t** NG; **b** Enrico Ferorelli; **60** JK 1599; **61t** NG; **bl** Enrico Ferorelli; **br** Photo Ángel Serrano Castro, INKO Producciones Fotográficas, S.L.; **62t** IG (MARI); **b** JK 1599; **63tl** SM; **tr** SM after SH; **b** SH; **65c** SH; **b** Takeshi Inomata; **66-7** Richard Schlecht/NGS; **67** l & r PW; **68** PW after IG; **69l** PMHU; **c** PMHU; **70t** PMHU; **b** JK 5458; **71l** & r SM; **73** PMHU; **74** PMHU; **75t** PMHU; **b** JK 4464; **77** SM; **78** PMHU; **79c** SM; **bl** Collection Museum der Kulturen, Basel; **br** JM; **80** PMHU; **81tl** IG; **tr** JK 927; **bl** SM; **cb & br** NG; **82l** IG; **c** IG; **r** SM; **83** NG; **84** PW after A.F. & D.Z. Chase; **85l** & c UPM, photos SM; **r** SH; **86** UPM, C. Beetz; **87** NG; **88** UPM, photo SM; **89** t SH; **bl** UPM; **90** UPM, C. Beetz; **91** NG; **92b** Courtesy of D.Z. & A.F. Chase, Caracol Archaeological Project; **93t** NG; **b** PW after R. O'Connell & C. Palmer; **94** NG; **95** NG; **97tl** SH; **tr** Chip Clark; **b** NG; **98c & b** NG; **99** NG; **100** PW after May Lau et al.; **101l** Museum zu Allerheiligen, Schaffhausen; **c** MZ; **r** MNA; **102** SM; **103t** SM; **b** Jorge Pérez de Lara; **104** JK 4829; **106** Ramón Carrasco; **107t** SM; **c** PW after SM; **b** SM; **108** Museum zu Allerheiligen, Schaffhausen; **109** SM; **110** JK 2882; **111t** SM; **tr** SM after JK; **l** MNA; **r** PMHU; **114tl** NG; **bl** SM; **r** SM; **115** PMHU; **116** PW after IG; **117l** From Proskouriakoff 1950; **c** JK 2885; **r** PMHU; **119l** David Stuart; **120** From Proskouriakoff 1950; **121t** Robert Frerck/Odyssey; **b** NG; **122** MNA; **123** IG; **124t** BM; **b** NG; **125tl** & bl IG; **r** BM; **126** TW; **128** NG; **129** JK 2892; **130** IG; **131t** PMHU; **bl & c** BM; **132t** JK 2885; **b** IG; **133t** NG; **cl** PW after Stanislao Labra M.; **cr** IG; **134** PMHU; **135** JK 2823; **136tl** Enrico Ferorelli/NGS; **tr** Doug Stern/NGS; **bl** Doug Stern/NGS; **br** SH; **137** PMHU; **138** PW after L. Satterthwaite *Piedras Negras Archaeology: Architecture*, Philadelphia 1943; **139l** RJMA; **r** PMHU; **140** PMHU; **141t** NG; **b** NG; **142** JM; **143** JM; **144t** PMHU; **b** RJMA; **145t** TP; **c** PMHU; **146** TP; **147l** JM; **r** JM; **148** PMHU; **149t** JK 4892; **l** JM; **150t** Peter Mathews; **b** SH; **151l** UPM; **r** PMHU; **152l** SM after JM; **r** JK 4899; **153** PMHU; **154** PW after Barnhart; **155l**, c & r SM; **156** Dumbarton Oaks Collection, photo SM; **158** MGR; **160t** MGR; **b** TW; **161** LS; **162** MZ; **163** SM; **164** TW; **165** Jeremy A. Sabloff; **166t** SM; **b** NG; **167l** PW; **r** MGR; **168** SM; **169** LS; **170t** MZ; **b** Massimo Borchi/AWS; **171t** LS; **b** Dumbarton Oaks Collection, photo SM; **172** MZ; **173** Pre-Columbian Art Research Institute, April 2000, photo Mark Van Stone; **174t** JK 266; **b** SM; **175t** SM; **b** LS; **176** PW after Martinez E. & Becquelin; **177l** RD; **c** MZ; **r** NG; **178** RD; **180** MZ; **181** NG; **182t** RD; **b** NG; **183t** & b RD; **184t** The St. Louis Art Museum, Gift of Morton D. May; **b** NG; **185t** RD; **b** LS; **187t** RD; **c** Michael D. Coe; **188l** NG; **b** Peter Mathews; **189** IG; **190** PW after BF and Refugio Murcia; **191l** SM; **c** NG; **r** Bunny Coates; **193** BM; **194t** Enrico Ferorelli; **b** BF; **195t** Kenneth Garrett; **b** JK 6785; **196** Jean Pierre Courau; **197** NG; **198** NG; **199** SM; **200** SM; **201** NG; **202t** Kenneth Garrett; **cl** William L. Fash; **r** SM; **203t** SM; **b** Bunny Coates; **204l** LS; **c** SM; **r** © A.M. Gross; **205** NG; **207t** NG; **b** Christopher Klein/NGS; **208t** TP; **b** NG; **209l** JK 2908; **r** LS; **210** Bunny Coates; **211** NG; **212t** William L. Fash; **bl** H. Hohmann; **bc and r** BF; **213** BF; **214** PW after UPM; **215l** RS; **c** RS; **b** MEM; **216** RS; **217t** NG; **b** BF; **218** RS; **219** RS; **220l** RS; **r** PMHU; **221** Matthew Looper; **222t** BM; **c** K. Taube; **223l** & r BM; **224** BM; **225** RS; **226** IG; **228t** SM; **b** LS; **229r** Samuel K. Lothrop, *Metals from the Cenote of Sacrifice Chichen Itza, Yucatan*, Camb. Mass. 1952; **c** SM; **b** Massimo Borchi/AWS; **230t** Sächsische Landesbibliothek, Dresden; **b** NG.

INDEX